LEGENDS OF AMERICAN INDIAN RESISTANCE

LEGENDS OF AMERICAN INDIAN RESISTANCE

Edward J. Rielly

GREENWOOD

AN IMPRINT OF ABC-CLIO, LLC
Santa Barbara, California • Denver, Colorado • Oxford, England

Library of Congress Cataloging-in-Publication Data

Rielly, Edward J.
    Legends of American Indian resistance / Edward J. Rielly.
        p. cm.
    Includes bibliographical references and index.
    ISBN 978–0–313–35209–6 (hardback) — ISBN 978–0–313–35210–2 (ebook)
1. Indians of North America—Kings and rulers—Biography. 2. Indians of North America—History. 3. Indians of North America—Government relations. I. Title.
E89.R54 2011
970.004′97—dc22   2010054394

ISBN: 978–0–313–35209–6
EISBN: 978–0–313–35210–2

15 14 13 12 11   1 2 3 4 5

This book is also available on the World Wide Web as an eBook.
Visit www.abc-clio.com for details.

Greenwood
An Imprint of ABC-CLIO, LLC

ABC-CLIO, LLC
130 Cremona Drive, P.O. Box 1911
Santa Barbara, California 93116-1911

This book is printed on acid-free paper

Manufactured in the United States of America

The chapter on Sitting Bull is adapted from material in Rielly, E. J. (2007). *Sitting Bull: A Biography*. Westport, CT: Greenwood Press. Used by permission of ABC-CLIO, LLC.

Contents

Acknowledgments   vii

Introduction   ix

Timeline of Events in the History of Native American–U.S. Relations   xiii

Philip   1

Pontiac   19

Tecumseh   39

Black Hawk   63

Osceola   89

Sitting Bull   109

Crazy Horse   143

Chief Joseph   181

Geronimo   215

Dennis James Banks   249

Russell Charles Means   273

Mary Brave Bird   303

Bibliography   321

Index   327

Acknowledgments

I am especially appreciative of the support that during my work on this book I have received from my home institution, Saint Joseph's College of Maine, and from the libraries of Saint Joseph's College and the University of Southern Maine. My editor at ABC-CLIO, Mariah Gumpert, has been consistently helpful and understanding. Of course, this book would not exist at all without the tremendous efforts by so many Indian leaders who have struggled to resist the destruction of their way of life or, in recent decades, to reclaim a heritage rich in cultural and spiritual values. Above all, I thank my wife, Jeanne, for her constant support.

Introduction

Long before Europeans arrived in North America, Indians from the Atlantic to the Pacific populated what would become the United States. They lived a life of relative freedom, able to maintain their traditional culture and practice their religious beliefs as their ancestors had done. This freedom, of course, was not absolute. American Indians' movements were limited by the availability of food, water, and other necessities such as materials for constructing their homes. They also had generally defined areas for living and hunting, and if they crossed into other Indian people's traditional areas, conflict was possible. Life was not easy, nor was it necessarily peaceful. Many Indian nations had traditional Indian enemies, and warfare was not uncommon.

Nonetheless, within these limitations, each Indian nation enjoyed considerable freedom. No nation told another nation what to do, and even warfare seldom threatened a people's very existence. From generation to generation, Indians lived according to their traditions and beliefs and were able to maintain a clear identity.

Then came the Europeans. With their arrival in the New World, life gradually—and in some cases suddenly—changed for the native peoples. A major cause of that change was the Europeans' desire for land. Land for Europeans was something to own, whereas Indians, although exercising territorial rights to traditional homelands and hunting grounds, did not own the land. They certainly did not individually own portions of the land. In their view, the land was to be reverenced, and one would no more cut open the land as European farmers did than one would cut open one's parent or grandparent. Likewise, no one would claim to own something that was viewed as essentially a spiritual entity.

As Europeans and their Euro-American descendants steadily moved westward from the seventeenth century through the nineteenth century, they took the land that they wanted, often by national policy. When Indians were in the way, they did their best to remove the native peoples. That removal might be by killing the Indians or, later, forcing the survivors onto reservations. These reservations usually consisted of land that the Euro-Americans did not want, typically the poorest of land. If they later decided that they did want some or all of the land set aside for reservations, they simply forced the Indians to move again. Illness was an effective ally of the Euro-Americans during this process of removal, and diseases such as smallpox that migrated to America with the Europeans wreaked great destruction on Indians, who had been unable to establish any immunity to them.

Euro-Americans, also by established policy, tried to remake the remaining Indians in their own image. They sought to change how Indians dressed, worked, worshipped, and were educated. As the United States grew and extended itself from Canada to Mexico, and from one ocean to the other, it attempted by national policy to effect, if not total annihilation, at least cultural genocide of the native peoples.

Yet Indians throughout these centuries of the new nation's expansion did not yield easily. Many Indian nations fought hard to maintain a way of life that to them was sacred, given to them by the Great Spirit. Leaders arose who used their intelligence, organizational skills, courage, and commitment to traditional values to resist Euro-American expansionism. If such efforts appear through a retrospective lens to have been doomed from the start, that simply makes the struggle even more heroic.

Later, as the twentieth century passed its midpoint, new leaders arose who attempted resistance once again. These modern leaders set out to resurrect much of past tradition, to secure the rights of Indians as citizens of the United States as well as their basic right to be Indian, and to create cultural, spiritual, and economic opportunities to make a better life for themselves. That better life looked forward to the future while also turning back to their ancestors' values. Something of the past, in fact, had survived, and the calling of the modern leaders was to build on that survival within the context of a very different world.

Survival in earlier centuries—not mere physical survival of an individual person, but survival of a people—had required resistance. In the modern world, survival and resistance also went hand in hand. Events such as the takeover of Wounded Knee in 1973 have been about both resistance and survival, even more so than individual political issues or government policies. They have also been about freedom—the freedom to live one's identity with pride and the opportunity to possess those qualities of life long granted to Euro-Americans: the right to life, liberty, and the pursuit of happiness.

Legends of American Indian Resistance examines the lives of 12 such leaders, ranging from Metacom (more commonly known as Philip) in the seventeenth century to three twentieth-century figures: Dennis Banks, Russell Means, and Mary Brave Bird. Each chapter explores especially that individual's method of resistance and his or her accomplishments. Biographical context is included to help readers come to know these Indian leaders more thoroughly.

The arrangement of chapters is designed to offer readers a coherent narrative of the Indian resistance movement. The approach is generally chronological, although some overlapping of individuals' lives regarding their dates occurs, as well as some overlapping of events. Both Sitting Bull and Crazy Horse, for example, played important roles at the Battle of Little Bighorn; years later, Dennis Banks, Russell Means, and Mary Brave Bird did the same during the takeover of Wounded Knee.

The narrative begins with Philip in the seventeenth century and the conflict commonly known as King Philip's War of 1675–1676. A discussion of Pontiac, who lived during the eighteenth century and is best known for his role in what is called Pontiac's Rebellion during the 1760s, follows. Tecumseh is the subject of the third chapter. Tecumseh was born in 1768, about a year before Pontiac's death, and died during the War of 1812, bridging the old century and the new. Black Hawk is the subject of Chapter 4. Although he was born in 1767, almost contemporaneous with Tecumseh, he is most prominently remembered in history for the conflict named after him—the Black Hawk War of 1832—and thus follows Tecumseh in this book.

Osceola, the subject of the fifth chapter, is the first resistance leader discussed in this book who was born in the nineteenth century. He died young, in 1838, after leading resistance in the Second Seminole War, which began in 1835. The discussion of his life logically follows the story of Black Hawk, who died in the same year, but who was born 37 years earlier than Osceola.

Chapters 6 and 7 cover two Lakota leaders, Sitting Bull and Crazy Horse, both of them born well after Osceola's birth (and in the case of Crazy Horse, after his death). Sitting Bull, almost a decade older than Crazy Horse, precedes him in this book. In addition to being older, Sitting Bull came to prominence earlier, and his influence in the nineteenth century extended farther than that of Crazy Horse, as reflected in the great gathering of Indians prior to the Battle of Little Bighorn in 1876.

Chief Joseph appears in Chapter 8, after the two Lakota leaders have been profiled. Although born in the same year as Crazy Horse, he outlived both Crazy Horse and Sitting Bull, dying in 1904. The most memorable historical event involving Chief Joseph also followed the defeat of Custer at Little Bighorn—his long, heroic attempt to lead his people to safety in Canada in 1877. Geronimo is the subject of the ninth chapter despite having been born in 1829, earlier than Sitting Bull, Crazy Horse, and Chief Joseph. This Indian leader lived a long life, dying in 1909, but he is an appropriate figure with which to conclude the narrative of the nineteenth century because he was the last prominent Indian resistance leader to surrender, doing so in 1886.

Dennis Banks, Russell Means, and Mary Brave Bird—three twentieth-century resistance figures—appear in the final three chapters, in that order. Their relative positions are consistent with both the dates of their birth and the points at which they came to prominence in the resistance movement. Banks co-founded the American Indian Movement in 1968, Means joined the organization about a year later, and Brave Bird, still a teenager, became well known at Wounded Knee in 1973.

At the end of each chapter is a list of recommended readings. A much fuller bibliography divided into print and nonprint sections appears near the end of the book. A timeline of important events in Indian history precedes the chapters. In addition, sidebars within the chapters offer supplemental information by discussing people, events, and organizations either not mentioned in the chapters or mentioned only briefly.

Choosing the 12 subjects covered in this book was a difficult task. Other Indian leaders certainly could have been included if this volume had been larger, but all 12 discussed at length in this book thoroughly deserve their inclusion here. Some important Indian leaders, such as Washakie of the Shoshones, are not included because they spent much of their lives working with, rather than resisting, the U.S. government. Some individuals considered for their own chapters are described within chapters or sidebars.

Much of the history education that students within the United States have long received has been from a decidedly Euro-American perspective, from the early Pilgrims through military figures such as George Armstrong Custer. Regrettably, history textbooks in their treatment of the twentieth century largely ignore Indians, as if in the late nineteenth century they ceased to exist.

In the 1960s, however, that veil of invisibility began to lift through the efforts of organizations such as the American Indian Movement, and through the vision and sacrifices of many individuals, some of whom appear within these pages. It is this author's hope that this book makes some small contribution toward creating a greater awareness of what Indians have endured throughout the centuries, what they have striven to do, and what they have accomplished by resisting efforts to deprive them of their identity and their way of life.

Timeline of Events in the History of Native American–U.S. Relations

1585	Sir Walter Raleigh sends soldiers and settlers to establish a colony at Roanoke; by 1590, the colony has disappeared.
1607	The British establish their first permanent settlement, Jamestown, among the Powhatans.
1620	The Pilgrims create Plymouth Colony and are greeted by British-speaking Squanto, a Patuxet living with the Wampanoags. Under the leadership of Massasoit, the Wampanoags befriend the Pilgrims.
1636–1637	The Pequot War between the Pequots and the British results in defeat for the Pequots, whose chief, Sassacus, is beheaded by Mohawk allies of the British.
1675–1676	King Philip's War pits the British against the Wampanoags under Metacom (known by the British as Philip) and their allies, ultimately leading to the killing of Philip and the enslavement of hundreds of Wampanoag survivors.
1711–1713	North Carolina Indians, including the Tuscaroras, oppose expanding European settlements, killing about 200 settlers on September 22, 1711. They are later defeated when the British and Indian allies capture the Tuscarora Fort in March 1713 and kill about a thousand Tuscaroras.
1715	British fur traders seize Yamassee women and children in South Carolina in payment for Yamassee debts, leading to the Yamassee War. During this conflict, approximately 400 British people are killed before the arrival of reinforcements forces the Yamassees to flee.

1722–1727	The Abenaki wars against the British occur in northern New England.
1736–1739	Chickasaws, who are loyal to the British, hand the French army two major defeats in the Southeast.
1756–1763	Indian nations take sides in the Seven Years' War (known in the United States as the French and Indian War) between France and England. In a prelude to the war, French and Indians defeat George Washington at Fort Necessity in Ohio on July 3, 1754.
1760–1761	Cherokees, who were previously British allies, turn against the British when colonists settle on their land but are forced by the British army to sue for peace.
1763	The Treaty of Paris ending the Seven Years' War removes the French as a major force in America and leaves their former Indian allies vulnerable to British retaliation.
1763	The Royal Proclamation establishes the Appalachian Mountains as a western boundary beyond which colonists are not to cross. England hopes that this move will limit warfare between settlers and Indians.
1774	Shawnees oppose colonists entering Kentucky and are defeated on October 10 by Virginian forces under Governor Lord Dunmore. Chief Cornstalk leads the resistance in the Ohio Valley but is killed in 1777 by Americans at Fort Randolph in West Virginia despite being under a flag of truce.
1775–1783	Both Americans and British seek Indian allies during the American Revolution. Among those groups assisting the Americans are the Oneidas, Tuscaroras, Delawares, Catawbas, and Housetonics (Stockbridges).
1778	White Eyes, a Delaware chief, is murdered by Americans, leading the Delawares to shift their allegiance to the British. The Delawares later become the first Indian nation to sign a treaty with the United States.
1782	Pennsylvania militia massacre 96 Delawares at a Moravian mission at Gnadenhutten.
1789	The U.S. Constitution empowers Congress, rather than the states, to negotiate treaties and regulate commerce with Indians. It also locates responsibility for Indian affairs in the War Department.
1790	Blue Jacket (a Shawnee) and Little Turtle (a Miami) lead resistance to U.S. encroachment on the Ohio Valley. "Little Turtle's War" continues throughout George Washington's presidency, with the pivotal battles being the Indians' defeat of General Arthur St. Claire in 1791 and General "Mad" Anthony Wayne's victory at Fallen Timbers in Ohio in 1794. The latter event leads to signing of the Treaty of Greenville the following year, in which Indians yield most of Ohio to the U.S. government.

1797	The American Philosophical Society of Philadelphia begins seeking archeological remains of Indians, initiating a 200-year-long practice of desecrating Indian graves. This practice continues until passage of the federal Native American Graves Protection and Repatriation Act (NAGPRA) in 1990.
1803	The Louisiana Purchase expands U.S. territory and sets up conflicts with western Indian nations.
1804–1806	The Lewis and Clark expedition meets Indian tribes, some of whom have not previously encountered Americans. Sacajawea, a Shoshone woman, assists the expedition as a guide and translator.
1805–1811	The Shawnee leader Tecumseh and his brother, the prophet Tenskwatawa, attempt to unify tribes east of the Mississippi River in opposition to American expansionism, especially in the Ohio Valley and Great Lakes regions.
1811	Governor William Henry Harrison of the Northwest Territory scores a major victory over the Shawnees at the Battle of Tippecanoe in Indiana on November 7.
1813	Tecumseh, fighting against the Americans in the War of 1812, is killed on October 5 near the Thames River in Canada.
1817–1818	The First Seminole War occurs in Spanish Florida.
1824	A Bureau of Indian Affairs is created within the War Department.
1827	White Cloud, a Winnebago and Sauk prophet, leads resistance to settlers in the Winnebago War in Wisconsin. After they are defeated, the Winnebagos are forced to relocate to Minnesota by 1840.
1830	President Andrew Jackson signs the Indian Removal Act on May 29 mandating removal of Indian tribes from the eastern half of the United States to beyond the Mississippi River. First to move are the Choctaws.
1832	Black Hawk leads resistance to settlers in Illinois and Wisconsin in the Black Hawk War. His defeat signals the end of major Indian resistance east of the Mississippi.
1835–1842	Osceola leads the Second Seminole War in Florida in opposition to efforts to relocate the Seminoles. Osceola dies in 1837 after being captured by U.S. troops.
1838–1840	Following the "Trail of Tears," Cherokees are forced to leave the Southeast for Indian Territory (the future Oklahoma).
1846–1848	War between the United States and Mexico results in large additions of land to the United States, including Texas, New Mexico, Arizona, and California. This expansion sets the stage for war between the U.S. government and the Apaches (initially led by Mangas Coloradas and Cochise).
1848	The discovery of gold in California leads to massive displacement of Indians.

1849   The Department of the Interior inherits responsibility for Indian affairs from the War Department.

1854   On August 18, U.S. troops led by Lieutenant John Grattan open fire on Brulés, killing their chief, Brave Bear. In response, warriors kill Grattan and all of his men in the opening salvo of the Sioux (or Plains) Wars.

1855   An attempt to place Yakimas on a reservation in Washington leads to a war that lasts for three years before the Yakimas are defeated.

1861–1865   Some Indian nations support either the North or South during the Civil War.

1862   A Dakota (Santee) uprising in Minnesota over land, food allotment, and financial injustices results in approximately 300 settlers dead, 38 Dakotas (including Little Crow) hanged in the largest mass execution in U.S. history, and the remaining Dakotas forced onto a South Dakota reservation.

1864   Colorado militia under Colonel John Chivington massacre hundreds of Cheyennes and Arapahos at Sand Creek in November.

1866   Oglala leader Crazy Horse leads a Lakota victory near Fort Phil Kearney in Wyoming on December 21, completely annihilating a force of 80 men led by Captain William Fetterman in ongoing efforts to shut down the Bozeman Trail.

1868   The second Treaty of Laramie establishes the Great Sioux Reservation in Dakota Territory with additional "unceded Indian territory" in eastern Wyoming.

1868   George Armstrong Custer and the Seventh Cavalry massacre approximately 100 peaceful Cheyenne villagers on November 27 in the Battle of the Washita in western Oklahoma. Among the dead is Chief Black Kettle, a survivor of the Sand Creek Massacre.

1870s   The U.S. government carries out a policy of slaughtering buffalos in an attempt to force the Plains Indians into accepting reservation life. Some 20 million buffalo are killed.

1872–1873   The Modocs in California turn to war as the government tries to force them onto a Klamath reservation; among the dead is Indian Commissioner Canby. Modoc leader Captain Jack is ultimately captured and executed, and the Modocs are dispersed to Oregon, Indian Territory, and Florida.

1874–1875   Comanche chief Quanah Parker leads a combined force of Comanches, Kiowas, and Cheyennes against the United States in the Red River War in Texas.

1874   Colonel Custer leads a gold-hunting expedition into the Black Hills, an area sacred to the Lakotas.

1876   Custer and his Seventh Cavalry command are defeated at the Battle of Little Bighorn in Montana. The total U.S. fatalities

	number 263, including Custer and everyone with him at Last Stand Hill.
1876–1886	The Apaches in the Southwest periodically wage war against the U.S. government, with Geronimo serving as the principal Apache war leader.
1877	Crazy Horse reports to Fort Robinson, Nebraska, on September 5, and is fatally wounded when he resists being jailed.
1877	Chief Joseph leads his Nez Perce on a 1,800-mile flight to Canada but is forced to surrender 40 miles short of the border.
1879	Richard Pratt, a former army captain, founds the Carlisle Indian School in Carlisle, Pennsylvania. The most famous of the Indian boarding schools, it attempts to transform Indian children into "imitation white people," while forcing them into abandoning their language, religion, and culture.
1881	Sitting Bull returns from Canada with the remainder of his people to surrender rather than see them starve.
1886	Geronimo surrenders in September, effectively ending the Apache wars.
1887	The U.S. Congress passes the Dawes Allotment Act. Its purpose is to break up communal reservation land, allot 160 acres per family, and sell off the remaining land.
1890	The Ghost Dance, preached by Wovoka, a Paiute prophet, spreads, offering hope that the past can be reversed, Euro-Americans removed, and Indian lands and peoples restored to the way they were before the coming of the Europeans.
1890	Indian police kill Sitting Bull on December 15.
1890	U.S. troops kill approximately 300 Lakotas, including Big Foot, at Wounded Knee, South Dakota, on December 29.
1899	The buffalo population declines to just a few hundred head.
1917–1918	The United States enters World War I; approximately 12,000 Indians serve in the military during the war.
1939–1945	Approximately 25,000 Indians serve in the military during World War II.
1944	The National Congress of American Indians is founded.
1949	The Hoover Commission recommends a policy of termination of federal–Indian relationships and assimilation of Indians into the broader American society.
1950	Dillon Meyer, Commissioner of Indian Affairs, pushes relocation of Indians to cities.
1953	House Concurrent Resolution 108 makes termination official U.S. policy. Shortly after its passage, Public Law 280 places Indians in several states under state jurisdiction.
1962	Under President John Kennedy, the federal government ends the practice of termination.

1964	Vine Deloria, Jr., becomes head of the National Congress of American Indians, retaining the position until 1967.
1966	Peabody Coal Company starts mining on Black Mesa in Arizona.
1968	The American Indian Movement (AIM) is started in Minnesota.
1969	Indians occupy Alcatraz Island in November, remaining there until June 1971.
1970	Indians occupy Mount Rushmore to protest desecration of the Black Hills.
1970	Members of AIM, including Russell Means and Dennis Banks, occupy *Mayflower II* in Plymouth, Massachusetts.
1973	Indians, led by members of AIM, occupy Wounded Knee for 71 days.
1975	Two FBI agents are killed on Pine Ridge Reservation; Leonard Peltier is convicted of their deaths in a controversial decision in 1977 that leads many to consider Peltier a political prisoner.
1979	The American Indian Religious Freedom Act becomes law, guaranteeing religious freedom to Indians.
1990	The Native American Graves Protection and Repatriation Act requires museums and other institutions to return Indian spiritual, cultural, and funerary artifacts as well as human remains to the Indian groups to which they belong.
1993	The Native American Free Exercise of Religion Act further strengthens Indians' freedom to practice their traditional religions.
2004	The National Museum of the American Indian opens in Washington, D.C.

Philip negotiates with Pilgrims at a treaty table, the proposed agreement spread out before him. (Library of Congress)

Philip (Metacom, Metacomet), circa 1639–1676

Philip, often referred to as King Philip, was the sachem (chief or leader, a term used primarily in relation to New England native peoples) of the Pokanoket, one of the groups making up the Wampanoag tribe. He ascended to this largely hereditary position in 1662 after the deaths of his father, Massasoit (Ousamequin), and his brother, Alexander (Wamsutta).

In some ways, Philip's life was a microcosm of Indian–Euro-American history, first in the American colonies and later in the United States. The Wampanoags, centered in Rhode Island, initially welcomed the European immigrants, but later came to regret their embrace of the newcomers. Ousamequin (more commonly referred to as Massasoit, a term that means "grand sachem" and that reflected his standing in relation to other Wampanoag sachems) befriended the Europeans who came to what would become Plymouth, Massachusetts, in 1620. These individuals were known as Pilgrims but are often identified with a second group of immigrants—Puritans—in English history. In reality, the Pilgrims and Puritans, although theologically similar—both "puritan" in their religious attitudes—differed in that the latter were committed to purifying Anglicanism but remaining within the Church of England, while the Pilgrims (also known as Separatists) desired to break entirely with the established church. Pilgrims, rather than Puritans, were the founders of Plymouth Colony.

The story of the first Thanksgiving is also the story of how the Wampanoags helped these individuals, who were fleeing oppression at home, to survive their early years in a new land. Tisquantum, a figure better known to American schoolchildren as Squanto, was a former English slave who returned to his native land only to find his people, the Patuxet, destroyed by illness. He was taken in by the Wampanoags and in turn befriended the English immigrants, helping to teach them the best places to fish and methods for growing corn.

Ultimately, however, it is Massasoit who deserves most of the credit for assisting the Pilgrims. In those first few years, the Pilgrims would have had great difficulty opposing a serious effort by Massasoit to eliminate them. Massasoit may have seen in these new residents a useful ally against native adversaries such as the Narragansetts (who became allies of the Wampanoags in King Philip's War) and the Mohegans (who supported the English in that conflict), but there also was considerable benevolence in the sachem's decision to extend a helping hand.

Before long, a major role reversal was in process: The former benefactor was increasingly facing encroachments on his land, often through land purchases imperfectly understood or unfairly administered. The Pilgrims (and Puritans) believed that they had been ordained by God to find a new home in this new land. The influential minister Increase Mather (father of another famous minister, Cotton Mather), argued passionately, for example, that taking the Indians' land was part of God's preordained plan: "the Heathen People amongst whom we live, and whose Land the Lord God of our Fathers hath given to us for a rightfull Possession."[1] While this drive to conquer—and sometimes to exterminate—would often exhibit a more secular coloring in later years, it would remain deterministic in nature. That is, if this movement was not actually perceived as being God's plan, then at least it was securely rooted in the nature of things.

Within a decade and a half of Philip's ascendancy to the role of Pokanoket sachem, the future for Indians in New England would largely be settled. King Philip's War marked the end of the American Indian as a political and military force in New England and almost led to the total demise of American Indian culture in the region. Some groups would survive, but just barely. After the 1670s, Euro-Americans occupied the dominant position along the eastern seaboard and could begin their drive to conquer the rest of the vast continent.

PRELUDE TO WAR

Philip's New England

By the mid-1670s, when war broke out between New England tribes and the Euro-Americans, the non-native population of the region stood at about 36,000 to 45,000, with approximately 17,000 in Massachusetts Bay Colony, with Boston as its principal town; 5,000 in Plymouth Colony to the south; 10,000 in Connecticut; 3,000 to 4,000 in Rhode Island; and some 5,000 to the north in Maine. The New Englanders were spread out in approximately 110 towns or villages, most located near the coast or along rivers. Elsewhere, the land was heavily wooded and intersected by paths primarily known to the native population.[2]

At this time, Euro-Americans outnumbered Indians by two to one. In large part, this ratio emerged because of diseases that ravaged the region in the seventeenth century, reducing the Indian population from a high estimated at about 90,000 to perhaps 10,000 to 20,000 people by 1675.[3] Although the native peoples belonged to a variety of tribes (including the Wampanoag, Narragansett, Niantic, Mohegan, Pequot, Massachusetts, Nipmuc, and Abenaki), they shared membership in the Algonquian language family and thus were able to communicate with and understand one another.

Euro-Americans had been trading with the Indians, especially for furs, since the early sixteenth century. When the non-native population began increasing by the middle of the seventeenth century, the Indian possession most in demand increasingly became the land itself. Native peoples were at a distinct disadvantage in land deals, as they neither engaged in private ownership of the land nor shared the Euro-American view of permanent habitations and, therefore, had difficulty fully grasping those concepts. The new arrivals wanted to establish villages and farms that would be their permanent homes. The native peoples, by contrast, saw land occupancy as temporary, moving with the seasons and shifting village sites to accommodate their needs. When Euro-Americans spoke of "owning," the native peoples were apt to register instead the principle of temporary use.

The English were punctilious about following their moral principles, and those principles included buying rather than stealing. They generally paid for the land but seemingly were not required, within their moral code, to give fair value as it would be computed from a native point of view. As the English saw it, the land was barely being used, so its value, they mistakenly and conveniently assumed, was not great to the current inhabitants, who could simply move on to other land. Nor did the buyers always define to a fine point the precise amount of land they were buying. When Philip catalogued his grievances against the English in a conversation with John Easton, deputy governor of Rhode Island, one of his complaints was that buyers often claimed more land than the Indians had agreed to sell. That June 1675 exchange, when Easton was trying to persuade Philip to forgo war, elicited an outpouring of charges that obviously had been festering over treatment by the English, as the Pilgrims still thought of themselves. According to Philip, the English were ungrateful for the help that his father had given them, had poisoned Philip's brother (a claim quite possibly wrong but widely believed by the Wampanoags), got Indians drunk and then cheated them, allowed cattle to destroy the Indians' cornfields, and provided unfair treatment in the English courts. Even the fact that crimes involving native peoples were always dealt with in the newcomers' courts demonstrated the Euro-Americans' view of their own superiority and proprietorship of the region.[4]

New Names and Early Relations with the English

Wamsutta became sachem of the Pokanoket band of the Wampanoags in 1661 upon the death of his father, Massasoit. At some point shortly after his accession, he asked the local English authorities to give him and his younger brother, Metacom, English names. The precise reason for the renaming is unclear, although assuming new names at important moments in one's life was a fairly common experience in many Indian cultures. Douglas Edward Leach states that the new names were given and received as signs of friendships.[5] The renaming could, therefore, have signified a continuation of the friendly relationship that Massasoit had cultivated with the English for more than 40 years. Eric Schultz and Michael Tougias note that the names also marked the beginning of a new period in the sons' lives and would have facilitated Wampanoag–English interaction.[6] Certainly, the English would have felt more comfortable referring to "Alexander" and "Philip," the new names for Wamsutta and Metacom respectively. These names, hearkening back to heroes of antiquity—Alexander the Great and his father, the Macedonian king— reflect the royal heritage of the brothers as well as a pre-Christian culture, the latter consistent with the newcomers' view of native culture.

The evidence indicates that Alexander intended to continue his father's peaceful coexistence with the English, although he lacked the lengthy relationship that his father had experienced with local leaders such as the Plymouth Colony governors Edward Winslow and William Bradford and the inevitable goodwill that Massasoit had accrued, especially for his assistance during the Pilgrims' early years on the continent. The English in Plymouth Colony, who consistently feared Indian hostilities, heard rumors that Alexander might be discussing a military alliance with the Narragansetts and were upset at his selling land to the Rhode Island colonists. In 1635, Roger Williams had been expelled from Massachusetts Bay Colony (settled by the Puritans) for affirming freedom of conscience in religion and denying the right of officials to interfere with people's religious beliefs—ideological stances sharply at odds with those more heavily influenced by Puritan attitudes. Williams ultimately founded a settlement near Providence, secured a charter from England, and established a colony that granted its citizens political and religious freedom. By 1675, many Quakers, who were especially despised by the Puritans, also lived in Rhode Island. To the English of Plymouth and Massachusetts, then, doing business with Rhode Island seemed at least ungrateful and unfriendly, if not outright treacherous.

The new sachem, newly named, was summoned to explain his actions. Alexander refused, and a contingent of English under Major Josiah Winslow (son of Edward Winslow, the former governor of Plymouth who had died at sea in 1655) was dispatched in July 1662 to bring him in. Alexander and some companions were taken to Duxbury, Massachusetts, and interrogated. This experience of being treated like a common criminal must have been both humiliating and infuriating for a leader.

Alexander then became ill, in what would become one of the great health-related mysteries in American history. Despite his illness, he was permitted to journey north to Massachusetts Bay Colony, after which he returned and stopped at Major Winslow's home at Marshfield. There Alexander became progressively worse but nonetheless started toward his home village, which was near present-day Bristol, Rhode Island, on Mount Hope Peninsula. Unfortunately, he died on the way.

The cause of his death remains uncertain. According to M. A. Dewolfe Howe, a Plymouth Colony physician, Dr. Fuller, treated Alexander with a "working physic."[7] If the problem had been appendicitis (one of the theories advanced to explain the illness), administering a strong laxative might have worsened Alexander's situation considerably. Philip, however, had another, simpler explanation: His brother had been poisoned. That seems unlikely given the repercussions the English surely knew would have followed, but what especially mattered was that the new sachem, Philip, thought so, and he continued to blame Winslow for his brother's death.

King Philip

Philip thus became his people's third sachem in about a year. The English referred to him as King Philip, and by that name he has been remembered over the centuries. The royal title may have been an echo of the settlers' English past, although their own troubles with kings had precipitated their departure from England. If William Hubbard, a Boston clergyman, is to be believed, the title may have reflected their dislike of kingly attitudes. Writing immediately after King Philip's

War, Hubbard describes "*Philip*, commonly for his ambitious and haughty Spirit nick-named *King Philip*, when he came in the Year 1662, in his own Person with Sausaman his Secretary and chief Councellor to renew the former League that had been between his Predecessors and the English of *Plimouth*...."[8]

Philip undoubtedly took on his new role in sadness and anger. After all, his brother had been treated more like a servant than a king in being taken prisoner to answer for his conduct—and possibly had been murdered. Without the old relationships that had helped to sustain his father's friendship with the English, and with a growing list of grievances, Philip faced the challenge of leading his people and trying to maintain peace with the English while also opposing English encroachments on Wampanoag land and rights.

A key event in King Philip's deepening distrust of the British occurred in April 1671. Hugh Cole, a resident of Swansea, a town located just north of Mount Hope Peninsula at the very edge of Plymouth Colony, charged that Philip's Wampanoags and the Narragansetts were preparing to go to war against the English. Philip, perhaps remembering what had befallen his brother and wanting to avoid being forcibly compelled to answer English questions, agreed to meet with officials from Plymouth and Massachusetts Bay colonies at Taunton, Massachusetts. His decision to attend the meeting was probably aided by the choice of representatives sent to invite him: James Brown, an old friend of Philip's who lived at Swansea, and the venerable Roger Williams. Brown and Williams, in fact, agreed to remain behind as hostages while Philip went to Taunton.

At Taunton, Philip found himself surrounded by English in whom he had little trust, and he may have feared being taken prisoner. Whatever the motivation, he agreed to a document known as the Taunton Agreement. He accepted the written statement asserting that he had broken his commitment to submit himself to the King of England and Plymouth Colony and that he now repented of his actions, renewed his friendship with the English, and promised to turn over all English weapons in his people's possession. It was a humiliating admission for someone called a king, and Philip may have put his mark to the document only to get out of the situation and return home. It is unlikely that he had any intention of turning over weapons, nor did he do so. That failure to carry out the terms of the agreement then subjected Philip in September to a fine of 100 pounds in goods.

Striking the Match

The next few years yielded no great crises but instead a steady uncertainty about each other's intentions. With growing distrust and probably an accumulation of weapons on Philip's part, and a constant fear of Indian attack on the part of the English, the fuel needed only a match to ignite a full-blown conflagration.

That match was struck in June 1675. Sassamon, a Christian convert who had long been close to the English—even attending Harvard College and teaching at an Indian village—was discovered apparently murdered. Sassamon had returned to his Wampanoag village in the 1660s, where he originally served Philip as something of a general assistant. Eventually, he fell out of favor with Philip and was expelled from their village. In January 1675, Sassamon warned Josiah Winslow, who had become governor of Plymoth colony in 1673, that the Wampanoags were planning to go to war against the English. A few days later, Sassamon was discovered dead in Assawompsett Pond near present-day Lakeville, Massachusetts.

Nothing might have come from the death had not Patuckson, another Christian Indian, testified in June that he had seen three Wampanoags kill Sassamon. The accused were Tobias (a counselor to Philip), Tobias' son Wampapaquan, and an individual named Mattachunnamo. Clouding the question of Patuckson's veracity today (but apparently not for the English then) was the accuser's indebtedness to Tobias as a result of his gambling.

The accused maintained their innocence but were quickly convicted by a jury—not of their peers, however, but rather 12 Englishmen. An auxiliary jury consisting of a small number of Indians, almost surely chosen to convey an impression of fairness but also undoubtedly picked for their fidelity to the English, acquiesced in the guilty verdict. Tobias, Wampapaquan, and Mattachunnamo were hanged on June 8, although Wampapaquan survived when the rope tied around his neck (John Easton calls it a "halter") broke.[9] Perhaps trying to save himself and concluding that he could no longer harm people already dead, Wampapaquan admitted his guilt in the crime. Regardless of his motivation, it saved him for only about a month before he was hanged again, this time successfully.

The executions made war inevitable. If Philip were behind the murder, he would have been considered as guilty as his agents and would have had to fight to protect his own life. If he were innocent, he would have been thoroughly outraged and anxious to seek revenge. The English must have realized that Philip almost surely would have retaliated, and that knowledge was what led John Easton on his futile peace-keeping mission later that month during which he heard Philip's long list of grievances.

Easton—a Quaker, son of a former Rhode Island governor, and himself a former attorney general, the deputy governor during the war, and a future governor of the colony—did his best to find a way out of the dilemma. Like Rhode Island colonists generally, Easton was not under the theological influence of Puritan divines. Politically, Rhode Islanders had their own problems with the other colonies and for that reason, as well as their own religious convictions, were more attuned than other English colonists to native concerns. Easton suggested a creative approach involving arbitration, with an Indian sachem chosen by the Wampanoags and the governor of New York, Edmund Andros, settling the disputes between Philip and the English. Andros' generally positive relationships with the native peoples and strained relations with Connecticut, Plymouth, and Massachusetts Bay colonies made him a figure whom Easton apparently thought Philip might trust. The suggestion had some appeal to

Philip, but the situation in New England had deteriorated too far by that point. Easton's *A Relacion of the Indyan Warre*, written in 1675, is remarkably fair and balanced in assessing blame for the conflict. He clearly holds the English accountable for starting the war with the Narragansetts and is highly critical of the English clergy, chastising them for being "blinded by the spiret of persecution" and altering the gospel for their own purposes. Easton's short history of the beginning of the war is equally remarkable for abstaining from the rhetorical harshness and demonizing of Indians so prevalent in most contemporary accounts of the conflict.[10]

On June 20, 1675, a group of Pokanokets looted several houses in Swansea that the inhabitants, perhaps fearing an attack, had left. They set two of the houses on fire. Three days later, some Indians were again stealing from houses in Swansea when a man and a boy saw them. The boy had a gun, and the man told him to shoot. He did, and an Indian was fatally wounded. Shortly afterward, other Indians came to a Swansea garrison (village garrisons were fortified houses) to inquire why he had been shot. The boy replied in such a manner as to indicate that the shooting was of no importance, insulting the Wampanoags by denigrating their dead companion. Any chance that full-scale violence might be averted perished with the shooting and the boy's stated indifference to his victim's death.

KING PHILIP'S WAR

Building their Forces

Initially, neither side consisted of a unified military force. Philip brought with him to the conflict many of the Wampanoags, including the Pocassets under Weetamoe, widow of Philip's brother, Alexander. Weetamoe had remarried after Alexander's death but then abandoned her second husband, Peter Nunnuit, when he joined with the English. As her third husband, she took the Narragansett sachem Quinapin. Weetamoe was a female sachem—women were able to assume this leadership position when there were no qualified male descendants of the previous sachem.

A prominent Wampanoag sachem who rejected Philip's efforts to enlist her in the war, despite being his cousin, was Awashonks of the Sakonnets. Benjamin Church, the most successful English military leader of the war, met with Awashonks prior to the initial raids on Swansea and learned that Philip had sent six men to persuade her to join in the war. She, in turn, had instituted a dance—a ritual commonly held when a great decision was to be made—and invited Church to attend. That Awashonks was reluctant to agree to Philip's request was evident by her invitation to Church, and she not surprisingly agreed to remain at peace with the English. According to Church, he later visited the Pocassets and learned from Peter Nunnuit that Philip had held a similar dance and was preparing for war, convinced that the English were prepared to hold him accountable for Sassamon's death.

Pequot War

King Philip's War was not the first major conflict between the native peoples and the New England colonists. That distinction belongs to the Pequot war of the 1630s. In 1634, John Stone, an English coastal trader, was killed by a Niantic band subservient to the Pequots. The English held the Pequots accountable for his death and demanded financial restitution as well as the individuals who had killed Stone. However, Sassacus, the leading Pequot sachem, was either unwilling or unable to turn over the killers.

In July 1636, another group of Niantics allied with the Narragansetts killed a trader named John Oldham off Block Island. Massachusetts Bay Colony sent Captain John Endecott to put to the sword all males on Block Island and sail up the Connecticut River to find Oldham's killers, who reportedly had taken refuge with the Pequots. Endecott did as told but then continued to the mouth of the Pequot River (now the Thames) and burned a Pequot village.

The Pequots responded in force, killing settlers in the area. In May 1637, Connecticut Colony appointed John Mason to lead a militia against the Pequots. Mason attacked the Pequot village at Mystic, which was surrounded by a stockade. Faced with strong resistance, Mason gave up on capturing the village intact and instead put it to the torch, shooting inhabitants as they rushed out. Perhaps hundreds burned to death.

After the Mystic Massacre, the Pequots broke up into small groups to escape the English. Sassacus, who had been absent during the attack on his village, sought help from the Mohawks. To appease the English, however, the Mohawks killed the Pequots and sent Sassacus' head to the English as a peace offering. The surviving Pequots signed the Treaty of Hartford on September 21, 1638, essentially dissolving the Pequots as a people.

Among the surrounding tribes, the Nipmucs entered the war immediately. The Narragansetts initially resisted the call to arms, joining only after English heavy-handedness in dealings with them, such as forcing a treaty on the still-peaceful Narragansetts, ultimately drove them into alliance with Philip.

Early Battles

Nipmuc warriors under Matoonas achieved the first significant victory of the conflict, attacking Mendon in Massachusetts Bay Colony on July 14, 1675. A few days later, a large English force entered the Pocasset swamp on the opposite side of Mount Hope Bay from the peninsula on which Philip and his Wampanoags had their village. The English came upon a rear-guard force and lost seven or eight men. A smaller force then attempted to block Philip's escape. Nonetheless, Philip was able to move with his warriors across the Taunton River and reach Nipmuc country to the north. He was forced to leave behind approximately 100 women and children, most of whom were sold into slavery—an action that the English often took with Indians they considered hostile or recalcitrant.

A contingent of Mohegans under Oneko who were loyal to the English engaged Philip in battle on July 30 near Old Rehoboth, Rhode Island. Philip lost 23 of his men, but he and his remaining forty escaped and moved farther north to join Nipmucs at Menameset near where Braintree, Massachusetts, stands today. The growing force, along with a Nipmuc victory on August 2 known as Wheeler's Surprise, attracted additional allies in the escalating war against the English. In the Nipmuc battle, eight English colonists were killed in an ambush, and both Captain Edward Hutchinson and Captain Thomas Wheeler were wounded. Hutchinson later died of his injuries. Wheeler wrote an account of the battle, *A Thankefull Remembrance of Gods Mercy to Several Persons at Quabaug or Brookfield*, in which he describes the sudden attack, with the Indians sending "out their shot upon us as a *showre of haile*," and his men fleeing from the onslaught. The entire narrative represents an attempt, he writes, to show "what the Lord did against us in the Loss of several persons Lifes . . . and also what great things he was pleased to do for us. . . ."[11]

The Spreading War

Over the next several months, the war spread throughout the New England colonies, with town after town attacked, houses burned, and villagers killed. Fear spread like an epidemic throughout New England, and many of the colonists felt largely defenseless.

Philip's role in the war is impossible to determine precisely. He certainly was the most important figure in the conflict, but he may actually have participated in a relatively small number of attacks. His personal prestige was great, and he well understood how to fight effectively in the wooded terrain of New England. Yet his military tactics were not unique to him, but rather the traditional tactics of his people: small-scale hit-and-run attacks to spread fear, destroy food supplies, and, of course, kill the enemy. Although it would be erroneous to see Philip as a modern type of commanding general planning all of the individual battles, he certainly was a major recruiter. Regardless of how much he was in charge of the daily fighting, the English perceived him as their primary opponent.

Philip, for example, was not at the Great Swamp Fight in December 1675. There a combined army from Massachusetts, Plymouth, and Connecticut, mandated by vote of the United Colonies (also known as the New England Confederation, which was formed in 1643 to coordinate matters of importance to the three colonies), attacked a Narragansett village. The battle occurred in what was known as the Great Swamp, located at present-day South Kingstown, Rhode Island. The English feared that the Narragansetts were planning to enter the war and decided to engage in a preemptive strike. The battle, under the leadership of Governor Winslow of Plymouth, initially seemed to be a victory for the English, as approximately 600 Narragansetts died. However, the attack brought the Narragansetts into the burgeoning war, which ultimately cost the English dearly.

On January 27, 1676, the Narragansetts, furious at the English, attacked Pawtuxet, Rhode Island (encompassing parts of today's Warwick and Cranston). Winslow's army then began a pursuit of the Narragansetts, only to suffer a series of attacks and run out of food, finally being reduced to eating their horses. On February 3, Winslow gave up and sent his men home, ending a pursuit that history has come to call the "hungry march."

By the end of 1675, the Wampanoags, Nipmucs, and Narragansetts (the latter including their great sachem Canonchet) had joined together against the English. Philip, meanwhile, was in New York attempting to recruit the Mahicans to his cause. Philip was welcomed by the Mahicans at their village at Schaghticoke, north of Albany. He apparently recruited a sizable number of Mahicans, with the estimates ranging from about 400 to 2,100.[12]

Although New York Governor Andros generally had good relations with the native peoples, he feared that the New England war would spread into his own colony. As a consequence, he encouraged the Mohawks—the traditional enemies of the Wampanoags and other New England tribes—to attack Philip. The Mohawks attacked in late February, killing close to 500 of Philip's men. Philip survived the attack and returned to New England, where he continued to be an important figure in the war. Nevertheless, other sachems, such as Canonchet and the Nipmuc sachems Monoco and Muttawmp, were more directly involved in the ensuing battles.

Mary Rowlandson

No visual portrait of Philip exists. The most famous supposed portrait, an engraving by Paul Revere in 1772 for an edition of Benjamin Church's history of the war, is now widely agreed to be a composite copy of three engravings of other Indians, with details of dress added based on Church's description of Philip. A particularly interesting first-hand narrative account of Philip, however, occurs in Mary Rowlandson's memoirs of her time in captivity. Wife of a minister, Rowlandson was captured along with three of her children during a raid on Lancaster, Massachusetts, on February 10, 1676. During her three-month captivity, she was taken to see Philip. The Wampanoag sachem invited her to sit down and asked if she would like to smoke. Rowlandson admits in her account that she used to enjoy smoking a pipe, a practice that she assigns to the devil's temptations within a narrative filled with religious lessons.

During her stay in Philip's camp, she received a request from him "to make a shirt for his boy, which I did, for which he gave me a shilling." Rowlandson notes that she offered the money to her "master," the Narragansett sachem Quinapin, who was Weetamoe's third husband. Quinapin, however, told Rowlandson to keep the shilling, and she bought some horse meat with it. Philip's second request was for her to make a cap for his son; in turn, Rowlandson received an invitation to dinner: "I went and he gave me a pancake, about as big as two fingers; it was made of parched wheat, beaten, and fried in bear's grease, but I thought I never tasted pleasanter meat in my life." Apparently, Rowlandson's skill as a seamstress spread, for two women subsequently asked her to make a shirt for a husband and a pair of socks. In both instances, she received food in payment and then invited Weetamoe and Quinapin to dinner.[13]

Rowlandson's account of her interactions with Philip as well as with some of her other captors clearly shows that, although certainly a captive, she generally met with respect, especially from Philip, who treated her as a guest and almost a business associate.

Changing Fortunes

The war continued to go Philip's way throughout March as his Wampanoags and their allies scored a number of victories, including an ambush of a Plymouth Colony militia column that was making its way from Rehoboth, Massachusetts. On March 26, near where Central Falls, Rhode Island, now stands, the force of 63 men under Captain Michael Pierce was attacked. Forty-two members of the militia died in the fighting. Three days later, Canochet led a Narragansett attack on Old Rehoboth, Rhode Island, burning approximately 100 buildings, including the home of Roger Williams.

The tide began to turn in April, as the English continued to implement new tactics in large part modeled after those practiced so successfully by their adversaries. The English began to use Indian allies to locate the warring groups, deliberately tried to eliminate Indian food supplies, and, especially through the leadership of Benjamin Church, substituted surprise attacks for traditional formations and methods of engagement ill suited to wooded terrain. Church offers his own account of one such innovation in words apparently dictated to his son:

> And his manner of marching through the woods was such, as if he were discovered, they appeared to be more than they were. For he always marched at a wide distance, one from another, partly for their safety; and this was an Indian custom, to march thin and scatter.[14]

In more modern terms, Church had some of his men marching point, others guarding the flanks.

The turnaround was not, of course, instantaneous. On April 3, 1676, the English captured one of the greatest war leaders, Canonchet, who reportedly behaved so bravely and nobly at his execution that even the English onlookers were impressed. However, an assault on Sudbury, Massachusetts, west of Boston, on April 21, led by the Nipmuc sachem Muttawmp, was successful. In that battle, several groups of would-be rescuers also were attacked and suffered heavy casualties. The total English fatalities were high. The following day, the victors appeared at Marlborough and shouted 74 times, informing frightened inhabitants of the number of English they thought they had killed.

Another English disaster occurred on May 19, when approximately 150 men under Captain William Turner attacked an Indian camp at Peskeompskut on the Connecticut River near Deerfield, Massachusetts. The "Peskeompskut Massacre" ensued, with a large number of men, women, and children being killed when the attackers opened fire on their wigwams. When nearby warriors arrived, however, the English retreated. The retreat quickly turned into a disorganized flight, and 39 English soldiers, including Turner, were killed.

The attack on Peskeompskut, while disastrous for both parties, may have weakened Indian resolve. By this time, Philip was the most hunted leader among the warring groups and had to spend much of his time trying to avoid English search parties. He returned to his home ground at Mount Hope, and the number of Indian surrenders and captures increased rapidly.

During June 1676, Potuck led 80 Narragansetts in to surrender. Ninigret surrendered his Niantics on July 15. Shoshonin and 180 Nipmucs surrendered on July 25, with Shoshonin turning in another Nipmuc leader, Matoonas, apparently in an attempt to save himself. Matoonas was eventually executed (shot to death) on Boston Common.

On July 31, Philip's uncle was killed and his sister was captured. The next day, Church captured Philip's wife, Wootonekanuska, and their nine-year-old son, for whom Philip had requested Mary Rowlandson to sew a shirt and cap. Both would be sold into slavery, probably somewhere out of the colonies such as the West Indies, and disappear from history, although various legends came to be associated with the son's future. In one story he survived to become the ancestor of a family in Battle Creek, Michigan, whose family Bible notes that they are the descendants of Philip's son.

Despite the son's youth, there was considerable sentiment for executing him, with Increase Mather sanctioning this punishment. There also was clear recognition among the English of what the boy's capture would mean to Philip. Mather wrote of the capture of Philip's wife and son:

> Thus hath God brought that grand Enemy into great misery before he quite destroy him. It must needs be bitter as death to him, to loose his Wife and only Son (for the Indians are marvellous fond and affectionate towards their Children) besides other Relations, and almost all his Subjects and Country too.[15]

Church's account conveys a similar observation through the words of other Indians:

> "Sir, you have now made Philip ready to die, for you have made him as poor and miserable as he used to make the English, for you have now killed or taken all his relations." That they believed he would now soon have his head, and that this bout had almost broke his heart.[16]

William Hubbard refers to Philip's "Treasures, his beloved Wife and only Son."[17] What today would seem highly commendable—deep affection for one's children—was perceived, from a Puritan perspective, as a weakness to be eradicated. In fact, the Puritans tried to persuade Indian parents to be stricter disciplinarians and enforce Christian principles of conduct.

Philip suffered another blow around August 6 when his sister-in-law, Weetamoe, drowned while trying to escape from the English across the Taunton River. When her body was discovered, she was decapitated and her head placed atop a pole in Taunton.

DEFEAT

Philip's Death

Benjamin Church offers a vivid first-hand account of Philip's death. The climactic event in the war began with one of Philip's men informing Church where the sachem was camping at Mount Hope. According to Church, the informant acted because Philip had killed his brother for offering unwelcome advice, perhaps counseling surrender. Alderman, who killed Philip, has been named as the individual who supplied Church with intelligence about Philip's location, but Church's account does not identify the informer by name and implies that the informer and the killer were different men.

In any case, Church planned his strategy for an early morning attack on August 12. Captain Roger Goulding led a small group to flush out the hidden Indians and drive them toward Church's men. Among the men whom Church positioned to prevent Philip's escape were an Englishman (generally identified as Caleb Cook) and Alderman, a Wampanoag who had previously abandoned Weetamoe in favor of assisting Church.

Before Church's trap was completely laid, a shot rang out. Goulding had seen an Indian who he thought had discovered the ambush and opened fire, sending the Wampanoags into flight. According to Church's account:

> They were soon in the swamp, and Philip the foremost, who, starting at the first gun, threw his petunk [a pouch probably containing bullets] and powder horn over his head, catched up his gun, and ran as fast as he could scamper, without any more clothes than his small breeches and stockings, and ran directly upon two of Captain Church's ambush. They let him come fair within shot, and the Englishman's [Cook's] gun missing fire, he bid the Indian [Alderman] fire away. And he did so to purpose, sent one musket bullet through his heart, and another not above two inches from it. He fell upon his face in the mud and water, with his gun under him.[18]

Most of Philip's men escaped, but the great sachem lay dead. Church withheld the news from his men until they had completed searching the swamp, perhaps so they would not be distracted from their task. Then Church's men gathered, and he conveyed the news, to which the army responded with three loud cheers.

Church ordered Philip to be brought out of the mud, describing the fallen leader as "a doleful, great, naked, dirty beast."[19] Because, according to Church, Philip was responsible for many Englishmen lying unburied, he should be treated similarly. Church had one of his Indian allies behead Philip and quarter him, the standard English punishment for treason. Before carrying out his orders, the man noted that Philip had been a great man who inspired much fear in his enemies. Then Church gave Alderman Philip's head and one of his hands. The head would be mounted on a pole at Plymouth, where it remained for nearly 20 years. The hand, marked by a gun blowing up at some earlier date when Philip was shooting, remained with Alderman, who earned money by exhibiting it in a pail of rum. Church's men soon afterward received their pay at Plymouth: 4 shillings and sixpence per man for the battle. In addition, each head of a dead enemy brought 30 shillings. There was no extra sum for Philip.

The End of the War

Annawon, a veteran Wampanoag warrior and Philip's war leader, escaped the ambush at Mount Hope. By late August, he had been sighted near Rehoboth, Massachusetts. On August 28, Church's militia, guided by an elderly Wampanoag man, surrounded his camp in Squannakonk Swamp. The guide explained that he felt obliged to follow Church because he had spared his life but that he would not fight against Annawon. Realizing that his chance of escaping was small, and perhaps finally tired of the long conflict, Annawon surrendered.

Church's account evinces considerable respect for Annawon in the manner of one old soldier to another. The two dined together, and Church allowed Annawon to enter the woods alone. When he returned, he had with him a pack. In it was Philip's belt made of wampum and decorated with flower, bird, and animal designs. Annawon also pulled out of the pack two additional belts, two horns of powder that Philip had used to paint himself, and a red blanket. These items, the old warrior explained, Philip wore while conducting important business in his position as a leader. The conveying of the items to Church symbolically marked the end of the war (although fighting in New England would continue sporadically for some time) as well as the end of a rich cultural era for the Wampanoags and other New England native peoples.

Church intended that Annawon be spared, apparently drawing a distinction between the leader who makes war and a loyal soldier. That distinction, however, was lost on others. Church traveled to Boston, and when he returned to Plymouth he found that Annawon and another of Philip's captains, Philip's brother-in-law, Tispaquin, whose life Church also had promised to spare, had been executed.

Tispaquin's wife and son were sold into slavery. The Nipmuc leaders Monoco, Muttawmp, and Shoshonin were executed, the last despite having delivered Matoonas to the English. The war dragged on longer in Maine, where Abenaki victories continued throughout the fall of 1676. The fighting finally came to an end in August 1677, when Governor Andros, acting under the direction of the Duke of York, who feared that the war might allow the French to make inroads in English territory, negotiated a peace agreement. On April 12, 1678, the English and Abenakis signed the Treaty of Casco, formally concluding the conflict in the north.

Awashonks, who had rejected Philip's overtures to join him in the war, saw her land reduced to a small allotment in Little Compton, Rhode Island. After a few years, she was never heard from again. The Little Compton community died out, but small Wampanoag communities—on Martha's Vineyard and Cape Cod—survived the war and retained something of their culture.

Philip had been defeated and killed, but his name survived as a result of its link to the war that he fought. There would be no more significant Indian wars in New England, although the Abenakis of Maine would suffer harsh effects from the French and Indian War (1756–1763), losing most of their land by the time Maine became a state in 1820. The English had incurred heavy casualties during King Philip's War: One out of every 10 adult males in Massachusetts, for example, was either killed or captured.[20] Yet despite the major English losses, the war secured their dominion over New England. The region now was truly "New England."

The Pilgrims would move into American history books, where in a twist of fate they ironically would be remembered most of all for sitting down to dine with their Indian hosts. Schoolchildren by the millions would learn about the so-called first Thanksgiving but little of what transpired afterward.

NOTES

1. Increase Mather, *A Brief History of the War with the Indians in New-England* (1676) in *So Dreadfull a Judgment: Puritan Responses to King Philip's War, 1676–1677*, ed. Richard Slotkin and James K. Folsom (Middletown, CT: Wesleyan University Press, 1978) 86.

2. Alan and Mary Simpson, eds., Introduction, *Diary of King Philip's War 1675–76*, by Colonel Benjamin Church (Chester, CT: Pequot Press, 1975) 2; first published in 1716 as T. C. [Thomas Church], *Entertaining Passages Relating to Philip's War Which Began in the Month of June 1675*. Subsequent references are to the Simpson edition and noted as Church. Also Eric B. Schultz and Michael J. Tougias, *King Philip's War: The History and Legacy of America's Forgotten Conflict* (1999; Woodstock, VT: Countryman Press, 2000) 21–22.

3. Francis Jennings, *The Invasion of America: Indians, Colonialism, and the Cant of Conquest* (New York: Norton, 1975) 29; Douglas Edward Leach, *Flintlock and Tomahawk: New England in King Philip's War* (1958; New York: Norton, 1966) 1.

4. John Easton, *A Relacion of the Endyan Warre* (1675), in *Narratives of the Indian Wars 1675–1699*, ed. Charles H. Lincoln (New York: Scribner's, 1913) 10–11.

5. Leach 23.

6. Schultz and Tougias 22.

7. M. A. Dewolfe Howe, *Bristol, Rhode Island: A Town Biography* (Cambridge, MA: Harvard University Press, 1930) 28.

8. William Hubbard, *A Narrative of the Troubles with the Indians in New-England* (1677), ed. Samuel G. Drake in two volumes as *The History of the Indian Wars in New England from the First Settlement to the Termination of the War with King Philip, in 1677* (1865), reprinted (New York: B. Franklin, 1971) 1: 52.

9. Easton 8.

10. See Easton throughout; also Leach 34.

11. Thomas Wheeler, *A Thankefull Remembrance of Gods Mercy to Several Persons at Quabaug or Brookfield* (1676), published in Slotkin and Folsom's *So Dreadfull a Judgment* 237–55.

12. Jennings 314; George W. Ellis and John E. Morris, *King Philip's War* (New York: Grafton, 1906) 165–66.

13. Mary Rowlandson, *The Soveraignty* [sic] *and Goodness of God, Together with the Faithfulness of His Promises Displayed; Being a Narrative of the Captivity and Restauration of Mrs. Mary Rowlandson* (1682), in *So Dreadfull a Judgment* 337.

14. Church 140.

15. Mather 136.

16. Church 147.

17. Hubbard 263.

18. Church 153.

19. Church 154.

20. Lincoln 4.

RECOMMENDED READING

Bourne, Russell. *The Red King's Rebellion: Racial Politics in New England 1675–1678.* New York: Atheneum, 1990.

Britt, Albert. "King Philip: The Wampanoag Mystery." *Great Indian Chiefs: A Study of Indian Leaders in the Two Hundred Year Struggle to Stop the White Advance.* 1938. Freeport, NY: Books for Libraries Press, 1969. 29–66.

Hubbard, William. *A Narrative of the Troubles with the Indians in New-England* (1677). Ed. Samuel G. Drake as *The History of the Indian Wars in New England from the First Settlement to the Termination of the War with King Philip, in 1677.* 2 vols. 1865; New York: B. Franklin, 1971.

Leach, Douglas Edward. *Flintlock and Tomahawk: New England in King Philip's War.* 1958. New York: Norton, 1966.

Philbrick, Nathaniel. *Mayflower: A Story of Courage, Community, and War.* New York: Viking, 2006.

Rowlandson, Mary. *A True History of the Captivity and Restoration of Mrs. Mary Rowlandson. Women's Indian Captivity Narratives.* Ed. Kathryn Zabelle Derounian-Stodola. New York: Penguin Books, 1998. 1–51.

Schultz, Eric B., and Michael J. Tougias. *King Philip's War: The History and Legacy of America's Forgotten Conflict.* 1999. Woodstock, VT: Countryman Press, 2000.

Simpson, Alan and Mary, eds. *Diary of King Philip's War 1675–1676,* by Colonel Benjamin Church. Chester, CT: Pequot Press, 1975.

Pontiac and other Indians talk with Major Gladwin, British commander of Fort Detroit, in 1763. (The Print Collector/Heritage-Images)

Pontiac
circa 1720–1769

Pontiac of the Ottawas was possibly the most influential Indian leader of his day, at least in the Midwest. A war (sometimes referred to as a conspiracy) is named after him, and his military and political efforts in the early 1760s had some impact, at least indirectly, on the coming American Revolution. Yet current knowledge of Pontiac's life is circumscribed within the span of approximately 20 years, and the date of his birth is at best a matter of educated guesswork.

The paucity of knowledge concerning most of Pontiac's life as well as the common terminology for his opposition to British rule during and after the French and Indian War (known in England as the Seven Years' War) reflect the Euro-American perspective. Pontiac's life, while historically significant, also serves as an exemplum of how Indian history has been largely filtered through a Euro-American lens. If a person or incident did not directly affect the descendants of Europeans, then little, if any, notice was taken by those soldiers and settlers who were pushing their way westward. The Indians' oral tradition also played a major role in historical forgetfulness: A tradition that is largely devoid of written documents and depends on cultural continuity for transmission obviously falters when that continuity is disrupted, if not thoroughly eliminated.

THE FRENCH VERSUS THE ENGLISH

Early References to Pontiac

The earliest surviving written reference to Pontiac is in a French document dated 1757. It purports to be a copy of a speech that Pontiac gave defending an alliance with the French, encouraging the French to make good on promises they had made to the Ottawas, and describing an attempt by George Croghan, a trader and British official with close Indian ties, to entice the western tribes away from the French. The document, which was part of the personal papers of Sir William Johnson, superintendent of the British Indian Department in the north, unfortunately was destroyed in a fire. Only a brief summary of its content remains, making verification of the document impossible.

It is possible (though the event is undocumented) that Pontiac was present during a victory by the French and their Indian allies over the British general Edward Braddock as he approached the French garrison, Fort Duquesne, on July 9, 1755. Howard Peckham, in his highly respected *Pontiac and the Indian Uprising*, suggests that Pontiac likely was present—a reasonable conclusion regarding a respected warrior probably somewhere in his thirties at the time. Francis Parkman, in his *The Conspiracy of Pontiac* (published in 1851 and revised by the author in 1870), an important study of Pontiac and the French–British conflict that has been supplanted in parts by recent historians, places him at the battle. Parkman, however, is less than definitive about Pontiac's role: "It is said that he commanded the Ottawas at the memorable defeat of Braddock...."[1]

Clearly, Pontiac must have demonstrated his ability in war and his capacity for leading prior to 1760, when he firmly enters the English (and later American) historical annals. He probably was a war chief. As Peckham points out, this position—far from being hereditary—was open to just about any male who proved his skill in combat and his ability to lead others into battle.

Allying with the French

During the French and Indian War, Pontiac was strongly supportive of the French, although it is a testament to the Euro-American mindset that Pontiac was seen by contemporary British and some later historians as being manipulated by the French for their own ends. The term "conspiracy" was applied by Parkman and others to Pontiac's efforts beginning in 1760, with the French viewed as co-conspirators urging the Ottawas and their other Indian allies to oppose British rule.

It is true that the French needed Indian support to have any chance against the British, but allying themselves with the French was a conscious political decision on the part of Pontiac and other Indian leaders, who saw the French as far less harmful to native interests than the British. The French were not present in large enough numbers to seem like an overpowering presence and generally were not viewed by Native Americans as a threat to take over traditional Indian lands. Gregory Evans Dowd, in his *War Under Heaven: Pontiac, the Indian Nations and the British Empire*, argues that the small French population in North America was both a disadvantage and an advantage for the French. The native peoples saw the French as less ominous. At the same time the French, who were clearly unable to dominate their neighbors yet greatly in need of their support against the British, treated Indians as allies—in other words, as something at least approaching equals. The especially small number of French women who immigrated to the New World also led to a lot of intermarrying of male French settlers with native women, further establishing close connections, understanding, and mutual respect between the two peoples.

British Attitudes and Policies

The British apparently saw Pontiac as an unusually perceptive figure among what they believed to be a generally ignorant mass of savagery. However, he was far from alone in recognizing that the French could serve Indian interests both as trading partners and by helping to keep the British in check. Dowd succinctly contrasts French and English goals in relation to two native peoples in terms that Pontiac and his allies would have recognized as more broadly applicable to all Indian nations: "Finally, the French came among the Ottawas to gain their trade, their souls [by conversion to Christianity], their hand in marriage, or their comradeship in arms, but the British especially came among the Delawares to gain their lands."[2]

The British shared little of the French desire to intermingle with the native population, erroneously judged Indians to be savage and untrustworthy, and viewed them as neither allies (too close to being equals) nor subjects (individuals to whom certain rights and privileges belong). At best, they were viewed as separate peoples under the control and protection of the Crown. That status was reinterpreted by the still-new United States in 1831–1832, in the words of Chief Justice John Marshall of the Supreme Court, as "domestic, dependent nations."[3]

What the British did during the French and Indian War, through the actions of military officers and colonists, was to denigrate Indians verbally, mistreat their women, engage in heavy hunting on traditional native hunting grounds (thus decreasing the availability of game for everyone), and threaten native retention of the land itself. They also made trading more difficult by isolating trading centers on a small number of distant posts, charging high prices for British products, and curtailing the sale of ammunition.

In addition, the British, especially after the French capitulation in North America on September 8, 1760, established a policy of greatly reducing the practice of gift giving. Believing that they no longer had to worry about Indian support of the French and, therefore, had less reason to win their friendship, the British, under orders of commander-in-chief Sir Jeffery Amherst, sharply scaled back the practice of giving gifts. Gifts were not primarily an economic issue for the Ottawas and other native peoples, nor were they viewed principally as material possessions. Rather, the giving of gifts was perceived as a way to show respect for the recipient in a culture, such as that of the Ottawas, in which generosity was a prized value.

By 1762, the Ottawas and other native groups were increasingly angered and threatened by a growing wave of mistreatment at the hands of the British and resolved to fight back. They did not yet realize that the conflict between the French and the British, which had largely ceased in North America in 1760 but had continued in Europe, was finally drawing to a close. Ultimately, it would end with the Peace of Paris, signed on February 10, 1763.

PONTIAC'S STRATEGY

Religious Traditions

As Pontiac prepared for war, he held out the hope that the British could be pushed back across the Alleghenies. To do so required a strong alliance of native peoples as well as support by the French. The number of soldiers confronting the Ottawas and their allies was not overwhelming. Dowd estimates that the number of British soldiers available to defend British interests in the region was roughly equivalent to the number available to Pontiac and his allies, somewhere in the vicinity of 3,500 men.[4] The British had their forts to protect them, but many were garrisoned in small numbers. Even so, frontal attacks, Pontiac knew, would be highly costly, if not at times suicidal. Thus cleverness was essential—a quality that the British were consistently ready to condemn as duplicitous, at least in part because the British remained wedded to a military philosophy featuring attacks in formation that confronted the enemy head on. Such fighting was not conducive to frontier warfare, which Pontiac well knew.

Pontiac also could draw on his religious traditions in planning military tactics. This religion enshrined trickery within the behavior of Nanabush, whom the Ottawas considered the creator of the world. Nanabush combined a variety of qualities—some good, some bad—much like the humans whom he supposedly created. He was viewed as persuasive, crafty, and capable of considerable trickery, and thus fell within the broader native framework of the Trickster figure.

Pontiac was respected for his spirituality as well as for his political and military acumen. He may even have been a *mide*—that is, a type of highly regarded shaman or holy man. When Pontiac heard of the revitalization visions of Neolin, known as the Delaware Prophet, he recognized in his teachings an inspirational underpinning for efforts to defend the Ottawas' homeland, drive back the intruders, and restore a world that seemed to be dissolving around them.

Neolin's Teachings

By at least 1761, Neolin was spreading his message of how he had learned in a dream that he was to travel to the Master of Life, the creator, and how he subsequently set out to do just that. A difficult journey led him finally to the Master, who instructed him in terms common to revitalization visions: rejection of Euro-American clothes, weapons, and other items; encouragement to drive the intruders out of native lands; and a variety of religious rituals that would protect the Indians and bring them victory. Regarding religion, Neolin's teachings were decidedly nontraditional, as he would replace such fundamental practices as vision quests, medicine bundles, and dances with, instead, a single-minded devotion to the Master of Life and use of a prescribed, written prayer. Neolin's narrative of seeking the Master of Life also included visions of heaven and hell and following of the straight and narrow path as opposed to the broad road, ideas clearly borrowed from Christian teaching.

Neolin's story offered a strong religious framework for the political and military effort that Pontiac knew would be essential to achieve his goals. Consequently, he decided to make overt use of Neolin's prophetic teachings as he prepared for war.

Preparations for War

In late 1762, Pontiac sent messengers with wampum belts and symbolic tomahawks in search of allies throughout the upper Midwest and down through Illinois. This effort was not intended to create one unified, centrally directed army, but rather to encourage local attacks on British installations throughout

From Pontiac's Speech, May 5, 1763

"It is important for us, my brothers, that we exterminate from our lands this nation which seeks only to destroy us. You see as well as I that we can no longer supply our needs, as we have done, from our brothers, the French. The English sell us goods twice as dear as the French do, and their goods do not last. Scarcely have we bought a blanket or something else to cover ourselves with before we must think of getting another; and when we wish to set out for our winter camps they do not want to give us any credit as our brothers, the French, do.

"When I go to see the English commander and say to him that some of our comrades are dead, instead of bewailing their death, as our French brothers do, he laughs at me and at you. If I ask anything for our sick, he refuses with the reply that he has no use for us. From all this you can well see that they are seeking our ruin. Therefore, my brothers, we must all swear their destruction and wait no longer. Nothing prevents us; they are few in numbers, and we can accomplish it. All the nations who are our brothers attack them—why should we not attack? Are we not men like them?"

Source: Translated by R. Clyde Ford from the French of the anonymous *Journal of Pontiac's Conspiracy*, in *The Siege of Detroit in 1763*, ed. Milo Milton Quaife (Chicago: R. R. Donnelley and Sons, 1958) 22.

the area between the Allegheny Mountains and the Mississippi River. Neither the Ottawas nor other native groups had single, autocratic leaders; decentralization and decision making by consensus were the norm. A leader such as Pontiac might plan, encourage, and motivate, but he could not expect to simply issue an order and receive total compliance—and Pontiac was far too perceptive to believe that he could.

The need for persuasion made Neolin's teachings all the more important, and Pontiac incorporated them into his address to his local allies gathered at his own village about 10 miles southwest of Detroit. There, at two councils—on April 27 and May 5, 1763—he spoke to Ojibwas, Potawatomis, and Hurons. The first two, like the Ottawas, were Anishinabeg, Algonquian-speaking groups that were culturally close but politically distinct. The name "Ottawa" came from the word for trade—an appropriate sobriquet for a people historically known for their experience in trading and skill at diplomacy. These two closely linked qualities had helped make the Ottawas both experienced and effective at interacting with other peoples. If an individual were to arise who might be able to bring together groups that very much prized their separate independence, it made sense that he would come from the Ottawas.

Pontiac shared with his auditors the story related by Neolin but may have softened the prophet's anti-French tone. The Master of Life, according to Neolin, not merely condoned the type of action that Pontiac urged on his listeners, but actually commanded it; at the same time the Master of Life reassured his followers that this goal could be achieved. Even so, clever tactics were also necessary, and the lessons of Nanabush offered a model of effective deception. The first step to taking Fort Detroit, which the British had inherited from the French after the capitulation of 1760, was to reconnoiter the interior of the fort.

The Plan to Capture Fort Detroit

On May 1, Pontiac persuaded Major Henry Gladwin, the fort's commander, to allow a ceremonial dance. While most of the visitors performed the dance, others carefully took notice of the location of such facilities as barracks and powder magazines in preparation for a future effort to capture the fort. At the conclusion of the dance, Pontiac set up a council with Gladwin for May 7.

The plan might have worked if Gladwin had not received intelligence from an Indian informer about Pontiac's true intent. Consequently, when Pontiac arrived on May 7 with approximately 300 Anishinabeg and Wyandots hiding weapons under their blankets, the British were ready. Pontiac had arranged a signal for attack: reversing a wampum belt to show its green rather than white side. However, 120 soldiers were arranged on the ramparts with weapons aimed at the visitors. Pontiac quickly realized that his men would have been slaughtered and left the white side of his wampum belt exposed.

Trying to make the best of a dangerous and embarrassing situation, Pontiac asked Gladwin why his men were in such a warlike posture. Gladwin made no effort to hide his knowledge of the plot, and Pontiac tried to persuade him that someone ("some bad bird") had lied about Pontiac's intentions.[5] Although it was not uncommon for Indians to believe that they could communicate with animals, especially birds, it seems likely in this case that Pontiac was speaking figuratively rather than mystically, referring to actual human beings.

Why Gladwin allowed Pontiac to enter the fort in the first place and, after having allowed him in, did not arrest Pontiac remain unanswered questions. Certainly the action that he took was risky and permitted Pontiac to try again, which, of course, is what he did. Peckham suggests that Gladwin may have been trying to defuse the situation and prevent a war by demonstrating his own superior knowledge and sufficiently humiliating the Ottawa leader to undermine his credibility. He may also have feared that taking Pontiac prisoner would precipitate a full-scale attack on a fort that, although reasonably strong, was constructed of wood and could be set afire. Parkman conjectures that Gladwin may have feared being considered dishonorable if he had detained Pontiac before he had actually committed a violent act against the British, and that he may have perceived the plot to be a local, temporary concoction that would be dropped once the initial foray was repulsed.

Pontiac returned to Fort Detroit the following day bearing a sacred calumet, or peace pipe. Gladwin refused to see Pontiac, but Captain Donald Campbell, the former commander of the garrison who had a history of friendly interactions with the Ottawas, met with him. They agreed that a general council would occur the next day.

PONTIAC'S WAR

Attack on the Fisher Family

On Monday, May 9, 1763, Pontiac returned yet again to the fort, accompanied by several hundred followers. Gladwin refused admittance to the large group and insisted that all save about 50 of the leading men leave. Instead, the entire group departed. Later in the day the fighting began as Pontiac's men started firing on the fort and the two gunboats, the *Michigan* and *Huron*, anchored near the fort in the Detroit River.

On the same day, a war party crossed to Isle au Cochon (currently Belle Isle) in the Detroit River, where the British kept a herd of cattle. The raiders killed two soldiers, a farmer named James Fisher, and Fisher's wife and one of his children. They took another soldier and the three remaining children prisoner. One of the children, seven-year-old Betty Fisher, was murdered the following year—drowned, apparently at the direction of Pontiac, who threw her in the Maumee River in a fit of anger when she soiled her blanket and sought warmth at Pontiac's fire. The act was surely the most offensive single incident of the Ottawa war chief's entire life.

A French sawyer on the island, François Goslin, apparently panicked and tried to escape, only to be killed when he was mistaken for being English. As a general rule Pontiac and his allies during the war remained friendly with the French who lived near the fort, seeing them as potential allies. To maintain a good relationship with the French, Pontiac occasionally even attended Mass with them. Although he needed to requisition supplies from French villagers (known as *habitants*), he generally gave them a bill of sale with his mark (reportedly a picture of a raccoon) for cattle or grain that he took.

Death of Captain Campbell

A party of Wyandots approached the fort on May 10, offering to negotiate a peace agreement. Later in the day, they returned with Ojibwas, Ottawas, Potawatomis, and three *habitants*. Gladwin agreed to permit Campbell, accompanied by Lieutenant John McDougall, to go with the supposed peace party; he kept two Potawatomi hostages in an effort to ensure the safe return of the British officers.

Campbell and McDougall were taken to the home of Antoine Cuillerier, a half-brother of the former French commander of Fort Detroit. There, little in the way of negotiations ensued, and the two men became prisoners. Pontiac named Cuillerier interim commander of the fort until the arrival of his brother, former commander François de Belestre; dispatched a party of Indians and French to Illinois to seek help from Chevalier Pierre Joseph Neyon de Villiers, the French commander of Fort de Chartres, located north of Kaskaskia near the Mississippi in southwestern Illinois; and issued a call for Gladwin to surrender immediately. Gladwin naturally refused. In late July, Pontiac received a letter from de Neyon stating that the French commandant had heard of a possible peace agreement between the French and British (which had occurred in February) and, therefore, could not assist Pontiac. In addition, a letter from de Neyon to the French *habitants* in the Detroit area urged them not to enter the conflict between Pontiac and the British.

Pontiac's force grew throughout May and June. Realizing that a frontal assault on the fort would result in heavy Indian casualties, he settled in for a siege. At the same time, Pontiac tried to prevent the fort from receiving reinforcements and supplies by attacking boats approaching on the river and attempting to disable the *Huron* and *Michigan* gunboats.

Meanwhile, Campbell and McDougall remained prisoners. On July 2, McDougall, along with two traders, escaped and reached the fort safely. McDougall reported that he tried to persuade Campbell to escape as well, but the overweight and nearsighted officer decided against the attempt, perhaps believing that he would slow down the group. Given his history of friendly relations with the Ottawas, he also may have believed that he was in no great danger. If so, he was tragically in error.

Gladwin ordered a detachment to leave the fort on July 4 and destroy an earthen fortification that the besiegers had constructed. The British exchanged fire with the Indians and French, and in the encounter the nephew of a Chippewa chief named Wasson was killed. Wasson, angered by both his nephew's death and what he considered insufficient effort by Pontiac, demanded custody of Captain Campbell. Pontiac turned his prisoner over to his irate ally. Wasson took Campbell to his own camp, stripped the officer, and killed him with a tomahawk. He then scalped his victim and ate his heart before throwing the body into the river, where it floated past the fort and was recovered by the British. The killing infuriated Pontiac, but he was not about to disrupt his alliance over it.

The Spreading War

As Pontiac continued the siege of Detroit, other forts were being attacked, many of them falling or being abandoned by troops too few in number to defend them. Between May 16 and June 2, Ottawas, Ojibwas, Miamis, Potawatomis, and Wyandots took Forts Sandusky (near the current Sandusky, Ohio), St. Joseph (near Niles, Michigan, in southwestern Michigan), Miami (near the modern Fort Wayne, Indiana), Ouiatenon (on the Wabash River near Lafayette, Indiana), and Michilimackinac (on the south shore of the Straits of Mackinac joining Lakes Huron and Michigan). In each case, clever stratagems led to victories. What Pontiac had attempted at Detroit worked at the first two forts that fell, with entry gained supposedly to hold council meetings and without the commanders suspecting any hostile intent. Both forts were taken in May before word had spread of the attempt at Detroit. At Ouiatenon, many of the soldiers were tricked into leaving the protection of the fort for a supposed council.

A different opportunity presented itself at Fort Miami, where the Miami girlfriend of the commander lured him outside the fort's walls on the pretext of helping with her ill sister. Outside, the commander was shot to death, and the remainder of the small garrison surrendered. The tactic at Fort Michili-mackinac was even cleverer. Ojibwas (also known as Chippewas) entertained their Sauk visitors with a game of lacrosse that lasted for hours. Troops also watched the game while leaving the gate to the fort stand open. Finally, the ball rolled through the open gate. Players, clearly unarmed, rushed after it, only to receive weapons from women spectators who had hidden them under their blankets. The surprised soldiers found themselves quickly taken prisoner or killed.

As the summer advanced, additional British forts fell or were abandoned—most notably Fort Presque Isle at present-day Erie, Pennsylvania. On June 19, a force of Ottawas, Ojibwas, Senecas, and Hurons built breastworks atop two nearby hills from which to fire on the fort. Burning arrows set portions of the fort on fire, and the troops retreated to the blockhouse. Finally, they had little recourse but to surrender. The only three forts in the region to survive were Forts Pitt (formerly Fort Duquesne), Niagara, and Detroit.

The Continued Siege

Pontiac continued trying to isolate Detroit. To do so, however, he had to stop Gladwin's use of his gunboats to ferry men and supplies to the fort as well as to provide firepower to keep the besiegers at a distance. In fact, the guns onboard the boats were so powerful that the British could bombard Pontiac's village from the river. The *Huron* began its round trips to Niagara in late May and continued to do so throughout the summer. Pontiac tried drifting burning rafts downriver, hoping to set one of the boats on fire, but the British were able to intercept the rafts. A massive attack on the *Huron* by canoe in September came closer than any other effort, but the crew was able to unleash broadsides of grapeshot at the canoes and turn back the attack.

While the *Huron* ferried troops and supplies, the *Michigan* usually remained nearby to defend the fort. When four other gunboats became available in July and were brought across Lake Erie by Captain James Dalyell, Gladwin began using the *Michigan*, in addition to the *Huron*, to resupply the fort. The *Michigan* broke up in windy weather on Lake Erie on August 28, 1763, but by that time Gladwin had access to a sufficient fleet without it.

Captain Dalyell persuaded Gladwin to let him lead a force of 247 men out of the fort early in the morning of July 31 on what he hoped would be a surprise attack on Pontiac's forces. However, Pontiac had learned of the plan and was waiting. By eight o'clock, the battered troops were back in the fort, having suf-fered 20 fatalities, including Dalyell, with more than 40 additional men wounded and others taken prisoner. Several soldiers had died in Parent's Creek, their blood staining the water red, resulting in the creek becoming known as Bloody Run. The conflict earned the name the Battle of Bloody Bridge, a term referring to the location of the troops on the bridge over Parent's Creek when Pontiac gave the order to fire on them.

Lifting of the Siege

As the stalemate continued at Fort Detroit as well as at Forts Pitt and Niagara, and with no substantial French help likely to arrive (de Neyon had again responded to Pontiac's entreaties with a call for peace) and Pontiac's force shrinking, Pontiac began to make peace overtures. A truce (but no formal peace treaty) was negotiated in late October 1763. After crops were harvested for the year, Pontiac left the area to establish a winter village approximately 90 miles southwest of Detroit on the Maumee River.

The fatalities suffered on both sides during 1763 are impossible to determine precisely. Gladwin claimed that Pontiac and his allies had lost 80 to 90 warriors in the Detroit region, and others obviously died in battles elsewhere. Peckham estimates that approximately 450 British soldiers were killed in addition to civilians.[6]

Pontiac was well aware that the war which had begun so promisingly in the spring now looked much less hopeful. Forts Pitt and Niagara remained under British control. Among events elsewhere, the British had scored a significant—though not unqualified—victory in the Battle of Bushy Run. Colonel Henry Bouquet had led a force of approximately 500 men west toward Fort Pitt during the summer of 1763, stopping at other garrisons on the way. Meanwhile, Delawares, Mingos, Shawnees, and Wyandots were besieging Fort Pitt in late July but left to try to intercept Bouquet. On August 5, 26 miles east of the fort on Edge Hill, Bouquet's troops came under attack. The attacking force encircled Bouquet's men, but two British companies managed to break out without being seen, outflanked the Indian forces, and forced them into a fast retreat.

Bouquet led his men to Bushy Run, where they were able to get water to drink; this location, rather than the site of the battle, gave the conflict its name. At Bushy Run, Bouquet again was attacked, but the Indians withdrew and Bouquet continued on to Fort Pitt, bringing reinforcements but leaving the bulk of his supplies behind. Both sides suffered heavy losses, with Bouquet losing approximately 50 men.[7] Nonetheless, despite the disappointments of 1763, Pontiac was not yet ready to give up the fight for good.

Seeking French Aid

In 1764, Pontiac's focus, as well as that of the British, turned toward the area that would become the state of Illinois. By the early eighteenth century, this region had become part of the French province of Louisiana, an area ceded to the British in 1763. In the mid-1760s, however, it still was uncontrolled by and inhospitable to the British. The future state became part of the Northwest Territory in 1787, was incorporated into Indiana Territory in 1800 when the Northwest Territory was partitioned, and was established as a separate territory including much of present-day Wisconsin and part of Minnesota in 1809. Finally, the area comprising present-day Illinois earned statehood in 1818.

With French influence still strong in the area, Pontiac again sought de Neyon's help, leading a delegation to visit him in April 1764. Pontiac presented the conflict not only as a political and military issue between the French and the British, but also in religious terms of Catholic (France) versus Protestant (England). Pontiac did not arrive empty handed: He carried with him symbols of military alliances in the form of wampum belts. In addition, he occupied a position of strength occasioned by the recent failure of Major Arthur Loftus to disrupt convoys from New Orleans that traveled up the Mississippi resupplying Indians in the Illinois region.

Although de Neyon was sympathetic to Pontiac, he again stated that given the establishment of peace between England and France, he could do nothing to help. Despite Pontiac's inability to enlist the French in his cause, a variety of Indian peoples were busy recruiting allies against the British throughout Illinois, and the British remained unable to exercise any significant control over most of the region.

BRITISH INDIAN POLICIES

Royal Proclamation of 1763

Back in Ohio, the British hoped to establish peace through a combination of legislation and political alliances that would isolate those Indian groups— including the Shawnees, Delawares, and Pontiac's Ottawas—whom they held responsible for resistance to British rule, prevent confrontations between Europeans and Indians, and avoid the considerable financial expense of fighting Indian wars. The Royal Proclamation of 1763 was directed toward keeping settlers out of traditional Indian lands, thereby maintaining both political and fiscal stability in the existing British possessions. The royal edict prohibited settlement west of the Appalachian Mountains and attempted to regulate Indian trade. It also clarified that, from the British perspective, Indians were not "subjects" but rather individuals under the protection of the British. Consequently, they lacked the legal rights enjoyed by subjects in England and in the colonies.

As subsequent history shows, the proclamation would prove at best a brief partial impediment to westward expansion. Colonists strongly objected to this attempt to keep them from settling beyond the Appalachians. Moreover, they found the policy to be one of many reasons ultimately to break free of the mother country, although historians remain divided about the extent to which the Royal Proclamation helped bring about the American Revolution.

The Iroquois League

There was much more to Indian policy, however, than the Royal Proclamation of 1763. Sir William Johnson, superintendent of the Indian Department in the north, attempted to reinforce British relations with the Iroquois League, a confederation of the Cayuga, Mohawk, Oneida, Onandaga, and Seneca nations, and after 1710 the Tuscaroras—often referred to as the Five Nations, and later the Six Nations. The arrangement between England and the Iroquois, referred to as the Covenant Chain, included British acknowledgment of Iroquois rule over the Shawnees. Johnson decided to ignore Seneca involvement in Pontiac's war, a political compromise given the Senecas' membership in the Six Nations. Peace overtures went out to other native peoples as well, with Johnson trying to isolate the bands whose actions he most wanted to curtail.

Ultimately, little of Johnson's plan went precisely according to his hopes. The Shawnees would strongly resist domination by the Iroquois, as the later efforts of Tecumseh demonstrated (see Chapter 3). Even the Iroquois tended to put their own interests first, as the expedition led by Colonel John Bradstreet illustrates.

Colonel Bradstreet's Peace

Johnson formed a strong force consisting of approximately 1,200 British soldiers and 650 Indians (largely Iroquois) that was ready by August 1764 to march westward from Fort Niagara under the command of Colonel Bradstreet to force acquiescence by the Ottawas, Shawnees, and Delawares to British rule. Bradstreet, however, seemed more inclined to make peace rather than war, and the Iroquois likewise preferred negotiation with Shawnees and others rather than risking combat. Thus, when Bradstreet reached L'Anse aux Feuilles on the southern shore of Lake Erie near Fort Presque Isle around the middle of August, he engaged a delegation of Indian representatives, including Shawnees and Delawares, in peace discussions. The agreement, concluded on August 12, included a promise by Bradstreet to send a message to Colonel Bouquet urging him to abandon his plans at Fort Pitt to attack the Shawnees and Delawares.

Bouquet, Johnson, and Thomas Gage (who had replaced Jeffery Amherst as commander-in-chief in North America at the end of 1763) all rejected Bradstreet's peace agreement. Bradstreet, however, was unaware of the anger that his actions had generated and dispatched a party that included Lieutenant Thomas Morris, a college-educated, French-speaking soldier who would later make a career as a poet and writer, to spread the news of the peace of L'Anse aux Feuilles. Thomas King, an Oneida chief, was among those accompanying Morris. Up the Maumee River from Maumee Bay, near present-day Toledo, Ohio, Morris' party was captured by Ottawas. After meeting with Thomas King, Pontiac agreed to talk with Morris. Pontiac then told Morris that he would consider peace and gave the British soldier permission to continue his journey up the Maumee. Pontiac sent along his nephew, a French trader named St. Vincent, and a wampum belt that referenced 180 villages. The belt, Pontiac assured Morris, would guarantee him safe passage.

Despite the protection afforded by Pontiac's belt, Morris ran into trouble at a Miami village. After being ordered to turn back, he set off for Detroit. Neither Bradstreet nor Bouquet ended up doing much fighting in 1764, but they achieved additional peace arrangements and managed to negotiate the return of several hundred British captives, some of whom had become thoroughly acculturated to their new communities and were reluctant to return to British civilization. There had been no military defeat of Indians in the Ohio region, and Pontiac remained free, still determined to resist the British.

FINALLY, A PEACE AGREEMENT

Lieutenant Fraser

Pontiac's actions in late 1764 and throughout the winter are uncertain. By April 8, 1765, however, Pontiac had arrived with other Ottawa warriors at Fort de Chartres in Illinois, still hoping to enlist others in his opposition to the British.

During the same month, a party led by Lieutenant Alexander Fraser arrived at the fort with the goal of asserting British domination. Fraser warned Louis St. Ange de Bellerive, who had succeeded de Neyon as commandant, against helping the Indians fight the British. Although less than pleased by the threat, St. Ange reminded Fraser that he could not control what Pontiac or any other Indian did and then invited his guests to dinner.

After the meal, Pontiac arrived with a number of supporters and took Fraser captive. Pontiac relented from this action at St. Ange's urging and allowed Fraser to remain in the fort, although the small contingent of troops (approximately 50) could offer Fraser only limited protection.

Fraser met with Pontiac the following day and assured him that the Shawnees, Delawares, and Iroquois had already made peace. Pontiac, based on conversations with Shawnees over the winter, did not believe that they had come to any significant agreement with the British and also argued that the British–French treaty of 1763 did not apply to the Illinois region. Nonetheless, Pontiac began to become concerned that the Great Lakes region might be lost and expressed a more conciliatory tone toward Fraser. He defended his brief capture of Fraser the night before as an attempt to ensure the officer's safety and expressed a willingness to speak with George Croghan, who was reportedly on his way toward Fort de Chartres.

Croghan never arrived, and Fraser remained in the area for about six weeks developing great respect for Pontiac's leadership, intelligence, integrity, and humanity. Finally, having decided to return to Ohio and demonstrating a fondness for the British officer, Pontiac urged Fraser to leave for his own protection, fearing what might happen in his absence. Fraser took the advice and departed on May 29, descending the Mississippi to New Orleans, with the British consequently failing once again to secure Illinois.

Croghan had left Fort Pitt in May 1765 expecting to join Fraser in Illinois. On June 8, however, he was taken captive by Kickapoos and Mascoutens. Croghan was finally released in July, perhaps in part because of a message from Pontiac expressing a willingness to hold discussions with him. Pontiac's growing acceptance of the need to discuss peace was at least partly a response to the general movement of native peoples in the Midwest toward peace agreements, most recently the Miamis.

Negotiations

Pontiac, accompanied by Iroquois, Delaware, and Shawnee representatives, met Croghan near the present-day location of Allerton in east-central Illinois. The parties then returned to Ouiatenon, where they formally discussed a cessation of hostilities. Pontiac insisted that he had never sold any land to the British and that he would not yield to British rule. Nonetheless, he was ready to cease fighting.

Croghan respected Pontiac's intelligence and the respect that other Indians had for him, but had little sympathy for the Indian point of view. Indeed, he noted in a letter back to Fort Pitt that he hoped to undermine Pontiac's standing with his own Ottawas. Croghan's and Pontiac's parties left Ouiatenon for Detroit on July 25 after Croghan had informed General Gage that it was now safe to send troops to Fort de Chartres.

An Agreement

On August 17, Pontiac and Croghan reached Fort Detroit—the same fort that just two years earlier Pontiac and his allies had tried so hard to capture. Pontiac, along with Chippewas, Hurons, and Potawatomies, met with Croghan on August 27, at which time Croghan stressed the benefits of peace. The meeting resumed the next day. Pontiac declared his desire for peace, promised to send a pipe to Sir William Johnson, and asked that his people be extended credit to purchase powder and lead for hunting. A week later, on September 4, Pontiac restated his long-held position that his people had never sold land to the French or the British, so they should receive payment for land that the British were using for forts and trading posts. On this point, the British had no intention of yielding, although some individuals, both French and British, perhaps to avoid conflicts with Pontiac, sought and received deeds from him for parcels of land.

The agreement ended Pontiac's military efforts against the British. Croghan, reflecting on his interaction with Pontiac, concluded that the Ottawa leader enjoyed more respect from the collective Indian nations than any other Indian received even from his own people.

SOME OLD FRIENDS AND ADVERSARIES

Robert Rogers

Pontiac's last few years are primarily veiled in obscurity, with documents of the era offering only occasional glimpses of the man who brought together so many Indian peoples to attempt what in retrospect appears clearly to have been an impossible objective: to turn back the tide of westward Euro-American expansion. In June 1766, Pontiac appeared along the Detroit River with members of several other groups, including the Ojibwa, Potawatomi, Wyandot, and Illinois. For some reason lost to history, Pontiac stabbed a Peoria chief named Black Dog, seriously wounding him. The occasion for the gathering was to meet with Hugh Crawford, who had been dispatched by Sir William Johnson with wampum belts to meet and escort a number of chiefs who had fought against the British to a meeting at Fort Ontario at Oswego, New York. There they were to ratify the peace agreements agreed to in the previous year. The fight between Pontiac and Black Dog may have resulted from the tensions between the Ottawa leader and other chiefs over a supposed annuity paid him by Johnson.

Pontiac and the others accompanying Crawford traveled, ironically, on the *Victory*, which had been used to resupply Fort Detroit in 1763. They reached Fort Erie on June 28, where Pontiac encountered an old acquaintance, Robert Rogers, who was traveling to Michilimackinac to become commandant of the garrison there. Rogers had just returned from England, where he had published *A Concise Account of North America*. He also had witnessed his stage play, a drama based on Pontiac's efforts against the British called *Ponteach, or, The Savages of America*, be both performed and published.

In *A Concise Account*, Rogers describes his friendship with Pontiac (spelled "Ponteack"), including the protection and assistance that Pontiac provided to Rogers and his military detachment in 1760 prior to Pontiac's war against the British. He recounts his own sending of a bottle of brandy to Pontiac in 1763 when Rogers was escorting provisions to the besieged Fort Detroit. According to Rogers, Pontiac was warned not to drink the brandy for fear it was poisoned. In response, the Ottawa chief, supposedly referring to the 1760 meeting, "laughed at their suspicions, saying it was not in my power to kill him, who had so lately saved my life." Rogers praises Pontiac highly, noting how honored and respected he is by other Indian nations, possessing the "greatest authority of any Indian Chief that has appeared on the continent since our acquaintance with it." Rogers also cites Pontiac's "great strength of judgment, and a thirst after knowledge."[8] Rogers surely would have informed Pontiac of these literary tributes to his former friend and adversary.

Thomas Morris

Continuing to Fort Niagara, Pontiac had a reunion with Thomas Morris, who had become the fort's commander. Morris, like Rogers, paid high tribute to Pontiac in print. In *The Journal of Captain Thomas Morris*, which he wrote in 1764 and published in 1791 within *Miscellanies in Prose and Verse*, Morris also perceived Pontiac as first among chiefs, with "a more extensive power than ever was known among that people; for every chief used to command his own tribe: but eighteen nations, by French intrigue, had been brought to unite, and chuse this man for their commander...."[9]

Sir William Johnson

Pontiac and his party reached Fort Ontario in early July, but had to wait until about July 22 for the arrival of Johnson, who was recovering from an illness. Johnson finally arrived and convened the conference on July 23. The superintendent brought out the pipe that Pontiac had sent to him through Croghan the year before and passed it around—a wise political move given Johnson's desire to have his guests recommit to peace. According to the British account of the conference, Pontiac responded respectfully and positively while promising a formal response the next day. When the conference reconvened, Pontiac apparently promised to take Johnson "by the hand," assured Johnson of his determination to maintain peace, and presented at least seven wampum belts that essentially served in place of a written contract.[10]

After a two-day halt because of inclement weather, the conference continued for several more days. Pontiac spoke a number of times, delivered additional belts, promised to retrieve war belts that had been sent to various Indian nations, and, if the British account is accurate, may have erred by presenting himself too much as the supreme leader of the peoples gathered at the conference. Howard Peckham surmises that Johnson may have tried to position Pontiac in such a way as to create resentment toward him, thereby undermining the standing of the individual whom the British may have most feared could lead further rebellions against their rule. Rumors of Pontiac receiving a pension from the British also apparently engendered resentment on the part of some of the Detroit-area Indians. Norman McLeod, the Indian commissary at Fort Ontario, reported to Johnson that a French trader had passed along the pension rumor and predicted that Pontiac would be murdered within a year if the British appeared to be favoring him. The prophecy of Pontiac's death would indeed come true, just not quite so soon, and not necessarily because of perceived British favoritism.

THE FINAL YEARS

Alexis Cuillerier

Pontiac appears only occasionally in the historical annals over the next three years. The case of Elizabeth Fisher surfaced in 1767 when Alexis Cuillerier (whose father, Antoine Cuillerier, had been a close friend of Pontiac's at Detroit) was arrested and jailed in Detroit for his part in killing young Betty Fisher. Jean Maiet, a friend of the accused, offered damning testimony that implicated Pontiac in ordering Cuillerier and Maiet to drown the girl.

Cuillerier subsequently escaped, but Pontiac traveled to Detroit to try to prevent any further action against his young friend, who also was the nephew of the former French commander of Fort Detroit, François-Marie Picoté de Belestre. Pontiac's appearance created a problem for the British, for they had no wish to consider Pontiac's role in the murder. Instead, many officials believed, it was more important to preserve Pontiac's valued role as a leader in maintaining the peace. Nor was Pontiac considered a British subject under British law, but rather was viewed as the leader of a separate nation. In any case, conflicting testimony led to the case against Cuillerier being abandoned—much to the relief of the British, who seemingly had little enthusiasm for confronting the suspect's prominent family or his Ottawa supporter.

Growing Hostility Toward Pontiac

During the years immediately following the conference with William Johnson, Pontiac accumulated a growing number of enemies among his own Ottawas and other Great Lakes area Indians. Jealousy and rumors of British favoritism played roles in the burgeoning hostility, as did anger by younger militants who wanted to renew the fight against the British. Shawnees were especially vehement about reestablishing an alliance against the Euro-Americans, and Peorias remained angry over Pontiac's stabbing of Black Dog. In a message to Lieutenant Jehu Hay at Fort Detroit, Pontiac complained in May 1768 that young Ottawas had mistreated him, showing little respect for his accomplishments—a generational and ideological rift that led Pontiac to leave his village on the Maumee River and move near Ouiatenon. He told Hay that he was hunting to pay off debts and planned to travel to Illinois shortly to find his wife's brothers. His letter does not reveal why he needed to find his in-laws.

In Illinois, Pontiac visited Fort de Chartres, received presents, and reiterated his commitment to peace. He left Illinois at some point, perhaps to return to the Ouiatenon area. In the spring of 1769, he returned to Illinois. Rumors swirled that Pontiac was planning to bring a sizable number of warriors and attack the Illinois Confederation—which included the Kaskaskias and Peorias—although the cause of Pontiac's supposed anger toward them is not known. However, when Pontiac did return, he did so in peace, accompanied by two sons but overall a small number of companions, his following having continued to disintegrate.

Murder of Pontiac

The Peorias, perhaps because of fear of Pontiac and an exaggerated view of his current power, or perhaps simply out of a desire to avenge his earlier wounding of Black Dog (whose village was near Cahokia, an old French settlement currently within the suburb of East St. Louis), decided to get rid of Pontiac once and for all. The task was delegated to a nephew of Black Dog.

Pontiac's death has been recounted in widely differing ways over the years, but the account by Howard Peckham is now generally accepted as about as definitive as is possible to discover given the paucity of information about the once great leader's end. According to Peckham, the nephew struck up a friendship with Pontiac as a way to stay close to his intended victim. On April 20, 1769, Pontiac and his new friend were in a store in Cahokia. Pontiac, who was unarmed, left the store, with the assassin following behind him. Outside the store, the Peoria hit Pontiac in the head with a club, knocking him to the ground. He then stabbed Pontiac, killing him.

In the aftermath of the assassination, the Peorias became terrified of retribution and tried to shift the blame to the British, claiming they were put up to committing the act. Louis St. Ange de Bellerive, former French commander at Fort de Chartres, who at that time resided at St. Louis, may have believed British complicity to be a reality: He informed northern Indian tribes that the assassin had acted on British orders. Nonetheless, he refused protection to the frightened Peorias who had crossed the Mississippi to seek his help, probably not wanting to be caught between the Indians and the British. Lieutenant Colonel John Wilkins, the current commander at de Chartres, also refused the Peorias' request for protection at the fort, although he did send them powder and lead with which to protect themselves if necessary.

Francis Parkman suggests that considerable retribution followed, writing "that over the grave of Pontiac more blood was poured out in atonement, than flowed from the veins of the slaughtered heroes on the corpse of Patroclus; and the remnant of the Illinois who survived the carnage remained for ever after sunk in utter insignificance."[11] Peckham points out, however, that this was not the case. The only violent response that can be directly attributed to Pontiac's death was committed by Minavavana, a Chippewa chief and former ally of Pontiac. Convinced that the clerk who waited on Pontiac had been involved in the murder, an accusation for which there is no surviving evidence, Minavavana appeared at Cahokia with two of his warriors in April 1770. Unable to locate the clerk, they killed two other employees of the company that operated the store.

After Pontiac's Death

The precise location of Pontiac's grave is not known. His body was interred either in Cahokia or in St. Louis. A common, although not universal belief is that the body was transported to St. Louis at St. Ange's request. Peckham lists a number of possible St. Louis sites for the grave in his book.

Pontiac had been instrumental in mounting a formidable alliance to resist the British, with the effort immortalized historically under his name, albeit often reduced in scope to a "rebellion" or "conspiracy." No such unified effort had been accomplished before, although a later, similar effort against the new American nation would be inspired and led by the Shawnee Tecumseh (see Chapter 3).

Francis Parkman deserves considerable credit for keeping Pontiac in the historical eye with his publication of *The Conspiracy of Pontiac*, despite the occasional inaccuracies found in the book. In addition, American culture has kept Pontiac's name alive in a variety of ways. Detroit automakers, for example, turned to the man who once attempted to capture Fort Detroit when they named one of their automobile makes the Pontiac. In addition, the Ottawa leader's name adorns at least seven towns from Rhode Island to Kansas as well as lakes in Michigan and the Province of Quebec.

NOTES

1. Francis Parkman, *The Conspiracy of Pontiac*, 10th ed. (New York: Collier Books, 1962) 154.
2. Gregory Evans Dowd, *War Under Thunder: Pontiac, the Indian Nations and the British Empire* (2002; Baltimore: Johns Hopkins University Press, 2004) 34.
3. Dowd 177–90.
4. Dowd 117.
5. Howard H. Peckham, *Pontiac and the Indian Uprising* (1947; Chicago: University of Chicago Press, 1961) 131.
6. Peckham 238–39.
7. Peckham 210–13.
8. Robert Rogers, *A Concise Account of North America* (London, 1765) 240–44.
9. Thomas Morris, *Journal of Captain Thomas Morris from Miscellanies in Prose and Verse* (Ann Arbor: University Microfilms, 1966) 6–7.
10. Peckham 290–97.
11. Parkman 478.

RECOMMENDED READING

Cave, Alfred A. "The Delaware Prophets." *Prophets of the Great Spirit: Native American Revitalization Movements in Eastern North America*. Lincoln: University of Nebraska Press, 2006. 11–44.

Dowd, Gregory Evans. *War Under Thunder: Pontiac, the Indian Nations and the British Empire*. 2002; Baltimore: Johns Hopkins University Press, 2004.

Jennings, Francis. *Empire of Fortune: Crowns, Colonies, and Tribes in the Seven Years War in America*. New York: Norton, 1988.

Parkman, Francis. *The Conspiracy of Pontiac*. 10th ed. New York: Collier Books, 1962.

Peckham, Howard H. *Pontiac and the Indian Uprising*. 1947. Chicago: University of Chicago Press, 1961.

Quaife, Milo Milton, ed. *The Siege of Detroit in 1763: The Journal of Pontiac's Conspiracy and John Rutherfurd's Narrative of a Captivity*. Chicago: R. R. Donnelley and Sons, 1958.

Todish, Timothy J., and Todd E. Harburn. *A "Most Troublesome Situation": The British Military and the Pontiac Indian Uprising of 1763–1764*. Fleischmanns, NY: Purple Mountain Press, 2006.

Tecumseh, called the Moses of his people, died fighting on the side of the British in the War of 1812. (Library of Congress)

Tecumseh
1768–1813

Tecumseh—whose name has been spelled a variety of other ways, including Tecumtha, and which means "Panther Passing Across"—received his name from the meteor that, according to Shawnee tradition, occurred at his birth. The natural phenomenon, associated by the Shawnees with a spirit residing in the physical form of a panther, was all the more relevant in the case of Tecumseh, as his father belonged to the Panther clan of the Shawnees.

The name would fit the man. Tecumseh became a dynamic, powerful, and visionary leader who fought the final battle against Euro-American encroachment on Indian lands in the Ohio Valley. He was a political genius who understood the importance of alliances at the same time that he became a courageous military leader. His sympathy for prisoners and humane treatment of them, along with his belief that war should be fought only against combatants, deviated sharply from the general rule of warfare fought by Euro-Americans and Indians alike.

Tecumseh was an inspiring orator recognized by friend and foe for his military and political skill. William Henry Harrison, then governor of Indiana Territory, labeled him the Moses of his people after their first meeting, in 1810.[1] In death, he was idealized by many Euro-Americans, especially in the East, as the ultimate "noble savage," although there was nothing savage about him.

TECUMSEH AND HIS PEOPLE

Tecumseh's Shawnees

By the time Tecumseh was born in 1768 to Methotasa and her Shawnee husband, Pucksinwah, near the Mad River in western Ohio, the Shawnees had long been struggling to retain their homeland. Many Shawnees, starting in the second half of the seventeenth century, had journeyed south; others had moved across the Mississippi to Missouri in the face of attacks by Iroquois. Some would return, and others would join the exodus. Still others would stay and fight for their land, by the middle of the eighteenth century principally against advancing Euro-Americans.

The Shawnees, looking for help in retaining their homeland, established alliances with the French against the British (and American colonists) and later with the British against the French during the French and Indian War, more commonly known in Europe as the Seven Years' War (1756–1763). A conflict at the conclusion of that war, occasioned by Treaty of Paris provisions granting Algonquian land to the British and led by the Ottawa war chief Pontiac (known as Pontiac's Rebellion; see Chapter 2), resulted in the Royal Proclamation of 1763 that forbade colonial settlements west of the Appalachian Mountains. The restriction angered colonists, including George Washington, Thomas Jefferson, and Patrick Henry—land speculators all, who saw the Crown inhibiting their ability to do business in what was still Indian land. Unable to keep Euro-Americans out of the restricted areas, in 1768 England turned trade over to the colonies to regulate, and speculators in droves sought land grants west of the Appalachians.

Sir William Johnson, the British Indian superintendent, negotiated the Treaty of Fort Stanwix with the Six Nations of the Iroquois in 1768, the year of Tecumseh's birth. The British considered the Iroquois to have dominion over the Shawnees, but in fact the Iroquois had no legal standing to speak on their behalf and did not control, much less own, the land on which the Shawnees lived and hunted. The Iroquois agreed to yield much of that land to the colonies, including most of what is now Kentucky and West Virginia and part of western Pennsylvania. The boundary line between Indian land and areas open for colonization became the Ohio River, which essentially forms the boundary for much of the present state of Ohio.

The Shawnees, of course, did not recognize the Treaty of Fort Stanwix. Nevertheless, almost as soon as the treaty was signed, colonists began to trespass on what Shawnees saw as their land. One of the early transgressors was the renowned American folk hero Daniel Boone, who entered Kentucky from North Carolina. Over the years, Boone would establish a settlement in Kentucky (Boonesborough), fight the Shawnees, be captured, and even become an adopted son of a Shawnee war chief, Black Fish.[2]

The major battle between Shawnees and colonists during Tecumseh's childhood occurred in 1774. In the Battle of Point Pleasant across the current state line in West Virginia, a force led by the Shawnee Cornstalk launched a strike on a large contingent of Virginia militia led by Colonel Andrew Lewis. Lewis's advance was part of a campaign launched by Lord Dunmore, Virginia's governor, in retaliation for raids by a Mingo chief, Tachnedorus (commonly known as John Logan). Logan's raids were intended to seek revenge for the murder of a group of Mingo women and children, including Logan's wife and sister, by colonists. Cornstalk's attack cost the Virginians approximately 75 to 80 lives, while the attackers suffered about 30 fatalities. In the end, the Shawnees began to run out of ammunition and withdrew, leaving the battered Virginians to claim victory. After the battle, Cornstalk and a number of other Shawnee leaders agreed to give up their hunting grounds in Kentucky, return prisoners, and permit unimpeded travel on the Ohio River. Dunmore agreed, in turn, that colonists would not hunt north of the river and that British traders would be permitted to return to Shawnee land.

The Young Tecumseh

Tecumseh's early years were marred by several events that had to have been unsettling for him. At the age of six in 1774, he lost his father, Pucksinwah, at Point Pleasant. In 1777, Cornstalk, along with his son and two others, was murdered by a mob at Fort Randolph in Point Pleasant, which Cornstalk was visiting to help create maps of the Ohio Valley. Cornstalk's murder precipitated raids into Kentucky in the spring of 1778. In turn, these events elicited an attack led by Colonel John Bowman in May 1779 on the chief Shawnee village of Chillicothe, which, according to Allan Eckert, was on the Little Miami north of the current town of Xenia, Ohio.[3] Bowman's raid induced approximately

1,000 Shawnees—including Tecumseh's mother, Methotasa, and one of her daughters—to relocate to Missouri.

Tecumseh remained behind with no parents but with six siblings, including his oldest brother, Chiksika (sometimes spelled Cheeseekau), whom he deeply admired, and the two surviving members of triplet boys born in 1775. One of them, Lalawethika, would become a controversial but important spiritual leader of the Shawnees. Tecumseh, though, was hardly deserted. His father's family was obliged by Shawnee family traditions to support the children, and the oldest girl in the family, Tecumpease, had married a Shawnee and taken the young children into her home.

Chiksika felt especially close to Tecumseh and took the boy with him on hunting trips. In late 1783, Tecumseh broke his leg hunting buffalo when he apparently tried to leap onto the back of a buffalo and kill it with a knife. Chiksika and his friends stayed with Tecumseh for several months while the leg healed. By this time, Tecumseh was well on his way to manhood and, by his own later account, had been inebriated during the hunt. At the time, he decided never to drink again. He became an ardent opponent of alcohol for the rest of his life, thus rejecting not only a potential source of personal weakness but also a Euro-American weapon wielded to subjugate native peoples by encouraging indebtedness and social dissolution.

Tecumseh's first battle against Euro-Americans did not go well. In an attack on Kentuckians entering Ohio, probably in 1786, the adolescent Tecumseh panicked and fled when Chiksika was wounded. The injury to his brother was minor, and Tecumseh never again would come up short in battle. In attacks on flatboats carrying immigrants on the Ohio River, he fought bravely. It was also at this time (possibly in 1788) that he established his firm attitude against mistreating prisoners. When his war party burned a prisoner to death, Tecumseh strongly objected to the action and determined that he would not again fail to protect prisoners under his supervision.

In September 1786, Kentuckians under George Rogers Clark and Benjamin Logan attacked Shawnee villages to avenge assaults in Kentucky actually carried out not by Shawnees, but rather by Mingo and Cherokee war parties. In one attack by the Kentuckians, Melanthy (Moluntha), an elderly chief loyal to the new American nation, approached holding aloft a United States flag. His protestation of loyalty, however, did not prevent his murder.

The Shawnees did not allow these assaults to go unavenged, and Tecumseh played an important role in the response. He joined Chiksika in raiding settlements in Tennessee and Kentucky. Over the next several years, Tecumseh was often at Chiksika's side, as he was when his beloved brother and mentor was killed during an attack on a small settlement, probably in Tennessee in 1788 or 1789. As with many events concerning Tecumseh, there is uncertainty regarding the date of Chiksika's death.

During Tecumseh's absence from Ohio, the Shawnees moved northwest, near the confluence of the Maumee and Auglaize Rivers (where the city of Defiance is currently situated), a location where they more easily could obtain supplies from the British at Detroit. Although the American Revolution had ended in 1783, the British retained their fort at Detroit and Fort Michilimack-inac (the latter on Mackinac Island in the Straits of Mackinac joining Lakes Huron and Michigan), ostensibly because of debts owed by American merchants. Even stronger motives for maintaining their forts, however, were their desire to retain control of the fur trade with Indians and their fear that another war might break out between England and the United States. For both of these reasons, Canadian officials sought to maintain good relations with the Shawnees and other Indians in the Northwest Territory (the area comprising the current states of Ohio, Michigan, Indiana, Illinois, Wisconsin, and eastern Minnesota).

During this time, the U.S. government erected Fort Washington on the Ohio River at the site of present-day Cincinnati. In 1790, Arthur St. Clair, governor of the Northwest Territory, established an army of close to 1,500 soldiers at Fort Washington. General Josiah Harmar led the troops northward in September, while Major John Hamtramck came up the Wabash River from Fort Knox at Vincennes in southwestern Indiana. Two attacks by Shawnees and Potawatomis on Harmar's men killed close to 200 soldiers and forced a withdrawal by both contingents.

Tecumseh the Warrior

During the summer of 1791, Governor St. Clair prepared for another assault on the Shawnees. After assembling an army of 2,300 men, most of whom were undertrained militia, he set off from Cincinnati in September. Tecumseh's role in this battle, if any, is unclear. He may have led a scouting party that tracked the military force and reported its movements to a waiting body of warriors. By the fall, this Shawnee force had grown in number to approximately 1,000 and, well supplied by British traders, was primed to repel the invaders. According to some accounts, Tecumseh by this time was a war chief.

On November 3, St. Clair's army camped near the Wabash River in western Ohio. Before dawn on November 4, the large Indian force attacked, albeit apparently without Tecumseh, who seems to have taken a position with his scouts behind the line of St. Clair's advance to prevent a surprise arrival of reinforcements. Within hours, St. Clair, having suffered about 650 fatalities and hundreds of additional men wounded, ordered a retreat.

After the substantial victory over St. Clair, Tecumseh fought several successful skirmishes. In December, Kentuckians under Robert McClelland launched a surprise attack on a Tecumseh-led hunting party along the Great Miami River in western Ohio, while the Shawnees were rising in the morning. Tecumseh and his men attacked the Kentuckians, who had hesitated to approach close to the camp, and drove them off, killing two of the men. The following spring, a party of about three dozen Kentuckians led by a prominent frontiersman named Simon Kenton attacked Tecumseh near what today is Hamilton, Ohio, just north of Cincinnati. Again Tecumseh and his men drove off the attackers. Kenton led another band of men against Tecumseh in 1793, attacking while the Shawnees slept near where Paint Creek meets the Scioto River. Tecumseh led his men on a successful drive through Kenton's lines to retrieve their horses, which were behind the Kentuckians. Mortally wounded in the encounter, according to the early Tecumseh biographer Benjamin Drake, was John Ward, a "white Shawnee" captured at the age of three and brother to James Ward, ironically one of the men accompanying Kenton.[4]

The United States proposed an agreement with the Shawnees that included their relinquishing any claims to Ohio east of the Muskingum River—a land mass accounting for roughly one-third of the future state. Tecumseh, along with many other Shawnees, rejected the deal, and the government continued to prepare for a military solution. As the British began construction of Fort Miami in northwestern Ohio near modern-day Toledo, and British agents close to the Shawnees such as Alexander McKee and Matthew Elliott encouraged the Shawnees to remain steadfast in their opposition to U.S. pressure, the U.S. prepared for military action. Major General Anthony Wayne became the new military commander in the region and began construction of Fort Greenville and, north of it at the site of St. Clair's defeat, Fort Recovery, both in central Ohio near the Indiana line.

A joint force of Shawnees (apparently including Tecumseh), Delawares, Potawatomis, Ottawas, and Chippewas attacked Fort Recovery and a pack train approaching the fort on June 30, 1794. The Shawnees and Delawares successfully routed the pack train, killing about half of the 30 soldiers accompanying it and capturing the horses. The other three Indian groups assaulted the fort but suffered heavy losses, withdrew, and returned to their villages.

Battle of Fallen Timbers

At the time of the attack, Wayne was still at Fort Greenville. In early August, he led his troops north to the Auglaize River, only to find that the Shawnees had abandoned their villages there. At the confluence of the Auglaize and Maumee Rivers, he constructed Fort Defiance (a name also given to a later fort built in Wisconsin during the Black Hawk War).

Tecumseh and the other war chiefs decided to meet the enemy at Roche de Bout north of the Maumee. A recent storm had knocked down a lot of trees in the area, which would give the site its more lasting name, Fallen Timbers. On August 20, 1794, Wayne advanced to meet about 400 defenders, including Tecumseh and two of his brothers, Sauwauseekau and Lalawethika. In the face of the greater numbers and strong discipline on the part of the advancing force, the Shawnees retreated and took up positions behind some of the fallen trees. Sauwauseekau died in the battle, becoming, along with Tecumseh's father and his brother Chiksika, the third member of the family to die fighting the Euro-Americans in defense of Shawnee land.

The Battle of Fallen Timbers was a major defeat for the Shawnees, although Tecumseh fought bravely. According to Benjamin Drake, after Tecumseh's rifle malfunctioned, he borrowed a fowling piece and continued to urge his companions to fight before finally leading his men out of the battle when the situation became hopeless. They then rejoined the main body of Shawnees, who had retreated. Wayne's army burned Shawnee cornfields; scalped and mutilated Indians who had fallen in the battle; tortured to death a wounded "white Shawnee," Charles Smith, by quartering him; and even disinterred and mangled bodies.

The defeat induced many of the Shawnees, including the war chief Blue Jacket, who had led the confederacy of Indian peoples at Fort Recovery and Fallen Timbers, to agree to a peace treaty. The Treaty of Greenville, signed on August 3, 1795, cost the Shawnees southern, eastern, and central Ohio, leaving them with approximately the northwest quarter of the present-day state. The Shawnees and the other tribes in the region received in compensation $20,000 worth of trade goods and annuities that varied from $500 to $10,000; the Shawnees, for example, received $1,000. The Indians were permitted to hunt in the lands they had ceded until settlers moved in. The compensation for the land that changed hands as a result of this agreement came to approximately one cent for every six acres.[5] Tecumseh, however, did not accept the treaty.

As with other treaties between Indians and the U.S. government, Euro-Americans quickly violated the terms of the Treaty of Greenville, intruding on Shawnee land north of the Greenville line. The Ohio River, which had served as the border between Indian and U.S. lands, now became an easy conveyance for those who were not about to let an agreement with Indians hinder their movements throughout all of Ohio as well as Indian lands to the west. Euro-American hunters almost wiped out the deer population, fur-bearing animals declined, and increasing numbers of Shawnee men struggled to provide for their families.

THE GREAT STRATEGIST

A Partnership of Brothers

In April 1805, an event occurred that would have far-reaching consequences for Tecumseh and his resistance efforts. His erstwhile ne'er-do-well brother, Lalawethika—something of a joke among his fellow Shawnees with his corpulence, alcoholism, eye blinded by an accident with an arrow, and lack of distinction as a warrior—had a vision. In Lalawethika's trance, he received a view of what must be done to create a better world. It was one of many revitalization visions that American Indians—not all of them previously accepted as shamans, or holy men—experienced in the nineteenth century, including the Paiute Wovoka's vision that led ultimately to the Ghost Dance among the Lakotas, the death of Sitting Bull, and the massacre at Wounded Knee. Certainly there was nothing in Lalawethika's earlier life to stamp him as an individual likely to receive any sacred messages.

Nonetheless, Lalawethika had a vision to share, and it resonated mightily with a people wondering which direction they could take to stem the tide of Euro-American expansion. According to Lalawethika, he had been transported to a spirit world at the command of the Master of Life. There, on a mountaintop, he had gazed at a paradise teeming with game and fertile lands where the souls of good Shawnees would dwell forever. Sinful Shawnees would instead burn in a giant wigwam, an image not much different from the Christian concept of hell. But how to merit this paradise? The answer, according to the vision, was to adhere to the traditional ways in behavior, clothing, and food. Shawnees must renounce the productions of the Euro-Americans, principally residents of the new American nation, who—unlike the Shawnees, British, and French—were born not of the Master of Life but of the Evil Spirit; such dualism was again evocative of Christian concepts, particularly the moral dualism associated with God and Satan. As in the early Puritan settlements, Lalawethika's new social and religious vision posited the existence of witches doing the Evil Spirit's work. Ultimately, this teaching would lead to identification of supposed witches among some Indian tribes that adopted Lalawethika's teachings and four executions carried out by the Delawares.

According to Lalawethika, the Master of Life called upon the Shawnees and other native peoples to avoid alcohol and sexual promiscuity, eschew personal ownership of the land, acquire wealth only to share it with others, abandon their medicine bundles as now unnecessary (a radical concept that must have been extremely difficult), and participate in new songs and dances mandated in the vision. They also were to venerate and keep close at hand a sacred string of beans supposedly made from this new prophet's flesh—an object that evokes still more Christian images, especially the Catholic concepts of the rosary and the Eucharist.

Adherence to this vision, according to Lalawethika, would lead to the Euro-American conquerors eventually being covered over by the earth. Like other native revitalization visions, there was something of a time machine element to the future. Essentially, the world would be turned back to what it had been before the coming of the Euro-Americans, although Lalawethika did not seem to recognize, as he explained his distinctions regarding people's origins, that ultimately the American soldiers and colonists had come from the same place as the British.

In addition, Lalawethika informed his adherents that he had been given a new name—Tenskwatawa, which means "Open Door." He now was the doorway into the future, which would simultaneously be a journey into the past.[6]

Tecumseh apparently believed at least some of his brother's vision. Of course, as perhaps the finest political strategist of all American Indians, he must have also understood the political ramifications of the vision—how it could help him to unite tribes in a pan-Indian alliance necessary to preserve Shawnee land. Accordingly, Tecumseh accompanied Tenskwatawa to Greenville, the site of the infamous Greenville Treaty agreement, where the man now often referred to as the Prophet established a new village.

William Henry Harrison, the governor of Indiana Territory, which had been separated from the Northwest Territory in 1800, claimed that Tenskwatawa was a liar and a charlatan. Harrison, like many other U.S. figures, shared a general suspicion and fear of revitalization movements that might inspire continued resistance among the native peoples. Addressing the Delawares, Harrison denounced Tenskwatawa and suggested that they test the Prophet by asking him to make the sun stand still, the moon to change its course, or the dead to return. In fact, astronomers had ascertained that a solar eclipse would occur on June 16, 1806—a projection that Tenskwatawa apparently had learned about when the scientists visited Ohio. He rose to Harrison's challenge and said that he would make the sun darken (that is, stand still). When the sun did go dark, Tenskwatawa appeared to possess the ability not only to predict the future but also to work miracles. Thus, while hoping to undermine the Prophet's standing and influence, Harrison unwittingly contributed to solidifying his reputation.

Tecumseh now had an important partner—his brother the Prophet—in what would become the final attempt to preserve Shawnee land and the Shawnee way of life. Many other Shawnees, however, chose accommodation with the U.S. government and rejected the path advocated by Tecumseh and Tenskwatawa, fearing that the new movement would engulf them in renewed conflict. Among the leaders of the opposition to the brothers was Black Hoof (Catahecassa), who moved to a new village, Wapakoneta, on the Auglaize River, to cooperate in an experimental agricultural community supported by the Quakers. During the early years of the nineteenth century, many of the area tribes signed treaties yielding large chunks of their land to the U.S. government. The chiefs signing those treaties, however, did not represent the will of all of their people. Young warriors especially gravitated to Greenville to adopt the Prophet's vision and accept Tecumseh's political leadership.

In 1807, Governor Edward Tiffin of Ohio, which had become a separate territory in 1799, demanded a conference with local Indians in response to the killing of several farmers. The gathering occurred in June at Springfield on the Mad River in west-central Ohio. Tecumseh attended the parley, seeking to convince authorities that he was committed to peace, as part of an effort to ensure that he would not be pulled into large-scale war before he was ready. Knowing that his own men had not killed the farmers, he blamed Black Hoof—an accusation that almost brought the two Shawnee factions into combat right then. The situation was defused, and it turned out that, in fact, Potawatomis were responsible for the deaths.

The Springfield conference elicited no agreements from Tecumseh, and increased tensions between Britain and the United States made Indian loyalty a major political and military issue. Thomas Kirker, who had become acting governor of Ohio Territory in March 1807 when Tiffin resigned to become a United States senator, was especially concerned about the growing impact of Tenskwatawa's vision and called for another conference, this one at Greenville. Tecumseh did not participate, but he did escort the U.S. officials back to Chillicothe in September. There, he gave a three-hour address that included an extensive history lesson on past treaties and an analysis of the current situation. He acknowledged present realities, affirmed that he would not try to force settlers from their homes on former Shawnee land, but vowed to permit no more loss of land north of the Ohio River. The speech reportedly was extremely effective, and Governor Kirker concluded that Tecumseh's intentions were essentially peaceful. According to R. David Edmunds, the speech marked a shift within the Shawnee community at Greenville away from the expectation of a religious revitalization solution to a political approach to halt encroachments on their land.

Building an Indian Confederacy

Tecumseh now turned his attention toward forming an alliance of Indian peoples that would be strong enough to resist the United States. This endeavor was especially difficult because it challenged traditional tribal independence and, even within tribal groups, the practice of leading by consensus rather than by dictates handed down by individual chiefs. Main Poc, a prominent Potawatomi war chief, for example, was highly skeptical of Tecumseh's plan. Main Poc was also viewed as a shaman because he was born with no fingers on his left hand (a disability interpreted as a sign of the Great Spirit's favor). He invited the brothers to Potawatomi land in eastern Indiana where the Tippecanoe River meets the Wabash. With the Greenville location surrounded by Euro-American and Indian adversaries and largely depleted of game, Tecumseh agreed. In April 1808, Tecumseh, the Prophet, and their followers left Ohio behind and moved westward to establish a new village known as Prophetstown on the Wabash approximately 2.5 miles from the mouth of the Tippecanoe.

As Prophetstown was being constructed, Tecumseh traveled to Fort Malden near Amherstburg in Canada across the border from southeastern Michigan. He met with Canada's Deputy Superintendent of Indian Affairs William Claus on June 13. Each party had its own agenda. The British anticipated a possible war with the United States and needed Indian allies to provide a military buffer between the United States and Canada as well as combatants in case of an attempted invasion from the south. Tecumseh's interests lay not with defending Canada, but rather with protecting Indian land from further confiscation.

Claus agreed to supply Prophetstown with food and ammunition, but neither he nor Tecumseh wanted any precipitous fighting to break out. Canada did not want Indian–U.S. conflicts to thrust it into a war; Tecumseh assured the British that his intentions were strictly defensive. With each side having felt out the other's intentions, Tecumseh returned to his new Indiana home in July.

No sooner had he returned to Prophetstown than he set about recruiting various Indian groups to join his planned confederacy. He met with the Senecas and Wyandots in Ohio but encountered strong resistance to his plans by prominent chiefs, including Tarhe of the Wyandonts. It was a difficult time for the Shawnee leader: Not only was he struggling to extend his confederacy, but his people suffered through a difficult, hungry winter in 1808–1809 and a serious outbreak of illness. Many who had come to Prophetstown—among them Chippewas and Ottawas—returned to their previous homes in the spring.

Tecumseh headed west in April 1809 to recruit confederacy members among the Sauks, Foxes, and Winnebagos in Illinois. Meanwhile, Tenskwatawa traveled to Fort Wayne to meet with John Johnson, the new Indian agent there, and to Vincennes to confer with Governor Harrison. These attempts to allay the fears of U.S. officials concerning an Indian uprising apparently had little effect, and Harrison moved forward on agreements with the Miamis, Delawares, and Potawatomis in an attempt to isolate the recalcitrant Shawnees. Harrison tried to keep his efforts hidden from Tecumseh, although at some point prior to the signing of the Treaty of Fort Wayne on September 30, 1809, he learned what was under way.

The agreement was signed by chiefs who were carefully selected for their loyalty to the United States and, at least in some cases, whose cooperation was induced with bribes. Its unpopularity drove many of these chiefs' followers to Tecumseh, who could readily offer an "I told you so" message to those who felt betrayed by their overly compliant leaders. Edmunds sees the treaty as another major turning point in the shift from Tenskwatawa's visions to Tecumseh's leadership—from revitalization visions to political and military strategizing.

The spring of 1810 brought to Prophetstown growing numbers of recruits, including Kickapoos, Miamis, Delawares, Sauks, Foxes, and Potawatomis. Even the hold that Tarhe and other pro-U.S. chiefs held over the Wyandots began to slip, and many of their warriors joined the growing force under Tecumseh.

Tecumseh and William Henry Harrison

Governor Harrison sent emissaries to meet with Tecumseh and Tenskwatawa in the summer of 1810. One of the messengers, Joseph Barron, urged Shawnee representatives to visit Washington, D.C., to meet with President James Madison. The Prophet threatened Barron with death, but Tecumseh took charge of Barron's safety, even having Barron sleep in his own lodge to ensure that no harm came to him. Tecumseh finally agreed to meet with Harrison at Vincennes, the capital of Indiana Territory from 1800 until 1813.

Tecumseh arrived at Vincennes on August 12 and met with the governor for several days. It was Harrison's first meeting with Tecumseh, and he was greatly impressed with his guest's intelligence and leadership qualities. At one point, Tecumseh's Shawnees and Harrison's soldiers almost came to blows, a confrontation that likely would have left both leaders dead. Despite the nearly disastrous incident, Harrison reported to Secretary of War William Eustis that Tecumseh was the principal leader of the Indians resisting the United States, the "Moses" of his people.

The meeting seemed to allay Harrison's fears of an imminent military confrontation with Tecumseh. While the Shawnees were experiencing a relatively calm autumn, Tecumseh again visited Canada and conferred with a long-time supporter, Indian agent Matthew Elliott, whose marriage to a Shawnee may have contributed to his loyalty. Tecumseh wanted a continued flow of supplies and ammunition, and Elliott tried hard to comply with his requests, even though his efforts to meet Shawnee needs sometimes exceeded official British policy. During the harsh winter of 1810–1811, Elliott helped to make sure that pack trains made regular trips south to Prophetstown.

Then, in the spring of 1811, the lull was shattered through no fault of Tecumseh, who tried diligently to keep his followers from starting a war. Main Poc's Potawatomis attacked Illinois settlements. Harrison apparently knew that Tecumseh and the Prophet were not involved, but he nonetheless sent intermediaries to Prophetstown. An incident in June contributed to Harrison's suspicions when, with Tecumseh in Michigan, Tenskwatawa directed the seizure of a cargo of salt intended for distribution to several tribes.

Harrison somewhat irrationally accused Tecumseh of plotting his murder, an accusation for which no evidence apparently existed and which was not Tecumseh's intention. Despite this inflammatory claim, he also invited the two brothers to visit President Madison in Washington, D.C., and to come to Vincennes to meet with him. Tecumseh had recruited many of the tribes from the former Northwest Territory to his confederacy but was still unready for military action. He was unwilling to journey to Washington at the time, but was willing to meet with Harrison in Vincennes so long as he did not convey a sense of weakness by appearing to be acquiescing to a summons.

Tecumseh's compromise was to go to Vincennes, but with a large supporting cast of warriors befitting his position. Harrison feared conflict and had some 800 soldiers awaiting Tecumseh, although the Shawnee's large contingent was a public relations maneuver rather than a prelude to combat. Tecumseh arrived on July 27, 1811, and the meetings lasted for almost a week. Tecumseh, always politically astute, did not rule out going to Washington in the future, thereby buying more time to enlarge his confederacy.

Tecumseh may, indeed, have been willing to visit Washington if events had worked out as he wished. He certainly tried consistently to keep his options open, but was, if anything, perhaps too truthful. He admitted to Harrison that after their meetings concluded, he was going farther south to recruit more members for his confederacy. Perhaps he hoped that Harrison would understand the difference between a political alliance that if necessary could be used militarily and a strictly military alliance. What Tecumseh was attempting to fashion, after all, was not radically different from the sorts of unions that the colonies had entered into, and that now constituted the states of the United States of America.

Shaking the Earth

Whatever Tecumseh's motivation, informing Harrison of his plans proved to be a mistake. Tecumseh journeyed to Alabama, Mississippi, and Georgia to meet with Chickasaws, Choctaws, and Creeks but enjoyed substantive success only with the last group. Especially important was his arrival on September 19, 1811, at the Creek town of Tuckabatchee, located where the Coosa and Tallapoosa Rivers form the Alabama River in present-day Elmore County, Alabama.

Also present at Tuckabatchee was Indian agent Benjamin Hawkins, who was trying to gauge the level of support for Tecumseh. Tecumseh tried to wait Hawkins out so he could recruit without the agent listening. Hawkins inadvertently contributed to Tecumseh's success when he announced that a federal road would be constructed across Creek land. Even with monetary inducements from tolls and gifts, the Creeks only reluctantly agreed to a deal that they felt was being forced on them. Hawkins finally left on September 28; the Creeks, angry at being pushed into an agreement they did not want, then listened sympathetically to Tecumseh's call for a confederation of Indian peoples.

Tecumseh spoke eloquently, skillfully drawing upon history as it affected his listeners and recapitulating their current situation. Others in his party, especially Seekaboo, pushed Tenskwatawa's revitalization vision. Ultimately, those who accepted the vision came to be known as "Red Sticks" because of the red war clubs they used in forming war parties. Supposedly merely shaking the red sticks at an enemy would sink him into boggy ground and make him helpless.

The most dramatic element in this multipronged recruiting pitch was Tecumseh's use of signs. A comet that coincided with Tecumseh's visit to the Creeks recalled vividly his birth and name. In addition, Tecumseh may have predicted an earthquake. He reportedly promised that when he was ready to strike at the oppressors, he would stamp his foot and the whole earth would shake. Whether he actually made this prophecy is uncertain; the story may have been added after the fact. In either case, earthquakes did occur early in the morning of December 16, 1811, not long after Tecumseh had left the South for his return to Indiana.

Known as the New Madrid earthquakes because the epicenter was near New Madrid, Missouri, the tremors were the most severe recorded in the United States as of that time. The shocks came in waves, beginning early in the morning of December 16 and recurring throughout January and February, totaling close to 1,900 aftershocks by March 15. For a people steeped in a culture that readily accepted natural phenomena as reflective of a spiritual reality, many people, especially among the Creeks, saw in the earthquakes a convincing expression of Tecumseh's power.[7]

Attack on Prophetstown

Harrison, fully recognizing Tecumseh's political skill and wanting to destroy the confederacy before its leader returned, had taken advantage of Tecumseh's absence to move on Prophetstown. In a letter to Secretary of War William Eustis on September 8, 1811, Harrison wrote:

> The implicit obedience and respect which the followers of Tecumseh pay to him is really astonishing and more than any other circumstance bespeaks him one of

those uncommon geniuses, which spring up occasionally to produce revolutions and overturn the established order of things. If it were not for the vicinity of the United States, he would perhaps be the founder of an Empire that would rival in glory that of Mexico or Peru. No difficulties deter him. His activity and industry supply the want of letters.[8]

Certainly part of Harrison's admiration for his adversary, as Robert M. Owens has pointed out, came from Tecumseh's actions being far more politically comprehensible to him than the vision-based behavior of the Prophet.[9]

After a positive response from Eustis regarding Harrison's plans, he assembled a force of approximately 1,000 men, including both regular troops and militia from Indiana and Kentucky. The soldiers started north on September 26. On the way, Harrison constructed Fort Harrison at the current site of Terre Haute, Indiana, and dispatched a perfunctory offer to Tenskwatawa to disband his group of warriors as a way to avoid conflict. He continued forward at the end of October, built Fort Boyd as a supply post, and came within 12 miles of Prophetstown by November 5.

Tenskwatawa had been ordered by his brother to avoid any military confrontations with the U.S. government but seemed unsure how to respond to the advancing army. On November 6, he offered to meet with Harrison, who halted long enough to comply but took precautions against a surprise attack, which Tenskwatawa was, in fact, planning. The Prophet assured the Prophetstown warriors that they would be invincible to bullets and apparently intended to have Shawnees sneak into the enemy camp and kill Harrison. However, early in the morning of November 7, sentries spotted the infiltrators and raised an alarm. Nonetheless, two of the Prophet's men got close to Harrison—but then mistook his aide, Colonel Abraham Owen, for the governor, killing the aide instead.

Heavy fighting caused heavy casualties on both sides. After roughly two hours, the Indians withdrew, giving Harrison the field and the right to declare victory in the Battle of Tippecanoe. The victory, in turn, offered Harrison a memorable slogan for his successful presidential campaign in 1840, when he and his running mate, John Tyler, ran as "Tippecanoe and Tyler, Too."

The battle marked the downfall of Tenskwatawa. Survivors angrily denounced him for his false promises, and many warriors abandoned the confederacy that Tecumseh had worked so hard to assemble. Knowing that Harrison would soon arrive at Prophetstown, the residents abandoned the village, leaving the advancing army to burn down the homes and destroy the food that had been left behind. Had Tenskwatawa not been Tecumseh's brother, he probably would have been killed by his former followers.

What awaited Tecumseh on his return to the area in January 1812 was not just a destroyed village, but a shattered confederacy. He bitterly upbraided his brother and threatened to kill him if he again jeopardized his efforts. The defeat also emboldened Tecumseh's Indian opponents, some of whom plotted to kill him but were unable to execute their plans.

THE WAR OF 1812

Moving Toward War

Tecumseh again set about putting his considerable leadership skills to work. He sought to keep Harrison at bay by promising to visit Washington after the corn was planted. He also sent a delegation to Vincennes to tell Harrison that the group had broken with Tecumseh, even drawing a different interpretation from the earthquakes, which the emissaries said signified that the Indians should make peace with the United States. Harrison was deceived, reporting to the Secretary of War that the Indians now desired peace—and perhaps wanting too much to believe that his military victory had achieved far more than it really had.

With Tecumseh's own personal reputation still intact and shored up by the ongoing earthquakes (despite what he had counseled his followers to tell Harrison), he began to draw more supporters to his side. The British, for their part, realized that war was now imminent and continued to woo the Shawnees. In addition, Tecumseh, who had established a temporary residence approximately 15 miles from Prophetstown, returned to the site of the former village and continued trying to delude Harrison about his intentions.

Tecumseh attended a conference with U.S. officials in May 1812 on the Mississinewa River in Indiana. Isadore Chaine of the Wyandots visited Tecumseh, ostensibly to tell him that he should no longer fight the United States, but actually to convey from the British a black wampum belt representing war. Tecumseh spoke at the gathering, denouncing the attack on Harrison at Tippecanoe as well as recent raids by Main Poc's Potawatomis. He further asserted that if he had been home, there would have been no battle with Harrison. All of this was undoubtedly true, but for reasons other than what Tecumseh probably hoped Harrison would infer. Tecumseh certainly preferred to achieve his goals politically, but he also knew that war was likely. He simply wanted to enter it, if necessary, on his terms.

Tecumseh left for a return trip to Amherstburg in Canada during June, arriving there at the beginning of July. Meanwhile, the United States continued moving inexorably toward war with Great Britain. U.S. war strategy had been formulated in the spring of 1812 to include a three-pronged attack on Canadian forces focused on Detroit, Niagara, and Lake Champlain. The army of the West was placed under William Hull, the governor of Michigan Territory and since April 1812 also a brigadier general. President Madison sent Congress a message supporting war on June 1. The House of Representatives voted in favor of war on June 4, and the Senate followed suit on June 17. The House agreed the next day to amendments added by the Senate, and Madison formally signed the declaration.

Battle of Brownstown

As Tecumseh made his way to Canada, Hull led reinforcements to Detroit, arriving on July 6. Six days later, Hull crossed the Detroit River and captured Sandwich (site of the present-day city of Windsor, Ontario), located north of Fort Malden. Tecumseh attempted to hold together his alliance, but many Wyandots vacillated, first joining Tecumseh and the British, and then switching back to the United States after Hull's victory at Sandwich. After the British in turn captured Fort Michilimackinac, many switched sides yet again, returning to support the British.

With Hull in need of supplies, a pack train under Captain Henry Brush started from Ohio to Michigan, and Hull sent Major Thomas Van Horne with 150 soldiers to meet it. Tecumseh, who was at Brownstown, Michigan, south of Detroit at the time, learned of Hull's orders when a dispatch rider was captured. Tecumseh expected to be reinforced by approximately 100 British soldiers under the command of Brevet Major Adam Muir. However, on August 5, despite Muir's failure to arrive, Tecumseh led an attack that sent Van Horne's troops fleeing in panic and inflicted major casualties on the Americans, including 19 killed, in what has been called the Battle of Brownstown.

Hull took most of his force back across the Detroit River to Detroit. He then dispatched, under Lieutenant Colonel James Miller, another relief force to Brush, whose supply train remained at the River Raisin in southern Michigan. Colonel Henry Proctor (who would be promoted to brigadier general the following year after a major victory at the same river) sent more British troops and Indians to Muir at Brownstown. On August 9, Muir led his troops, with Tecumseh in charge of the Indian allies, to a Wyandot village called Monguagon, located five miles north of Brownstown. Some of Muir's men mistakenly fired on Potawatomis, thinking they were Miller's men. In addition, a British bugler sounded the call to advance, but it was misinterpreted as ordering a retreat.

Tecumseh, however, remained at his post with his Shawnees in a cornfield, and ordered a withdrawal only after realizing that the British had withdrawn. Tecumseh was wounded, apparently painfully but not especially seriously. The wound has been reported variously as a leg wound caused by buckshot or a neck wound. It is also possible that Tecumseh actually suffered the wound during the earlier Battle of Brownstown. The Americans claimed victory, although they had suffered even more fatalities than the British–Indian force (about 18 Americans killed compared to 15 British–Indian deaths).[10]

Attack on Detroit

Major General Isaac Brock arrived at Fort Malden in the middle of August 1812 to assume command of operations in the west. He and Tecumseh immediately established considerable rapport and respect for each other. When Brock decided to attack Detroit, Tecumseh strongly seconded the decision, appreciating the new commander's decisiveness. Tecumseh is reported to have remarked of Brock admiringly, "This is a man!"[11] Both men exuded

Wampum

The description of Tecumseh provided by Captain John Glegg includes a medallion of King George III attached to a multicolored wampum string that the Shawnee leader wore around his neck. When Isadore Chaine of the Wyandots visited Tecumseh in 1812, he brought a black wampum belt from the British to signify that the British and Shawnees should ally themselves against the United States in case of war.

Rather than a form of Indian currency, as is often thought, wampum was primarily a medium for what today we would call official documents—treaties, contracts, and records of transactions, usually of a public nature. The word *wampum* comes from a Narragansett word for white shell beads. Wampum consisted of pieces of shells and later beads acquired from Euro-American traders. Originally, the beads were either white or purple–black. Holes were drilled through the beads with a flint drill rolled between the hands, which permitted the beads to be strung. Several wampum strings were often woven together into belts, usually three to four feet long and four or five inches wide. The belts usually consisted of multiple colors with designs (human figures, geometric patterns, and other images). The colors and figures were symbolic, making their narrative easily read by those who understood the language of wampum belts. Indian leaders often spoke while accompanied by a wampum belt to which they would refer. Belts also were used to convey tribal history and traditions.

Both durable and easily transported, the belts were practical and often quite beautiful. The latter quality made them attractive to traders and collectors of Indian artifacts and, therefore, quite valuable monetarily. The value that Euro-Americans often placed on wampum belts did lead to their use in trading at times, but that remained a secondary purpose.

leadership, and an aide to Brock, Captain John Glegg, recorded a detailed description of the Shawnee leader that conveys not only Tecumseh's appearance but also his character:

Tecumseh's appearance was very prepossessing; his figure light and finely proportioned; his age I imagined to be about five and thirty [actually about forty-four]; in height, five feet nine or ten inches; his complexion, light copper; countenance, oval, with bright hazel eyes beaming cheerfulness, energy and decision. Three small silver crowns, or coronets, were suspended from the lower cartilage of his aquiline nose; and a large silver medallion of George the Third, which I believe his ancestor had received from Lord Dorchester, when governor-general of Canada, was attached to a mixed coloured wampum string, and hung around his neck. His dress consisted of a plain, neat uniform, tanned deer-skin jacket, with long trousers of the same material, the seams of both being covered with neatly cut fringe; and he had on his feet leather moccasins, much ornamented with work made from the dyed quills of the porcupine.[12]

Hull deserted Sandwich on August 11, taking his troops across the river to Detroit. Brock formally requested Hull's surrender on August 15, but Hull refused to capitulate. As the British began bombarding American positions, Tecumseh drew a map of Detroit and its surroundings for Brock. The plan was for Tecumseh to lead his warriors across the river during the night, surround Detroit, and attack the town the following morning while the British marched on the fort. Hull was facing a force of about 1,100 British and 600 Indians; he had about 1,000 of his own men after sending 400 of his troops to the River Raisin under Lewis Cass and Duncan McArthur to meet Brush, who was still there. The mission may have been designed to get the two officers out of the way, as they strongly objected to Hull's refusal to attack Fort Malden and Hull's overall lack of leadership.[13]

Much to Brock's surprise, Hull surrendered on August 16, lowering the American flag in the early afternoon. Many of his men had deserted when the British began their advance, and Hull may have wanted to ensure the safety of the women and children under his protection. Cass and McArthur, who had failed to reach Brush, were on their way back to Detroit when the surrender occurred and had no recourse but to join in the surrender. In all, Hull surrendered approximately 2,200 men, 39 large guns, 3,000 rifles and muskets, and extensive ammunition and supplies. All of Michigan Territory was now under the control of the British, and Tecumseh had helped to save Canada, albeit only temporarily.

Indian and British efforts in the immediate aftermath of the victory at Detroit had mixed results. U.S. forces abandoned Fort Dearborn, site of the future city of Chicago, on August 15 in the face of hostilities by Potawatomis and were attacked two miles away from the fort. They suffered heavy casualties, and those soldiers who were not killed outright were taken prisoner. Potawatomis then attacked Fort Wayne on September 5 and sent for reinforcements. Tecumseh tried to persuade the British to provide help. Finally, he succeeded and headed for Fort Wayne with 600 warriors while 250 British under Muir also set out. However, William Henry Harrison arrived at Fort Wayne with more than 2,200 men on September 13; by the time Tecumseh reached the fort, the attackers had been repelled.[14]

The British, who were camped on the Maumee River on September 25, learned that most of Harrison's army under General James Winchester was approaching. Muir hesitated, embarked on several small-scale retreats, and finally took his soldiers back to Detroit. When various Indian groups also departed, including the Ottawas and Chippewas, Tecumseh was forced to follow suit. Tecumseh was disappointed by the indecision and vacillation, and must have longed for General Brock; Brock had departed for the Niagara area, leaving Henry Procter in command in the Detroit area. On October 13, Brock was killed in battle while trying to rally his men for a counterattack against a large U.S. force that had crossed the Niagara River and taken Queenston Heights.

Tenskwatawa had remained at Prophetstown when Tecumseh rejoined the British. When the Prophet learned of the Indian successes, he planned an attack on Fort Harrison. This effort, which was primarily carried out by Kickapoos and Winnebagos, was defeated by Captain Zachary Taylor— another future President of the United States who would use his Indian-fighting career to help further his political ambitions. Tenskwatawa and his dwindling number of followers then moved farther northwest in Indiana and, in December, into Canada. The two brothers reunited and spent the winter of 1812–1813 back in Indiana, taking no role in the British victory by Colonel Procter and the Wyandot chief Roundhead over General Winchester at the Battle of Frenchtown on the River Raisin in January 1813. Tecumseh, however, continued recruiting in Indiana and Illinois for his Indian confederacy. Despite the earlier setbacks, he saw the confederacy, in alliance with the British, as the last, best way to retain Shawnee land in the upper Midwest.

Tecumseh's Treatment of Prisoners

In March 1813, Tecumseh started toward Amherstburg with his followers, not realizing that before long he would wage the final battle of his life and make one last unsuccessful effort to resist the mighty tide of U.S. expansionism in the Ohio Valley. The man who would ultimately defeat him, his old adversary William Henry Harrison, was busy that spring constructing a new fort, Fort Meigs, near present-day Maumee south of Toledo in northern Ohio. The fort was a handy jumping-off point for liberating Detroit and invading Canada, and Procter realized that it was a target he had to attack.

On April 24, a joint British and Indian force under Procter and Tecumseh left Amherstburg to destroy Fort Meigs. By May 1, Procter, now a brigadier general, had his artillery in position. Harrison, however, had constructed earthen walls inside the fort to reinforce the wooden stockade. Consequently, the artillery barrage had little effect. Because Harrison knew that reinforcements were on the way, he rejected Procter's ultimatum to surrender.

One contingent of the reinforcements, some 800 men strong, under Lieutenant Colonel William Dudley, landed across the Maumee River from Fort Meigs on May 5. Dudley captured one of Procter's two batteries but committed a serious blunder by pursuing the fleeing Indians. As Dudley's men moved deeper into the woods, they encountered a large force under Tecumseh and quickly attempted to retreat. While British were retaking the battery, approximately 550 of Dudley's 800 men were either killed (including Dudley) or captured.

The prisoners were taken to Fort Miami, an abandoned British post, and forced to run the gauntlet between two lines of Indians. Some of Dudley's men died in the process, and others were killed after they survived the terrifying run. All of this activity occurred unbeknownst to Tecumseh, who was conferring with Major Adam Muir at the recaptured battery. When Tecumseh learned what was happening, he rode quickly to the torture site, stopped the Indians from harming any more prisoners, and sharply upbraided Procter and the other officers for not protecting the prisoners.

Tecumseh's rescue of the prisoners contributed enormously to the Shawnee leader's reputation, not only in the immediate aftermath of the battle, but also down through the years. John Sugden discusses the incident in detail and remarks that "perhaps more than any other incident in Tecumseh's life this one lingered in the memory." He adds, "Tecumseh's defense of the American prisoners became a cornerstone of his legend, the ultimate proof of his inherent nobility ...."[15]

Writing within 30 years after the incident, Benjamin Drake offers an account of a British officer present during Tecumseh's arrival at Fort Miami relayed through a correspondent of Drake's. The account is likely romanticized but offers the prevailing view of Tecumseh's behavior:

> Whilst this blood-thirsty carnage was raging, a thundering voice was heard in the rear, in the Indian tongue, when, turning round, he saw Tecumseh coming with all the rapidity his horse could carry him, until he drew near to where two Indians had an American, and were in the act of killing him. He sprang from his horse, caught one by the throat and the other by the breast, and threw them to the ground; drawing his tomahawk and scalping knife, he ran in between the Americans and Indians, brandishing them with the fury of a mad man, and daring any one of the hundreds that surrounded him, to attempt to murder another American.[16]

Despite Dudley's catastrophic defeat, the combined force could not capture Fort Meigs. Procter, much to Tecumseh's disappointment, ordered his men back to Canada on May 9. Driving the U.S. military out of the upper Midwest was far more important to Tecumseh than defending Canada. Nonetheless, he maintained his alliance with the British despite serious misgivings about Procter's decision-making and leadership capabilities.

Acceding to Tecumseh's wishes, Procter agreed to another attack on Fort Meigs in July. The British made little use of artillery, however, and did not try to storm the fort. A stratagem by Tecumseh, although creatively conceived, failed. His plan was to simulate a battle against advancing U.S. reinforcements that would lure the soldiers in the fort, now under the command of General Green Clay, out into the open to help the fictitious troops. Clay, however, knew that no reinforcements were scheduled to arrive and suspected a trick.

When the second attempt to capture Fort Meigs failed, Procter agreed to attack Fort Stephenson on the Sandusky River. Procter launched the attack on August 2, but again his artillery was not able to batter down the fort's walls. During the early evening, the British began a frontal attack, but the fort's single cannon, aimed at the attackers who were attempting to scale the surrounding moat, caused heavy British casualties. Tecumseh viewed the attack as suicidal and did not have his men participate. The British began their journey back to Canada the next day, and many members of Tecumseh's confederacy—which included Sauk, Fox, Menominee, and Chippewa warriors, including the great Sauk warrior Black Hawk (who had also participated in the attacks on Fort Meigs)—departed for their home villages.

The Final Battle

After U.S. ships under Captain Oliver Perry destroyed Captain Robert Barclay's British fleet on Lake Erie, and with Harrison preparing to invade Canada, Procter decided to withdraw from Amherstburg, abandon Detroit, and take his army to the Niagara area. Learning of these plans on September 18, 1813, Tecumseh strongly opposed Procter and argued for staying and fighting. Because it was not Canada that drew Tecumseh into the war but his own homeland, the prospect of retreating into Canada held little appeal for him. A few days later, Procter explained in a face-to-face meeting with Tecumseh that recent reversals gave him little choice. At that point, Tecumseh reluctantly agreed to accompany him up the Thames River, in southeast Ontario above Lake Erie. In the final analysis, he knew that the Shawnees' only hope still lay with the British ultimately winning their battle with the Americans.

In late September, Procter burned the Amherstburg shipyards, Fort Malden, and anything else that might be useful to Harrison. Some Indian allies, including the Potawatomi chief Main Poc, left the British side to return to Michigan. Those remaining with Tecumseh numbered approximately 3,000, including men, women, and children. Despite the departures, Tecumseh's confederacy had continued to hold together reasonably well given the circumstances, and included Kickapoo, Potawatomi, Winnebago, and Wyandot representatives in addition to Shawnees. Most continued with Procter up the Thames toward Chatham, although en route about half of the 3,000 abandoned the British.

Tecumseh, who had stayed behind in Amherstburg to watch the movement of Harrison's forces, arrived at Chatham on October 2. The next day, Procter led a further retreat toward the Indian village of Moraviantown. Tecumseh waged a delaying tactic, destroying bridges along the route Harrison was following. At McGregor's Creek, as the British approached Chatham on October 4, Tecumseh's warriors fired on the advancing army, but artillery fire drove them away. In the exchange, Tecumseh suffered a slight wound to his left arm.

That night, Tecumseh led his war party to the British camp near Moraviantown. Tecumseh reportedly believed that he was on the verge of defeat and seemed to anticipate his own imminent death. Various accounts note his distribution of personal items such as his pistols; a sword to be conveyed to his son, Paukeesaa, who was then about 17 and had not yet distinguished himself as a warrior; and, to Black Hawk, a tomahawk that he had received from his brother Chiksika.

The next morning, October 5, Tecumseh planned strategy with Procter and arranged to evacuate the women and children in his party. In the afternoon, with Harrison's troops approaching, Procter organized his British soldiers in two lines across the road approximately two miles west of Moraviantown north of the Thames. Tecumseh and his men positioned themselves to the right of the British troops in the thickets. The river protected Procter's left flank.

Harrison arrived in the middle of the afternoon and attacked the British forces. Although the British had one cannon, they did not discharge it. The infantry fired about two volleys, and then the British fled, their resistance lasting only a few minutes. Procter quickly left his men to their own fate and rode off, pausing long enough at Moraviantown to have a quick drink without dismounting and then galloping off into infamy. He was court-martialed in Montreal in December 1814, publicly reprimanded, and suspended without pay for six months. The charges were detailed and quite specific, but ultimately came down to incompetence in planning and executing the battle. His military career was over, and he died in 1822 in England.[17]

Tecumseh, however, was ready to fight. Although his once-grand confederacy had shrunk to about 500 men, it still included a remarkable range of warriors: Creeks, Delawares, Foxes, Sauks, Kickapoos, Winnebagos, Wyandots, Potawatomies, Ottawas, Ojibways, and his own Shawnees. Tenskwatawa was present but did not engage in the fighting, confining himself to exhorting others. He survived the conflict to live an increasingly anonymous life, dying in 1836.

Tecumseh and his warriors succeeded initially in driving back Harrison's infantry. With the quick defeat of the British, however, the full brunt of the army could be directed against the Indians. Mounted militia under Colonel Richard Johnson crowded close to the brush from which the Indians were firing. Tecumseh fought bravely, firing his musket and encouraging his men. Finally, one soldier found his mark, shooting Tecumseh in the chest.

The identity of the man who killed Tecumseh remains uncertain, although Johnson accepted (if he did not directly claim) that distinction during his political career, running under the nickname "Old Tecumseh" in his Congressional and vice-presidential campaigns in the 1820s and 1830s. Johnson reached the apex of his career as President Martin Van Buren's vice president in 1837. Allan Eckert offers a detailed and reasonably persuasive argument that a private named David King was the man who shot Tecumseh, but the identity of the shooter probably will never be known with absolute certainty.[18]

Another enduring mystery surrounding Tecumseh's death is what happened to his body. Many slain Indians were mutilated, but whether Tecumseh suffered that fate is not definitely known. Nor has anyone been able to identify absolutely the great Shawnee leader's burial place. Sugden asserts that soldiers scalped the corpse and ripped strips of skin from the body. The famous politician Henry Clay was said to have exhibited a strip of Tecumseh's skin in Washington. Eckert notes that Simon Kenton claimed to have deliberately identified the wrong body as Tecumseh in an effort to spare him the indignity of mutilation. He comes to the conclusion that the body was not mutilated and that during the night it was removed by some of Tecumseh's followers and buried.[19] As with the identity of Tecumseh's slayer, the final word on this mystery likely will remain unsaid.

The death of Tecumseh did not end opposition to efforts by the United States to take over traditional Indian lands, but for all practical purposes it did end serious resistance in most of the Old Northwest Territory. The War of 1812 ended officially on Christmas Eve 1814. The Shawnees never again would be a bulwark against U.S. expansionism and as a people would prove increasingly peripatetic, wandering among Ohio, Missouri, Kansas, Texas, and Oklahoma. Death, however, did not diminish Tecumseh. His reputation would grow and endure, with the Shawnee leader being exalted by romantic primitivists and serious historians alike. Today few American Indian leaders occupy such a respected position as Tecumseh, who worked tirelessly, if ultimately unsuccessfully, to unite Indians throughout the United States in an attempt to preserve a way of life that he believed Shawnees and other native peoples had a right to maintain.

NOTES

1. Letter to Secretary of War William Eustis, quoted in R. David Edmunds, *Tecumseh and the Quest for Indian Leadership* (Boston: Little, Brown, 1984) 132.

2. Edmunds, *Tecumseh* 93–98.

3. Allan W. Eckert, *A Sorrow in Our Heart: The Life of Tecumseh* (1992; New York: Bantam Books, 1993) 815–16.

4. Edmunds, *Tecumseh* 34–35; Benjamin Drake, *Life of Tecumseh, and of His Brother the Prophet; with a Historical Sketch of the Shawanoe Indians* (1841; New York: Arno Press and *The New York Times*, 1969) 71–78.

5. Eckert 916; Charles J. Kappler, ed., *Indian Affairs: Laws and Treaties*, 2 vols. (Washington, DC: Government Printing Office, 1904), 2: 39–45.

6. See Edmunds' chapter "Red Messiah" in *Tecumseh* 73–98, Colin G. Calloway's chapter "The Visions of Tenskwatawa and Tecumseh" in his *The Shawnees and the War for America: The Penguin Library of American Indian History* (New York: Penguin, 2007) 126–54, and Edmunds' *The Shawnee Prophet* (1983; Lincoln: University of Nebraska Press, 1985).

7. See the chapter "Red Sticks and Earthquakes" in John Sugden's *Tecumseh: A Life* (New York: Henry Holt, 1997) 237–51.

8. Letter from William Henry Harrison to William Eustis, September 8, 1811, in Douglas F. Clanin, ed., *The Papers of William Henry Harrison, 1800–1815*, available on microfilm (Indianapolis: Indiana Historical Society, 1999).

9. Robert M. Owens, *Mr. Jefferson's Hammer: William Henry Harrison and the Origins of American Indian Policy* (Norman: University of Oklahoma Press, 2007) 212.

10. Edmunds, *Tecumseh* 176; Sugden 297.

11. Edmunds, *Tecumseh* 177.

12. Quoted in Edmunds, *Tecumseh* 178; Sugden 300.

13. Edmunds, *Tecumseh* 178.

14. Sugden 304, 314.

15. Sugden 334–38.

16. Drake 181.

17. Gilpin 227; Sugden 384; volume 16, pages 179–83, of *Michigan Pioneer and Historical Collection*, published by the Michigan Historical Society in Lansing, Michigan, in 40 volumes, 1877–1929.

18. Eckert 976–80.

19. Sugden 379; Eckert 984–86.

RECOMMENDED READING

Calloway, Colin G. *Crown and Calumet: British–Indian Relations, 1783–1815.* Norman: University of Oklahoma Press, 1987.

Calloway, Colin G. *The Shawnees and the War for America: The Penguin Library of American Indian History.* New York: Penguin, 2007.

Drake, Benjamin. *Life of Tecumseh, and of His Brother the Prophet; with a Historical Sketch of the Shawanoe Indians.* 1841. New York: Arno Press and *The New York Times*, 1969.

Eckert, Allan W. *A Sorrow in Our Heart: The Life of Tecumseh.* 1992. New York: Bantam Books, 1993.

Edmunds, R. David. *The Shawnee Prophet.* 1983. Lincoln: University of Nebraska Press, 1985.

Edmunds, R. David. *Tecumseh and the Quest for Indian Leadership.* Boston: Little, Brown, 1984.

Gilpin, Alec R. *The War of 1812 in the Old Northwest.* East Lansing: Michigan State University Press, 1958.

Ohio Historical Society. "Tecumseh" (and related links). *Ohio History Central: An Online Encyclopedia of Ohio History.* http://www.ohiohistorycentral.org/entry.php?rec=373.

Sugden, John. *Tecumseh: A Life.* New York: Henry Holt, 1997.

The American steamship the *Warrior* fires on Sauk trying to cross the Bad Axe River during the Black Hawk War of 1832. (Library of Congress)

Black Hawk (Makataimeshekiakiak) 1767–1838

Makataimeshekiakiak, better known to history as Black Hawk, became the most famous Indian of his time despite never holding the position of a chief. That fame derived from his lifelong accomplishments as a warrior, his efforts to resist the takeover of his people's homeland, and, in defeat, his public journey throughout several eastern cities. That journey secured his image in the East as a symbol of nobility and courage, though many Euro-Americans in the Midwest continued to demonize him. Even in the Midwest, where Black Hawk had fought his battles, often against tribal enemies and sometimes against the United States, he eventually would become an exemplum of injustice against the region's native inhabitants. Part of Black Hawk's legacy is the long list of Midwestern sites named after him and his Sauk people, including the professional hockey team known as the Chicago Blackhawks.

EARLY YEARS

Black Hawk's Family

Little is known of Black Hawk's earliest years. According to his own account of his life, which was published in 1833 after his defeat in the Black Hawk War, he was born in 1767, shortly after his people had migrated to a fertile area where the Rock River met the Mississippi River in northwestern Illinois. Today the city of Rock Island sits on that site. His father was named Pyesa, and his mother Kneebingkemewoin, or Summer Rain, although she is not identified by name in the autobiography. The parents may have had another son in addition to Black Hawk, or perhaps even more children, although no evidence of their existence remains.

Black Hawk was proud of his family heritage, especially of his great-grandfather, Nanàmakee, and his own father. According to Black Hawk, Nanàmakee, then living near Montreal, received a message from the Great Spirit that he would meet a white man who would be like a father to him. Consequently, Nanàmakee went off with his two brothers and encountered a white man who said that he was the son of the King of France. The man, possibly the French explorer Champlain, who first arrived in Canada in 1603, presented Nanàmakee with a medal. Upon returning to the Sauk, Nanàmakee received the highly valued medicine bag from his father, Mukatàquet, who was the principal chief of the Sauk. Black Hawk would inherit the same medicine bag many years later.

The Sauk

The Sauk left the Montreal area around 1629, when the British temporarily captured Quebec from the French. They resided first on Mackinac Island in northern Michigan, but later moved near present-day Green Bay, Wisconsin. After establishing an alliance with the Fox, the Sauk eventually moved westward in Wisconsin and then down to northern Illinois at the confluence of the Mississippi and Rock Rivers.

Black Hawk (whose given name actually meant Black Sparrow Hawk, but who later shortened the name to the one by which he came to be widely known) notes that few significant events occurred during his youth, suggesting that he led what was for Sauk children a typical existence. That would have involved a seasonal pattern of work (and certainly play as well, including horse and foot races and lacrosse). During the winter, the Sauk endured some hardships, but led (for the times) a reasonably comfortable life in the other seasons. The young Black Hawk spent spring, summer, and fall in the location that he came to love and would try as hard as he could to preserve. The later Black Hawk War cannot be understood without also understanding what the Sauk village, called Saukenuk, meant to Black Hawk and his people.

Spring was the time for planting not just corn (the Sauk's most important crop), but also a variety of other foods, including beans, melons, squash, and pumpkins. All of these crops were planted together in the same fields. Plums, crab apples, and assorted berries also enriched the Sauk people's diet. During the summer, the Sauk hunted for buffalo, deer, and smaller game. Nevertheless, as largely an agricultural people, they never depended on the buffalo as extensively as did many other Indian nations, including the Lakota. Some members of the community, including women and older men, worked lead mines, selling the lead to the Euro-Americans. Others fished and wove mats for flooring.

Harvesting occurred in the fall. Before winter hit in force, the Sauk moved to their winter hunting grounds west of the Mississippi. They left behind a store of corn buried and ready for the next spring planting. During the winter, the Sauk hunted and trapped to trade skins and also engaged in making maple sugar. In the spring, they returned to Saukenuk.

One of the most important areas at Saukenuk was the cemetery, which tied past and present together for the Sauk. In his autobiography, Black Hawk describes the Sauk practice of visiting graves and keeping them in good shape. According to Black Hawk, mothers went to the cemetery to mourn their children, and sons to honor their fathers. Maintaining this connection was of great importance to him: Even years later, after the loss of Saukenuk seemed inevitable, he asked for permission to be buried there. It is no wonder, then, that when the time came to defend Saukenuk, Black Hawk was prepared to do just that.

The Warrior

Long before Black Hawk faced the United States in battle, he had established his warrior credentials against the traditional Sauk enemies, especially the Osage. According to his autobiography, Black Hawk wounded his first enemy at the age of 15, which would have been about 1782. Not long after this initial encounter, he volunteered to accompany his father in a campaign against the Osage. It is clear from his own account that Black Hawk's motivation was largely to prove to his father his worthiness as a son. During the battle, Black

Hawk watched his father kill one of the enemy and then, determined to impress his father, rushed against another of the Osage. Black Hawk knocked him to the ground with a tomahawk and then ran him through with a lance. He removed the fallen warrior's scalp and presented it to his father, who, according to the son's account, said nothing but gazed approvingly at him. After the battle, Black Hawk participated in his first Scalp Dance, a communal celebration that sometimes, at least, included women of the village.

A few months later, Black Hawk for the first time led men into battle. His small party of seven attacked a much larger Osage force (according to Black Hawk 100, although he surely would not have been able to take an exact count); in the encounter, Black Hawk killed one Osage and then led his men on a successful retreat without incurring any casualties. Afterward he gathered a much larger force (numbered at 180 in the autobiography) and again sought out the Osage. Reaching the Osage camp, they found the enemy gone. Disappointed, most of Black Hawk's men returned to their own village, while Black Hawk and five other men continued their pursuit. They finally caught up with the Osage warriors, killed two of them, and returned in victory. At the age of 19, Black Hawk led another large expedition against the Osage. This time, the Sauk found their adversaries and engaged in a major battle. Black Hawk records six kills himself (five men and one woman), and puts the total Osage dead at approximately 100 with the loss of 19 of his own men.[1]

The victory temporarily induced the Osage to remain in their own territory, but another traditional enemy awaited Black Hawk—the Cherokee. This battle, fought a few miles below St. Louis, apparently not long after the victory against the Osage, brought a great change to Black Hawk's life. His father, Pyesa, suffered a mortal wound to which he soon succumbed. Black Hawk assumed command during the battle and led the Sauk to another victory, with the Sauk losing only 7 men to the Cherokees' 28.[2] As always, these numbers come from Black Hawk recalling the battles many years later and may not be completely accurate.

The sacred medicine bag, which had been in Pyesa's possession for safekeeping, passed to Black Hawk upon his father's death. The medicine bag was a bundle, likely made of animal skin, birch bark, or a fabric, containing a variety of objects that possessed spiritual and cultural significance (such as cedar leaves, a hawk skin, a buffalo tail, and sacred tobacco). When going into battle, the keeper of the medicine bag led the band of warriors, holding the bag against his chest. While departing from the battle, he walked last with the bag on his back. This strategy ensured that the medicine bag always remained between the Sauk war party and the enemy, thereby providing protection against a surprise attack.[3] The medicine bag represented the Sauk people and also connected Black Hawk with his ancestors—his great-great grandfather, Mukataquet, had passed the medicine bag on to his son, Nanàmakee, and ultimately, through Pyesa, to Black Hawk. Black Hawk's status among the Sauk thus arose from two sources: his skill and success as a warrior and his role as keeper of the medicine bag.

Medicine Bundle

The medicine bundle that Black Hawk carefully guarded was an important element in Sauk culture. Sacred bundles were also important among the Fox, Shawnee, Comanche, Kiowa, Chiricahua Apache, Seminole, Creek, and Choctaw, as well as many other native peoples. Different types of bundles existed. For example, the naming bundle was used during a child's naming ceremony. The war bundle offered protection and success in battle. The medicine bundle also provided assistance in a range of everyday activities, including hunting.

The medicine bundle included a variety of charms, objects, or substances that could induce supernatural powers to aid the possessor of the bundle. Sacred bundles also might contain fetishes and amulets: A fetish was believed to be the repository of a living being, while an amulet symbolized a divine being that aided the individual for honoring it by carrying the token.

Sauk and Fox war bundles typically included portions of the buffalo, eagle feathers, and parts of other animals. The buffalo and eagle were especially honored as sacred. War whistles, cedar leaves to burn as incense, herbs and roots, and paint also were common in war bundles. Sauk medicine bundles included a variety of charm medicines, often paint, and sometimes medicines believed to bring success in a specific endeavor such as hunting, gambling, or war.

M. R. Harrington, writing in *Sacred Bundles of the Sac and Fox Indians* (1914), describes medicine bundles as minor bundles and implies that they were more individual and less communal than war bundles. Black Hawk, however, describes his medicine bundle (medicine bag) in his autobiography with great reverence and notes that he carried it on military expeditions. He gives the history of the bundle, explains how he came to inherit it (on the death of his father), and describes it as having widespread application to his people.

Black Hawk deeply mourned Pyesa's death. He blackened his face, fasted, and prayed to the Great Spirit. While he hunted and fished, he apparently (so far as one can tell from his autobiography) did not take a leadership role for five years. Black Hawk's period of mourning was unusually long given that Sauk typically mourned the death of close relatives for six months to a year. Whether this hiatus also involved abstinence from war is uncertain.

In his autobiography, Black Hawk compresses a lengthy period of time into a few pages, noting that by his thirty-fifth year, which would have been about 1802, he had fought extensively against a variety of enemies, such as the Osage, Cherokee, Chippewa (also known as the Ojibwa), and Kaskaskia. Black Hawk and his Sauk continued fighting the Osage as well as the Lakota well beyond that date.

THE TREATY OF 1804

The Louisiana Purchase

The first decade of the nineteenth century marked a major turning point in the life of Black Hawk and the fortunes and ultimate destiny of the Sauk. The Louisiana Purchase of 1804 set in motion a chain of events that ultimately would lead to the defeat and removal of the Sauk.

In 1803, the United States purchased from France for approximately $15 million a vast tract of land west of the Mississippi River known as Louisiana, which Napoleon had acquired through a treaty with Spain in 1800. The acquisition doubled the size of the United States and included traditional hunting grounds of the Sauk in what would become Missouri and Iowa. During 1804, the United States took possession of this new area, substituting American administrators for European ones. Among those who lost their jobs was the individual whom Black Hawk referred to as his "Spanish father"—Charles Dehault Delassus, the Spanish governor of the upper portion of Louisiana. Delassus had shown considerable respect to the Sauk and had given them many presents as well as provisions over the years. Suddenly, however, Americans, of whom Black Hawk was highly suspicious, were in power and seemed to favor the Osage over the Sauk. The U.S. military, for example, stopped a Sauk war party of some 300 from attacking the Osage.

The Sauk also were concerned about the presence of increasing numbers of Euro-Americans on the Cuivre (Quiver) River north of St. Louis. In 1804, after four Sauk hunters killed three settlers, two Sauk chiefs journeyed to St. Louis to condemn the killings and inquire about a just retribution. The Sauk practiced a system of justice that included the option of paying a price for the dead person to the victim's relatives, a concept practiced in England during the Middle Ages and known there as *wergild* (literally, "man-price").

The two Sauk instead were sent home with orders to hand over the guilty men and arrange for a group of Sauk to attend a treaty council with William Henry Harrison, who had been appointed by President Thomas Jefferson to negotiate land concessions with the Indians. Harrison was also governor of the Indiana Territory and of the northern part of the Louisiana Purchase (the District of Louisiana). He would become President of the United States in 1841, only to die one month later.

A small group of Sauk and Fox traveled to St. Louis to deliver one of the murderers and meet with Harrison. The Sauk apparently believed that the primary purpose of their trip was to resolve the killings. The prisoner was jailed and subsequently either escaped or was released before being shot and killed by a guard. It later was discovered that the killings of the settlers had actually been in self-defense, and President Jefferson forwarded a pardon. The notification, however, came too late to save the accused.

Desire for Land

The larger issue for the United States was its desire to acquire land from the Sauk and Fox, and that was what Harrison was charged to do. The details of what transpired in St. Louis are hazy. Somehow five Sauk and Fox, including the Sauk Quashquame, ended up signing a treaty that granted to the United States all of their land east of the Mississippi between the Illinois River in the south and the Wisconsin River in the north. The area extended east to the Fox River in Illinois. Also included was a section of land west of the Mississippi in Missouri. This area east of the Mississippi included the village of Saukenuk. In return, the Sauk and Fox received an immediate payment of $2,234.50 in goods and an annual payment of $1,000 ($600 to the Sauk, $400 to the Fox). The Sauk and the Fox were permitted to live and hunt on the land until the federal government sold it.

Many things were wrong with this treaty. The five signers almost surely did not understand the full implications of the agreement. Even if they did, the five individuals were not authorized to finalize such a sale. The Sauk required any transfer of land to be discussed by the tribal council (usually consisting of approximately 12 chiefs) and by the whole community. A consensus of both men and women was further required before such a sale could occur.[4] Because these procedures had not occurred, few, if any, Sauk believed that they truly had sold off their land, and certainly not their revered Saukenuk. The Sauk continued to live on their land after 1804 in the same manner as before, and did so for many years, contributing to their belief that they had not sold the land.

In time, however, the Treaty of 1804 would come to affect the Sauk profoundly. In the aftermath of what came to be known as the Black Hawk War, Black Hawk would lament that the Treaty of 1804 "has been the origin of all our difficulties."[5]

THE WAR OF 1812

Tecumseh and the British Alliance

By 1811, Tecumseh of the Shawnees was attempting to establish a confederacy of Indian peoples, its center located where the Tippecanoe River meets the Wabash River in Indiana. Although Black Hawk shared with Tecumseh strong anti-American feelings and a decided preference for the British, he did not at that time join the Shawnee leader. As Tecumseh was traveling farther south trying to recruit allies, William Henry Harrison led a force of approximately 1,000 men toward the Shawnee stronghold. On November 7, 1811, the Indians attacked Harrison's force. Harrison lost 68 men to about 50 Indian fatalities, but when the battle was over, he held the field, claiming victory. This encounter would help propel Harrison and his future vice-presidential running mate, John Tyler, to victory in the presidential election almost 30 years later under the slogan of "Tippecanoe and Tyler, Too." Harrison claimed that the British had armed Tecumseh—a claim that helped justify an attack on the Shawnee and, if not true, would at least become prophetic. Certainly, after the Battle of Tippecanoe, Tecumseh had no doubt about the wisdom of solidifying an alliance with the British.

Black Hawk, while still not allied with Tecumseh, participated in a raid on Fort Madison, located at the site of the present town of Fort Madison, Iowa, in the far southeastern corner of the state, on September 5, 1812. The attack was a joint Winnebago–Sauk effort that lasted for four days. Attempts to set the fort on fire failed, and the attackers withdrew after having lost one Winnebago and killed one soldier and two woodcutters who were attacked at the beginning of the siege when they left the fort without being aware of the force that had surrounded it.

Black Hawk records in his autobiography that shortly after this attack on Fort Madison, he learned of an impending war between the United States and Britain. For years, a number of tribes, including the Sauk, had traveled annually to Fort Malden at Amherstburg in Canada to receive gifts. In fact, the route across Illinois, Indiana, and Michigan had become known as the Great Sauk Trail. The British, in turn, were receiving intelligence about U.S.–Indian tensions, including Indian grievances that might play into Britain's hands in its uneasy relationship with its southern neighbor.

The United States, which was only three decades removed from securing its independence from Great Britain, also worried over the role that Indian tribes might play in any future confrontation with Britain. In 1812, several Sauk chiefs were invited to accompany William Clark—of Lewis and Clark fame, and later Territorial Governor of Missouri (1813–1820) and Superintendent of Indian Affairs for the upper Michigan and Missouri River regions (1822–1838)—to Washington, D.C. There they met with President James Madison. According to Black Hawk, who did not make the trip, Madison urged the Sauk to remain neutral in any conflict between the United States and Britain. The returning Sauk believed that they had been promised credit at Fort Madison for guns, ammunition, and other goods necessary to carry out their winter hunting. Consequently, the Sauk decided to remain at peace.

That decision would quickly change when the Sauk arrived at Fort Madison in preparation for the winter season. The trader insisted that he had no authorization to extend credit, leaving the Sauk in a precarious position regarding their ability to engage in a successful hunt that was necessary for their very survival.

While the Sauk tried to determine what to do, they learned of the arrival down the Mississippi of a British trader named Edward La Gouthrie. He presented the Sauk with gifts of tobacco, pipes, and wampum (shell beads made into strings or belts and used mainly for communication). La Gouthrie also gave the Sauk, on credit, the goods that they needed for the winter. He further urged

Black Hawk to gather a large number of warriors and go to Robert Dickson, who was at Green Bay with 12 boatloads of guns, ammunition, and supplies. Dickson (whose named is spelled Dixon in Black Hawk's autobiography) was a British trader recruiting Indians as allies of the British in their war against the United States, known to history as the War of 1812.

Black Hawk gathered together a party of 200 men and set off for Green Bay. For Black Hawk, the deciding factor in choosing to ally himself with the British was what he saw as U.S. deceit in reneging on the offer of credit promised by President Madison.

Black Hawk's Sauk joined with a number of other groups at Green Bay, including bands of Ottawa, Kickapoo, Potawatomi, and Winnebago. Dickson armed the Indian forces and treated Black Hawk with great respect, referring to him as General Black Hawk and awarding him a medal, British flag, and formal commission in writing. Dickson's promises, as Black Hawk remembered them, included assurances that the British would help drive the Americans out of Indian lands, and that after defeating the U.S. soldiers at Detroit the Sauk could return to fight the army along the Mississippi.

Black Hawk's Entrance into the War

Black Hawk left Green Bay in charge of some 500 warriors. They passed Chicago and the deserted Fort Dearborn and joined the British army south of Detroit. On January 22, 1813, the British under Henry Procter and their Indian allies engaged U.S. forces under General James Winchester in the Battle of Frenchtown on the River Raisin just west of Lake Erie in the southeastern corner of Michigan. Winchester's troops fought well, earning Black Hawk's respect. In fact, Winchester initially was victorious but failed to establish a perimeter defense after his early success, and a counterattack ultimately overwhelmed his troops.

Winter brought a lull in the hostilities, and Black Hawk remained with the British near Detroit. By May 1, he was participating in an assault by a 5,000-strong British and Indian force against Fort Meigs on the Maumee River in northern Ohio. Again General Procter (who had been promoted from colonel to brigadier general after his River Raisin victory) led the combined army, this time facing General William Henry Harrison. The Indian allies were led by Tecumseh.

The attackers surrounded the fort, but U.S. reinforcements arriving by boat attacked the British artillery. They forced the British back but in turn were surrounded, with most of the 800 soldiers being captured and many forced to run the gauntlet. Approximately 40 were killed during the torturous run until Indian leaders brought their men under control. Black Hawk claimed to have stopped the killing because he considered it cowardly to kill unarmed prisoners, although Tecumseh is more likely to have actually brought the carnage to a halt.[6] As the siege of the fort dragged on, however, Black Hawk and his Sauk eventually tired of the inconclusive effort and left. Procter finally withdrew his forces on May 9.

Black Hawk participated in another attack on Fort Meigs in July, and an assault on Fort Stephenson at Lower Sandusky, Ohio, on August 2. Both of these efforts were led by Procter, and both were unsuccessful, with a frontal attack on Fort Stephenson producing a large number of British casualties. Black Hawk praised the British soldiers' courage but thought that the tactic of attacking openly was foolish.

Precisely when Black Hawk left the British to return to Saukenuk is unclear. His autobiography seems to state that Black Hawk took 20 of his braves and left for home while the British were preparing to abandon their attempt to capture Fort Stephenson. Other accounts place him at the Battle of the Thames, which occurred on October 5, 1813.[7] The Thames River runs through southeast Ontario, Canada, above Lake Erie. It was in this engagement, a major victory by Harrison over the British, that Tecumseh died.

The day before the battle, Tecumseh, according to his biographer Allan W. Eckert, had a premonition of his death and gave away some of his most prized possessions, including a tomahawk to Black Hawk, who subsequently fought near Tecumseh during the battle. Not long before his death, Black Hawk apparently spoke of being in the battle. Benjamin Drake, in his biography of Black Hawk published around the time of his subject's death, cites two individuals recalling Black Hawk telling them of his involvement in the Battle of the Thames, one in a newspaper article and another in a letter to the biographer. The newspaper account recalls Black Hawk reminiscing about "being at the right hand of Tecumthe, when the latter was killed at the battle of the Thames."[8]

Black Hawk returned home sometime in 1813 but did not completely abandon his support of the British. When the British captured the fort at Prairie du Chien, Wisconsin (then in the Michigan Territory), in 1814, they invited Black Hawk to join them once more in waging war against the United States. Black Hawk left to do that and quickly caught up to several boats carrying U.S. soldiers to Prairie du Chien. The boats, under the command of Major John Campbell, had stopped at the Sauk camp just the night before and been welcomed, but that was prior to the British invitation. When one of the boats ran aground, Black Hawk and his warriors fired on the men and set the boat afire. Another boat returned to rescue the stranded soldiers. When the Sauk explored the cargo on the beached boat, they discovered several barrels of whiskey. Black Hawk, who strongly opposed use of whiskey by his people and the distribution of it by traders, dumped the contents into the river. Not surprisingly, the defeat of the reinforcements was a cause for rejoicing by the British at Prairie du Chien.

In early September, the British came down the Mississippi by boat and unloaded, according to Black Hawk, "a big gun," leaving several soldiers in charge of its use. There may actually have been several pieces of artillery.[9] The Sauk prepared a site from which to fire the gun or guns and did not have to wait long. That evening eight U.S. boats under the direction of Zachary Taylor—another Black Hawk adversary who would later become President of the United States (in 1849)—arrived but were driven off by the Sauk and the British gunners. Taylor then took his detachment downriver and constructed Fort Johnson near the current Warsaw, Illinois; however, he abandoned the fort after just a few weeks.

End of the War and the Treaty of 1816

The war between Britain and the United States formally ended on Christmas Eve 1814. Unfortunately, the news did not travel fast enough to prevent the Battle of New Orleans, a bloody victory by Andrew Jackson's forces over the British on January 8, 1815, during which the British suffered some 2,000 casualties.

Although the War of 1812 was over, Black Hawk found himself in a battle against a party of soldiers in the spring of 1815. Known as the Battle of the Sink Hole, the encounter looked ominous for Black Hawk and his men, who numbered close to 20. Surrounded, they took refuge in a sinkhole, and some of the Sauk began singing their death songs. Despite their apparent advantage, the soldiers then withdrew, having lost two men—Captain James Craig and Lieutenant Edward Spears—and having killed just one of Black Hawk's men.

The U.S. government, having made peace with the British, invited the Sauk and other Indian nations to make peace as well. Consequently, in September 1815 the Sauk began to make their way toward Portage des Sioux a few miles above the mouth of the Missouri River. When a Sauk chief fell ill, however, the party paused while the Fox representatives continued onward. When the chief subsequently died, the Sauk, seeing his death as a cautionary sign against continuing the voyage, returned to Saukenuk. As a result, the Sauk from Saukenuk did not sign the treaties of September 13 and 14, 1815, although the Sauk living along the Missouri River did sign the agreements.

The following year, the Sauk were summoned to another treaty signing. William Clark, the territorial governor of Missouri, awaited them at St. Louis, where the Sauk were accused of having committed serious crimes. The Sauk chiefs denied the accusations but signed the treaty on May 13, 1816. Although not a chief, Black Hawk also signed, only later coming to understand that the treaty effectively gave away Saukenuk and much else by reaffirming the Treaty of 1804. A few days before, on May 10, construction had begun on Fort Armstrong, situated on Rock Island, an island that served as the Sauk garden, supplying them with such delicacies as strawberries, blackberries, plums, and apples. The Sauk believed that a good spirit lived underneath the area where the fort was built, but Black Hawk notes in his autobiography that the construction drove the spirit away, with a bad spirit replacing it.

At some point, apparently over the next few years, Black Hawk lost a son and a daughter to death. Nevertheless, the Sauk continued with their seasonal migrations between Saukenuk and their winter hunting grounds in relative peace. The treaties of 1804 and 1816 receded from their consciousness as no one tried to take their village away from them. According to the treaties they had yielded the area to the Americans, yet in practice it still seemed to be thoroughly theirs despite the presence of Fort Armstrong.

LEAD-UP TO THE BLACK HAWK WAR

A Changing World

From 1815 to the middle of the third decade of the nineteenth century, Black Hawk seemingly lived the life of a private citizen within the Sauk community at Saukenuk on the Rock River. His glory days as a warrior appeared largely behind him. Events were unfolding, however, that would propel him back into the world of warfare and make him more famous (and infamous in some people's minds) than ever.

The war that came to bear his name—the Black Hawk War—grew out of major economic and social changes that were occurring along the Mississippi River. Euro-Americans were advancing on several fronts, squeezing the Sauk and other Indian nations while also bringing pressure to bear on U.S. officials to accommodate this rising tide of pioneers. Illinois was admitted as a state in 1818, and its population grew to more than 150,000 by 1830. Large tracts of land in the state had been set aside (initially 2 million acres, and later another 1.5 million acres) to accommodate land grants made available to men who would enlist in the military during the War of 1812. Enlistees were offered 160 acres, an area later doubled when the government had trouble finding enough willing soldiers. Many of the men who received these allotments sold them to land speculators, who then resold the land to settlers for a tidy profit.[10]

As settlers encroached on Sauk land from the south and east, Euro-Americans were establishing mining centers along the Mississippi River in Iowa, in northwestern Illinois, and in what would become southwestern Wisconsin. Galena, Illinois; and Shullsburg, Mineral Point, Dodgeville, Gratiot, and many other Wisconsin towns grew up around mining sites. Alexander Hamilton's son, William, established a mining settlement called Hamilton's Diggings near the present Wiota, Wisconsin. Some Sauk individuals also worked in lead mines, and the Fox operated mines at Dubuque. By 1832, however, Euro-Americans had taken over the Fox diggings at Dubuque's Mines, and the era of Indian mining came to an end in the Mississippi region.

Changes in the fur-trading business also negatively affected the Sauk. The "factory system" consisted of federally owned trading posts run by "factors," agents appointed by the government. Indian traders received reasonably fair treatment in terms of credit and prices paid for their goods. In 1822, the federal government abandoned this system both because of the high cost of maintaining it and as a result of extensive lobbying in Congress by John Jacob Astor, who soon succeeded in establishing a near-monopoly for his American Fur Company. As Indians became entrapped in a debt-ridden web of credit and endured low compensation for the furs and skins they sold, they had to shoot or trap even more animals. Overhunting, by reducing the number of animals nearby, forced hunters into hunting and trapping grounds that were traditionally the domain of other tribes, with the obvious result of increased intertribal conflict. A peace conference dealing with these issues, for example, was held at Prairie du Chien in August 1825, hosted by Lewis Cass, governor of Michigan Territory, and William Clark, who was in charge of Indian affairs in the regions of the upper Mississippi and Missouri Rivers. The Sauk, Fox, Iowa, and several other groups attended, including such traditional Sauk enemies as the Sioux. The conference lasted about two weeks and resulted in boundary lines being accepted by the participants, although given the socioeconomic forces at work, the agreement did not—really, could not—establish lasting peace among all of the participants.

Also during this time, the U.S. government's policy toward whiskey changed. Up to that point, the government factory system had kept alcohol out of the trading business. When Thomas McKenney, formerly the chief administrator of the factory system, became director of the War Department's Indian Office, he maintained this opposition to selling whiskey to the Indian tribes. Conversely, the American Fur Company, realizing that it could use whiskey sales to increase its own profits, lobbied against the prohibition, arguing that without a change in policy the company would lose out to the British Hudson's Bay Company. In 1828, the policy was changed to allow traders to have whiskey for their own employees. That may have opened the door just a crack, but the door quickly swung wide open, and soon Sauk were trading their furs for whiskey. Much to Black Hawk's disgust, some began trading even their guns and traps for whiskey, thus going into debt and at the same time losing their ability to get the hides necessary to pay off their debt.

Black Hawk himself did not drink alcohol and strongly discouraged both its sale by Euro-Americans and its consumption by his own people. When settlers started moving into Black Hawk's village, one of the ongoing sources of conflict was their introduction of whiskey. Black Hawk records in his autobiography how he pleaded with the new arrivals not to sell it. When one refused to stop, Black Hawk led a small group of his men to the man's house, took his barrel of whiskey, and dumped out the liquor. The Sauk's concern, as he expressed it, was not just that his people were being taken advantage of, but also that while drunk they might kill some of the settlers.

Intrusion of Euro-Americans

The first invasion of Saukenuk by Euro-American settlers occurred during the winter of 1828–1829, when Black Hawk and his Sauk were away for the season. Under the terms of the Treaties of 1804 and 1816, the Sauk no longer owned their village. However, the years that had passed since those agreements, coupled with their at best imperfect understanding of what the treaties said, had contributed to the Sauk's perception that Saukenuk remained theirs and would continue to do so. Even a reminder the previous spring by Thomas Forsyth, Indian agent at Rock Island, that the Sauk no longer owned the land on which their village stood and his recommendation that they make that year their last one at Saukenuk failed to shake Sauk confidence in the permanence of their home.

Black Hawk, by then 62 years old, heard of the arrival and returned alone to Saukenuk, an arduous trip for a man of his age to make alone in winter. Black Hawk knew little English but attempted to make the settlers understand that they were living in homes that belonged to someone else and that they must leave. He also sought out Antoine LeClaire, a government interpreter at Fort Armstrong, and George Davenport, the Rock Island trader who would be instrumental in founding the city of Davenport, Iowa, for advice and help. LeClaire provided Black Hawk with a letter to the settlers that failed to effect their departure. Davenport offered the unwelcome advice that the Sauk should abandon Saukenuk and establish instead a permanent summer residence west of the Mississippi. Black Hawk then traveled north to Prairie du Chien to talk with John Marsh, the Indian affairs subagent who was married to a Métis-Sioux woman. When Marsh echoed Davenport's advice, Black Hawk returned down the Rock River to the village of Wabokieshiek, also known as the Winnebago Prophet. Wabokieshiek counseled Black Hawk to return to Saukenuk in the spring and suggested that there would be no serious trouble.

A large number of Sauk and Fox decided to abandon their villages, and the settlers apparently believed that none of the Sauk would be returning to Saukenuk. Black Hawk, however, had no intention of leaving the village with its healthy cornfields, its bountiful gardens, and, of course, its much-revered cemetery. He returned with a large contingent of Sauk in the spring, as he had been doing for his whole life.

Many disputes arose between the Sauk and the settlers, including problems over whiskey. The settlers—squatters in the eyes of Black Hawk—insulted Sauk women, burned down Sauk lodges, and wrote to Illinois Governor Ninian Edwards to complain of the Sauk presence. Complicating life for Black Hawk was a resurgence of conflict with the Sioux and the political opposition of Keokuk, who was both the official tribal council speaker and a war chief. Keokuk was a major leader of what might be called, depending on one's point of view, either the peace or the accommodationist faction of the Sauk. Keokuk strongly encouraged accepting the U.S. directive to move.

After Black Hawk and the Sauk left in the fall of 1829, their village, along with all of the other Sauk land along the lower Rock River, was offered for sale at the federal land office in Springfield, Illinois. The trader George Davenport bought 3,000 acres. Faced with the prospect of actually paying for their land, most of the squatters abstained, preferring to get land for nothing. While their land was being placed on the sale block, the Sauk were enduring a harsh winter, the heavy snow hampering their hunting.

In the spring of 1830, Black Hawk returned again to Saukenuk. Forsyth, whom Black Hawk viewed as a friend but who feared that the present stalemate might encourage conflict, recommended to William Clark that a large show of force led by General Henry Atkinson, commander of the troops at Jefferson Barracks, St. Louis, supplemented by several hundred militia might compel the Sauk finally to abandon Saukenuk. Tensions among the Indian tribes as well as between settlers and Indians were weighing heavily on Forsyth.

Worsening Relations

Wyncoop Warner, Indian affairs subagent at Galena, Illinois, relayed from the Winnebago an invitation for the Fox to send representatives to Prairie du Chien for peace discussions. Joseph Street, the Indian agent at Prairie du Chien, wrote to Warner expressing concerns about the safety of the Fox and especially urging that they be alert to possible danger from the Sioux. Warner apparently did not receive the letter, having left Galena before its arrival. Warner arrived at Prairie du Chien on April 28, at which time Street urged him to return and tell the Fox not to come. Somehow Warner missed the Fox as he returned, and 18 Fox, unarmed, continued on their journey by canoe. On May 5, 1830, they stopped to rest and were attacked by Sioux and Menominee warriors. All of the Fox were killed except for one boy, whose arm was broken before he was sent back to his people to tell them what had happened. The Fox who were working the Dubuque mines left to avoid attacks by the Sioux, and settlers quickly took over the mines. The stage was set for even more intrigue and violence.

With the situation deteriorating, the U.S. government made some local changes in its personnel. John Marsh was fired in the spring of 1829 from his position at Prairie du Chien. Warner was next to go, losing his position as sub-agent at Galena in June 1830. Later that summer, Forsyth was replaced at Rock Island by Felix St. Vrain, a sawmill operator with political connections to William Clark.

While Black Hawk and the Sauk were suffering through yet another unusually harsh winter, St. Vrain was urging use of force to prevent the Sauk from returning to their summer home. At the same time, John Reynolds, who had been elected governor of Illinois in 1830, was hearing reports of Sauk offenses against the settlers. Reynolds, who had served in the militia during the War of 1812, thought of himself as a strong and decisive leader and enjoyed being referred to as the "Old Ranger." He hated Indians, and was convinced that fighting Indians would secure his political popularity.

Black Hawk, recognizing the increasingly precarious nature of his situation at Saukenuk, reluctantly agreed to sell the land if George Davenport would negotiate the agreement with William Clark. Davenport suggested a sum of $6,000. Clark, however, rejected the offer, declaring that he would not buy what the Sauk no longer had the right to sell. It was in the long run a foolish decision by Clark, who probably could have prevented a war for a modest monetary figure.

Reynolds called up the Illinois militia in late May 1831, a month after Black Hawk's return to Saukenuk. Having a lot of inexperienced militia brandishing their weapons and possibly provoking conflict did not appeal much to the military. Upon hearing of Reynolds' plans, Major General Edmund Gaines, who commanded the military's Western Department, informed the governor that he had ordered six companies of troops to leave Jefferson Barracks for Fort Armstrong. Gaines made it clear that he would handle the situation himself.

Gaines arrived at Rock Island on June 4 and called a conference of Sauk leaders for the following day. Black Hawk at first was absent from the gathering, but before long he arrived with a large contingent of warriors, all of them painted, armed, and singing war songs. The dramatic entrance was intended to provide an intimidating effect, and the conference continued nonviolently but with considerable disagreement for three days. The Sauk denied that they had sold their land, at least legally. Sauk women proclaimed, with Black Hawk's support, that the land could not be sold without their approval because the cornfields and gardens belonged to them. Gaines, however, was insistent: The Sauk would have to move within three days. Even Keokuk argued that the season was too far advanced to permit planting crops elsewhere, an objection that Gaines at least somewhat countered by promising to provide enough corn to replace their lost harvest.

Concerned that the Sauk might fight rather than leave, Gaines unsuccessfully sought reinforcements from Fort Crawford at Prairie du Chien before reluctantly requesting militia support from Reynolds. The volunteer force of 1,500 men arrived at Rock Island on June 25. On the following day, the attack on Saukenuk began. Artillery hit the village, but when the joint force entered Saukenuk they found it deserted.

So long as Black Hawk had only the regular army to contend with, he was determined to remain at Saukenuk but not offer resistance when the soldiers arrived. When he learned of the approaching militia, however, he wisely recognized that their combination of hatred for Indians and lack of discipline would prove a lethal combination. To avoid an encounter with them, the Sauk crossed the Mississippi and camped below Rock Island. The militia meanwhile behaved abominably, tearing down fences, destroying crops (including many belonging to settlers), and digging up the Sauk dead and desecrating the corpses.

The next month brought an unhappy acceptance of the loss of Saukenuk. Twenty-eight Sauk leaders signed the Articles of Agreement and Capitulation. The Sauk, including Black Hawk and his followers, were never again to make their home there. Among the signers was Black Hawk. According to Lieutenant George McCall, General Gaines's aide-de-camp, Black Hawk slowly rose to sign the document, his face conveying "a deep-seated grief and humiliation that no one could witness unmoved."[11] The agreement reaffirmed the treaties of 1804, 1816, and 1825. The corn that Gaines gave the Sauk proved insufficient, reducing the Sauk to secretly returning to Saukenuk in the dead of night to steal their own corn.

It was apparently during this difficult summer of 1831 that Black Hawk approached George Davenport with his request to be buried in the Saukenuk cemetery. Davenport agreed to the request, which likely gave Black Hawk some comfort. In fact, he would no more return to his home in death than he would in life.

A violent conflict with the army and militia had been averted, but the summer of 1831 would not remain violence free. A large party of Fox (and perhaps some Sauk), seeking revenge for the massacre of the Fox peace delegation the year before by Sioux and Menominees, attacked a Menominee camp just outside Fort Crawford early in the morning of July 31. Approximately 25 men, women, and children were killed without anyone at the fort knowing what was happening. The attack, which did not include Black Hawk, elicited condemnation from U.S. officials, including President Andrew Jackson, and a demand for the attackers to be handed over to U.S. authorities.

THE BLACK HAWK WAR

British Promises

During this period of the early 1830s, Black Hawk listened closely to advice from the British. He traveled to Malden in Canada during the summer of 1830, receiving assurances that the "American Father" would treat the Sauk fairly. The next summer, Neapope, a young Sauk war chief, made the same trip, returning in the fall. Whatever Neapope was actually told in Canada, his message to Black Hawk—at best a misunderstanding of what he had heard—helped propel Black Hawk into making decisions that would result in the war that bears his name.

According to Black Hawk, Neapope told him that the British reaffirmed Sauk rights to the land along the Rock River. Further, the British would help the Sauk if war broke out between Black Hawk's people and the U.S. government. Neapope had stopped at the Prophet's village on the way home and claimed that he had received more promises from the British there—in this case, that they would supply the Sauk with guns, ammunition, and other supplies. The Prophet supposedly also stated that several other Indian nations (the Chippewa, Ottawa, Potawatomi, and Winnebago) would fight alongside the Sauk. None of this information turned out to be true, and Black Hawk in his autobiography noted Neapope's falsehood. Yet Black Hawk was not alone in believing that the British would come to his help; throughout the region, concern about another British–Sauk alliance and a broader war between Britain and the United States was widespread among settlers and U.S. officials.

Black Hawk's Strategy

Fortified by Neapope's promises, Black Hawk and his group (often referred to as the "British band" of Sauk) crossed the Mississippi River on April 5 or 6, 1832, carrying with them a British flag and intent on returning to Saukenuk. Various estimates place the total size of Black Hawk's party at around

2,000, including women, children, and some 500 to 700 warriors. Some traveled by canoe toward their home village, others overland by horseback. On April 8, General Atkinson left Jefferson Barracks with six companies of the Sixth Infantry for Fort Armstrong at Rock Island, arriving on the night of April 11–12.

Black Hawk had crossed the Mississippi with a fallback position. If returning to Saukenuk did not prove feasible, he had an offer from the Prophet to go to his village on the Rock River north of Saukenuk and grow corn there. The Prophet exercised poor judgment in telling Felix St. Vrain, the Rock Island Indian agent, of his offer, and St. Vrain in turn relayed that information to Major John Bliss, commander at Fort Armstrong. Not surprisingly, Bliss began to prepare for war.

Approximately a week after arriving at Fort Armstrong, General Atkinson met with Keokuk and other chiefs who were not with Black Hawk. Atkinson also made hurried preparations for the anticipated showdown with Black Hawk, communicating with troops at Fort Crawford at Prairie du Chien and Fort Winnebago on the Wisconsin River at Portage. He traveled personally to Fort Crawford; then, after returning to Rock Island, he accepted as prisoners three of the men who had attacked the Menominee camp the previous year. That the remaining participants were supposedly with Black Hawk simply fueled the general's outrage.

Atkinson also exchanged letters with Governor Reynolds, perhaps reasoning that Black Hawk feared the militia more than the regular military and might be induced to surrender if he knew that he would be facing Reynolds' men. The governor wasted no time mobilizing the militia for the second year in a row.

On April 24, by which time Black Hawk was camped at the Prophet's village, he received a communication from Atkinson urging him to recross the Mississippi. On the same day, Black Hawk received a visit from Henry Gratiot, a subagent to the Winnebago who also ran a mining operation at Gratiot's Grove (the future Gratiot, Wisconsin). Gratiot learned of Black Hawk's plans to lead his group farther north, to another Winnebago camp on the Pecatonica River in what would become southwestern Wisconsin, and of his willingness to fight if Atkinson pursued him.

During the latter part of April, the militia, approximately 2,000 strong, gathered at Beardstown near the Illinois River. The militia departed on April 30, heading north to Yellow Banks, where Black Hawk had crossed the Mississippi. At that point, however, General Atkinson had not yet received authorization from his superiors to call the militia into action. This situation changed on May 5, when General Alexander Macomb, commanding general of the U.S. Army, ordered Atkinson to take decisive action against the Sauk and authorized him to use the militia to do so. Atkinson subsequently ordered Colonel Zachary Taylor, recently reinstalled as commander at Fort Crawford, to bring a contingent of troops to Fort Armstrong.

By May 8, Taylor with his force and Reynolds with his militia were at Fort Armstrong. The following day, Atkinson began his campaign against Black

Hawk. By this time, Black Hawk's situation was deteriorating. His people were low on food, and some of his companions were deserting him. In another blow, he had not received any military support from the Winnebago or Potawatomi or any supplies from the British.

Stillman's Run

The first major engagement of the Black Hawk War occurred on May 14, 1832. Black Hawk was camped in north-central Illinois on the Kishwaukee River, not far south of the present site of Rockford. Governor Reynolds, determined to gain the glory himself for defeating Black Hawk, ordered one of his militia officers, Brigade Major Nathaniel Buckmaster, to dispatch Major Isaiah Stillman in search of Black Hawk. Stillman led a force of about 130 volunteers northward. Another contingent of about 150 men accompanied Stillman under the command of Major David Bailey. At about 2:00 P.M. on May 14, one of Stillman's scouts sighted two Indians and, according to Stillman, killed both of them. Later that same day, Black Hawk learned of a large force of men approaching and sent more of his own men under a white flag to meet them. These Sauk also came under fire. Accounts vary regarding the fate of the men, although there is agreement that some were killed and some were taken prisoner. Stillman reported that six Indians were involved, with three killed and three captured. Black Hawk's account describes his sending three men with a white flag, all of whom were taken prisoner. He reportedly sent five more warriors to follow and see what would take place with the first set. Black Hawk states that this group was pursued by the soldiers and fled, with two being killed.[12]

As Stillman's men approached the Sauk camp, Black Hawk ordered his men, who numbered only about 40, to mount their horses and charge the attackers. Black Hawk expected that he and his men would be killed, but the sudden assault by the Sauk so confounded the militia, whose numbers far exceeded the Sauk force, that they turned and fled. This action earned them lasting ignominy along with a permanent name for their encounter: Stillman's Run. During the battle, 12 of Stillman's men were killed but none of Black Hawk's band died, except for the members of the peace delegation.

Continued Fighting

Black Hawk's victory over Stillman was followed by a number of raids on settlers' homes and farms. In an engagement on May 24, a Winnebago party killed four men at Kellogg's Grove west of the site of Stillman's Run and near Kent, Illinois. The dead included the Rock Island agent Felix St. Vrain. Unable to catch Black Hawk and increasingly scorned by angry and frightened settlers, the militia largely disbanded by the end of May. Approximately 300 agreed to serve an additional 20 days to provide some sense of protection for the area. A notable member of this group was young Abraham Lincoln, who had been serving as a captain but was reduced in rank to private in the abbreviated militia.

The most frightening attack on settlers took place on May 21, although the attackers were Potawatomi rather than Sauk. At Big Indian Creek in Illinois, 15 men, women, and children were killed and severely mutilated. Two teenage girls, Sylvia and Rachel Hall, were taken captive. Some Sauk who had accompanied the Potawatomi took the girls to Black Hawk's camp. There they were kept unharmed, but were forced to travel with the Sauk for several days until they were released. Nonetheless, Black Hawk received the blame for the attack, largely because he was the most famous Indian leader involved in the war.

Another attack that spread fear occurred on June 14 south of Dodgeville, Wisconsin, on a farm owned by Omri Spafford. Six men were working in a cornfield when they were attacked, and Spafford and three others were killed. Two days later, along the Pecatonica River, 30 volunteers under the command of Henry Dodge (some of them out of Fort Defiance south of Mineral Point) fought what became known as the Battle of Pecatonica. Dodge, who had founded a mining settlement that he named after himself, was a tall, swashbuckling, natural leader, and later became governor of the state of Wisconsin.

Dodge and his men followed a war party across the east branch of the Pecatonica. There, near present-day Woodford, Wisconsin, they killed all nine members of the party, all of them Kickapoo. Black Hawk was not there, as he had not been at the Spafford farm. Nonetheless, this battle—really more of a small skirmish—helped settlers regain some confidence that they could defeat Black Hawk's Sauk and their allies. The Battle of Pecatonica, small as it was, removed at least some of the fear and uncertainty that had arisen in the wake of Stillman's Run and the succession of sporadic raids against which the farmers and villagers seemingly had no defense.

In fact, some of Black Hawk's battles were far less than total successes. An attack on the Apple River Fort south of Galena, Illinois, on June 24, resulted in the death of one soldier and the capture of livestock and supplies but a quick abandonment of any attempt to capture the fort or set it afire. A second battle of Kellogg's Grove two days later against a militia force led by Major John Dement resulted in the death of five of Dement's men and a large number of their horses. For their part, however, the Sauk lost two chiefs and seven other warriors.

Black Hawk's Retreat

As the summer progressed, Black Hawk and his people, who numbered approximately 1,000, increasingly faced hunger and the stress of not knowing when their pursuers might locate them. Camped in the swampy terrain near Lake Koshkonong southeast of where Madison is now situated, the Sauk were reduced to eating their horses, digging up roots, and stripping bark for their food. The elderly began to die.

Black Hawk decided to lead his party west to the Wisconsin River and take the river route down to the Mississippi, which he hoped to cross to safety. Desperate to reach the Wisconsin as quickly as possible, the Sauk left a long line of supplies behind them, making pursuit easy for anyone who picked up their trail, as Henry Dodge and his force had done. Dodge's men caught up with the Sauk on July 21 near the Wisconsin. Neapope and a contingent of 20 warriors remained behind and faked attacks in an effort to slow down the pursuers and allow the main body of Sauk to cross the river. As the Sauk were crossing to an island in the middle of the Wisconsin, Dodge's forces arrived. Black Hawk led about 50 warriors against them, while his remaining men tried to help the women and children cross. The Sauk tried a frontal attack and then attempted to flank Dodge, who gave permission for a bayonet charge that drove the Sauk back from the heights (known as Wisconsin Heights) to the woods and grass along the river. During the battle, Black Hawk's horse was twice wounded. Strangely enough, Dodge did not continue the engagement, a development that astonished Black Hawk.

The Sauk completed their crossing of the river, having managed to escape a disastrous defeat. The number killed by Dodge's troops is unknown. Black Hawk put the figure at six, by all other accounts far too low. Estimates from the other side ranged from 40 or more (Dodge's report) to close to 70. Dodge's men and their Winnebago scouts scalped many of the fallen Sauk.

On the other side of the Wisconsin, Black Hawk's party split. Some started downriver toward the Mississippi, Neapope and one companion left to sit out the rest of the war at a Winnebago village, and Black Hawk and the remaining Sauk started overland toward the Mississippi north of Prairie du Chien. Many of the latter band of Sauk were forced to walk because of a shortage of horses. Most members of the first party, which consisted primarily of women, children, and elderly men traveling in hastily constructed canoes, met disaster at the hands of troops from Fort Crawford stationed at the mouth of the Wisconsin. Many were either killed or captured outright, while others escaped the troops only to perish from starvation or be hunted down and killed by Menominee recruited by the army.

Black Hawk and his companions continued toward the Mississippi. On August 1, they were on the east bank about two miles south of the Bad Axe River when Black Hawk saw a steamboat, the *Warrior*, approaching. Black Hawk was acquainted with its captain, Joseph Throckmorton. Intending to surrender so as to save the children and women, he hoisted a white cloth and called out to Throckmorton. Two factors conspired to thwart Black Hawk's plan. First, the military had chartered the *Warrior* to carry about 20 troops to a Sioux village; thus, in addition to a six-pound cannon, the boat carried a cargo of soldiers. Second, Throckmorton apparently did not recognize Black Hawk and suspected an ambush. He dropped anchor and called out an invitation for a representative to come to him in a boat. Having no boat, the Sauk could not comply, and Throckmorton, assuming a refusal and trickery, ordered the cannon to open fire, as did the soldiers. As night fell, Throckmorton left for Prairie du Chien, leaving 23 Sauk reportedly killed.

After the *Warrior* departed, Black Hawk told the Sauk that those who wished could cross the river. Black Hawk himself, accompanied by the Prophet and a small group of Sauk, headed north to take refuge with the Chippewa. He also directed a party of about 20 warriors to take up position east of the Mississippi and, if the soldiers arrived, lead them away from the main band.

Slaughter on the Mississippi

Early in the morning of August 2, a party of Henry Dodge's scouts under Captain Joseph Dickson of Platteville encountered the decoy group. In the ensuing fighting, eight Sauk were killed. By eight o'clock, General Atkinson's main body of soldiers, some 1,000 strong, reached the river. Some Sauk desperately tried to fashion rafts to cross the river, while others tried to swim across.

The attack by Atkinson's force was supplemented by the return of the *Warrior*. The resulting slaughter yielded 150 or more dead.[13] Approximately 200 Sauk managed to cross the Mississippi. In the following days, many who had initially escaped were caught and killed by militia and Sioux. Major General Winfield Scott, who in June had been put in charge of defeating the hostile Indians in Illinois and the Michigan Territory, later apologized for the killing of women and children.

Black Hawk and the Prophet, among a party of about 30, made their way westward, establishing a temporary camp near the present town of Tomah, Wisconsin. There they were discovered by a Winnebago and subsequently convinced to come to the Winnebago village at Prairie La Crosse (now La Crosse) and surrender. Black Hawk left the precious medicine bag that had long been in his possession with the Winnebago chief and, along with the Prophet, traveled to Prairie du Chien.

On August 27, 1832, Black Hawk and the Prophet arrived at the home of Joseph Street, the Indian agent at Prairie du Chien. Black Hawk was wearing a new suit of white tanned deerskin that the Winnebago women had made for him so that he could surrender with dignity. Street was amazed by his sudden arrival and delighted that the famous Black Hawk was putting himself under Street's control and effectively ending the war. Street then turned Black Hawk over to Colonel Zachary Taylor at Fort Crawford.

A Prisoner

Lieutenant Jefferson Davis (later to become famous as the president of the Confederacy during the Civil War) escorted both Black Hawk and the Prophet to Jefferson Barracks. Along the way, they paused at Rock Island, where General Winfield Scott came out in a boat to see them rather than have the party land and possibly contract cholera, which had spread among the military that year. Black Hawk spent the winter imprisoned and in chains. Also imprisoned were Black Hawk's sons (Nasheweskaska and Wathametha), the Prophet,

Neapope, and several other Sauk. During his incarceration, Black Hawk received visits from such luminaries as the writer Washington Irving and the painter George Catlin, who completed portraits of several of the prisoners. George Davenport, Antoine LeClaire, and Keokuk also visited, the latter bringing with him Black Hawk's wife, Singing Bird, and their daughter, Nauasia.

Despite their past differences, Keokuk appealed directly to President Andrew Jackson to have Black Hawk released. Instead of being freed, however, Black Hawk was sent to Washington, D.C., as part of a six-man group that also included the Prophet, Neapope, and Black Hawk's son Nasheweskaska. Lieutenant Thomas Alexander, two other soldiers, and an interpreter, Charles St. Vrain, accompanied them. They arrived in Washington on April 24, 1833, and met briefly with President Jackson. They then were sent to Fort Monroe in Virginia to be imprisoned. At Fort Monroe, Colonel Abraham Eustis treated them more as guests than prisoners, removing their shackles and holding dinners in their honor. A long stream of painters came by to execute their portraits, contributing to a continuing elevation of Black Hawk among the Euro-American public, especially in the East, as the prime exemplum of the "noble savage."

After about a month at Fort Monroe, the decision was made to release Black Hawk but bring him back to the Midwest on a journey through several major cities to impress on him the might of the United States and the futility of further opposition. On June 4, 1833, the group, led by Brevet Major John Garland, departed Fort Monroe.

The caravan's progress introduced Black Hawk to adulatory crowds in Norfolk and then in Baltimore, where the old Sauk warrior attended a performance of the play *Jim Crow* in an audience that included President Jackson, who greeted his former enemy pleasantly after the performance. It then wended its way through Philadelphia and New York. Newspapers chronicled Black Hawk's journey under the heading "Blackhawkiana." Detroit, closer to the location of the Black Hawk War, gave Black Hawk a very different welcome, burning him in effigy. After arriving back at Prairie du Chien, Black Hawk informed Street that he had left his medicine bag with the Winnebago chief and urged him to retrieve the sacred bag and return it to him. Street assured Black Hawk that the medicine bag was safe and that he would forward it. In his autobiography, Black Hawk expresses his hope that Street will follow through on his promise. At the time he created the autobiography, Street obviously had not sent the medicine bag along, and there is no follow-up documentation as to whether he ultimately did so.

The Final Years

As the summer wound down, Black Hawk returned to Fort Armstrong, where he dictated his autobiography to Antoine LeClaire. John B. Patterson, acting editor of the *Galenian* newspaper, helped put the account in an orderly form.

Also at Fort Armstrong, Black Hawk received the humiliating news that he was to be under the direction of Keokuk. Nonetheless, publication of the autobiography ensured Black Hawk's lasting fame and position as the greatest of the Sauk leaders.

Black Hawk lived out his remaining years in Iowa, dying on October 3, 1838, at the age of 72. He was buried sitting, wearing a military cloak given to him by President Jackson. Also interred with him were some of his prized possessions, including a cane he had received from Senator Henry Clay and two swords. Within a year, a man named Doctor Turner had dug up the grave and cut off and stolen his head. Within a few more months, Turner came back for the rest of the body. Turner then put the skeleton on display in his office until Governor Robert Lucas of Iowa Territory had the body removed. It later went on display at the Burlington Geographical and Historical Society in Burlington, Iowa. This building burned down in 1855, with the fire consuming the final physical remains of the legendary warrior.

Over the decades following Black Hawk's surrender, the combined Sauk and Fox population declined dramatically, dropping from about 6,000 in 1833 to fewer than half that number by 1845.[14] Eventually, Black Hawk's people were moved to Kansas, and then to Oklahoma. Not until 1912 did many Americans again think about the Sauk, when a grandnephew of Black Hawk named Jim Thorpe won the pentathlon and decathlon at the Olympics in Stockholm, Sweden.

NOTES

1. Black Hawk, *An Autobiography*, ed. Donald Jackson (1955; Urbana: University of Illinois Press, 1990) 47–48.

2. *Autobiography* 48–49.

3. Kerry A. Trask, *Black Hawk: The Battle for the Heart of America* (New York: Henry Holt, 2007) 20–22.

4. Anthony F. C. Wallace, "Prelude to Disaster: The Course of Indian–White Relations Which Led to the Black Hawk War of 1832," *The Black Hawk War 1831–1832*, ed. Ellen M. Whitney, vol. 1 (Springfield: Illinois State Historical Library, 1970) 6–7.

5. *Autobiography* 54.

6. *Autobiography* 67; R. David Edmunds, *Tecumseh and the Quest for Indian Leadership* (Boston: Little, Brown, 1984) 193; John Sugden, *Tecumseh: A Life* (New York: Henry Holt, 1998) 334–38.

7. Allan W. Eckert, *A Sorrow in Our Heart: The Life of Tecumseh* (1992; New York: Bantam Books, 1993) 804–13.

8. Benjamin Drake, *The Great Indian Chief of the West or, Life and Adventures of Black Hawk* (1838; Cincinnati: BiblioBazaar, 2006) 154.

9. *Autobiography* 80; Roger L. Nichols, *Black Hawk and the Warrior's Path*, American Biographical History Series (Wheeling, IL: Harlan Davidson, 1992) 56.

10. Trask 50–51.

11. George A. McCall, *Letters from the Frontiers: Written During a Period of Thirty Years' Service in the Army of the United States* (1868; Gainesville: University Presses of Florida, 1974) 241.

12. Trask 183–86; *Autobiography* 122–23.

13. Roger L. Nichols, *General Henry Atkinson: A Western Military Career* (Norman: University of Oklahoma Press, 1965) 173.

14. William Thomas Hagan, *The Sac and Fox Indians* (Norman: University of Oklahoma Press, 1958) 205–6.

RECOMMENDED READING

Black Hawk. *An Autobiography*. Ed. Donald Jackson. 1955. Urbana: University of Illinois Press, 1990.

Jung, Patrick J. *The Black Hawk War of 1832*. Norman: University of Oklahoma Press, 2007.

Mahan, Bruce E. *Old Fort Crawford and the Frontier*. 1926. Prairie du Chien, WI: Prairie du Chien Historical Society, 2000.

McLaughlin, Benjamin. *In Black Hawk's Footsteps: A Trail Guide to Monuments, Museums, and Battlefields of the Black Hawk War of 1832*. 3rd ed. Santa Fe: B. McLaughlin Publishing, 2005.

Nichols, Roger L. *Black Hawk and the Warrior's Path: American Biographical History Series*. Wheeling, IL: Harlan Davidson, 1992.

Thayer, Crawford B., ed. *Hunting a Shadow: The Search for Black Hawk: Black Hawk War Eye-Witness Series*. Menasha, WI: Banta Press, 1981.

Trask, Kerry A. *Black Hawk: The Battle for the Heart of America*. New York: Henry Holt, 2007.

Whitney, Ellen M., ed. *The Black Hawk War 1831–1832*. 4 vols. Springfield: Illinois State Historical Library, 1970–78.

After a military funeral, Osceola was buried near the entrance of Ft. Moultrie, Charleston, S.C. (Library of Congress)

Osceola
(Billy Powell)
circa 1804–1838

The American Indian leader most commonly known today as Osceola lived a short life, with an even shorter public existence as an important resistance leader. In his brief time upon the stage of Indian opposition to Euro-American efforts to usurp Indian lands and obliterate Indian culture, Osceola embodied narrative patterns that are easy to romanticize: the brilliant young leader who dies before his time, the comet that strikes out with great heat and light but quickly dissipates, the tragedy of unrewarded genius.

All of these narrative trajectories are at least partly true, but they need not be, and should not be, romanticized. Osceola was, after all, a real person whose actual efforts, if ultimately in a largely lost cause, had a profound impact during his lifetime and continue to reverberate today in the nation's historical memory.

BILLY POWELL

Born into Two Cultures

Osceola was born around 1804 in Tallassee, near today's Tuskegee, Alabama. He was born into a Maskókî (also spelled Muskoke) clan, a people more widely known by a name given to them by the British, the Creeks. Osceola, however, was perhaps more multicultural than any other prominent Indian resistance leader. His father was William Powell, an English trader; his mother, Polly Copinger, included among her ancestors a Scottish grandfather named James McQueen and a father named Copinger about whom little is definitively known but who may have been Spanish. Patricia Riles Wickman conjectures in *Osceola's Legacy* that Osceola's maternal grandfather may have been José Coppinger, the final Spanish governor of East Florida before the area was turned over to the United States in 1821, or a black slave previously owned by the Coppinger family who kept his former owner's surname.[1]

Osceola, by Wickman's reckoning just one-eighth Indian,[2] was known as Billy Powell in childhood; he continued to be known by this name by Euro-Americans even during adulthood, well after he received the Indian name Osceola sometime during his teen years. Growing up, Osceola was exposed not only to his native Creek language and the English of his father, but also possibly to Spanish; indeed, he is known to have spoken Spanish well as an adult. He must have seen himself within very different cultures, although in his own actions he clearly gave primacy to the Creek.

The Creek War

The Creek War of 1813–1814 was both a civil war among the Creeks and a struggle against the United States. It occurred at the same time that the United States was fighting the English and their Indian allies, including the great Tecumseh of the Shawnees, in the War of 1812. Some elements of the Creeks wanted to remain at peace with their Euro-American neighbors, while other

Creeks saw the United States as a serious threat to their way of life and felt solidarity with the native peoples fighting farther north. A prominent figure in the Creek War was Peter McQueen, Osceola's clan grandfather, a brother of Osceola's maternal grandmother.

The officer most responsible for the U.S. victory in the Creek War was the unrelenting future President, Andrew Jackson. Jackson arose from his sick bed, where he was recuperating from wounds suffered in a duel, to lead the U.S. forces against the Creeks. Among the men serving under him were Davy Crockett, the hero of the Alamo during the Texas Revolution against Mexico, and Sam Houston, president of the Republic of Texas during the 1830s and 1840s prior to its being admitted as a state in 1845.

After Jackson's decisive victory over the starving Creeks, he imposed on them the Treaty of Fort Jackson, which forced the Creeks to yield 23 million acres of land, or approximately half of their traditional territory, and ended Creek domination of the Southeast. The land seized in the treaty represented roughly half of the current state of Alabama and a significant portion of Georgia.

Moving South

Jackson's oppressive treaty, which was designed to compensate the United States for the financial cost of the conflict with the Creeks, had an immediate effect on Osceola's family. Deprived of their ancestral home, large numbers of Creeks migrated to Florida. Among those embarking on this sad journey were Osceola's parents, William Powell's two daughters by a previous marriage, Peter McQueen, and other members of the clan who may have included siblings of Osceola (although no definitive record of other children of William and Polly remains). At some point during the trip, William Powell and his two oldest daughters turned east and settled near the Chattahoochee River along the Alabama–Georgia line.

OSCEOLA'S TEEN YEARS

The First Seminole War

Several significant events occurred in Osceola's life during his teens. Peter McQueen, the most important member of his clan—an extended family defined by the matriarchal structure of Creek society—died in 1818 or 1819. An ardent defender of Creek life and opponent of the United States, McQueen had an enormous influence on young Billy Powell, who grew up to firmly embrace his mother's culture rather than his father's. This was a choice entirely consistent with Creek culture: In this culture, a man married into his wife's clan but did not become a member of that clan, resulting in children adopting the primacy of the mother's relatives.

Then came the First Seminole War and the reappearance of Andrew Jackson as a disruptive and dangerous force in Osceola's life. The Creeks (or Maskókîs) were related culturally, linguistically, and often by blood to the Seminoles of Florida, but the latter were a distinct group by the eighteenth century, albeit one that continued to absorb Creeks from farther north. The Seminoles, in fact, readily welcomed the migrating Creeks as well as runaway African slaves. Much writing about the war has drawn no distinction between Creek (or Maskókî) and Seminole, placing both groups under the Seminole name.

Florida itself was widely seen by its northern American neighbor as at least a nuisance, and at worst a serious threat to the safety and economy of the United States. Jackson embodied these various grievances against Florida, deploring the support that it offered as a refuge to Indian and slave alike. At the time, the U.S. government was engaging in negotiations to acquire the Spanish possession, but the process was proceeding much more slowly than Jackson wished.

Jackson saw an opportunity to achieve several goals at once with a forceful military excursion into Florida. He could not only put an end to problems with Indians in the region and remove a haven for runaway slaves, but also sidestep the prolonged negotiations by simply taking Florida by force. Jackson implored President James Monroe to let him seize Florida. In return, he received an ambiguously worded directive seeming to give him that authority without actually stating it in explicit language. In other words, Monroe was covering himself with plausible deniability should Jackson's military foray backfire.

Jackson invaded Florida in March 1818. At the time, Peter McQueen was still alive and considered one of the leading Creek refugee leaders. Florida Indians wisely did their best to avoid Jackson's army, but Jackson did capture Pensacola and appoint one of his officers as governor of West Florida. Jackson then returned to the United States at the end of May—and his invasion blew up on the diplomatic front. President Monroe and his Cabinet considered abandoning their support of Jackson to mollify Spanish anger, but at the urging of former President John Quincy Adams decided not to discipline him. The decision not to scapegoat Jackson saved his career, securing a future that would see him become President of the United States. In that role, he would continue contributing to the destruction of Osceola's people and their way of life.

Green Corn Ceremony

Shortly after Jackson's invasion of Florida, Osceola moved with his mother and other relatives farther south into central Florida. At some point during these years, possibly when he was 18, during 1822, Billy Powell became Osceola. He received his new name during the annual Green Corn Ceremony, which included four days of fasting by young men, usually in their teen years, as they received a ceremonial name and entered into adulthood.

This important communal ceremony included dancing and feasting, all within a serious ritualistic framework that occurred in the summer, approximately late June to early July, during the corn-growing season. Already identified as a future leader, in no small part because of the prominence of Peter McQueen and other male figures in his mother's clan, Osceola was chosen to assist at the Green Corn Ceremony. His duties included locating the herbs, such as button snakeroot, for the ceremonial black drinks that served as emetics to further the participants' purification, and sweeping the dance circle prior to the night's dance. The new name that Billy Powell received refers both to the sacred black drink and to the singing that accompanied the drink. The sacred event, which lasted five days, also included ball games, which Osceola was not permitted to participate in until after his renaming, and court sessions at which crimes were identified and adjudicated.

The Green Corn Dance began at midnight just as the fifth day of the ceremony was starting. Dawn brought with it the ritual scratching on the bodies of the participants to purify their blood. During the final evening, the medicine bundle was examined to see if any additional objects had been inserted into it to enhance its protective properties.

At the conclusion of the Green Corn Ceremony that included Billy Powell's renaming, the young warrior was ready to embark upon a career that would enshrine the name "Osceola" permanently in American history. However, his contemporary Euro-Americans continued to refer to him regularly as Billy Powell. Even as Osceola, he still had much to prove to his own Creeks. Osceola never became a chief. Instead, his ability to lead men into battle depended on his courage, his skill as a warrior, and his capacity for instilling confidence in other warriors.

Apprenticeship to Abiákî

An important part of Osceola's education occurred through his apprenticeship to Abiákî (Abéca), a prominent medicine man committed to resisting Euro-Americans and revered for his medicines believed to protect men in battle. Abiákî imparted his knowledge of the supposed protective powers of plants and chants to Osceola, probably beginning when his student was still Billy Powell.

As U.S. efforts to remove the Creeks and Seminoles from the Southeast and transport them beyond the Mississippi to what would become Oklahoma intensified, mentor and student would become firm allies. Osceola learned to employ a variety of strategies to resist the U.S. government, drawing in part on Abiákî's wisdom.

OSCEOLA'S PUBLIC LIFE

Jackson Becomes President

Life for Osceola, given his background, education, and leadership qualities, could have been productive and peaceful, possibly in Florida or, more likely, farther north. (Florida had been a possession of the United States since 1821, although it would not earn statehood until 1845.) Multicultural, in appearance as much Euro-American as Indian, and speaking English (and possibly Spanish) as well as his native Creek language, Osceola could look back on a long string of European ancestors. He clearly saw himself as Creek but seemed to move easily between the two worlds. He might have found his way farther north to live and work within the United States or have even gone to Europe to fashion an entirely new existence for himself. But he did not make those choices: Instead, he stayed to fight and die for the people who gave him one-eighth of his genetic makeup but also the traditions and history that he accepted as his own.

Andrew Jackson, who was firmly rooted in only one world, became President of the United States in 1829 and held that office until 1837. In those years, he did all he could—and with considerable success—to eliminate the last vestiges of Indian power not just in the Southeast, but everywhere east of the Mississippi River.

Early in his first term as president, Jackson happily signed into law the Indian Removal Act of May 28, 1830. This federal legislation legalized what had been Jackson's personal policy choice—the removal of all Indians in the Southeast to Indian Territory beyond the Mississippi. Many congressmen in the North opposed the legislation because it would increase the white population in the slave-holding South. The law also called for the removal from the Seminoles and Creeks all slaves (and many former slaves living with the Indians), an issue that had contributed to U.S. justification of the First Seminole War.

Treaty of Payne's Landing

The Indians of the Southeast still had to agree or be forced to accept their removal, of course. The U.S. government recognized that the former option was far less costly in terms of both money and the lives of soldiers as well as other Euro-Americans who might be caught in another war. To pursue this approach, James Gadsden, a personal friend of President Jackson, was named as a special agent to negotiate with the Indians.

Gadsden selected Payne's Landing on Oklawaha River near present-day Eureka, Florida, as the site for a meeting that convened in early May 1832. The treaty was signed on May 9, but no written record of the discussions was retained. Fifteen Indian signatures appear on the document, but they do not include the signature of Osceola. Osceola, who was neither a chief nor a supporter of the treaty, was present at the meeting as a *tustenuggee*—that is, a sort of policeman designated to keep order. The treaty included the signing mark of Micanopy, a prominent hereditary leader who favored emigration, although he later claimed that his mark had been forged. In fact, rumors circulated that many—even all—of the marks were either forged or coerced. Given the absence of any minutes of the proceedings, it is impossible to tell whether the signings were genuine and the subsequent disclaimers simply represented efforts to back away from an unpopular agreement.

And unpopular the treaty was—with Osceola and many other Creek and Seminole residents of Florida. Under the provisions of the treaty, the Indians were to give up their land, move to their assigned home beyond the

Mississippi, and become part of one Creek nation that would include those Creeks whom Osceola's people had fought in the Creek War. In return, they would be paid $15,400 after their arrival in their new home and receive an annual annuity of $3,000 for 15 years, a sum to be divided among those who had earlier acquiesced to their removal as well as the present inhabitants of Florida. Each person, upon arriving in the Indian Territory, also would receive a blanket and frock, and the U.S. government would write off claims of up to $7,000 for slaves and other stolen property. Finally, the articles stipulated that the exodus from Florida must be completed within three years.[3]

The Treaty of Payne's Landing also included an ambiguous provision early in its Preamble. Seven chiefs were to travel to the western lands to inspect their new home. Then, "should they be satisfied with the character of that country, and of the favorable disposition of the Creeks to reunite with the Seminoles as one people," the agreement would be considered binding.[4] The pronoun "they" appears remarkably unclear in its reference, alternately referring to the seven chiefs or to the entire Seminole nation (the latter interpretation was certainly inaccurate, as U.S. officials made no apparent distinction between the Florida Seminoles and Creeks who had migrated to Florida). In fact, the seven chiefs, under their own legislative traditions, would not have been authorized to speak for everyone but would instead have been required to return and let their people collectively decide whether to move.

John Sprague, a U.S. army officer, asserts in his book *The Origin, Progress, and Conclusion of the Florida War*, published in 1848, that a seven-person delegation, accompanied by Indian Agent John Phagan, made the journey in the fall of 1832 to inspect the assigned land. Strangely, Abiákî, whom Sprague refers to as Sam Jones, was to be among the seven chiefs and also is listed as one of the signers of the treaty; his inclusion lends credence to accusations that the signing marks were fraudulent, given his well-known opposition to removal. The revered medicine man, however, did not make the trip, being replaced by John Hicks. Nor did he sign the supplemental Additional Treaty of March 28, 1833, although the document includes the mark for John Hicks (Euchee Billy) and the notation "representing Sam Jones."[5] Uncertainty in determining who did and did not support the Treaty of Payne's Landing and its follow-up can also be explained (as with many other treaties forced upon Indians by the U.S. government) by the Indians' inability to read English, making them dependent on U.S. government officials' explanations of what the wording meant.

Apart from the ambiguous wording of the treaty, it contained enough that was clearly stated to arouse the opposition of Osceola. Over the following two years, Osceola became widely known to Euro-Americans as he visited military compounds and may have worked as a guide. At the same time, he continued to rise in stature among his own people as an opponent of removal.

Osceola was indeed impressive. Highly intelligent, articulate, and passionate, he combined political insights with his training in medicine. He was somewhat tall for the times, standing approximately 5 feet 10 inches with fine, handsome features and a penchant for dressing well. He surely made a striking impression on non-Indians in his intricately designed knee-length dress-frock topped off with a turban sporting large plumes.

Osceola often appeared at Fort King near the present site of Ocala in central Florida. Likewise, his mentor, Abiákî, visited the fort to sell fish, earning him the nickname "Sam Jones" after a character in a popular poem, "Sam Jones the Fisherman of Sandy Hook." Both Osceola and the older man were well aware that they were visiting people with whom they might soon be at war and recognized that they should learn as much as possible about them and their habits.

Friendship with John Graham

Osceola's interactions with soldiers cannot be accurately explained solely as a clever ploy to reconnoiter the enemy in preparation for a conflict that Osceola knew was likely to come. Starting with his English father, he had known Euro-Americans all of his life and was able to judge them as individuals, even counting some as his friends.

A compelling example was a graduate of West Point named John Graham, who was approximately 10 years younger than Osceola. The two met at Fort King. By 1835, they had become, in the words of a first-hand observer, John Bemrose (an unusually observant and literate enlisted man), "inseparable." According to Bemrose, who wrote his reminiscences about 30 years after his experiences in the Second Seminole War, the two men "were seen daily together."[6]

The friendship between Osceola and Lieutenant Graham developed out of the officer's kindness toward a daughter or niece of Osceola's and included the giving of various gifts. One such gift was a frock, which Graham hiked three miles to Osceola's village to present to the girl. The two men visited for several hours that day. At some point during the conversation, Osceola offered to teach Graham a bit of his own language, while Graham agreed in turn to help Osceola improve his English. The visit was the first of many by Graham. Osceola also gave Lieutenant Graham a number of presents, including a plume of white crane feathers.

When war broke out, Osceola cautioned his warriors during the First Battle of the Withlacoochee not to fire on Graham. Those orders may have saved the young officer's life, but he would survive his friend by only three and one-half years, succumbing to yellow fever on July 30, 1841. He left behind his widow, the daughter of Florida's governor, Robert Raymond Reid.

WILEY THOMPSON

The Fort King Council

Wiley Thompson was appointed as the Indian agent at Fort King in late 1833. He had fought with Andrew Jackson during the Creek War and owed his title of general to his having been a major general of the Georgia militia. His overarching responsibility was to persuade the remaining Creeks and Seminoles in Florida to agree to move west. This task ran up against the firm wall of Indian resistance and led Thompson into a protracted relationship with Osceola, which would ultimately lead to the agent's death.

Thompson convened a gathering of Indian leaders at Fort King on October 21, 1834, with the hope that he could persuade them to leave Florida. At this meeting, Thompson distributed what was supposed to be the final annuity paid to the Indians before their departure. The meeting resumed two days later, with Thompson assuring those present that the Creeks who had previously moved were anxiously looking forward to the Seminoles from Florida joining them, where together they could form a great nation.

That evening, the leaders met apart from Thompson, although he had informers present to keep him abreast of what was discussed. Osceola sat near Micanopy, who was prone to changing his mind and waffling on the matter of emigrating. Osceola adamantly objected to moving, and, expressing his position with great eloquence and power, helped to convince most of those present to remain in Florida. He also urged that those who supported migrating be considered enemies. When the group of leaders met with Thompson to convey their decision, Osceola gave a powerful speech denouncing Thompson's plan. There was no longer any question in Thompson's mind about Osceola's status as a leader.

Osceola's Arrest

Thompson was not about to give up his effort to persuade the Creeks and Seminoles still in Florida to leave. Recognizing Osceola's influence, Thompson lavished attention and gifts upon him, including a silver-mounted flintlock rifle. Upon failing to achieve acquiescence from Osceola, and after having an angry confrontation with him in June 1835, Thompson decided to have his perceived nemesis arrested.

Putting the young Creek leader in irons and jailing him, Thompson hoped, might bring him around to accepting migration. The actual result was the personal shaming of Osceola and his decision to be more strategically clever in his opposition. Consequently, Osceola sent word to Thompson on the day after his arrest that he was ready to sign the Payne's Landing Treaty. He also promised, as a condition of his release, that he would return in five days with others who also would sign the treaty. In fact, Osceola did return, bringing a contingent of about 80 of his people. Along with Osceola, they agreed to the treaty provisions. The agreement deceived Thompson, who concluded that his arrest had achieved its intended end. Thompson would later pay for the arrest and his misjudgment of Osceola's intentions with his life.

THE OUTBREAK OF WAR

Killing of Charley Emathla

Osceola wasted no time preparing for the war that he now concluded could not be avoided. He arranged a traditional ball game at Fort King, an event that was both a sport and a cultural tradition that, through competition, reminded the participants of their common background. Along with reaffirming cultural identity, the contest gave Osceola a cover for acquiring additional ammunition, which the U.S. military provided as prizes.

The Indian war council sought to build unity by declaring that any Indians who agreed to follow the Payne's Treaty plan and began to make arrangements to leave Florida would be put to death. Among those preparing for departure was Charley Emathla, who had been among the group visiting Indian Territory in 1832. Emathla had started selling his livestock, a precondition stated in Article V of the Treaty of Payne's Landing. That decision and preliminary action brought Emathla into conflict with the warning from the council of chiefs.

Needing a leader that people would follow to carry out its prescribed punishment, the council chose Osceola to administer its judgment. On November 26, 1835, Osceola and a small group of followers attacked Emathla as he was returning home with his two daughters. The girls were unharmed, but Emathla died from multiple gunshot wounds. He was carrying gold and silver coins from the sale of his livestock. Osceola denounced the coins as having been earned with Indian blood and threw the money away.

Battle of Black Point

Approximately three weeks later, on December 18, Osceola engaged in his first battle with U.S. troops in what came to be known as the Battle of Black Point. Osceola and approximately 80 warriors ambushed a military baggage train that was on its way to Alabama. As Osceola was securing the baggage train, a militia force of about 30 under the command of Captain John McLemore (later a major) arrived but quickly retreated when most of the men refused to attack the Indians. A relatively minor incident in itself, the engagement was the first battle of the Second Seminole War.

Thompson's Death

Next up was General Wiley Thompson, who had jailed Osceola the previous year and who was the primary local figure involved in trying to force the Florida Indians to move to Indian Territory. Although Osceola certainly had no love for Thompson, his killing of Thompson was not an act of personal revenge but rather the fulfillment of another council dictate.

Thompson dined with Lieutenant Constantine Smith and Captain Thomas Lendrum on December 28, 1835. After the meal, late in the afternoon, Thompson and Smith left Fort King for what they thought would be a pleasant stroll to the store run by the sutler Erastus Rogers.

Suddenly, a group of Indians led by Osceola appeared, easily killing Thompson and Smith. As the primary object of the attack, Thompson was shot several times and scalped. At the same time, another group attacked Rogers' store, killing him and his two clerks as they ate their supper. Rogers, who was apparently much disliked by his Indian customers, was shot 17 times.

Dade's Column

On the same day, shortly after dawn, yet another group under Micanopy and the creek war leaders Jumper and Alligator was preparing to attack a military column led by Major Francis Dade that was moving toward Fort King. Micanopy had wanted to wait until Osceola arrived, but Jumper argued successfully for moving ahead with the attack.

Early in the morning, Dade's column entered the trap prepared for them. The first shot struck Dade. Within seconds, half of Dade's men were dead; others were wounded. Captain George Washington Gardiner rallied his men and got them to take cover. Gardiner ordered the quick construction of a triangular barricade made from trees that his soldiers hurriedly cut down. While still on his feet and trying to save his men, Gardiner was shot and killed. The survivors took refuge within the barricade, which was only two feet high.

Before long, only three men remained alive within the small enclosure, with three wounded men outside it. Ultimately, three soldiers and an interpreter survived the battle. The U.S. dead numbered 107, with the attacking force suffering just three fatalities.[7] On orders from Osceola, the Indians did not mutilate the bodies, although some members of a group of former slaves allied to the Seminoles exacted revenge for their previous enslavement on some of the bodies.

THE SECOND SEMINOLE WAR

First Battle of Withlacoochee

After the Battle of Black Point, the almost total elimination of Major Dade's column, and the killing of General Wiley Thompson, there was no doubt but that Florida was now engulfed in a war. It eventually became known as the Second Seminole War, although the combatants included Creeks as well as Seminoles. In fact, the most prominent figure on the Indian side in this conflict with the United States was the Creek Osceola.

By far the best known of the Indians who took up arms to oppose migration, Osceola was soon being credited for almost every military action taken by the Indians of Florida, whether or not he actually participated in them. For the U.S. military, he became the face of the enemy, even after his health began to decline, limiting his effectiveness as a warrior and reducing his involvement as a leader of the resistance.

The first major battle of the Second Seminole War occurred on December 31, 1835, along the Withlacoochee River southwest of Fort King, not far from Osceola's village. Osceola led about 220 warriors and some 30 blacks. During the battle, Osceola suffered an apparently minor wound to an arm or hand, although rumors circulated that he had been badly injured or even killed in the battle. Osceola was reported to be wearing a U.S. army coat during the engagement, perhaps a gift from Wiley Thompson.[8]

Early in the morning of the final day of the year, General Duncan Clinch and a force consisting of about 250 regulars and 500 Florida volunteers reached the north bank of the Withlacoochee. Finding no feasible ford across the river, Clinch used an old Indian canoe left at the river to ferry the regulars across, seven or eight at a time, with the soldiers steadily bailing out the canoe to keep the leaky vessel from sinking. The canoe may have been left at Osceola's direction to induce a crossing that would limit the number of soldiers who would be able to make it across the Withlacoochee and at the same time to set up an ambush. After crossing, Clinch took his men about 400 yards south of the river and stopped to rest.

At that moment, Osceola's warriors began shooting. Caught in a serious trap with the volunteers still north of the river, Clinch finally ordered bayonet charges to repel the attackers. Meantime, most of the volunteers would not cross the river, probably because their period of enlistment was up the following day and they did not want to put themselves in jeopardy so close to the end of their service. Ultimately, between 30 and 60 volunteers did cross. The regulars then retreated toward the volunteers and took up a defensive position, thereby preventing the Indians from separating them from the river.

Osceola directed the firing, urging his men to try to shoot the officers. He may also have taken part in the shooting, although that remains uncertain. General Clinch had his horse shot out from under him, and there were reports that a musket ball went through his hat.

Realizing that he had inflicted significant damage on the military but that he could not encircle them, Osceola called for a withdrawal. Clinch took advantage of his opponents' departure by constructing a wooden bridge and taking his men back across the river. There were not a high number of fatalities in the battle (which had lasted about 90 minutes)—3 Indians and 4 U.S. soldiers—but the military suffered many more wounded than did the Indians, 50 to 5.[9]

The outcome was not a clear victory for either side, but it certainly convinced both parties that the Indians could more than hold their own against the U.S. military. They had gained confidence by stopping the advancing army, and Osceola had demonstrated his ability as a war leader. From this point on, U.S. officials would identify Osceola as their prime enemy, and defeating him would become tantamount in their minds to winning the war. That, of course, was a simplistic overstatement of Osceola's role and a serious reductionist assessment of the opposition, but understanding the complexity of Indian life in any of its dimensions was something that U.S. political and military officials were seldom very good at doing.

Additional Battles

The war continued through 1836 with the U.S. military trying unsuccessfully to capture Osceola (still usually referred to as Powell by his adversaries).

In late February, troops under General Edmund Gaines were locked for days in a precarious position by surrounding Indian forces in a second battle along the Withlacoochee. Then came a ceasefire on March 6 and a parley, with Osceola, Jumper, and Alligator representing the Seminoles and Creeks. Osceola remained adamant about not leaving Florida, but he and his associates agreed to accept the Withlacoochee River as a boundary line between U.S. and Indian lands. Gaines responded that he lacked the authority to make such an arrangement but stated that he would relay the offer to government officials; he suggested that Osceola stay south of the river until an answer was forthcoming. Regardless of whether the talks had any chance of success, the arrival of a relief column under General Clinch, which immediately began to shoot, ended the discussion and the Indians withdrew. In the battle Gaines lost 5 men, with an additional 46 being wounded, and two of his own teeth were knocked out by a bullet.

Additional battles during the year included an attack on U.S. forces on July 19 at the Battle of Welika Pond and a November attempt to capture Osceola's stronghold, known as the Battle of Wahoo Swamp. The former was an engagement at the north-central settlement of Micanopy, named after the pro-emigration leader. Osceola attacked a wagon train escorted by 60 men. Five soldiers were killed and six wounded before troops from Fort Defiance (one of several U.S. forts by that name) came to the train's rescue.

In November, forces under Lieutenant Colonel Benjamin Pierce (recently promoted from major at the recommendation of General Richard Call) joined Call's troops near the scene of Major Dade's earlier defeat. Also present was a group of Creek volunteers who were prepared to fight for the United States. Call had been harassing Osceola, burning three of his deserted villages and inflicting moderate casualties, including approximately 45 fatalities. The great prize remained Osceola's stronghold.

Osceola was prepared when the joint forces approached in the morning of November 21. Osceola and his men fired but soon began to pull back, firing from tree to tree, with the pursuers floundering after them through the swamp. Call's forces finally struggled to reach a stream and again engaged the Indians in a gun battle. The time was about 3:30 P.M. Fearing that the dark water was deep, and realizing that the day was rapidly coming to an end and that his soldiers were tired, Call decided not to attempt a crossing. That decision was a stroke of luck for Osceola: The stream was actually only three feet deep, affording a potentially easy crossing that would have put Call within easy striking distance of Osceola's stronghold.

As the war continued through 1837, Osceola's active participation and leadership role declined, to a considerable extent apparently because of his health problems. Osceola was not alone in falling ill amid the inhospitable topography and climate exacerbated by serious shortages of food. In fact, illness was common among the U.S. troops, seriously undermining military efforts. Nonetheless, U.S. soldiers methodically destroyed whatever they could find that might assist their adversaries, including their crops.

General Thomas Jesup

Brevet Major General Thomas S. Jesup replaced General Call as commander of the Florida forces on December 9, 1836. Jesup brought to his new post a determination to achieve what no one else had been able to manage—the capture of Osceola, who remained in the military imagination both the will and the backbone of Indian opposition.

The experienced Jesup had served with distinction in the War of 1812. By 1818, he was a quartermaster general with the rank of brigadier. In 1828, he earned a promotion to major general. Jesup proved to be a formidable opponent for Osceola, one who would earn lasting fame and infamy for the manner in which he finally brought down his opponent.

On the Run

As rumors of Osceola's declining health (apparently recurring fever occasioned by malaria) circulated during the spring of 1837, troops again approached his stronghold, forcing Osceola to remain steadily on the move. Jesup had established a circle of forts around the Withlacoochee area, and Osceola understood that his people would have to spread out in smaller groups to avoid the potentially large-scale disaster that likely would occur if Jesup attacked Osceola's primary village—"Powell's town" as the military referred to it.

Osceola moved to the Panasoffke Swamp on the Withlacoochee to take up residence at a village of former slaves. (Today Lake Panasoffke lies west of Leesburg.) At least part of Osceola's motivation was to defend the runaways, many of whom fought bravely alongside him in the war. East of the village was Fort Mellon, commanded by Lieutenant Colonel William Harney. Osceola spent the night of May 7 as the guest of Colonel Harney, to whom he spoke of bringing the war to a close. Harney apparently believed that Osceola was sincere, but the visit likely was intended to slow down military efforts with a strategically misleading suggestion of peace.

Adding to the pressure on Osceola was the capitulation of several prominent leaders to the U.S. forces on March 6, including Micanopy and Jumper. Jesup tried to entice Indians to yield by agreeing that they would be permitted to take with them to the west any blacks to whom they had rightful ownership. In the face of considerable opposition claiming that he was permitting the property of white slave owners to escape, Jesup later modified the provision to exclude runaway slaves and ordered the Indians to turn over all runaway slaves. Using a variety of carrot-and-stick methods, Jesup sent a message to Osceola warning him that he was importing bloodhounds from Cuba to hunt Osceola down for hanging.

Still Resisting

Osceola's bouts with fever during 1837 seriously hindered his military activities and reduced the number of warriors around him, a natural development given that a leader who was unable to fight would be unlikely to have a large group of able-bodied men waiting beside him when they could be productive elsewhere. Yet despite his health problems, Osceola remained unwilling to surrender. In May 1837, he attempted to unify his allies and improve their morale by arranging a ball game at Fort Mellon. In an attempt to divert U.S. authorities from his true purpose, Osceola led them to believe that the game was designed to encourage Indians to come together with the intention of emigrating to Indian Territory.

Osceola later reported to Colonel Harney that he could not keep his own appointment to report for emigration in early June because he had hurt his foot in the game. The report of the injury may have been true, but in any case it offered a useful excuse not to appear. Instead, Osceola and Abiákî gathered a force of some 200 warriors and traveled to Fort Brooke (where the city of Tampa would eventually arise). There Micanopy, Alligator, and Jumper, among a group of about 700, had gathered prior to emigration. The three men, from Osceola's perspective, had betrayed the cause and led many others astray.

During the night of June 2, Osceola and his party went about awakening those who had gathered at the fort, urging many to abandon the emigration, threatening some, and leading the contingent out of Fort Brooke, from where they eventually scattered to various sites. Micanopy was stripped of his leadership role after again proving that he could not be trusted to resist efforts to remove the Florida Indians, and his place was taken by Abiákî. The successful removal of the 700 people from Fort Brooke led General Jesup to request that he be relieved of his command. That request was denied, leaving Jesup to decide that victory could never come while Osceola remained at large.

OSCEOLA'S CAPTURE

Jesup's Treachery

General Jesup decided that what he considered Osceola's duplicitous behavior required drastic action. If the Indians could not be persuaded or coerced to surrender and agree to being removed from Florida, they would have to be exterminated. Further, no traditional niceties of military conduct would be allowed to get in the way of victory. Indian allies of the United States would be permitted, if not actively encouraged, to take a no-holds-barred approach to defeating Osceola and his people.

On September 9, 1837, U.S. forces captured Philip, Micanopy's brother-in-law, who was one of the most important war leaders. Philip was incarcerated at Fort Marion, where he was permitted to send for his son, Coacoochee. Coacoochee arrived with another warrior, Blue Snake, bearing a white flag—the traditional, almost sacrosanct symbol of peace, and hitherto a virtual guarantee that those so appearing would be permitted to arrive, talk, and leave in peace. Not so with Jesup: When the two men arrived to meet with him, the general had them arrested.

Jesup then laid his trap for Osceola. On October 20, Osceola sent a trusted black fighter, Juan Caballo (also known as John Horse), to Brigadier General Joseph Hernandez, a militia commander at St. Augustine and an unsuccessful candidate for the U.S. Senate in 1845, to request a meeting with Jesup. Jesup told Hernandez to agree to the meeting and arrest Osceola when he arrived.

On October 21, Osceola, accompanied by Coe Hadjo, a pro-emigrationist, awaited Hernandez about eight miles south of St. Augustine. Hernandez arrived with two companies of troops (about 250 men), while Jesup remained at Fort Peyton nearby.

Hernandez easily found Osceola's camp with a white flag flying over it. This flag had been made from the white cloth that Jesup had earlier supplied to the Indians so that they could surrender without harm. Osceola asked Coe Hadjo to speak on his behalf. After some discussion, Hernandez motioned for the troops to come closer. Perhaps not surprised by the stratagem, Osceola offered no resistance. He, Coe Hadjo, 71 warriors, 6 women, and 4 blacks were taken prisoner and marched to Fort Marion at St. Augustine.

The method whereby Jesup had taken Osceola prisoner would subject him for the rest of his life to severe criticism, both within Congress, where an extensive debate about his actions occurred in the spring of 1838, and beyond the halls of Congress in the press and in public discourse. The stigma of dishonor went with him to his grave and has endured permanently in accounts of the Second Seminole War. The one place where his actions did meet with almost total approbation was Florida, among the Euro-Americans who looked forward to the removal of Osceola and the other Indians.

Imprisonment

Osceola was joined later that fall at Fort Marion by several family members, including his two wives (Uichee and Ahlikchen) and two children. He remained at the fort for about 10 weeks, during which time his health declined. In December, a measles outbreak killed 15 prisoners, although Osceola apparently did not contract the disease. Conditions were unsanitary, and lice became a serious problem. Dr. Frederick Weedon, a surgeon under contract to the army who also was a brother-in-law of Wiley Thompson, was at Fort Marion and would continue to treat Osceola during the final months of his life.

While at Fort Marion, Osceola turned down a chance to escape with Coacoochee and 18 others on November 29. Osceola cited his health as a reason for staying behind, but he also was awaiting his family members and worried about their fate if he escaped.

Osceola and the others held at Fort Marion (including Micanopy, who had surrendered at Fort Mellon on December 3, and Philip) were transported aboard the steamer *S.S. Poinsett* to Fort Moultrie on Sullivan's Island in the harbor of Charleston, South Carolina. They arrived at the fort on New Year's

Day 1838. Accompanying the Indians were Dr. Weedon and Captain Pitcairn Morrison, the officer in charge of Seminole emigration. Many of those incarcerated, including Osceola's wives and children, eventually were shipped west. Osceola, however, would soon die at Fort Moultrie.

Osceola's Final Days

Osceola was treated reasonably well at Fort Moultrie, where his accommodations were large enough to include his wives and children. He was permitted the freedom to walk about the fort, he had a pallet on which to sleep beside a fire, and he retained at least some of his weapons.

Considered a major celebrity, Osceola was able to receive visitors, including two of the leading painters of his day, George Catlin and Robert John Curtis. Osceola agreed to pose for both, donning his best clothes, including a turban with plumes and a variety of ornaments. He sat in the middle of a room, moving about as he wished, while the two painters worked at opposite sides of him.

Curtis painted one portrait of Osceola, a moving view that captures the pensive humanity of the leader so close to the end of his days. Catlin took longer with his work, finishing several portraits of the Indians held at Fort Moultrie, including two of Osceola. His full-length painting, *The Black Drink*, depicts Osceola facing left, with his eyes slightly uplifted and steadying a rifle by its barrel with its stock resting on the ground. The Creek's facial expression in Catlin's bust-length *Osceola, the Black Drink, a Warrior of Great Distinction*, is more thoughtful, perhaps melancholy, and less inspiring than the full-length painting. The full-length Catlin painting is now in the American Museum of Natural History; his other portrait resides in the Smithsonian American Art Museum. The Charleston Museum houses Curtis' portrait.

Death and Burial

Osceola grew more ill on January 26, a day after Catlin completed his paintings. Dr. Weedon blamed his growing illness on fatigue occasioned by posing for the portraits. Weedon summoned another physician, Benjamin Beard Strobel, of the Medical School College of South Carolina, but Osceola's condition quickly worsened.

During the morning of January 30, Osceola, although unable to talk, managed to put on his best clothes, which his wives brought him. He painted half of his face red, placed his knife under his belt, put his turban with its three plumes on his head, and rested. He then managed to arise and shake hands with family members, Dr. Weedon—who left behind an account of these final actions—and others who were in the room. After being lowered again onto his bed, Osceola withdrew his knife, laid it across his chest, and, armed and wearing the paint of a warrior, awaited death, which came that evening shortly after 6:00 P.M.

Osceola's Missing Rifle

Osceola had many of his most prized personal possessions about him when he died at Fort Moultrie on January 30, 1838. They included a rifle immortalized by George Catlin in his full-length portrait of the hero of the Second Seminole War. Unfortunately, the rifle, along with many other valuable items, disappeared shortly after Osceola's death.

Dr. Frederick Weedon took many of the artifacts with him, among them Osceola's gun, which was soon sent on to a Mr. J. W. Jackson in Albany, New York. Jackson was apparently a friend of Weedon's. The gun, based on Catlin's painting, was a flintlock with a metal butt plate and a metal patch box. It corresponds roughly to an earlier description of a silver-mounted rifle that Osceola possessed and which he may have received from Wiley Thompson when the agent was trying to woo Osceola to accept removal to Indian Territory.

Patricia Riles Wickman, in her book *Osceola's Legacy*, describes an attempt by a Utah dealer in the 1980s to sell a carbine that he claimed to be Osceola's rifle. It turned out not to be the genuine article. Osceola's gun remains undiscovered, perhaps long ago encrusted with rust and discarded. Of course, it may also be standing silently in a corner of some dusty attic awaiting discovery. Should the gun ever come to light, it will take its place among the most valued of artifacts associated with the great Indian leaders who devoted themselves to trying to keep alive their people's culture, even their very existence.

Osceola received a military funeral and was buried near the entrance to Fort Moultrie. Prior to the burial, Dr. Weedon, assisted by Dr. Strobel, removed Osceola's head (without the knowledge or consent of Osceola's family). Weedon took the head to St. Augustine and kept it within preservatives in his drug store, seemingly for scientific purposes. This indefensible indignity shocked many people when it came to light, although that apparently did not deter others, including curiosity seekers, from going to view it. The head was transferred a few years later to Dr. Valentine Mott of the Medical College of the City of New York. The current whereabouts of Osceola's head are unknown, although it may have been consumed in a fire at the Medical College that occurred in the 1860s.

The Aftermath

The Second Seminole War did not immediately end with the death of its most famous combatant. Fighting continued, although the Indians held with Osceola at Fort Moultrie were sent westward near the end of February. General Jesup asked to be relieved of his command, and his wish was granted in April 1838. Brigadier General Zachary Taylor, a future President of the United States, succeeded him as commander of the Florida forces. As the war dragged on, Taylor was followed by several other commanders. Finally, starving and emaciated, and threatened with the execution of several of their leaders who were being held prisoner, many of the resisters surrendered in 1841. Additional holdouts were pursued throughout the following year, with the war officially pronounced over on August 14, 1842.

At the supposed conclusion of the Second Seminole War, some 300 Creek and Seminole Indians remained in Florida. Most withdrew into the Everglades. According to John Mahon, more than 3,800 Indians were shipped westward by the conclusion of 1843. Those remaining in Florida gradually declined in number, dropping to fewer than 100 by the 1850s.[10] By the 1880s, they began to interact again with the descendants of Europe, and their population slowly began to increase—each man, woman, and child still in Florida a living testament to Osceola's determined refusal to give up.

NOTES

1. Patricia Riles Wickman, *Osceola's Legacy*, rev. ed. (Tuscaloosa: University of Alabama Press, 2006) 39.
2. Wickman 6.
3. William and Ellen Hartley, *Osceola: The Unconquered Indian* (New York: Hawthorn Books, 1973) 93–94.
4. John K. Mahon, *History of the Second Seminole War: 1835–1842* (Gainesville: University of Florida Press, 1967) 76.
5. John T. Sprague, *The Origin, Progress, and Conclusion of the Florida War* (1848; Gainesville: University of Florida Press, 1964) 78.
6. John Bemrose, *Reminiscences of the Second Seminole War*, ed. John K. Mahon (Gainesville: University of Florida Press, 1966) 21.
7. Hartley and Hartley 149.
8. Mahon 111.
9. Mahon 111.
10. Mahon 321.

RECOMMENDED READING

Bemrose, John. *Reminiscences of the Second Seminole War*. Ed. John K. Mahon. Gainesville: University of Florida Press, 1966.
Hartley, William, and Ellen Hartley. *Osceola: The Unconquered Indian*. New York: Hawthorn Books, 1973.
Laumer, Frank. *Dade's Last Command*. Gainesville: University Press of Florida, 1995.
Mahon, John K. *History of the Second Seminole War: 1835–1842*. Gainesville: University of Florida Press, 1967.
Sprague, John T. *The Origin, Progress, and Conclusion of the Florida War*. 1848. Gainesville: University of Florida Press, 1964.
Tebbel, John, and Keith Jennison. *The American Indian Wars*. 1960. Edison, NJ: Castle Books, 2003.
Wickman, Patricia Riles. *Osceola's Legacy*. Rev. ed. Tuscaloosa: University of Alabama Press, 2006.

Sitting Bull poses for the camera holding a calumet in a photograph taken in the early 1880s after his surrender. (Library of Congress)

Sitting Bull (Tatanka-Iyotanka) 1831–1890

Sitting Bull was the greatest American Indian leader of his time. His virtues encompassed all of the most desirable characteristics of his Hunkpapa culture. He was enormously brave, demonstrating his courage in single combat, by risking his life to count coup, and in other ways, such as sitting down in full view (and shooting range) of U.S. soldiers and calmly smoking his pipe—what his nephew White Bull called the bravest act he ever saw. Courage was a requisite for a leader, and it helped Sitting Bull earn his position as a war chief.

What set Sitting Bull apart from other leaders was not just his courage or skill in battle against Indian enemies such as the Crows or against U.S. troops, but rather the wide range of his attributes. He was a true spiritual leader who felt very much in touch with Wakantanka and by all accounts sincerely believed that he had received visions and dreams in which the spirit world communicated with him. Closely attuned to the world around him, he also believed himself able to understand the communications of animals and birds.

The most significant of Sitting Bull's visions occurred shortly before the Battle of Little Bighorn. After participating in the Sun Dance, he received a vision of soldiers falling from the sky upside down, which he interpreted to mean a great victory for his people in the upcoming battle. That vision inspired and emboldened the Lakotas, helping to ensure a decisive victory over George Armstrong Custer and his Seventh Cavalry in one of the most famous battles in American history.

THE RISE OF A LAKOTA LEADER

Sitting Bull's Youth

Sitting Bull was a Hunkpapa, a group within the Lakota division of the people often referred to as the Sioux. Neither the location nor the precise date of his birth is known with certainty. Sitting Bull's two most prominent biographers, Stanley Vestal and Robert Utley, conclude that he most likely was born at Many Caches, named for storage pits on the south bank of the Grand River, near present-day Bullhead, South Dakota. They also opt for 1831 as the probable year of his birth, a time when the Lakota Sioux were approaching their peak as the most dominant people of the Great Plains. Vestal, who conducted extensive interviews during the 1920s and 1930s with elderly Lakotas who as young men had known Sitting Bull, suggests that he was born in the late winter of 1831.

Sitting Bull's original name was Jumping Badger. His father carried the name that he later would impart to his son: Tatanka-Iyotanka, or Sitting Bull. The mother's name was Her Holy Door. An older sister, Good Feather, preceded Jumping Badger by six years. Another sister, Brown Shawl Woman, also known as Twin Woman, would follow Jumping Badger. Fool Dog, the son of the elder Sitting Bull and an earlier wife, also was a member of the family. Before long, Jumping Badger inherited a nickname, Hunkesni, which means slow in the sense of being deliberate in action. In later years, this trait would manifest itself in the careful planning and wisdom that, along with his courage and spiritual nature, helped make Sitting Bull deeply respected and honored.

A Respected Warrior

Long before Sitting Bull earned fame fighting the U.S. cavalry, he had earned acclaim among the Lakota as a fearless and highly skilled warrior. He counted his first coup when he was about 14 years of age against the Lakota's traditional enemy, the Crow. His father celebrated his son's achievement with gifts of a lance and shield as well as his own name, which he replaced for himself with Jumping Bull. In subsequent battles against the Crow as well as against other tribal enemies, Sitting Bull continued to win renown. Many of these battles he later commemorated in his series of pictographic autobiographies.

Sitting Bull also became a member of such prestigious akicita societies as the Strong Heart and Kit Fox Societies. These societies were open only to the most successful warriors and supplied the Lakota with *akicitas*, individuals charged with enforcing tribal regulations. He also was instrumental in forming the elite Midnight Strong Heart Society.

As his successes in battle earned him white eagle feathers, Sitting Bull also received red feathers in acknowledgment of the wounds he suffered. Sitting Bull's attributes extended well beyond his skill in combat, as he earned great respect for his hunting prowess, his personal generosity and kindness, his loyalty to family members, and his status as a Wichasha Wakan (a holy man) closely in touch with Wakantanka through dreams and visions.

Early Euro-American Encounters

Sitting Bull had mixed feelings about the white-skinned traders from the East, but he had no natural hatred toward Euro-Americans. On the whole, he simply wanted them to leave his people alone. He and his Hunkpapas, as well as the larger Lakota community, saw other Indian tribes, such as the Crows, as their natural enemies and the source of honor in war. Only when it became obvious that Euro-American incursions into Lakota territory endangered their way of life, as well as their very lives, did Sitting Bull come to view the intruders as enemies.

By the 1850s, Sitting Bull and tribes of the Great Plains in general increasingly understood this growing threat. The U.S. government by then was actively moving on several fronts to make westward expansion easier and safer. The government wanted to establish travel routes and, in the next decade, lay down railroads. To make crossing the country less threatening, treaties such as the Fort Laramie Treaty of 1851 sought to limit tribes to certain areas and to prevent both intertribal warfare and conflict with travelers. At the same time, the government continued to construct military forts throughout Indian land.

During the decade, Sitting Bull and his Hunkpapas continued their battles with the Crow and other Indian enemies. At the same time, they occasionally engaged Euro-Americans when they passed too closely by Hunkpapa territory. Although direct attacks on forts were not common, an assault on Fort Union in northeastern Montana took place on August 11, 1860. Sitting Bull likely participated in this battle, although no definitive record places him there. Approximately 250 Hunkpapas and Lakota Blackfeet attacked the fort. Initially, the soldiers inside withheld fire while the attackers killed cattle and burned wagons, firewood, and haystacks. When they tried to set fire to the fort, soldiers finally started shooting, and the Lakotas withdrew.

At the beginning of the 1860s, two factions began to grow farther apart within the Lakota community. One group, led by Bear's Rib, sought accommodation with the U.S. government, believing that this approach was the only way to achieve peace, prevent great destruction to their people, and retain at least something of their old way of life. Sitting Bull would increasingly become the leader of the other faction, which saw the newcomers as a deadly threat to Lakota traditions and values. Sitting Bull sought peace with the U.S. government, but a peace that would preserve the Lakota culture. He saw the reservation culture as fundamentally incompatible with the Lakota way of life, and he would maintain that position as long as he had the capacity to do so.

Warfare with the United States

Pursuing refugees from an uprising by Dakotas (the eastern division of the Sioux) that occurred in Minnesota during 1862, General Henry Sibley, who had served as Minnesota's first governor after statehood was achieved in 1858, led an army from Minnesota into Dakota Territory. General Alfred Sully led another army up the Missouri River. The army's July 1863 encounters with the Lakota Hunkpapas and Blackfeet, who had been joined by a large contingent of Dakota warriors, at the Battles of Dead Buffalo Lake and Stony Lake in present-day North Dakota signaled the beginning of open warfare between Sitting Bull's Hunkpapa and the U.S. military. Both battles were victories for the army, whose cavalry and artillery forced their adversaries to retreat westward. Sitting Bull apparently participated in these battles.

Almost exactly one year later, on July 28, 1864, Sitting Bull was involved in another battle with General Sully's troops. The site of the conflict was Killdeer Mountain in northwestern North Dakota. One of General Sully's soldiers rode too far in advance of the rest of the troops and was ambushed and killed by three Dakota warriors. The cavalry arrived quickly thereafter and shot the three Dakotas, after which one of the soldiers cut off their heads. General Sully ordered the heads to be hanged on a hill as a very visible warning against further transgressions. Outraged by this incident, the Sioux gathered about 3,000

Inkpaduta

Inkpaduta (circa 1815–circa 1879) may have been the most demonized Indian leader in history. Some of that reputation is his own fault. For example, he is notorious for leading a band of his fellow Dakotas on brutal raids in 1857 against settlers around Spirit Lake in northwestern Iowa and at Springfield in southern Minnesota. Altogether, these raids resulted in 39 deaths, including women and children. Two women taken prisoner during the attacks were also later killed.

The attacks cannot be justified, but the common depiction of Inkpaduta as a bloodthirsty monster who lived to kill whites is far from the truth. As Paul N. Beck points out in the first scholarly biography of Inkpaduta ever written, *Inkpaduta: Dakota Leader* (2008), Inkpaduata lived at peace with Euro-Americans for much of his life and was a close friend to some of them. That he became radicalized toward Euro-Americans is certain, but they clearly contributed to setting him on that path.

In 1854, Henry Lott and associates murdered Sintominiduta, a Dakota chief and relative (some say brother) of Inkpaduta, along with Sintominiduta's mother, two wives, and two of his children. Inkpaduta turned to the authorities, including the military, for justice, but Lott was never arrested. Then in February 1857, Inkpaduta and his band, who were living peacefully at Smithland, Iowa, were forced to leave. Even more significantly, they were required to surrender all of their guns, putting their very survival at risk because they were unable to hunt or protect themselves from enemies such as the Omahas.

Inkpaduta may have participated in the Dakota War of 1862 and was present at the Battle of Little Bighorn in 1876, by which time he was a revered figure for rejecting reservation life. In neither battle, however, did he play a particularly prominent role. Inkpaduta was widely hunted by the military but never captured. He eventually died in Canada, reportedly of pneumonia.

warriors. The large assemblage included Sitting Bull, his uncle Chief Four Horns, and his nephew White Bull, who at age 14 was preparing for his first battle against U.S. government forces.

On July 28, Sully's army of approximately 2,200 soldiers approached the Sioux camp near the base of Killdeer Mountain. The Sioux, including Lakotas, Dakotas under Inkpaduta, and Yanktonais, went out to meet the army, but the army's firepower—rifles and cannons versus the Indians' muskets and bows and arrows—proved too strong for the Indians.

The Sioux steadily fell back toward their village and then continued their retreat, taking what they could with them. Advancing soldiers destroyed most of their provisions and tipis. Perhaps 100 Sioux died in the Battle of Killdeer Mountain, while Sully's forces lost only two men. Inkpaduta survived and led the remaining members of his Dakota group farther east, leaving behind Sitting Bull and the rest of the Sioux.

This event marked Sitting Bull's first major battle with a large government force, and despite the defeat he was not ready to give up. Over the next week, his Hunkpapas were joined by additional Miniconjou, Sans Arc, and Brulé, as well as Cheyenne warriors. From August 7 to August 9, they tried to take advantage of the rugged terrain of the Badlands near Heart River in North Dakota by harassing the army's advance or rear guard and killing livestock. Artillery, however, kept them from closing in and doing much damage. With the attackers' casualties mounting and the Sioux running short of supplies, Sitting Bull wisely urged withdrawal.

The next battle with Euro-Americans would leave Sitting Bull wounded. Near the end of August 1864, Sitting Bull's Hunkpapas spotted a train of approximately 100 wagons commanded by Captain James L. Fisk, who with a force of 500 soldiers was escorting a party of miners. For several days, Sitting Bull observed and waited for an advantageous moment to attack without taking on the entire body of travelers.

On September 2, a wagon broke down, and about a dozen men, most of them soldiers, stopped to make repairs. Sitting Bull led approximately 100 warriors toward the wagon. According to Utley, it was at this time that Sitting Bull was wounded. Because there was more honor in physically touching and struggling with an enemy than in killing him from a distance, Sitting Bull rode up to a mounted soldier and started to struggle with him, trying to throw the soldier to the ground. The soldier pulled his pistol and shot Sitting Bull in the left hip, with the bullet coming out his back. Jumping Bull, Sitting Bull's adopted brother (named by Sitting Bull after his own father), and White Bull reached their wounded war chief and led him to safety. Jumping Bull, who had learned some basic medicine, managed to stop the bleeding and bandaged Sitting Bull.

The remaining group of men who had stopped with the wagon were killed or wounded, and the Hunkpapas withdrew after additional soldiers arrived from the wagon train. The miners and soldiers then created a simple fort by circling their wagons and piling sod against them. This rudimentary fort they named Fort Dilts after Jefferson Dilts, one of the men killed in the recent fight.

It was also during this period that Sitting Bull helped to save a woman named Fanny Kelly, who was captured by an Oglala Sioux war party. Over a period of five months in captivity, Kelly was forced to travel and live with the Oglalas until she was traded to the Hunkpapa Brings Plenty, who made her his wife. She was with the Lakotas during the battle of Killdeer Mountain and the attack on Captain Fisk's wagon train.

Several offers to purchase Kelly's freedom were made by emissaries from her husband, but Brings Plenty resolutely refused all offers. Finally, Sitting Bull, with his friend Crawler, summoned the reluctant trader to his tipi and compelled him at gunpoint to yield the woman. Although Sitting Bull was primarily responsible for securing Kelly's freedom, she declined to acknowledge her debt to him in her memoir, which was published in 1871.

THE POSSIBILITY OF PEACE

Father De Smet's Peace Initiative

Father Peter John De Smet, a Jesuit Roman Catholic priest who had worked closely with a variety of Indian groups since 1838, was convinced that war for the Indians meant extinction. He consequently set out on April 21, 1868, to persuade Sitting Bull to discuss peace with members of the Indian Peace Commission that was established by the U.S. Congress on July 20, 1867.

When Sitting Bull learned that the Black Robe's party was on its way, he sent a delegation of 18 men to accompany and protect the visitor. On June 19, Father De Smet neared the camp, where he was met by Sitting Bull and some 400 warriors dressed in their best and singing in greeting. The most prestigious of the Hunkpapas joined Sitting Bull in this extraordinary reception, including Four Horns and Gall; the latter was a longtime friend of Sitting Bull who eventually would turn against him during their reservation years. Unfurled on the priest's carriage was a large banner, De Smet's "standard of peace"; it depicted the Virgin Mary surrounded by stars on one side of the banner and the name of Jesus printed on the other. The Virgin Mary was a reassuring and popular image among the Hunkpapas, who related to her as someone similar to White Buffalo Woman, who according to Lakota belief had descended from Wakantanka with the gift of the sacred Buffalo Calf Pipe.

On June 20, a large council lodge was constructed of 10 tipis. The crowd was immense, perhaps numbering 5,000, and probably included many people from other Lakota tribes, who gathered to hear what the Black Robe had to say. De Smet spoke with great conviction, urging his listeners to stop fighting and meet with the commissioners at Fort Rice. He then had the Holy Virgin banner set up in the lodge and said that he would leave it as a sign of his commitment to the welfare of the Sioux.

Black Moon, a cousin of Sitting Bull's, gave an answering address, expressing respect for De Smet's message but also citing a range of Euro-American injustices, including establishing forts, slaughtering buffalo, cutting timber, and, of course, killing Indians. Sitting Bull then spoke. He announced that Hunkpapa representatives would return with Father De Smet to Fort Rice near the confluence of the Cannonball and Missouri Rivers in North Dakota to meet with the commissioners and reiterated his desire to be a friend to his current enemies.

After finishing, Sitting Bull shook hands with Father De Smet. As soon as Sitting Bull sat down, though, he jumped back up to say that he had forgotten certain points he wanted to make. He asserted that he would not sell any portion of his land and repeated some of his enduring conditions for peace: abandonment of forts and an end to cutting of timber along the Missouri River. These final comments elicited great applause from his audience.

The council had been an extraordinary event, bringing together two of the greatest spiritual leaders of nineteenth-century America, the revered Wichasha

Wakan, Sitting Bull, and the dedicated Jesuit, Father De Smet. The two men genuinely respected and liked each other, but their respective aspirations for peace—noble but essentially incompatible within that historical moment— were doomed to failure.

After saying Mass early in the morning of June 21, Father De Smet started his return journey to Fort Rice, accompanied by a group of lesser chiefs, including Gall and Bull Owl. Sitting Bull and a group of akicitas rode along as far as Powder River, both to protect and to honor the Black Robe. Sitting Bull then shook hands with De Smet, reaffirmed his comments of the previous day, and returned to his village. He had instructed Gall to accept no presents, listen to the commissioners, and tell them that they must remove the soldiers and stop the steamboats from coming up the rivers. Sitting Bull had promised to accept the decisions made by Gall and the rest of the contingent in council, but he clearly expected any agreement to include his often stated requirements, which he considered non-negotiable.

The Fort Laramie Treaty

Gall told the commissioners (Generals Alfred Terry, William S. Harney, and John B. Sanborn) what his people expected them to do. He then signed the Fort Laramie Treaty, making his mark by, according to the common expression, "touching the pen." On the treaty Gall is noted by another name of his, The Man That Goes in the Middle.

The Fort Laramie Treaty established the Great Sioux Reservation in the Dakota Territory west of the Missouri River. It identified the land north of the North Platte River and east of the Bighorn Mountains (roughly eastern Wyoming) as "unceded Indian territory" open to the Sioux for hunting as long as enough buffalo still roamed there "in such numbers as to justify the chase." The treaty promised that "no white person or persons" would be permitted to enter the area without permission of the Sioux. A provision especially impor- tant to the Oglala chief Red Cloud was included, declaring that the forts along the Bozeman Trail, which stretched from Julesburg, Colorado, to the gold fields in Montana, would be vacated. A provision that later would prove troublesome to the government stipulated that no reservation land could be taken without approval of "three-fourths of all adult male Indians occupying or interested in the same . . . ." The Indians, in exchange, would cease warfare and maintain peace.[1]

The Fort Laramie Treaty did not meet Sitting Bull's requirements, yet Gall signed it on July 2, seemingly doing an about-face after previously stating his position. Most likely, Gall, who was unable to read the treaty, assumed that it included what he had said it was to include and did not understand that the treaty had been completely drafted prior to his statement.

The Fort Laramie Treaty offered Sitting Bull several options: become a res- ervation Indian, try to compromise with the Euro-Americans while retaining as much of the old way of life as possible, or hold fast to Lakota traditions and culture. Sitting Bull chose the third option.

A RETURN TO WAR

Resumption of Hostilities

In February 1869, only a few months after proclamation of the Fort Laramie Treaty, the War Department violated the provision that allowed Indians to hunt in the unceded land. It issued a statement declaring that Indians traveling beyond the reservation were subject to military jurisdiction and would be considered hostile.

With the Bozeman Trail forts dismantled, Sitting Bull concentrated on the upper Missouri River area. A large number of Sitting Bull's pictographs from this period show his increasing military focus on Euroamericans.[2] Just a few months after the signing of the Fort Laramie Treaty, Sitting Bull led a raid against Fort Buford in northwest North Dakota—a fort he had especially resented since its construction in the mid-1860s as an intrusion into Hunkpapa territory. The attack killed 3 men, wounded 3 others, and captured more than 200 cattle. Sitting Bull followed this action with additional harassing raids against Fort Buford as well as raids against Forts Rice, Stevenson, and Totten, the latter in the Devil's Lake region of northeast Dakota Territory.

Another significant attempt to harm Fort Buford took place in September 1870. With a Hunkpapa, Miniconjou, and Cheyenne force numbering 200, Sitting Bull attacked the cattle herd attached to a camp of woodsmen working for Durfee and Peck, the company hired to supply wood to the fort. One of the men, Charles Teck, was driving oxen about 500 yards from the camp and was cut off. Teck made a heroic stand, shooting several of his attackers until he ran out of ammunition. He then used his rifle as a club, but was soon overwhelmed.

Shifts in Strategy

After this attack on the woodcutters, Sitting Bull made a strategic decision to adopt a more defensive posture. In Robert Utley's words, he shifted his military policy from being the lance of his people to being their shield.[3] He would fight the Euro-Americans, but only when they posed an immediate threat to the welfare of the Lakotas.

By this time, the nonreservation Lakota area had shifted westward, pushed by the carving out of reservations toward the east and pulled by the migration of the buffalo to the west. Lakotas now viewed their territory as stretching westward from the Powder River to the Bighorn and north to the Missouri River, then northwest to the Musselshell. However, it was an area not long left to their control.

One of the wisest of the Hunkpapa leaders, Sitting Bull's uncle Four Horns, recognized that resisting the Euro-Americans required more unity than the Lakotas had traditionally exercised. A new type of war pitted them against a highly organized enemy, and the Lakotas must adapt, he believed, if they were to survive. In response, Four Horns devised a plan to unify all of the Sioux still resisting U.S. government expansion under one supreme leader, Sitting Bull, who had been a war chief since about 1857. He was a proven leader, courageous warrior, accomplished hunter, and revered Wichasha Wakan. He was the one man, Four Horns believed, who could lead successfully in this new and necessary position.

Although the precise date of Sitting Bull's elevation to supreme leader is uncertain, it likely took place after the Fort Laramie conference, in 1869, on the middle Rosebud Creek in Montana.[4]

Sitting Bull's Bravest Act

As much as Sitting Bull wanted to be left alone by the Euro-Americans, that was not to be. An especially obtrusive incursion was that of the Northern Pacific Railroad, which was planned to run directly through Lakota hunting grounds to connect St. Paul, Minnesota, with Seattle, Washington. Trains frightened buffalo, seriously undermining the Lakotas' very survival. U.S. government and military officials knew the provocative nature of the railroad—and they recognized that the Lakotas surely would resist it.

In the fall of 1871 when the U.S. cavalry and a party of railroad surveyors appeared along Yellowstone River (which the Lakotas called the Elk River), Sitting Bull paid close attention but did not immediately attack. In the summer of 1872, two additional groups of Northern Pacific engineers returned, accompanied by two sizable military forces: 600 soldiers under Colonel David S. Stanley out of Fort Rice, and 500 soldiers under Major Eugene M. Baker from Fort Ellis near Bozeman, Montana.

In August, warriors from several Lakota tribes had come together at the Powder River in southeastern Montana for a Sun Dance to prepare for a military expedition against their Crow enemies. The large force started moving west to engage the Crows. Then scouts reported soldiers nearby on the north bank of the Yellowstone near the mouth of Arrow Creek. This party consisted of Major Barker's troops plus 20 railroad workers.

While chiefs discussed whether to continue after the Crows or confront the soldiers, a number of young warriors escaped the notice of the akicitas who were trying to prevent any unsanctioned attacks and made the decision for the chiefs. The soldiers and railroad employees took refuge in a dry riverbank while these Lakotas fired from higher ground and raced "daring lines" past the shooting soldiers.

The encounter, known as the Battle of Arrow Creek, did not prove decisive for either party. In the end, the attackers, faced with the U.S. military's usual superior firepower, withdrew. Yet the railroad employees were so badly

Sun Dance

Among all Lakota religious ceremonies, the Sun Dance was the most significant. The Sun Dance, which was held in honor of Wi, the sun god, occurred annually, typically around June, and was designed to foster spiritual and social rebirth for the Lakotas. The buffalo god, Tatanka—god of ceremonies, health, and provision—also figured importantly in the ceremony. After the dance was finished, the tribe would set out on its buffalo hunts.

The central portion of the Sun Dance (preparation of the Sun Dance Lodge and the dancing itself) took four days, with the actual dancing occurring on the third and fourth days. This period was preceded by eight days of reflection, instruction, and preparation. The Sun Dance took place in a dance lodge specially constructed for that purpose. The dancing area consisted of the open, middle portion of the lodge.

The Sun Dance Pole, made from a cottonwood tree, was the most important structural element in the Sun Dance Lodge. The pole was erected in the middle of the inner circle, surrounded by stakes driven into the ground. Male dancers were tied to the stakes, with the Sun Dance Pole reserved for an individual seeking to establish his special holiness and qualifications to be a holy man (a Wichasha Wakan). Two sets of parallel slits would be cut in the dancer's chest, or sometimes in the back, and two wooden skewers inserted under the skin. A rope then was tied to each skewer and connected to the pole or a stake. The dancer would dance until he pulled free, his skin ripping open in the sacrificial act.

The Sun Dance involved many rituals and symbols, including fasting requirements, painting of bodies and clothing in colors that conveyed spiritual meanings, and ritualistic use of a buffalo head and a sacred pipe.

shaken by the encounter that they turned northward to the Musselshell River rather than continue down the Yellowstone, returning as quickly as possible to Fort Ellis.

The battle was most memorable for a display of courage by Sitting Bull unlike anything that either side had ever seen. It resulted from the need for Sitting Bull to reestablish his authority over the young warriors who were inclined to let their impetuosity overrule their better judgment. He set aside his weapons and, picking up his pipe and tobacco pouch, strolled into the area between the two warring forces. With bullets kicking up dust around him, he struck fire with his flint and steel, lighted his pipe, and calmly smoked. Then he invited others to join him. White Bull, another Lakota named Gets the Best of Them, and two Cheyennes reluctantly accepted. After finishing his smoke, Sitting Bull carefully cleaned out his pipe, then returned at a leisurely pace while the other four raced to safety in such a hurry that Gets the Best of Them forgot his arrows, which White Bull retrieved. It was, according to White Bull, the bravest act ever by Sitting Bull.[5]

Custer in the Black Hills and Other Incursions

Rumors of gold in the Black Hills of Dakota Territory, an area within the Great Sioux Reservation, had circulated for some time. In July 1874, Colonel George Armstrong Custer, under the direction of General Philip Sheridan, led an exploratory expedition that included miners and newspaper correspondents. The official reason for the expedition was that Custer was merely searching out a good site for a fort that could support the reservation Indians at the Red Cloud and Spotted Tail agencies in northern Nebraska and also protect the railroad.

The correspondents, who wanted to please their editors with stories that would sell papers, sent out glowing reports of the rich deposits just waiting to be excavated. Custer, always anxious to enhance his fame, proclaimed that the area was replete with "gold among the roots of the grass." Not surprisingly, given these promises of riches in the face of the still-raging economic depression of 1873, prospectors and mining companies rushed to the area.[6]

The Black Hills were of great importance to the Lakotas. Known as the Paha Sapa ("The Hills That Are Black"), the area also was called a "Meat Pack" by Sitting Bull because of all the game that lived there. The Black Hills also offered valleys protected from the wind and a seemingly inexhaustible store of firewood. Lodgepole pine supplied strong, straight poles for tipis. Although Sitting Bull preferred the Plains as his primary home because he could hunt buffalo there, he valued the Black Hills as a ready supply of food and wood when needed. He also sensed a mystical presence in the hills to which many young Lakota men went for their first vision quest and certainly had no intention of turning them over to the U.S. army or miners.

As miners and settlers rushed into the Black Hills, Sitting Bull was primarily occupied with developments farther west. Sitting Bull's old enemy, the Crow, continued to be an irresistible magnet for hostilities. Sitting Bull's men repeatedly harassed the Crow agency in southern Montana. They stepped up their attacks in the summer of 1875, when the agency was moved farther away from Fort Ellis, near Bozeman, Montana, to a site about 14 miles south of the Yellowstone near Stillwater River. Sitting Bull's war parties regularly hit wagon trains hauling supplies for construction of the new agency on the premise that government agents or anyone else assisting the Crows also made themselves enemies of the Lakotas.

Sitting Bull also faced intrusions into his Montana lands by organized groups determined to make their fortune either by prospecting or by trading. In February 1874, a large party of some 150 men heavily armed with rifles and two cannons and calling itself the Wagon Road and Prospecting Expedition set out from Bozeman, Montana, down the Yellowstone in search of gold, crossing the iced-over river below the mouth of the Bighorn. On April 4, Sitting Bull led several hundred warriors against the intruders' camp, but the prospecting expedition, which primarily consisted of experienced frontiersmen, was able to repel the attackers. Three times, Sitting Bull attacked but was compelled to retreat. The Lakota attacks caused few casualties among the would-be prospectors but took a heavy toll on their livestock. Coupled with bad weather, the fighting led the Yellowstone Wagon Road and Prospecting Expedition to abandon its plans and return to Bozeman.

A second Bozeman expedition, led by Fellows D. Pease, moved into Lakota land in the summer of 1875 with the intention of building a trading post near the confluence of the Yellowstone and Bighorn Rivers. Pease and his party proceeded to build several log huts connected by a protective wall of tall wooden posts. The Lakotas whittled away at Pease's settlement, over time killing six members of his party and wounding many more through the winter of 1875–1876. Fort Pease, though, remained an annoying presence to Sitting Bull. It would not be completely abandoned until March 1876. By that time, the original trading plan had long since been discarded, and the site had become a precarious refuge for fewer than 20 wolfers who had to be rescued by a cavalry column out of Fort Ellis.

The Sun Dance of 1875

Continuing to face traditional Indian enemies as well as a variety of newer adversaries, including soldiers, miners, and settlers, Sitting Bull tried again to create a more unified force of native peoples in the summer of 1875. The agent of unification was an especially large Sun Dance that, Sitting Bull hoped, would more closely bind together his Hunkpapas, Spotted Eagle's Sans Arcs, the Oglalas led by Crazy Horse and Black Twin, the Miniconjous of Makes Room and White Bull, and the Northern Cheyennes led by Little Wolf and a revered holy man named Ice.

Sitting Bull was both the primary force behind this remarkable Sun Dance and the principal performer at it. Ice had given him a black war horse, and Sitting Bull rode this mighty horse to the Sun Dance lodge. Streaks of white adorned the horse, and Sitting Bull, wearing only a breechcloth, moccasins, and war bonnet, had painted his own body with yellow clay. Strips of black paint covered his forehead and portions of his face, including his chin. His wrists and ankles were circled by black bands, and a black disk on his chest and a black crescent on his right shoulder representing the sun and moon indicated that he had received visions and been in communication with the spiritual world. All of this created an extraordinarily dramatic spectacle, with the black on Sitting Bull's face symbolizing his past success in battle and the yellow covering his body representing destruction and violence. Those watching the ceremony knew that war was not far away.[7]

Following the Sun Dance, the large village moved to the Tongue River, likely near the state border in southeastern Montana northwest of present-day Sheridan, Wyoming. There in August 1875, Sitting Bull met a contingent of about 100 agency Indians accompanied by former friend Frank Grouard. This party had come to invite Sitting Bull and others resisting accommodation with the government to attend a council at Red Cloud Agency in northwestern

Nebraska in September, the goal of which was to negotiate a sale or long-term lease of the Black Hills.

At a council meeting the following morning, a series of speakers opposed going in to the agency. Crazy Horse, the great Oglala warrior, refused even to talk about the invitation, leaving Little Hawk to speak on his behalf. Sitting Bull, according to Grouard, gave a long speech in which he declared that he was no agency Indian, would never sell the Black Hills, and was prepared for war: "He told me to go out and tell the white men at Red Cloud that he declared open war and would fight them wherever he met them from that time on."[8]

THE PATH TO LITTLE BIGHORN

An Ultimatum

After the failure to secure an agreement to buy or lease the Black Hills, President Ulysses Grant met on November 3 to discuss the issue with a number of prominent government officials, including Secretary of the Interior Zachariah Chandler, Commissioner of Indian Affairs Edward P. Smith, Secretary of War William W. Belknap, and Generals Philip Sheridan and George Crook. Grant came to two major decisions. First, he would retain the prohibition on miners moving into the Black Hills but would not enforce the edict. Second, he authorized the use of force to make the hunting bands yield the unceded land (a clear violation of the 1868 treaty) and settle on the reservation. Implicit within these decisions was the transfer of responsibility for the hostile bands from Indian Affairs to the military, a position that Commanding General of the U.S. Army William Tecumseh Sherman and General Sheridan had been urging.

Grant, either at the same November 3 meeting or later, ordered or at least approved giving the tribes a deadline to enter the reservation, after which they would be considered hostile and be subject to military force to compel their acquiescence. The date chosen was January 31, 1876. On December 6, Commissioner Smith directed the Sioux agents to send runners out to inform the various villages of this directive.

The messengers were sent out during a particularly harsh winter. Thus, obeying the order, even if the tribes had wished to do so, would have been physically impossible. The message reached some bands at least as late as December 22; some villages, in fact, were never informed. To comply would have meant a forced march over hundreds of miles through blizzards and deep snow with women, children, and hungry, weakened horses. In addition, even if Sitting Bull and the other Lakotas had reached the agencies, they would have found little or no food there, as famine caused in part by failure to secure the necessary beef herds had hit most agencies by the middle of the winter. As a consequence, January 31, 1876—the deadline for hostile Indian bands to report to government agencies—passed with Sitting Bull still cherishing his freedom.

From his headquarters in Chicago, General Sheridan commanded the Military Division of the Missouri, which included all of the Plains. He wired General Crook and General Alfred Terry on February 8 that the War Department had ordered military action against hostile Indians. Sheridan envisioned a multipronged action. Crook would move from Fort Fetterman in Wyoming against Crazy Horse, who was believed to be in the vicinity of the headwaters of the Bighorn, Powder, Rosebud, and Tongue Rivers in north-central Wyoming. Terry's forces would converge from the east and west, with one column under Colonel John Gibbon moving eastward from Fort Ellis in Montana, and a second column under Lieutenant Colonel George Armstrong Custer departing Fort Abraham Lincoln in northern Dakota Territory and moving toward the west. These three forces would encircle the recalcitrant Lakotas and Cheyennes and crush them.

The bitter winter weather that would have precluded compliance with the January 31 directive also prevented Terry from moving forward with this plan. His troops were inadequately provisioned for the lengthy march that would be required to reach Sitting Bull and would have to await a spring thaw to permit more supplies to arrive by train on the Northern Pacific Railroad or by steamship.[9]

Gathering of a Great Force

As spring arrived, increasing numbers of hunting bands migrated to join Sitting Bull. Meanwhile, as the U.S. military prepared for what it hoped would be the final victory over Sitting Bull and the Plains Indians, the hunting bands gathered around their greatest leader.

Somewhere between May 21 and 24, while camped on the Rosebud, Sitting Bull felt an unseen force pulling him to a nearby butte. When he reached the top, he prepared through prayer and meditation to receive a message from Wakantanka. Then he fell asleep and dreamed of a dust storm rushing toward a white cloud. The cloud he recognized as a Lakota village near a snow-covered mountain, and behind the storm he saw soldiers. As the storm hit the cloud, lightning streaked through the sky and rain poured down. Yet after the storm had vanished, the cloud remained unscathed and drifted off beyond his sight.

Returning to his village, Sitting Bull recalled the dream for the other chiefs and interpreted it according to the wisdom he had received from Wakantanka. The cloud represented his village, which soldiers would attack. The soldiers would be defeated, however. Accordingly, directions were given to the scouts, also known as wolves, to watch carefully for the soldiers who Sitting Bull was certain would soon come.

The Great Sun Dance and Sitting Bull's Vision

Perhaps a week later, near the end of May, Sitting Bull asked his nephew White Bull, his adopted brother Jumping Bull, and a son of his friend Chief Black Moon to accompany him to the top of a hill. There Sitting Bull, having prepared by loosening the braids of his hair, removing his feathers, and washing off the red paint he often wore on his face, prayed. He asked that Wakantanka provide sufficient food for his people during the coming winter and inspire the Lakota bands to get along well together. In return, Sitting Bull would offer a whole buffalo and dance the Sun Dance. Sitting Bull and his three companions then performed a pipe-smoking ceremony.

Sitting Bull immediately set about fulfilling his promises. In addition to shooting three buffalo and offering the fattest one to Wakantanka, he began organizing a Sun Dance with Black Moon presiding and Sitting Bull himself as the chief dancer. Only Hunkpapas would participate in this dance, but members of the other bands were permitted to observe.

The usual preparatory ceremonies began about June 4. Once they were completed, Sitting Bull was ready to make a special offering of 100 pieces of his flesh. He sat with his back against the sacred Sun Dance pole while Jumping Bull knelt beside him. Starting near one of Sitting Bull's wrists and working his way up to near the shoulder, Jumping Bull 50 times inserted a small awl under the skin, lifted the skin flap, and cut off a piece of flesh with his knife. Then Jumping Bull repeated the process 50 times on Sitting Bull's other arm. The pain must have been excruciating for Sitting Bull, and his arms, covered in blood, began to swell badly.

For the rest of the day and that night, and into the next day, Sitting Bull danced, staring into the sun during daylight hours. Finally, he stopped, appearing to have passed out on his feet. Hunkpapas gently lowered him to the ground and brought him water.

When Sitting Bull regained consciousness, he told Black Moon of the vision he had received, and Black Moon shared it with the rest of the assembly. Sitting Bull had seen large numbers of soldiers, as thick as grasshoppers, descending from the sky into his camp, but they and their horses were falling upside down. The voice that Sitting Bull heard in his vision announced that the soldiers had no ears, meaning that they failed to hear what Sitting Bull had been saying about leaving his people alone. The upside-down image meant that the soldiers would be killed, but the victors were cautioned in the vision not to take any plunder. Some Indians also appeared upside down, indicating that Sitting Bull and his people would also suffer fatalities. However, the battle would be a great victory for Sitting Bull and his warriors.

The vision would soon prove prophetic, but it also helped pave the way for victory. Sitting Bull's vision increased the Indians' confidence regarding the impending battle. Coupled with his remarkable demonstration of self-sacrifice during the Sun Dance, it must have erased any doubts about Sitting Bull's leadership.

Battle of the Rosebud

As Sitting Bull was inspiring his followers with his historic vision, General George Crook was preparing to move north from the Sheridan, Wyoming, area in search of hostiles. By June 15, Crook had received reports that a large village was approximately 45 miles away from his present location. Believing that the expedition would be short, Crook decided to take only four days' worth of rations and leave his pack train behind.[10]

Crook departed early in the morning of June 16 with 100 soldiers, 85 volunteers in support roles, and 262 Shoshone, Crow, and Arikara (Ree) allies. The following morning, Crook reached the main branch of the Rosebud in Montana. By 8:00 A.M. on June 17, Crook had ordered his men to stop. The troopers unsaddled their mounts, and Crook and some of his officers played whist while his men drank coffee.

Suddenly, shooting could be heard beyond the bluffs to the north. Some 750 warriors led by Sitting Bull and Crazy Horse had encountered a party of Crook's scouts. The remaining scouts rushed to engage the attackers. The soldiers quickly organized themselves and entered the fray.

The fighting raged furiously, first between the two sets of Indians, then between Sitting Bull's warriors and Crook's entire force. The Sioux and Cheyennes attacked, withdrew, and then counterattacked when the enemy forces spread apart in pursuit.

Early in the afternoon, Sitting Bull's men withdrew, leaving 9 soldiers dead and at least 23 wounded, and likely even more with slight wounds. Crook's Indian scouts suffered 1 death, with 7 being severely wounded. Sitting Bull's attackers had suffered approximately 20 fatalities.

The battle was a major victory for Sitting Bull's men. The Sioux and Cheyenne forces had attacked when they wished, withdrawn when they wished, kept Crook from advancing toward their village, and driven him away to the south where he was of little immediate threat. Sitting Bull's warriors returned that night to sleep comfortably in their lodges. In contrast, Crook, in an effort to establish the appearance of victory, required his men to lie out on the dark and dangerous battlefield where they had more than met their match. The next day Crook withdrew and headed toward his base camp in Wyoming.

THE BATTLE OF LITTLE BIGHORN

Preparing for Battle

By June 24, Sitting Bull and his large following had moved into the valley of the river they called the Greasy Grass, better known to the rest of the world as the Little Bighorn. With agency Indians arriving steadily, the size of the village swelled by June 25, according to conservative estimates, to more than 1,000 lodges and approximately 7,000 people, close to 2,000 of whom were males capable of active engagement in warfare. The numbers may have been even higher. White Bull, for example, later estimated that there were 2,000 lodges and some 2,500 able-bodied warriors.[11]

Sitting Bull was certain that the soldiers would attack, because his vision was still unfulfilled. In the evening of June 24, a Saturday, Sitting Bull removed most of his clothing, loosened his hair, and painted himself. Wearing a breechcloth and carrying a buffalo robe and his pipe, and accompanied by his nephew One Bull, he walked to a nearby ridge across from the Cheyenne circle of lodges. There, near where Colonel Custer and his Seventh Cavalry would shortly make their last stand, he prayed to Wakantanka. Sitting Bull offered the pipe to the Great Mystery and prayed for protection for his people. As additional offerings, he left behind tobacco tied to sacred cherry wand sticks stuck into the ground.

A few days earlier, on June 21, on the Yellowstone River at the mouth of the Powder, General Alfred Terry had met aboard the supply steamer *Far West* with Colonel John Gibbon and Lieutenant Colonel George Armstrong Custer. The meeting was intended to finalize the military strategy for rousting the Plains Indians. At noon on June 22, both the Gibbon- and Custer-led troops departed camp below the mouth of the Rosebud. Terry accompanied Gibbon. Custer's Seventh Cavalry consisted of 33 officers and 718 enlisted men, but 2 officers and 152 men had been detached between June 10 and 22, most of whom were dispatched to serve at the Powder River depot. That left a fighting force of 31 officers and 566 men, plus about three dozen Arikara and Crow scouts and 15 nonmilitary participants, mainly quartermaster employees. The Seventh Cavalry consisted of 12 companies, each company numbering about 50 soldiers, well below the desired strength, with Custer's regiment overall at about 60 percent of full strength.[12]

Custer's Orders

By Saturday, June 24, Custer was detecting fresh signs of Indians in the direction of Little Bighorn. He planned to let his men rest the following day and attack on June 26, thereby permitting Terry and Gibbon to arrive from the north with reinforcements before engaging in battle.

The following day, June 25, from a ridge called the Crow's Nest, Custer's scouts pointed out signs of a large village in the distance, some 18 miles away. The bad news for Custer was that some of his troopers also reported a confrontation with Indians. Custer concluded that his presence was no longer a surprise and feared that the Sioux would flee before he could mount an attack. Accordingly, he decided to attack at once, even if both his troops and horses were tired.

By noon, Custer had his Seventh Cavalry on the move. Inexplicably, he split his command, embarking on a course of action that continues to perplex historians. He sent Captain Frederick Benteen with Companies D, H, and K southwest with the vague instructions to "move to the left, pitch into anything you come cross, and report to me." Custer later sent additional directions to Benteen telling him to move to a second set of bluffs if he saw no Indians from the first set.[13]

Custer had also detached Captain Thomas McDougall from the Seventh Cavalry's main body, directing him to escort the pack train with Company B. The pack train followed Benteen but stayed well behind him.

Custer then took his remaining forces down a tributary of the Little Bighorn that would later be named Reno Creek, where he further divided his force by sending Major Reno with Companies A, G, and M to attack the village. Custer assured Reno that he would support him.

Despite that promise, Custer did not follow in support across the Little Bighorn but instead stayed to the east of the river and with Companies C, E, F, I, and L turned north. From a ridge looking northwest, Custer received his first clear view of the village. Apparently only then realizing the enormity of the challenge, Custer sent Sergeant Daniel Kanipe to find McDougall and tell him to bring the pack train, which had all of the ammunition except what the soldiers had on their persons or in their saddlebags.

Major Reno's Attack

At approximately 3:00 P.M., Reno attacked. Almost instantly, he realized that his men had no chance to survive a direct assault on the mammoth village. Reno halted the charge short of the village, where he ordered his men to dismount. They formed a skirmish line facing the Hunkpapa circle.

The attack surprised the villagers. Sitting Bull's first thoughts apparently were for his family. He mounted his mother and a sister behind him on a horse and raced to a position away from the fighting. One Bull did the same for his mother. The rest of Sitting Bull's family also made it to safety.

Sitting Bull then hurried to his tipi to get his weapons. He gave his treasured shield as well as his bow and arrows and a war club to his nephew One Bull. The nephew reciprocated by offering his Winchester repeating rifle to his uncle and rode off to join the fight against Reno.

At that point, White Bull arrived at Sitting Bull's tipi. Sitting Bull had no time to prepare properly for battle. He wore no feathers and had no time to change his clothes or paint himself. Instead, he quickly mounted a black horse and rode about shouting encouragement to his warriors. Sitting Bull and White Bull, along with Four Horns, then joined the battle against Reno.

Reno and his men dropped to their stomachs to fire as the Indians attacked. Heavy fire forced the warriors back, but they quickly circled around Reno's left and attacked from the rear. Knowing that he would soon be completely surrounded, Reno ordered his men into a nearby timber. The battle continued there for about 30 minutes when Reno, recognizing that his troops were heavily outnumbered and their ammunition was running out, ordered his men to mount. He led them in a charge out of the timber and, in a race for their lives, about a mile upstream where they crossed back over the river. Some of the troopers were shot from their horses or killed as they floundered in the water. The survivors scrambled up a bluff, later to be named Reno Hill, east of Little Bighorn. There, shortly after 4:00, the badly outnumbered troopers prepared to make their desperate stand. Forty members of Reno's command were already dead. In the confusion, 17 soldiers had not heard the order to charge out of the timber and had been left behind, although many of them later made their harried way to the bluffs.

By about 4:20, Benteen arrived at Reno Hill. An hour later, the pack train joined them, by which time the fighting around Reno Hill had sharply decreased. Major Reno and the rest of the Seventh Cavalry members who had taken refuge on the bluffs still were wondering where Custer was; they were unaware that by the time the pack train arrived, Custer and all of his men were already dead.

Turning Toward Custer

When Reno recrossed the river to take refuge on the east side, Sitting Bull remained behind, leaving the pursuit to the younger men. East of the Little Bighorn, Indians continued to hunt down straggling soldiers. Sitting Bull urged his men to leave the soldiers on the hill alone so they could return to their people and tell of the great victory by the Lakotas and Cheyennes, but the warriors— especially the young men—were not yet ready to cease their attacks.

By this time, Custer and his five companies had begun approaching the village from the north. Turning from Reno, the Indians in overwhelming numbers converged on Custer's troops. Sitting Bull directed his warriors toward the new set of attackers and then returned to his village, riding around the Cheyenne circle of lodges to the western edge of the village, where a large number of women and children had gathered. There Sitting Bull helped stand guard against a possible attack by soldiers.

Custer had divided his remaining companies into two segments. The right wing consisted of Companies C, I, and L, under the command of Captain Myles W. Keogh. The left wing comprised Companies E and F, under the command of Captain George Yates, with Custer accompanying Yates. Custer and Yates entered a large dry gulch named Medicine Tail Coulee, which headed west toward the river and the village. Apparently at this point, villagers discovered Custer's forces, drawing warriors away from Reno and almost surely saving the lives of Reno and his men. Custer did not cross the river; instead, when shots were fired across the water at him, he turned back and moved farther north. Keogh's wing seems to have stayed somewhat behind Custer and Yates to wait for Benteen and the pack train. Custer may have been looking for a way to cross the river, but if so, he never had time to find a suitable place.

Company L, under Lieutenant James Calhoun (Custer's brother-in-law), formed a skirmish line on what later came to be known as Calhoun Hill, with Companies C and I behind in reserve. Company C tried a charge south but was forced to withdraw to Calhoun Hill, and the Lakota warriors, with Chief Gall among them, applied steady pressure to Keogh's troops. Then Crazy Horse made a daring run on horseback between Keogh's men on the hill and those in reserve. Many of the men on the hill broke ranks and fled northward, only to be cut down as they raced on foot or on horseback. The men who stood and fought were quickly overwhelmed.

Last Stand Hill

Custer and Yates with Companies E and F had proceeded to Cemetery Ridge in the present Custer National Cemetery. They then moved down into a basin below today's Last Stand Hill (also known as Custer Hill), and Company E dismounted. At that point, Indian warriors known as "suicide boys" because of their dangerous role rushed in to stampede horses.

Next, the troopers moved up Last Stand Hill, where they were joined by perhaps two dozen survivors of Keogh's command. About 45 soldiers charged toward the river, attempting to reach safety through some 1,500 warriors. They were either struck down at once or took temporary refuge in Deep Ravine, which runs to the south and west of the current Visitor Center of the Little Bighorn Battlefield National Monument, before being killed.

The remainder of Custer's men, numbering about 41, along with Custer himself, shot their horses and used them as breastworks. Soon they were all dead, including Lieutenant Colonel Custer and his brothers, Captain Tom Custer and younger brother Boston Custer, who had been brought along as forage master to secure food for the horses. The dead also included Custer's 19-year-old nephew, Armstrong Reed, who had come along for the adventure; the colonel's brother-in-law, Lieutenant Calhoun; and Mark Kellogg, a reporter for the *Bismarck Tribune*, the notes for his next newspaper article still in his pockets. According to Indian accounts, some soldiers, realizing their desperate situation, shot themselves rather than be captured. The last man fell on Last Stand Hill at approximately 4:45, about an hour after the first shots had been fired across the river at Custer's men.

Altogether, 210 men from the Custer–Yates–Keogh companies lay dead. The total Seventh Cavalry fatalities would number 263 by the end of the battle the following day.

While Custer and his men were fighting for their lives, Reno remained on his hill four miles away with no inkling of his leader's fate, although from that hill his men could hear gunshots. Captain Thomas Weir took Company D downstream toward the firing, and Captain Benteen followed with Companies H, K, and M. By now it was about 5:00, too late to help Custer. However, Weir got no farther than about one and one-half miles, to the high point later named Weir Point. From there, the troopers could see Indians riding around what they later learned was the Custer battlefield, sometimes shooting toward the ground. No one imagined that Custer's troops had been wiped out, and that the sporadic firing was probably to finish off some wounded soldiers. About 6:00, Indians started returning to the site of the earlier battle, and Weir and Benteen had to retreat to the hilltop where Reno had established his defense.

That night, Sitting Bull joined the warriors firing at the Reno and Benteen forces from a ridge northeast of the soldiers' position before returning to his village.

Withdrawal

The following morning, Monday, June 26, the battle continued but without Sitting Bull, who remained in the village until about noon, when he returned to the battle site. As he had the previous day, he urged warriors to leave the surviving soldiers alone. His request likely would not have prevailed had Terry and Gibbon's column not been sighted coming from the north. By dusk, the village had moved, leaving just two tipis behind as burial lodges for warriors killed in the battle. Altogether, between 30 and 100 Indians died in the Battle of Little Bighorn.

How much credit for the triumph over the Seventh Cavalry at Little Bighorn belongs to Sitting Bull cannot be measured precisely. Sitting Bull did not function as a commanding general, directing troops during the conflict. Once Reno had launched his first bullets at the village, the cavalry's defeat was all but certain given Custer's division of his troops and the numerical advantage enjoyed by the Indians.

Nonetheless, Sitting Bull had given his people the vision of a triumph over the soldiers and solidified their confidence and determination to remain free. His own refusal to surrender to the U.S. government served as a model of resistance. Certainly, as the greatest and most revered of the Plains Indians, he was the magnet that attracted the thousands of individuals who had gathered in the village by June 25 in the valley of the Little Bighorn. Without Sitting Bull, there would have been no victory. Sitting Bull unmistakably was the indispensable person, the pivotal maker of history during those June days.

AFTERMATH OF LITTLE BIGHORN

Slim Buttes

Sitting Bull was too wise not to realize the consequences of his victory. He knew that the soldiers would come again and try to kill him or take him prisoner. He also knew that such a large force of Indians as had gathered at Little Bighorn could not stay together and hope to find sufficient food for both people and horses.

The village moved eastward seeking buffalo, with part of the group moving up the Tongue River, which flows into the Yellowstone east of Little Bighorn, and the rest searching downstream. By August 1, the village had reassembled on Powder River. A few days later, the village split, with bands going in different directions after game. Sitting Bull led his Hunkpapas and some Miniconjous and Sans Arcs along the Little Missouri to Killdeer Mountain in northern Dakota Territory, where he had fought General Sully in 1864.

By early September, a contingent of Hunkpapas, Oglalas, Miniconjous, and Sans Arcs had congregated near Slim Buttes in Dakota Territory. Sitting Bull was there, in mourning for a son who had died after being kicked in the head, by either a horse or a mule.

Captain Anson Mills, under General Crook (who after receiving reinforcements had taken the field again in August) and with Frank Grouard scouting, discovered a small village of Miniconjous and attacked them. The inhabitants fled to the bluffs overlooking the village and fired down on the soldiers, who took up positions within the village. General Crook soon appeared with his main force, and Sitting Bull arrived to join the fighting as well, shooting from the bluffs and encouraging his warriors. Among the slain were women and children. Soldiers apparently enraged over the deaths of Custer and his men scalped some of the dead. The army moved out the next day. Crook took his troops to Deadwood, before ending his campaign in October at Camp Robinson in Nebraska. From Slim Buttes, Sitting Bull, with the Miniconjous and Sans Arcs who had been traveling with his Hunkpapa followers, turned toward the Yellowstone River.

Nelson Miles in Pursuit

Sitting Bull later led his entourage to Cedar Creek north of the Yellowstone, where they engaged in a buffalo hunt. The peaceful interlude was not to last long, however, as the Fifth Infantry under Colonel Nelson A. Miles was rapidly approaching.

Sitting Bull used Long Feather and Bear's Face to set up a meeting with Miles, which occurred on October 20. The negotiating party headed by Sitting Bull included White Bull and Jumping Bull.

Miles wore a fur cap and an overcoat trimmed with bear fur on the cuffs and at the collar, earning him the name "Bear Coat." The discussion broke up but resumed the next day, though to no avail. At about noon, Sitting Bull and his party rose in frustration and left the meeting. Both he and Miles returned to their men and prepared for battle.

The Battle of Cedar Creek was not long in coming. About one o'clock, Miles ordered his men forward. The affair proved to be far different from the Battle of the Little Bighorn, although many of the soldiers had at least brief thoughts of ending up the same way as Custer's men. The engagement consisted largely of some skirmishing and Sitting Bull's men steadily pulling back with the soldiers in pursuit. Casualties were light, with one Lakota killed and two soldiers wounded.[14]

Sitting Bull moved toward the Yellowstone and then, with 30 lodges, turned northward. By the end of October, Sitting Bull and his band were at Big Dry River, 25 miles south of Fort Peck, which had been constructed across the Missouri near where the Big Dry emptied into it. Bear Coat Miles, by now given sole responsibility for catching Sitting Bull, led his troops north from Tongue River in early November and reached Fort Peck by the middle of the month. Sitting Bull, now having gathered approximately 100 Hunkpapa lodges, had his scouts closely monitor Miles's location. As the soldiers followed the Big Dry toward the Missouri, Sitting Bull led his people eastward to the Red Water, also a tributary of the Missouri.

Because Sitting Bull was unaware that his friend Johnny Bruguier was gathering intelligence for the U.S. military, Bruguier was permitted to move freely about the Hunkpapa camp. On December 3, Bruguier left the camp. Three days later, he met Lieutenant Frank D. Baldwin, who commanded three of Miles's companies. Bruguier told Baldwin where Sitting Bull was located, near the mouth of the Milk River, and formally joined the army as a scout.

Baldwin led his men toward Sitting Bull's camp on December 7. With the troops advancing, the Hunkpapas were able to cross the ice-covered Missouri to the south bank and take up positions on high ground above the river, from which they fired down on Baldwin's men. A ferocious storm hit that night, and the soldiers, bitterly cold, marched back to Fort Peck.

Baldwin, his men riding in wagons drawn by mule teams, caught up with Sitting Bull again on December 18 at Ash Creek, southeast of Big Dry River. Most of the Hunkpapa warriors were out hunting, but those still in the camp (which numbered about 120 tipis) made a stand against the advancing soldiers while women and children took to the hills to escape. Several shots from a howitzer, however, sent the men retreating. There was no loss of life, but Sitting Bull lost his village and almost everything in it, including meat, blankets, several hundred buffalo robes, the tipis themselves, and a large number of horses and mules.

CANADIAN REFUGE

Leaving His Native Land

Sitting Bull had been considering crossing into Canada as a fall-back position if staying in the Plains became untenable, and in February 1877 he announced his intention to do just that. The pain of leaving his native land and moving across the border was eased somewhat by the Lakotas' historical association with the British and Canadians. They had been allies of the British during the French and Indian War, which culminated with the Treaty of Paris in 1763 and the awarding of New France (i.e., France's Canadian possessions) to Great Britain and Spain. That loyalty had persisted through the American Revolutionary War and the War of 1812. Sitting Bull still possessed the medals that his grandfather had received from King George III. In addition, some of Sitting Bull's closest associates, including his cousin Black Moon, already had made that journey north. Others who would precede him into Canada included his uncle Four Horns, who arrived in March.

Sitting Bull and his by now small village of about 15 tipis crossed the Missouri River from Fort Peck, where they barely escaped with their lives from a flash flood caused by melting ice. At a council of chiefs 60 miles northwest of Fort Peck, Sitting Bull announced his intention of continuing to Canada and watching from there to see what happened to those who turned themselves in to the agencies. He was determined not to surrender his weapons and horses;

if that was forced upon others, he vowed to remain north of the border. In early May 1877, Sitting Bull, whose assemblage had grown to about 135 lodges (totaling some 1,000 people), crossed the *chanku wakan*, the sacred road (also known as the Medicine Line or the Big Road) into Canada.

Major Walsh of the Mounted Police

Waiting to meet Sitting Bull were the Northwest Mounted Police, who had been formed just three years earlier. Especially anticipating Sitting Bull's arrival was the courageous, highly skilled, and thoroughly honorable Major James M. Walsh, commander of Fort Walsh. Inspector Walsh, known as "White Forehead" to Canadian Indians, decided to pay the new arrivals a visit. With scout Louis Lavalie translating, Walsh explained that the new arrivals were on British soil and must obey British laws.

Walsh added that he intended to enforce the law in regard to everyone and that each person living in Canada was entitled to justice. If Sitting Bull and his people obeyed the law, the police would protect them. And, he assured Sitting Bull, there was no danger from U.S. soldiers, who were not permitted to cross the line into Canada. For the first time in many years, Sitting Bull would not have to worry about a surprise attack. At the same time, his people would not be permitted to cross the border to the United States to fight or steal and then return.

And live in peace Sitting Bull generally did during his stay in Canada, albeit not always easily. Walsh proved a fair and sympathetic official who believed that the Lakotas had been treated badly by the U.S. government. He would be the first white man who truly functioned as an advocate for Sitting Bull.

Unfortunately, Walsh was himself limited by the position of his government toward Sitting Bull. The Canadian government would not force Sitting Bull to leave, but it very much hoped that he would voluntarily accede to the U.S. demand to return and live on a reservation. To facilitate that decision, Canadian officials tried to persuade the U.S. government to drop its demand for unconditional surrender and permit Sitting Bull and his people to retain their horses and guns. The United States alternated between desiring Sitting Bull's return and hoping that Canada would declare Sitting Bull's people Canadian Indians and, therefore, assume permanent responsibility for them. The presence of Sitting Bull on Canadian soil proved a continuing irritant to diplomacy between the two countries.

The Threat of Starvation

By 1880, with the buffalo disappearing and hunger growing, Sitting Bull increasingly faced great pressure to return to the United States and surrender. He could readily see the suffering of his people, but he also knew what surrender would mean—if not death for himself, then at least the end of the Lakota way of life and, to a great extent, the end of the Lakotas themselves.

Complicating matters for Sitting Bull was the loss of his friend Walsh. Because he was perceived as too sympathetic to the Lakotas, Walsh was transferred to Fort Qu'Appelle, 140 miles northeast; he had earlier shifted from Fort Walsh to Wood Mountain Post to be closer to Sitting Bull. His sympathetic ear was replaced at Wood Mountain by Inspector Lief N. F. Crozier. Both Crozier and Lieutenant Colonel Acheson G. Irvine, who was installed as commissioner of the Northwest Mounted Police in the fall, began to pressure Sitting Bull to return to the United States.

By late 1880, Sitting Bull was vacillating—first agreeing to return, then changing his mind. January 1881 found Sitting Bull's people with so little to eat that they bartered almost all of their remaining 150 buffalo robes to traders at Wood Mountain for food. Commissioner Irvine stressed that they would receive neither a reservation nor food in Canada. Under duress, more of Sitting Bull's people gave in and headed south.

The Surrender

On July 12, 1881, Sitting Bull began his own reluctant journey to surrender. Of the many prominent chiefs who once had ridden with Sitting Bull, by the summer of 1881 only Four Horns, ever faithful to his nephew, remained by his side. Sitting Bull's followers now numbered fewer than 200. No one, however, was certain that he would not change his mind, so a train of six wagons laden with supplies set out from Fort Buford to meet him and his companions. On July 16, the two parties met, and the Lakotas hungrily devoured the food. In addition, Captain Walter Clifford, in a small party of seven, rode out to meet Sitting Bull and reassured the chief that his daughter, Many Horses, who had earlier returned to the United States, was fine. Clifford commented regarding Sitting Bull, with unusual perception and sympathy, that "nothing but nakedness and starvation has driven this man to submission, and that not on his own account but for the sake of his children, of whom he is very fond."[15]

As the travelers made their way south, they passed the site of an old buffalo hunt. Stretching far into the distance lay buffalo bones, skulls, and partly mummified legs. Sitting Bull surely understood the significance of the scene—how quickly the connecting thread between past, present, and future had been broken. He could well have seen himself and his way of life there among the grass and flowers growing up around the bones. On July 19, 1881, Sitting Bull and the others in his party entered the parade grounds at Fort Buford. Sitting Bull dismounted and shook hands with Major David Brotherton, the Fort Buford commander, who agreed to postpone the formal surrender until the next day.

On July 20, 1881, at 11:00 A.M., the man who had gathered together a mighty army and handed the U.S. military an overwhelming defeat at Little Bighorn surrendered. Sitting Bull, his son Crow Foot beside him, sat next to Major Brotherton in the major's office. Sitting Bull laid his fine Winchester rifle on the office floor between his feet. When it came time for Sitting Bull to speak, he sat quietly for several minutes, then motioned for Crow Foot to hand the rifle to Brotherton. "I wish it to be remembered," Sitting Bull said, at least according to a *St. Paul Pioneer Press* reporter, "that I was the last man of my tribe to surrender my rifle." Brotherton later donated the rifle to the Smithsonian Institution.[16]

At the time, Sitting Bull appeared unable to face what the future held for him. He told Brotherton that he wished to be able to live where he chose, to hunt as he had, and to be able to visit Major Walsh and Captain Alexander Macdonell (the latter being another Mountie whom he had come to respect). None of this, of course, would be permitted. If he were psychologically in a temporary state of denial, the real world soon came rushing in on him. Not long after the surrender, Sitting Bull composed a brief, sad song:

> A warrior
> I have been
> Now
> It is all over
> A hard time
> I have[17]

RESERVATION LIFE

Standing Rock Reservation

Sitting Bull would spend most of the rest of his life on reservations, from 1883 until his death in 1890 on Standing Rock Reservation, which bridges northern South Dakota and southern North Dakota. His most notable period away from the reservation was the summer of 1885, when he toured with Buffalo Bill Cody's Wild West Show, starring with Cody and Annie Oakley in performances in Canada and the eastern United States.

Life at Standing Rock Reservation was vastly different from the way Sitting Bull had lived most of his life. No longer could he travel where he pleased, hunt the buffalo, or even exercise leadership as he had done on the Plains and in Canada. The agent at Standing Rock, Major James McLaughlin, was determined to carry out his government's national policy of bringing Christianity and "white civilization" to the Indian.

McLaughlin quickly labeled Sitting Bull an obstructionist—a "nonprogressive"—although the Hunkpapa chief tried hard to accommodate the agent while retaining as much of the Lakota way of life as possible. It was certainly a difficult balancing act. Sitting Bull settled into his final home in the spring of 1884 on the north bank of Grand River, not far from where he had been born in what must have seemed increasingly like another world. Sitting Bull worked effectively at farming, planting oats, corn, and potatoes, and raising horses, cattle, and chickens.

Despite these accommodations with McLaughlin, Sitting Bull continued to maintain the respect of most members of his Hunkpapa community. He spoke his mind to anyone he believed needed to know the truth as he saw it, including McLaughlin and prominent officials who visited Standing Rock.

Among the tools that McLaughlin and other agents used to impose their will on Indians and coerce them into desired patterns of behavior were the Indian police and Indian courts, as well as schools and religion. Sitting Bull had made extensive use of akicitas to keep his warriors in line, and many young males were more than willing to take on a similar role for the agent. Offenses that could lead to arrest and punishment included traditional religious practices such as the Sun Dance. Sitting Bull's death would later come at the hands of reservation police.

McLaughlin, playing off prominent Hunkpapa figures against one another, did his best to minimize Sitting Bull's influence and elevate the "progressives"—that is, individuals who responded positively to his directions. Gall, increasingly at odds with Sitting Bull and jealous of the respect accorded him, proved especially amenable to McLaughlin's wishes, because in serving the agent he also improved his own position at the reservation. McLaughlin and Gall both denigrated Sitting Bull's role at Little Bighorn, with McLaughlin labeling him a coward in his memoirs, *My Friend the Indian*.

Sitting Bull continued trying to maintain something of the old way of life, which included retaining as much land as possible for his people. Consequently, he generally opposed the U.S. government policy of encouraging allotment in severalty—that is, separate and individual ownership designed to convert Indians into imitation white farmers.

Life became increasingly difficult for Sitting Bull and his people. Crops on the reservation were poor in 1889, and a drought the next year reduced the harvest even more. In 1888, blackleg afflicted the Indians' cattle. It was followed by a reduction in beef rations in 1889 resulting from a budget cut mandated by Congress. Epidemics of measles, whooping cough, and influenza took many lives in 1889 and 1890, and an unusually harsh winter in 1889–1890 exacerbated the challenging conditions.

The Ghost Dance

The Lakotas desperately needed a source of hope, and that assistance arrived in the form of the Ghost Dance. Based on visions of a Paiute named Wovoka (also known as Jack Wilson) during the 1880s, the Ghost Dance spread to the Lakota reservation at Pine Ridge in the spring of 1890. The dance promised regeneration of the native peoples and the land, with the return of buffalo and other game. The conquerors were to be covered over by the new earth, returning the world to what it had been before the arrival of Euro-Americans.

How much of this vision Sitting Bull truly believed is impossible to say. He supported the Ghost Dance at his Grand River settlement on Standing Rock Reservation, where dances under his sponsorship were conducted enthusiastically beginning in the fall of 1890, although he himself never danced. If he did not believe the new vision entirely, he may have recognized that at least it gave his people hope—and so long as there was hope, they might yet find a way to achieve an acceptable balance of past and present.

The Final Struggle

Sitting Bull's refusal to acquiesce completely to James McLaughlin's plans for the Lakotas laid the groundwork for his arrest and death. The Ghost Dance was a precipitating factor, in that McLaughlin believed it was delaying the Lakotas' acceptance of the white man's world. He blamed Sitting Bull for encouraging the dance, just as he tended to blame the Hunkpapa chief for all opposition to his authority. McLaughlin recommended that the man he saw as the primary troublemaker and obstructionist be arrested and removed to a place where he could not interfere with McLaughlin and the U.S. government's plans for the Lakotas.[18]

McLaughlin planned to arrest Sitting Bull on December 20, 1890, but moved up the date when he heard that Sitting Bull was considering leaving Grand River for Pine Ridge Agency to meet with the Ghost Dance leaders. On Saturday, December 13, One Elk learned from his policeman brother, Iron Thunder, of the impending arrest and informed his close friend Jumping Bull, Sitting Bull's adopted brother, of the plan. Jumping Bull returned to Sitting Bull's cabin and helped to establish a guard throughout the night. In charge of the bodyguards was Catch the Bear, a bitter enemy of Bull Head, the tribal policeman charged with securing the arrest. Throughout the night, Sitting Bull and his guards reminisced about the old days, including the buffalo hunts. In the morning, on Sunday, December 14, Sitting Bull told his guards to leave and spent the day quietly in camp while others danced the Ghost Dance.

That night, Sitting Bull slept in his cabin without bodyguards. Also in the cabin were one of his wives, Seen by the Nation; his son Crow Foot, now 14 years old; one of his small children; One Bull's wife, Red Whirlwind; and two old men who were guests. Other members of his family, including another wife, Four Robes, slept in a nearby cabin of Sitting Bull's.

Sitting Bull awoke to pounding on the door, the rush of feet across his floor, and a flickering match that was quickly extinguished before another match successfully lit a candle. Sergeant Shave Head informed Sitting Bull of the arrest. The two old men were permitted to leave, and Seen by the Nation rushed to the other cabin to retrieve Sitting Bull's clothes. Sitting Bull resisted the hands that tried hurriedly to help him dress, and as he was shoved to the door braced himself against the doorframe.

As Sitting Bull emerged through the door, Bull Head and Shave Head were beside him, Sergeant Red Tomahawk at his back. They did not get far before Sitting Bull's Hunkpapa supporters surrounded the policemen. Catch the Bear confronted Bull Head and urged his fellow Hunkpapas to protect Sitting Bull. Jumping Bull, trying to prevent violence, urged his brother not to resist. Young

Wounded Knee

With Sitting Bull dead, Big Foot became the Lakota chief whom the military most wanted to apprehend. On December 28, 1890, at Porcupine Creek in southwestern South Dakota, Big Foot, who was seriously ill with pneumonia, saw soldiers nearby. Major Samuel Whitside informed Big Foot that he had orders to escort the Miniconjou chief and his people to a military camp at Wounded Knee Creek, a few miles closer to the Nebraska line. When they arrived at Wounded Knee, a count showed 120 men and 230 women and children. During the night, Colonel James Forsyth arrived with additional troops. As Big Foot slept fitfully, struggling to breathe, four Hotchkiss guns, each capable of firing nearly 50 two-pound shells per minute, were trained on the sleeping Indians.

The next morning, confiscation of weapons began. Forsyth sent troopers into the tents to search for weapons. Then the Indians were ordered to remove the blankets they were wearing in case they were concealing weapons underneath. The soldiers were unaware that Big Foot and his band were wearing Ghost Shirts, which they believed would protect them from the soldiers' bullets. When Black Coyote raised his rifle over his head and declared that he would not turn over his gun, soldiers grabbed him and spun him around. Somehow a gun went off.

That single shot instantly precipitated massive firing and chaos. The Hotchkiss guns rained death down on the Miniconjous. When the fighting was over, Big Foot and more than 150 Indians lay dead or mortally wounded, many of them women and children. Some estimates put the death figure as high as 300. Twenty-five soldiers were dead and 39 wounded, many from friendly fire as they grappled in close combat with the Indians. Sioux resistance, for all practical purposes, was over.

Crow Foot, according to some accounts, then upbraided his father for not showing his accustomed courage, although Vestal claimed that none of the policemen whom he interviewed heard any such statement from the boy.[19] The effort to spirit Sitting Bull away was delayed while policemen brought up his horse, which Sitting Bull had ridden in Buffalo Bill's Wild West Show and which the showman had given him as a gift.

Sitting Bull may have proclaimed his decision not to leave with the policemen. Most certainly, many angry supporters were calling out that they would not let him be taken. Suddenly Catch the Bear raised his Winchester rifle and fired, hitting Bull Head. As the wounded policeman fell, he aimed and fired, hitting Sitting Bull in the chest. Red Tomahawk at the same moment fired into Sitting Bull's head. Although Red Tomahawk is usually credited with killing the Hunkpapa leader, either shot, according to the army surgeon who examined Sitting Bull, would have been fatal.

The body of Sitting Bull was loaded onto a wagon underneath the dead tribal policemen and transported to Fort Yates. Sitting Bull was laid to rest among the soldiers who had once been his enemies. The placement might have seemed ironic to some, but placing one warrior among others probably would have appealed to Sitting Bull much more than being buried in the Catholic cemetery where the dead policemen were interred. When Fort Yates was dismantled in 1903, the bodies of the soldiers were moved, leaving Sitting Bull to lie alone.

Clarence Gray Eagle, son of Gray Eagle, Sitting Bull's brother-in-law who had joined the policemen to help arrest Sitting Bull, worked for years to have his remains moved from the military cemetery to a more appropriate site. As a child, Clarence Gray Eagle had watched Sitting Bull die and perhaps felt, if not guilt over his father's role, at least a sense of duty to honor the great leader with a more fitting burial location.

After Clarence Gray Eagle's efforts repeatedly failed, he and several other men descended on the grave during a night in April 1953 and removed Sitting Bull's remains. They reburied him on a high point overlooking the Missouri River near the town of Mobridge, South Dakota. For the new burial site, near where Sitting Bull had been born, the sculptor Korczak Ziolkowski created a 12-foot-tall monument to the Hunkpapa leader, honoring the stature and accomplishments of the man who altered history even if, finally, he could not completely stem its tide.

NOTES

Portions of this chapter were adapted from *Sitting Bull: A Biography*, by Edward J. Rielly. Westport, CT: Greenwood Press. Copyright © 2007 by Edward J. Rielly. Used by permission of ABC-CLIO, LLC.

1. Charles J. Kappler, ed., *Indian Affairs: Laws and Treaties*, 7 vols. (1904–41; Washington, DC: U.S. Government Printing Office, 1975–79) 2: 998–1007.

2. *The Kimball Pictographic Record*, in *Three Pictographic Autobiographies of Sitting Bull*, ed. M. W. Stirling (Washington, DC: Smithsonian Institution, 1938) illustrations 11–12, 14–22, 25–26.

3. Robert M. Utley, *The Lance and the Shield: The Life and Times of Sitting Bull* (1993; New York: Ballantine Books, 1994) 91.

4. Utley 87.

5. Stanley Vestal, *Warpath: The True Story of the Fighting Sioux Told in a Biography of Chief White Bull* (1934; Lincoln: University of Nebraska Press, 1984) 131–44.

6. *Private Theodore Ewert's Diary of the Black Hills Expedition of 1874*, ed. John M. Carroll (Piscataway, NJ: Consultant Resources Incorporated, 1976) 57–58; Stanley Vestal, *Sitting Bull: Champion of the Sioux*, 2nd ed. (1957; Norman: University of Oklahoma Press, 1989) 132–33; Utley 115–16; Charles M. Robinson III, *The Plains Wars 1757–1900* (Osceola, WI: Osprey Publishing, 2003) 58; Jeffrey Ostler, *The Plains Sioux and U.S. Colonialism from Lewis and Clark to Wounded Knee* (New York: Cambridge University Press, 2004) 59–61; Donald Dean Jackson, *Custer's*

Gold: The United States Cavalry Expedition of 1874 (1966; Lincoln: University of Nebraska Press, 1972); Ernest Grafe and Paul Horsted, *Exploring with Custer: The 1874 Black Hills Expedition*, 3rd ed. (Custer, SD: Golden Valley Press, 2005).

7. Utley 122–23, for details of the Sun Dance; and James R. Walker, *Lakota Belief and Ritual*, ed. Raymond J. DeMallie and Elaine A. Jahner (1980; Lincoln: University of Nebraska Press, 1991) 274–80 for the symbolism.

8. Joe DeBarthe, *Life and Adventures of Frank Grouard*, ed. Edgar I. Stewart (Norman: University of Oklahoma Press, 1958) 85–86.

9. John S. Gray, *Centennial Campaign: The Sioux War of 1876* (Ft. Collins, CO: Old Army Press, 1976) 31–44.

10. See Gray 110–24 for the detailed analysis of the Battle of the Rosebud on which this description is based.

11. Utley 142; Vestal, *Sitting Bull* 154; Gregory F. Michno, *Lakota Noon: The Indian Narrative of Custer's Defeat* (1997; Missoula, MT: Mountain Press Publishing Company, 2004) 3–20.

12. Except where specifically noted, this discussion of the Battle of the Little Bighorn is synthesized from many sources, most prominently Gray; Vestal, *Sitting Bull*; Utley; Michno; E. A. Brininstool, *Troopers with Custer: Historic Incidents of the Battle of the Little Bighorn* (1952; Lincoln: University of Nebraska Press, 1989); Jerome A. Greene, ed. *Lakota and Cheyenne: Indian Views of the Great Sioux War, 1876–1877* (Norman: University of Oklahoma Press, 1994); David Humphreys Miller, *Custer's Fall: The Native American Side of the Story* (1957; New York: Meridian, 1992); and a publication available at the National Monument: Mark L. Gardner, *Little Bighorn Battlefield National Monument* (Tucson: Western National Parks Association, 2005).

13. "Capt. Benteen's Own Story of the Custer Fight," in Brininstool 75–77.

14. Jerome A. Greene, *Yellowstone Command: Colonel Nelson A. Miles and the Great Sioux War, 1876–77* (1991; Norman: University of Oklahoma Press, 2006) 100–05; Robert Wooster, *Nelson A. Miles and the Twilight of the Frontier Army* (1995; Lincoln: University of Nebraska Press, 1996) 84–85.

15. Utley 230.

16. Vestal, *Sitting Bull* 233; John C. Ewers, "When Sitting Bull Surrendered His Winchester," in *Indian Life on the Upper Missouri* (Norman: University of Oklahoma Press, 1968) 175–81.

17. Utley 233; Frances Densmore, *Teton Sioux Music*, Smithsonian Institution, Bureau of American Ethnology, Bulletin 61 (Washington, DC: Government Printing Office, 1918) 459.

18. Much of this account is indebted to Utley.

19. Vestal, *Sitting Bull* 298.

RECOMMENDED READING

Buffalo Bill Historical Center. <http://www.bbhc.org/home/index/cfm> (information about the Plains Indians, William F. Cody, and other aspects of Western life).

Gray, John S. *Centennial Campaign: The Sioux War of 1876*. Ft. Collins, CO: Old Army Press, 1976.

Last Stand at Little Big Horn. Dir. Paul Stekler. *American Experience*. WGBH Educational Foundation and Thirteen/WNET, 1992.

MacEwan, Grant. *Sitting Bull: The Years in Canada*. Edmonton: Hurtig Publishers, 1973.

Philbrick, Nathaniel. *The Last Stand: Custer, Sitting Bull, and the Battle of the Little Bighorn*. New York: Viking, 2010.

Rielly, Edward J. *Sitting Bull: A Biography*. Westport, CT: Greenwood Press, 2007.

Sitting Bull. *Three Pictographic Autobiographies of Sitting Bull*, ed. M. W. Stirling. Washington, DC: Smithsonian Institution, 1938.

Standing Rock Sioux Tribe. <http://www.standingrock.org/> (information about the history of the Sioux and the reservation).

Utley, Robert M. *The Lance and the Shield: The Life and Times of Sitting Bull*. 1993. New York: Ballantine Books, 1994.

Vestal, Stanley. *Sitting Bull: Champion of the Sioux*. 2nd ed. 1957. Norman: University of Oklahoma Press, 1989.

Yenne, Bill. *Sitting Bull*. Yardley, PA: Westholme Publishing, 2008.

In a pictograph by Amos Bad Heart Buffalo, Major Reno flees pursuing Indians at the Battle of Little Bighorn, a decisive victory over Custer's Seventh Cavalry for the Sioux and Cheyenne forces led by Sitting Bull and Crazy Horse. (Stapleton Historical Collection/Heritage Images)

Crazy Horse
(Tasunke Witko, Curly Hair)
1840–1877

Crazy Horse (the name is a common translation of Tasunke Witko) continues to be revered as one of American Indians' greatest heroes in their resistance to U.S. efforts to conquer them and their land. Crazy Horse endures, firmly embedded in both history and legend, as a heroic figure full of contradictions, one difficult for even his fellow Oglalas to understand.

Usually quiet and aloof, Crazy Horse neither sought positions of leadership nor participated with any regularity in leadership councils that formulated policy regarding war and peace. An almost reclusive individual much of the time, he nonetheless was recognized by his contemporaries as one who led by example, exhibiting courage, wisdom, compassion, and spirituality. Both the colossal nature of his character and its mystery seem aptly embedded in the giant figure astride a horse that since 1948 has slowly been emerging out of a mountain in the sacred Black Hills of South Dakota.

CURLY HAIR

Early Years

From his birth, probably in 1840 near Bear Butte east of present-day Sturgis, South Dakota, Crazy Horse was different. His skin was unusually light complexioned, and his hair was curly, the latter characteristic earning him the nickname Pehin Yuhaha, which means "curly hair." His original family name has been lost to history. Crazy Horse was initially the name of his father, an Oglala Lakota. His mother, Rattle Blanket Woman, was a member of another Lakota band, the Miniconjous, and had given birth to a girl about four years before the birth of her son.

The future hero was born into a prominent family. His father's father, Makes the Song, was a respected holy man, and the spiritual realm would become an important part of the younger Crazy Horse's life. In addition, his father's younger brother, Male Crow, was highly regarded as a warrior.

Curly Hair was born at a time when Euro-Americans were becoming a serious threat to the Lakotas, although his first experiences with war were against Indian adversaries. When he was about four years of age, the renowned Male Crow led a party of about 160 men on a raid to steal Shoshone horses. When scouts reported an encounter with the enemy, Male Crow, despite strong efforts to dissuade him, led approximately 30 of his men against the Shoshones, who had been joined by Crows, longstanding enemies of the Lakotas.

Their vision dramatically impaired by a heavy snowfall, Male Crow and his companions found themselves surrounded by hundreds of warriors. Male Crow and all but one of his men were quickly killed, and the remaining 130 Oglalas fled in disgrace. The elder Crazy Horse apparently felt shamed by the rout and resolved to lead a large force against the Shoshones to gain revenge. He managed to put together a coalition of Oglalas, Cheyennes, and Arapahos in January 1845. Traders had supplied the group with liquor, however, and an extended drinking session led to conflict and the dissolution of the coalition. The young Curly Hair could hardly have avoided hearing recriminations over the failures of his uncle and father, perhaps contributing to the child's tendency to withdraw into himself. Often while growing up, for example, he would ride out by himself into the surrounding hills.

An unhappy marriage between his parents also likely contributed to the son's often self-imposed isolation. Rumors have made their way down to the present concerning unfaithfulness on the part of both husband and wife. Crazy Horse apparently questioned the reason for his son's light complexion, suspecting that he may not have been the child's father. Not long after the death of Male Crow and Crazy Horse's failed effort at revenge, Rattle Blanket Woman committed suicide by hanging herself from a tree.

Curly Hair's father soon took a new wife, Kills Enemy, daughter of Corn, a Miniconjou chief. Later, he also married Kills Enemy's sister, Iron Between Horns. The two sisters bore two daughters and a son, respectively, and their family connections made the young Curly Hair a nephew of Spotted Tail, who became a prominent Brulé leader.

Other members of the extended family who would have long-term relationships with Curly Hair were Iron Whiteman, High Backbone, and Touch the Clouds. He also established a lasting friendship with He Dog, who would live into his nineties and supply considerable information to early Crazy Horse biographer Mari Sandoz and journalist Elinor Hinman.

A Changing World

Curly Hair grew up in a rapidly changing world. By 1849, large numbers of Euro-Americans were crossing the Platte Valley in southeastern Wyoming, part of the Oglalas' traditional area, as they made their way along the Oregon Trail to the Northwest. The travelers brought with them a variety of diseases—including smallpox and cholera—that took the lives of several of Curly Hair's stepsisters.

In 1851, the Treaty of Fort Laramie was signed (although not by any Oglalas). It established tribal boundaries and promises of peace among tribes in exchange for $50,000 worth of goods annually for 50 years, a term reduced to 15 years by 1853. The treaty represented a major milestone in the effort by the U.S. government to take—by one method or another—most Indian land. The Oglalas at this time remained largely peaceful regarding the Euro-American intruders, but that situation would later change.

The year 1854 brought with it a major confrontation with the U.S. military involving the Brulés and a Miniconjou named High Forehead. In August, an apparently lame animal, variously reported as being a cow or an ox, wandered away from a Mormon wagon train and was shot by High Forehead. The Brulé chief Conquering Bear (sometimes referred to in historical accounts as Brave Bear or Scattering Bear), a cousin of Curly Hair's stepmothers, tried to avoid reprisals by offering to pay for the animal with ponies from his own herd.

Lieutenant Hugh Fleming, who was the commander of Fort Laramie, refused the offer and insisted that the offender be handed over for punishment.

Lieutenant John Grattan then persuaded Fleming to allow him to go to Conquering Bear's village and arrest High Forehead. Grattan arrived at the village with 31 men and demanded that the killer of the cow be turned over. A soldier fired, apparently before being ordered to do so, and struck one of the villagers. Conquering Bear tried to move away from Grattan but was shot. Five men were killed by the soldiers, but the Brulés reacted quickly and overwhelmed Grattan's men, killing all of them. Conquering Bear died a few days later. The incident, referred to in government reports as the Grattan Massacre, was the first battle in what would become known as the Sioux Wars, or the Plains Wars, and reverberated throughout the Lakota world as well as in the U.S. halls of government.

General William Harney arrived in 1855 at the head of a military force to try to end Indian hostilities, which had included attacks on emigrant trains and settlers' livestock. In addition, a new agent at Fort Laramie, Thomas Twiss, relayed a U.S. requirement that Lakotas who wanted to live in peace must move south of the North Platte River in southeastern Wyoming. On September 3, Harney attacked a Brulé camp near Fort Laramie on Blue Water Creek, killing 86 people and capturing 70 women and children.[1]

Still hoping to avoid war, a majority of the Oglalas, including Curly Hair's father, obeyed the directive to move south of the North Platte. Among those Lakotas who did not was Spotted Tail, who later in the year surrendered and was imprisoned at Fort Leavenworth. When he was released, in the autumn of 1856, he permanently renounced war, aligning himself with the Indians who, unlike Sitting Bull and the younger Crazy Horse, accommodated themselves to reservation life.

CRAZY HORSE THE WARRIOR

The Warrior's Road

In the year 1857, Curly Hair embarked on the path that would immortalize him as one of the greatest of Indian leaders. His first significant battle occurred in May 1857, when he participated in an attack on a Pawnee village in eastern Nebraska. Curly Hair outpaced the rest of his companions and rode into the village, causing panic among the Pawnees. Seeing a woman near him, he struck her, counting his first coup. The incident has elicited various accounts over the years. Sandoz wrote that Curly Hair killed an individual who he thought was a man, later deeply regretting his action when he discovered not only the individual's gender but also her young age. In a more recent biography, Kingsley M. Bray argues that Crazy Horse knew his victim was a woman but at first only counted coup on her. According to Bray, Curly Hair later killed her deliberately, perhaps to carry out a pledge to kill a woman made the previous year when he became a heyoka dedicated to honoring the Thunderbird, practicing humility, and raising people's spirits. He Dog had referred to Crazy Horse's killing of a woman, and Bray suggests that Sandoz fictionalized the incident so as not to present her subject in a bad light. Nonetheless, Bray's own narrative of the event is based heavily on conjecture.[2]

Curly Hair engaged in another battle on July 29, this one against the U.S. military. Influenced by Ice and Dark, two young men who were convinced that their power would protect their companions from the soldiers, Curly Hair rode with a group of Lakotas and Cheyennes against Colonel Edwin V. Summer into Kansas. The war party was resting their horses when suddenly about 300 soldiers appeared and charged. After releasing a barrage of arrows, the Cheyennes fled south and the Oglalas north. The encounter must have been a great disappointment to the young warrior, but he surely learned an important lesson that would serve him well later—that confronting the U.S. military in a direct head-to-head battle was a recipe for disaster.

War with the Crows

A large council of Lakota bands occurred in August 1857 near Bear Butte, South Dakota, to consider future directions involving both traditional, Indian adversaries, and the newer Euro-American enemies. Among the conclusions arrived at was a reaffirmation of the importance of the Black Hills, sacred site of so many Lakota vision quests and home to game, water, and timber essential to Lakota life. Also on the agenda was the desire by U.S. officials that Indian nations make peace with one another, a common provision embedded in government treaties to prevent intertribal warfare from spilling over and endangering settlers traveling across and settling in the territories west of the Missouri River.

Warfare with the Crows, however, was far too deeply rooted in Lakota culture to be abandoned at the stroke of a pen. War was the avenue by which a young Lakota could earn his status as a respected member of his people. It also was a way to gain horses, which were vital to a wide range of functions, including hunting and the constant moving of villages to find game and fresh grass. Also, excursions by settlers squeezed ever tighter the old hunting grounds, meaning that military action was necessary to push aside other tribes to gain their hunting grounds—and the Crows were essentially next-door neighbors to the Lakotas, making their traditional lands the most accessible and enticing. In addition, old enmities die hard, and the Lakotas were not about to try to make peace with the Crows or with other traditional enemies.

According to both Sandoz and Bray, it was at this gathering that Crazy Horse first encountered Sitting Bull, already a revered Hunkpapa leader. As described in Chapter 6, at Little Bighorn in 1876, Crazy Horse would help Sitting Bull achieve the greatest victory ever by American Indians over the U.S. military.[3]

Renaming

Among other enemies of the Lakota were the Gros Ventres (also known as Atsinas or Hidatsas). As a sedentary people living in earthen lodges, this group was especially susceptible to Euro-American diseases and had been severely weakened as a rival of the Lakotas by the ravages of smallpox. Nonetheless, when a raiding party that included Curly Hair encountered a group of Gros Ventres in 1857, fighting broke out. When Curly Hair's friend High Backbone had his horse shot out from under him, Curly Hair came to his rescue. He helped High Backbone onto his own horse behind him and rode to safety. Later in the battle, Curly Hair scored a number of successes, counting several first coups and taking two scalps while suffering a minor wound to an arm.

Each coup earned him an eagle feather, with the wound meriting a red one. The battle also brought Curly Hair something else—a new name. After the war party returned to camp, Crazy Horse transferred his name to his son, adopting Worm as his new name. Curly Hair was now Tasunke Witko, Crazy Horse.

Crazy Horse's Growing Reputation

Like other great Indian leaders before him, Crazy Horse earned his reputation as a great warrior not by fighting Euro-Americans but by demonstrating his courage and skill against traditional Indian enemies. In May 1858, when the newly renamed Crazy Horse participated in a raid west across the Bighorn Mountains, the Lakota party clashed with a group of Shoshones, Bannocks, and Crows. Crazy Horse suffered a wound to his left leg and later had his horse shot. Nonetheless, he persevered, and when an enemy rode toward him, Crazy Horse knocked the rider to the ground and killed him. He then mounted his victim's horse and rode to safety.

Two sons of the Miniconjou chief Black Shield were killed by Crows in the spring of 1859. Crazy Horse had been visiting his mother's people renewing old friendships, and along with other Oglalas he joined Black Shield on a retaliatory expedition. The Lakotas attacked a Crow party on June 12 along the Yellowstone River, killing about a dozen of the Crows.[4]

Among Crazy Horse's early military encounters, the engagement known as the Battle Defending the Tents achieved special attention. During the summer of 1863, a large party of Oglalas, Miniconjous, Arapahos, and Cheyennes approached a major Crow village in south-central Montana. As the attackers pressed a line of Crow warriors back against their village, Crazy Horse's horse was shot. On foot, he caught up with a Crow who was trying to reach the tipis and killed him before rejoining his own comrades, who exulted in his accomplishment. Ultimately, neither side could score a decisive victory. When the attackers learned that Crow reinforcements might be coming, they withdrew.

Not long afterward, Crows caught up with Crazy Horse's party. Once again, Crazy Horse lost a horse in battle. Even so, when he saw that his younger brother, Young Little Hawk, was in danger, he leaped onto another horse and rushed to his brother's rescue. Crazy Horse killed one of the Crows endangering his brother, and the others fled.

The Dancing Horseman

Biographers have devoted much attention to Crazy Horse's vision of a dancing horseman, but the earlier reporting of that vision has recently come into question. The account usually goes something like this: Crazy Horse went off alone to seek a vision but without following the customary ritual of purification in a sweat lodge. Nonetheless, after fasting, he saw a horseman who arose from a pond and seemed to be floating or dancing in the air. The horseman gave Crazy Horse certain directives, later interpreted for Crazy Horse by his father after the two, following the prescribed purification rituals, had gone off together to seek a renewed vision. Crazy Horse was to dress simply, wearing perhaps a feather but not a war bonnet. Before a battle, he must toss dust over his horse and himself and wear a small stone behind an ear. He was not to accumulate personal possessions. Bullets and arrows would not harm him, but the vision also included a battle in which some of Crazy Horse's companions attempted to hold his arms.[5]

The vision is typically interpreted by modern commentators (1) as helping to explain Crazy Horse's extreme generosity and simplicity of dress and (2) as foreshadowing his manner of death. Such interpretations have certain problems with them. In the latter matter of holding his arms, his companions in the vision seem to be trying to keep him from battle, and perhaps from endangering himself. The former implies a cause-to-effect sequence, with the vision fostering certain behavioral patterns. The vision was often located in the immediate aftermath of the so-called Grattan Massacre of 1854, when the adolescent Curly Hair was young enough still to be forming a self-image of what he should be regarding such matters as service, self-sacrifice, and modesty.

Bray argues that the vision actually occurred several years later, in 1860 or 1861, and that the vision has been misinterpreted over the years. Throwing of dust from a gopher burrow, for example, would cause sores, indicating that only a wakan (holy) person could do so without suffering the skin ailments such an action would usually cause. If Bray's hypothesis about the date is correct, the vision may have reinforced tendencies already strong within Crazy Horse rather than engendered any new patterns. Bray also contends that Sandoz incorrectly considered this experience to be Crazy Horse's only significant vision, whereas he actually experienced several. The true meaning of the horseman, for Bray, was that as a water spirit from the Underground, he succeeded, through his promise of invulnerability, in neutralizing the power of the Thunder Powers that resided in the Upper World and that were responsible for giving humans the gift of guns.[6]

Whatever the precise meaning of the vision and its causal impact on Crazy Horse, the great Oglala leader was remembered by contemporaries for living out several elements of the vision. He dressed quite simply, did not wear a war bonnet, and painted only hailstones and lightning streaks on his body. In addition, his generosity was extraordinary, as he gave freely to others what he captured in battle or shot during buffalo hunts. He also took great care to watch over his younger relatives and friends, including Young Little Hawk, and made concerted efforts to allow young men to count coups that he could readily have gained instead.

THE NEW ENEMY

The Bozeman Trail

By the middle of the 1860s, settlers and soldiers were replacing traditional enemies such as the Crows as the Lakotas' principal adversaries—certainly they posed the greatest threat to the Lakota way of life that had endured for generations. Gold discoveries in western Montana earlier in the decade and wagon trains heading west created a need for a ready path across traditional Lakota lands, and John M. Bozeman mapped such a route in 1863. The Bozeman Trail ran northwest from the North Platte River near Fort Laramie, ascended just east of the Bighorn Mountains, crossed over into Montana Territory, and continued to the present town of Bozeman, Montana.

While traffic along the Bozeman was increasing, military events were alarming the Lakotas and other Plains Indians, especially the massacre of some 150 Cheyennes and Arapahos—mainly women, children, and the elderly—by Colorado militia under Colonel John Chivington at Sand Creek, Colorado, in November 1864. The Cheyenne village was headed by Chief Black Kettle, who had consistently remained friendly to the U.S. government.

By 1864, Crazy Horse was engaging in raids along the North Platte. In 1865, Oglalas and Cheyennes planned an attack on the military at Platte Bridge Station about 130 miles north of Fort Laramie at the present location of Casper, Wyoming, partly in revenge for the Sand Creek massacre. By that time, some of the Sand Creek survivors had taken refuge with the Oglalas.

On June 26, Lieutenant Caspar Collins led 24 soldiers across Platte Bridge to escort a supply train heading east. Before reaching the supply train, Collins and his men came under fire, with Collins and five others shot down before they could retreat to their post. What Crazy Horse specifically did in the attack is unknown, although Mari Sandoz, seemingly without any clear evidence for the claim, describes Crazy Horse earlier that morning unsuccessfully leading a decoy maneuver against another group of soldiers, just as he later would do to better effect in the Fetterman battle.[7]

The Oglala–Cheyenne force then turned to the train still about five miles away. The five-wagon train and escort led by Sergeant Amos Custard were easily overrun. All of the soldiers were killed and the wagons burned, bringing the total number of soldiers killed that day to 28. The bridge and military post, however, remained standing and under U.S. military control.

The U.S. military moved aggressively to exert control over the Bozeman Trail. General Patrick Connor, who had recently been appointed commander of the Department of the Plains, established his headquarters at Fort Laramie and established a "take no prisoners" policy regarding male Indians older than the age of 12. Connor marched north along the Bozeman Trail. By the middle of August, he had his men erecting a military post named Camp Connor, later renamed Fort Reno, along the Powder River in northeastern Wyoming. The camp became a regular object of Crazy Horse's attacks over the next three years.

By early September 1865, forces under Colonel Nelson Cole and Colonel Samuel Walker, both part of Connor's command, were approaching Oglala and Cheyenne villages. Crazy Horse and his allies first encountered Walker's troops; then, about 15 miles away, they met Cole's men. Cole established a strong position, and High Backbone suggested trying to draw his troops out into the open by pretending to withdraw. After several hours, that stratagem failed to work, and Crazy Horse took action.

Crazy Horse rode furiously along the length of Cole's defensive line, inviting heavy shooting from the soldiers. Twice more he repeated his run, only to find the firing stop. He then rode directly toward the soldiers, but the guns remained silent. The maneuver accomplished nothing militarily but demonstrated to his own men his considerable courage as well as his seeming invulnerability. A bit later, when Cole ordered his howitzers into action, the Oglalas and Cheyennes withdrew. Cole and Walker, suffering the effects of unseasonably cold weather and hunger, moved on to Camp Connor. The following month, Connor withdrew most of the men back to Fort Laramie, leaving a skeleton crew behind.

Fort Phil Kearny

The split between those Indians who were willing to accept reservation life and those who were not continued to grow. Man Afraid of His Horse (an Oglala) and Spotted Tail (a Brulé) worked to develop support for moving to Fort Laramie in 1866, while Red Cloud, although willing to meet with treaty commissioners at Fort Laramie, refused to make any deals. Crazy Horse refused even to engage in talks with the commissioners.

Also in July, at the direction of Colonel Henry Carrington, construction began on another fort along the Bozeman Trail, Fort Phil Kearny, located at Little Piney Creek north of Fort Reno (formerly Camp Connor). This further movement into Lakota land was especially provocative and led to immediate attacks against the fort during its construction. In August, Carrington ordered another Bozeman fort to be built, C. F. Smith, across the border in Montana overlooking the Bighorn River.

These Bozeman forts were a source of great anger for Red Cloud, bringing him and Crazy Horse into a closer alliance than they had ever experienced before or would again. Crazy Horse harassed Fort Phil Kearny throughout

Red Cloud's Autobiography

Red Cloud has not fared well with historians over the past few decades. Next to Sitting Bull and Crazy Horse, he comes across as a leader more willing to accommodate himself to the wishes of the U.S. government and accept reservation life than to fight heroically to maintain his people's traditional culture and way of life. Even his role as a leader in the Fetterman battle has been called into question.

Historical evaluations of Red Cloud as a military leader usually focus almost exclusively on his resistance to Euro-American forces, while ignoring his actions against the Oglalas' traditional enemies such as the Crows, Pawnees, and Shoshones. That part of Red Cloud's life, however, is what he focuses on in the document that finally was published in 1997 as *Autobiography of Red Cloud*, edited by R. Eli Paul.

The "autobiography" dates from 1893, when Charles Wesley Allen, postmaster at the Pine Ridge reservation in South Dakota, decided to write Red Cloud's history. Allen enlisted as interviewer a veteran fur trader and longtime friend of Red Cloud's named Samuel Deon. For approximately six months, Deon sat with Red Cloud on a bench by the post office asking questions about Red Cloud's life. They would talk for two or three hours, after which Deon shared with Allen what Red Cloud had said and Allen wrote the narrative down in the third person.

Although much of the language is clearly Allen's, and the third-person approach is more typically biographical than autobiographical, the account offers valuable information about Red Cloud's early military successes and his rise to a position of leadership. Not surprisingly, Red Cloud ends his narrative before his encounters with U.S. soldiers. Living in peace on a reservation, he had no desire to resurrect stories about killing U.S. soldiers.

the fall of 1866, stealing horses and attacking soldiers when they could be found alone or in small groups. These efforts, however, produced little in the way of tangible results, leading Red Cloud, High Backbone, and Crazy Horse to decide on what they hoped would be a decisive blow.

The Fetterman Battle

In early December 1866, a combined Lakota, Cheyenne, and Arapaho force approached Fort Phil Kearny. The first blow was struck on December 6, when warriors attacked a party of woodcutters. Colonel Carrington sent Captain William J. Fetterman and Lieutenant H. S. Bingham to the rescue. Carrington and Lieutenant George Grummond led another force, hoping to cut off the attackers. Bingham and 15 of his men became separated from the rest of the soldiers, however. He and two of his men were killed, and the Indians withdrew.

For the next two weeks, Red Cloud kept up sporadic harassment of the fort, frustrating the soldiers, none more than Captain Fetterman, a veteran of the Civil War who possessed considerable regard for his own fighting ability and an equal amount of scorn for his adversaries. He boasted that with 80 men he could ride through the entire Sioux nation. By December 21, two days after another attack on the woodcutters and subsequent Indian withdrawal, he would get his chance for glory.

Crazy Horse was chosen to lead a contingent of 10 decoys in an effort to draw the soldiers out into the open and across a ridge north of Big Piney. At that point, the Indian forces figured, they could be ambushed and annihilated out of sight of the remaining soldiers in the stockade.

Again a wood train left the fort; at approximately 11 A.M., it was attacked. Apparently with some misgivings about his subordinate's judgment, Carrington put Fetterman in command of a rescue party of 50 infantrymen and 27 cavalrymen, the latter under Lieutenant Grummond. Two civilians raised the total, in an unintended twist, to the 80 of Fetterman's boast. Carrington ordered Fetterman to rescue the train and return immediately, and absolutely not to pursue Indians over Lodge Trail Ridge.

As Fetterman's men approached the wood train, which had formed a defensive circle, Red Cloud ordered his men to withdraw, seemingly removing from Fetterman his opportunity for a military victory. Then Crazy Horse and his fellow decoys appeared, and the soldiers opened fire. No longer having to protect the wood train, Fetterman led his men after the decoys. Crazy Horse and the other decoys took a number of actions to keep Fetterman following, such as yelling taunts and pretending that their horses were tired or hurt. Once the pursuers had crossed the ridge, the decoys sped away, then divided into two lines and rode intersecting paths, the signal for the large, hidden force to attack.

By this time the cavalry had moved well beyond Fetterman and his infantry. Grummond and the cavalry were overrun; then the attacking force hit the infantry while cavalrymen fled past them. The infantrymen were wiped out first, followed by the remaining cavalry. The entire event, from the moment of the ambush, took perhaps 30 minutes. About 12:45 P.M., a relief column under Captain Tenedore Ten Eyck reached the top of the ridge but remained there, watching huge numbers of Indians below. After the victorious warriors withdrew, Ten Eyck's men removed 48 of the dead.

The defeat of Fetterman would prove to be one of the most memorable moments in Crazy Horse's life, but not a particularly joyous one. Crazy Horse discovered that his childhood friend Lone Bear had been fatally wounded. The total number of Indian dead is uncertain but may have included about 11 killed during the fighting plus others, like Lone Bear, who succumbed to their wounds later.[8]

To Negotiate or to Fight

The next two years saw a divergence of focus between Crazy Horse and Red Cloud. Crazy Horse continued on the warrior's path, engaging the

Twenty-Seventh Infantry in February 1867 and detachments from Fort Reno in April. Also at this time, he began to establish a close relationship with Sitting Bull of the Hunkpapas, a relationship that would blossom into a close military alliance in which Crazy Horse would essentially serve as the older war chief's second-in-command, culminating in the victory over Colonel George Armstrong Custer and the Seventh Cavalry at Little Bighorn.

Crazy Horse returned to Fort Phil Kearny in early August 1867 to again attack the woodcutters in what would become known as the Wagon Box Fight. The infantry escorting the wood party had formed a circle of 14 wagon boxes to provide protection for their livestock. On August 2, Crazy Horse struck a small woodcutters' camp guarded by four soldiers. Four woodcutters and two soldiers were killed, and the attackers then turned to the corral. Inside the improvised stockade, Captain James Powell commanded 32 men and armed with the new Springfield breechloader, which could be reloaded quickly, they took a heavy toll on the warriors. When a relief column arrived and started firing howitzer shells, Crazy Horse and his men withdrew.

Simultaneously, efforts toward reaching a peace treaty at Fort Laramie were under way, headed by Red Cloud and the accommodationist Man Afraid of His Horse. Red Cloud was still demanding abandonment of the forts along the Bozeman Trail even as another post, Fort Fetterman, was being constructed between Fort Laramie and Fort Reno just south of the post at Platte Bridge Station, which had been renamed Fort Casper in honor of Lieutenant Caspar Collins (while misspelling his name). The small fort was closed upon completion of the new installation in 1867.

The Fort Laramie Treaty of 1868

In March 1868, the War Department, meeting Red Cloud's demand, ordered the Bozeman Trail forts (C. F. Smith, Phil Kearny, and Reno) closed. The treaty being readied at Fort Laramie also would establish the Great Sioux Reservation west of the Missouri River in the Dakota Territory. In addition, the treaty specified that a large segment of land north of the North Platte River and east of the Bighorn Mountains would be labeled "unceded Indian territory." According to the treaty, this unceded territory would remain open to the Lakotas as long as buffalo continued to be found there "in such numbers as to justify the chase." A provision that before long would create difficulties for the U.S. government was the acknowledgment that no reservation land would be taken from the reservation without the approval of "three-fourths of all adult male Indians occupying or interested in the same." For their part, the Indians were required to guarantee that they would live in peace with Indians and non-Indians alike. Each family head would receive 320 acres for a farm, a variety of agricultural supplies, and cattle. Education also would be part of the package designed to remake the reservation Indian into something resembling a white man.[9]

Spotted Tail readily accepted the treaty, but Red Cloud held out until the forts were actually abandoned, a process completed by August. On August 10, the Great Sioux Reservation was placed under General Harney as a separate military district, with local commanders responsible for the unceded territory. On November 4, Red Cloud arrived at Fort Laramie prepared to sign the treaty. Two days later, he made his mark, essentially withdrawing from the resistance effort and relinquishing Oglala military efforts to the leadership of Crazy Horse. From then on, the two Oglala leaders would go their separate ways, with Red Cloud becoming a reservation Indian and Crazy Horse aligning himself ever more closely with Sitting Bull on his way to becoming one of the greatest of Indian resistance leaders.

The Shirt Wearer

The respect with which Crazy Horse was viewed by his fellow Oglalas was evidenced in the summer of 1868 when he was named one of four new Shirt Wearers (along with American Horse, Sword Owner, and Young Man Afraid of His Horse, the last a son of the chief Man Afraid of His Horse). The Shirt Wearers occupied a position of considerable responsibility. They helped to select promising hunting areas and were called upon to settle a variety of issues, including personal conflicts, that might otherwise divide their people. They were expected to be models of generosity, especially toward less fortunate members of the community such as widows and orphans—a quality that Crazy Horse had long exhibited. In addition, the Shirt Wearers were deeply involved in helping to set tribal policy regarding such important matters as treaties and land use.

While Red Cloud and Man Afraid of His Horse continued to negotiate settlement of such issues as the locations of trading posts and government agencies, with Red Cloud journeying to Washington, D.C., as part of a delegation, Crazy Horse resisted any accommodation with the U.S. government. One of his encounters with the military, an otherwise relatively insignificant engagement on April 19, 1870, that resulted in no fatalities, led to the first notice of Crazy Horse by name in print. The account, by Fort Laramie chaplain Alpha Wright, appeared in the *Plattsmouth Herald* for May 5, 1870. At about the same time, Crazy Horse gave perhaps his first formal speech in council in which he shared his fear that Lakota land "will be taken under duress without payment."[10]

While Crazy Horse had come to see the encroaching Euro-Americans as his greatest threat, he had by no means set aside his people's longstanding conflict with the Crows. In fact, he seemed to relish resumption of that conflict as a sort of escape into the natural order of things. He threw himself into a raid against the Crows that would be known as the Fight When They Chased Them Back to Camp. The battle, which occurred in May, was a Lakota victory, and Crazy Horse distinguished himself by claiming the life of at least one Crow victim in the encounter.

Not long after the battle against the Crows, Crazy Horse suffered through the most negative period in his life. He apparently had been engaged in a relationship for some time with Black Buffalo Woman, wife of No Water. The jilted husband followed Crazy Horse, surprised him as he sat talking with Little Big Man and other companions, and shot Crazy Horse in the face. The bullet hit beneath Crazy Horse's nose, broke his jaw, and exited through his neck. In the confusion following the shot, No Water escaped, believing that he had killed his rival. The wound was actually not so serious as it had first appeared, and Crazy Horse recovered, although he was in pain for months and incurred permanent scarring.

Crazy Horse's friend Touch the Clouds succeeded in effecting a truce between Crazy Horse and No Water that included the return of Black Buffalo Woman to her husband. The incident led to Crazy Horse being removed as a Shirt Wearer, a decision that must have been humiliating but that also freed him from the need to engage in political and diplomatic actions that had never come naturally to him.

The same year saw Crazy Horse take a wife, Black Shawl, and lose a brother, Young Little Hawk, who was killed, according to differing accounts, by either U.S. settlers or Shoshone adversaries. When Red Cloud accepted a 35-year expiration date for retaining the unceded hunting grounds, Little Big Man agreed to the arrangement. As 1870 progressed, Crazy Horse continued to experience the year's turbulent pattern of ups and downs. His rejection as a Shirt Wearer was mitigated somewhat by his selection as a war chief, but another close friend, High Backbone, was killed by Shoshones.

The Northern Pacific Railroad

A new threat to the Lakota culture emerged in the early 1870s: the Northern Pacific Railroad, intended to link the Great Lakes with the Pacific Northwest, thus cutting across the northern tier of Lakota territory. The earlier meeting of the Central Pacific and Union Pacific at Promontory Summit, Utah, in 1869 had divided the two great buffalo herds, and the projected railroad threatened the source of Lakota livelihood even more. By 1872, the railroad issue had helped cement a strengthened partnership between Sitting Bull and Crazy Horse.

That relationship was much in evidence in the summer of 1872 when two sets of Northern Pacific surveyors, escorted by U.S. troops, approached Lakota lands. The military force numbered approximately 600 soldiers under Colonel David S. Stanley out of Fort Rice, near the confluence of the Cannonball and Missouri rivers in the future state of North Dakota, and 500 soldiers under Major Eugene M. Baker from Fort Ellis, near Bozeman, Montana.

Warriors from several Lakota bands had come together along the Powder River in southeastern Montana for a Sun Dance prior to an expedition against the Crows. However, Lakota scouts reported soldiers nearby along the Yellowstone River near the mouth of Arrow Creek, which turned out to be Baker's contingent. A group of young warriors rushed into battle, triggering a confrontation known as the Battle of Arrow Creek. The outcome of the battle was indecisive, but the railroad employees were badly shaken by the encounter and withdrew, along with their military escort, northward to the Musselshell River and returned to Fort Ellis.

The battle featured the famous display of courage by Sitting Bull, who reasserted his leadership after a claim by self-styled holy man Long Holy—namely, that he had the power to protect the Lakotas from enemy bullets—resulted in several young men following Long Holy's exhortations and being wounded. Sitting Bull, carrying his pipe and tobacco pouch, calmly strolled out between Lakota and U.S. lines and sat down. He leisurely smoked his pipe while bullets struck nearby and then beckoned others, including his nephew White Bull, to join him. After finishing his pipe, Sitting Bull slowly returned to his own line while his companions rushed as quickly as possible to safety.

Crazy Horse also distinguished himself during the battle. Exhibiting considerable courage himself, he raced his horse several times along the line of enemy troops, who unleashed a heavy barrage of fire at him. On his last run, he was followed by White Bull. However, Crazy Horse's mount was shot, leaving him to continue on foot until another Lakota came to his aid, and the two men rode together out of firing range.

The First Crazy Horse–Custer Encounter

In August 1873, Lieutenant Colonel George Armstrong Custer led two companies of his Seventh Cavalry as part of a military force under the command of Colonel David Stanley that was accompanying another party of railroad surveyors. This Yellowstone Expedition left Fort Rice on June 20 and by August 4 had followed the Yellowstone down to the Tongue River.

The Lakotas attempted the decoy strategy, with Crazy Horse waiting in ambush. Around noon, a small group of Indians charged soldiers who were standing guard while a patrol of about 20 men led by Custer rested. The patrol pursued the attackers, but Custer sensed the possibility of an ambush. Riding with his orderly ahead of the rest of his men, Custer forced a premature springing of the trap, whereupon he raced back to the rest of his patrol, who had formed a skirmish line in the tall grass. Despite the arrival of additional cavalry, Crazy Horse continued the battle for several hours before withdrawing.

The Lakota forces faced Custer again on August 11. In an attack designed to divert Custer from endangering a Lakota village that had hurriedly crossed the Yellowstone River as Custer approached, Crazy Horse and several hundred warriors engaged Custer. The fighting was intense, and the Lakotas withdrew, successfully keeping the cavalry at a distance while they crossed the river to join their families. Fortunately for Crazy Horse and his Lakota allies, the financial panic of 1873 came to their aid, temporarily ending railroad construction across their lands.

Crazy Horse, with the battle over, would have little time to enjoy village life. During the fall, his only child, a daughter named They Are Afraid of Her, died while he was absent fighting the Crows. She was only two and one-half years old and apparently much beloved by her father. Frank Grouard, a friend of

Sitting Bull and Crazy Horse who ultimately would throw in with the U.S. military against them, wrote that Crazy Horse's "grief was pathetic" over her death and described a trip he and the grieving father made to her burial scaffold. Crazy Horse supposedly climbed the scaffold and lay beside his dead daughter for three days and nights, mourning the child. The account has not been verified by anyone else and seems excessive even for a devastated father.[11]

BATTLE OF LITTLE BIGHORN

The Black Hills

The path to the Battle of Little Bighorn ran, to a great extent, through the Black Hills of Dakota Territory in what today is western South Dakota. When rumors of gold in the Black Hills began circulating widely, General Philip Sheridan, commander of the Army of the Missouri (an area including all of the Plains) sent an exploratory expedition under Colonel Custer into the area, ostensibly to locate an appropriate site for a fort that could support the reservation Indians at the Red Cloud and Spotted Tail Agencies in northern Nebraska. Later in the decade, Spotted Tail's Brulés and Red Cloud's Oglalas would be moved into South Dakota's Rosebud and Pine Ridge Agencies, respectively.

Custer left his headquarters, Fort Abraham Lincoln, in Dakota Territory (near the present town of Mandan, North Dakota) on July 2, 1874. Because the unstated motive for the expedition was to look for gold, Custer's party included miners to search for the precious mineral and newspapermen to report the findings. Obviously, once confirmation of the area's resources reached newspaper readers, there would be no stopping prospectors from pouring into the Black Hills, which were supposedly Indian lands within the Great Sioux Reservation. Although Private Theodore Ewert, a member of Custer's command, reported in his diary that "the earth containing the precious metal is so scarce that but a very few persons will be the lucky owners of any," the newspaper correspondents were not about to disappoint their editors and readers. They sent back glowing accounts of gold discoveries. Likewise, Custer, who was never averse to personal publicity, exaggerated the modest findings.[12]

The Black Hills, known to the Lakotas as the Paha Sapa (the hills that are black), were an important source of food because of the abundant game living in the area. The Black Hills also provided firewood; strong, straight pine poles for tipis; and spiritual sustenance because of the mystical presence that the Lakotas sensed in the region. Crazy Horse and many other nonreservation Lakotas were therefore deeply troubled by the sudden influx of Euro-Americans following Custer's excursion and were determined not to yield these sacred hills to the intruders.

General Sheridan ordered his commanders to stop civilian wagon trains from entering the Black Hills, but the effort to stem the tide was undertaken half-heartedly and with little success. In fact, over the next few months hundreds of miners staked claims to what they hoped would be rich gold deposits. An occasional eviction proved to be little deterrence to the flood of gold seekers. In an effort to avoid war over the Black Hills and maintain some semblance of legality, the U.S. government attempted to negotiate a financial arrangement with the Lakotas to buy or lease the area.

Faced with multiple worries—the continuing influx of miners and settlers as well as the possibility that reservation chiefs might agree to a deal relinquishing Paha Sapa—the northern Oglala Council gave Crazy Horse and his long-time companion He Dog the responsibility of protecting the Black Hills. During the summer of 1875, Crazy Horse acquired, very briefly, an unexpected ally in his efforts to preserve the hills: Brigadier General George Crook. Crook, who had become commanding officer of the Department of the Platte in April, established a deadline of August 15 for miners to leave the Black Hills and threatened expulsion if they refused.

The Allison Commission, led by U.S. Senator William Boyd Allison of Iowa, met with Lakota leaders at Red Cloud Agency in September and proposed leasing the hills and purchasing part of the unceded territory. Payments for the leased portion would be made to the next seven generations of Lakotas. Red Cloud agreed to the deal, but Little Big Man expressed his opposition by leading a mock charge of warriors firing their weapons toward the commissioners. Spotted Tail defused the situation; violence, if actually intended by Little Big Man, did not materialize. The deal, however, was dead, as the leaders who had to agree to achieve a peaceful transfer of the land—Crazy Horse and Sitting Bull—had boycotted the deliberations.

An Ultimatum

President Ulysses S. Grant, determined to acquire the Black Hills but hoping to limit the military cost of doing so, met on November 3, 1875, with several of his top officials, including Secretary of the Interior Zachariah Chandler, Commissioner of Indian Affairs Edward P. Smith, Secretary of War William W. Belknap, and Generals Philip Sheridan and George Crook. Grant came to two major decisions: (1) to maintain but not enforce the prohibition on miners entering the Black Hills, and (2) to force the "hunting bands"—that is, the nonreservation Lakotas—to yield the unceded lands and accept reservation life. To facilitate the latter aim, he transferred responsibility for the "hostile" groups to the War Department and, either at that meeting or soon thereafter, approved a deadline by which all of the resisting Lakotas would have to go into the reservations or face military force. The deadline of January 31, 1876, was completely unrealistic even if the bands had wanted to acquiesce: It barely allowed time to notify the widely scattered groups, let alone permit them to travel through the difficult winter weather to the reservations.

General Sheridan, apparently assuming noncompliance, planned his military action carefully. A multipronged approach was envisioned. Crook would move north from Fort Fetterman in Wyoming against Crazy Horse, believed to be in north-central Wyoming. General Alfred Terry would split his forces, with Colonel John Gibbon moving east from Fort Ellis in Montana, and Lieutenant Colonel George Armstrong Custer descending from Fort Abraham Lincoln and turning westward. The three prongs would encircle the Lakotas and their Cheyenne allies and destroy them, eliminating the primary opposition on the Plains, including the two men considered the greatest threats to the Euro-American plans: Sitting Bull and Crazy Horse. In reality, the harsh weather that would have prevented the Indian bands from complying with the ultimatum also prevented Sheridan from implementing his plans during the heart of winter, when he hoped to find the bands in their winter camps and more vulnerable to attack.

Powder River Battle

The first battle of the offensive was aimed at Crazy Horse but missed the mark as General Crook misjudged the location of his camp. Commanding the expedition under Crook, which departed Fort Fetterman at the end of February 1876, was Colonel Joseph J. Reynolds. Within days, however, the mammoth force—which consisted of 12 companies, 6 pack trains of mules, a supply train of 80 wagons, and assorted scouts and guides—had lost its beef herds, and Crook resumed operational control.

Frank Grouard, who had been befriended by both Sitting Bull and Crazy Horse, was among Crook's scouts and determined, erroneously, that Crazy Horse was camped on the Powder River in southeastern Montana. He found a village there, a few miles north of the Wyoming line, but it turned out not to be Crazy Horse's camp. A strike force of six companies under Reynolds moved to attack. Incompetence on the part of Reynolds, Captain Henry Noyes, and Captain Alexander Moore (all of whom were later court-martialed for their performance) allowed almost all of the approximately 735 villagers to escape, although the attackers were able to capture some 700 horses and destroy the village and its contents. Warriors from the village, however, followed Crook's forces and eventually recaptured about 550 of the horses.

Crazy Horse's involvement came later, as the villagers, largely destitute of food and warm clothing, completed their 40-mile trek to his village on March 23. Crazy Horse supplied what assistance he could, but his village was too small (about 50 tipis) to accommodate all of the new arrivals for long. Consequently, they continued north along the Powder River to Sitting Bull's village.

Battle of the Rosebud

As spring advanced, increasing numbers of hunting bands gathered along the Rosebud River, drawn together especially by the status of Sitting Bull as the de facto leader of the Lakotas and their allies who were resisting U.S. efforts to bring all Plains Indians into the reservations.

Crook, meanwhile, had returned to Fort Fetterman in preparation for another foray north. With more than 1,000 soldiers, including both cavalry and infantry, and 120 wagons, Crook departed on May 29, leading an even more formidable force than he had taken north a few months earlier.

In early June, Sitting Bull set in motion plans for a Sun Dance, the most important religious event for the Lakotas. The Sun Dance typically occurred over four days but followed about eight days of reflection, instruction, and preparation. The Sun Dance was held in honor of Wi, the spirit of the sun, and normally took place around June prior to the great summer buffalo hunts. The buffalo god, Tatanka, also figured prominently in the dance.

As a special offering to Wakantanka, Sitting Bull, sitting against the sacred Sun Dance pole, had his adopted brother Jumping Bull cut out 50 small pieces of flesh from each of the Lakota leader's arms. For the rest of the day, throughout the night, and into the next day, Sitting Bull danced, staring into the sun during the daylight hours. Finally, he appeared to pass out, and some of his Hunkpapas lowered him to the ground.

After his recovery, Sitting Bull shared the vision that he had received—surely one of the most famous and significant visions in history. Sitting Bull reported that he had seen large numbers of soldiers falling from the sky, numerous as grasshoppers; both the soldiers and their horses were falling upside down, symbolizing their defeat. The vision would prove prophetic within the month at Little Bighorn, but at the moment generated great confidence among the Lakotas that they would be triumphant in any confrontation with the army.

By June 16, the large group of Lakotas and Cheyennes had started moving west but received reports of a large enemy force nearby. Crook had received intelligence as well of a large village in the vicinity. With grass growing scarce at Crook's camp on the Tongue River, he moved to a site at the confluence of the two forks of Goose Creek, which flows into the Tongue. On June 14, according to Captain John G. Bourke (at the time a lieutenant), who served under General Crook and recorded his experiences in *On the Border with Crook*, two parties of Shoshone and Crow allies totaling 262 joined Crook's forces. On the day of their arrival, preparations were made to seek out the reported village.[13]

Crook left his wagons behind with an assortment of packers, teamsters, and wounded and sick soldiers under the command of Captain John Furey and set out early in the morning of June 16. Crook had his men primed for quick movement. Each soldier carried rations for four days, one blanket, and 100 rounds of ammunition. Infantrymen were mounted on mules that had been freed from their pack-train duties.

Crook moved northwest, with his men shooting buffalo along the way for additional provisions. That night, the sizable contingent bivouacked on the Rosebud and was under way again by daylight on the Seventeenth. Crazy Horse, well aware of the approaching army, was prepared for what he hoped would be a defining victory.

Crook brought his men to a halt about 8:00 A.M. for a rest. The men unsaddled their horses, and Crook joined some of his officers in a game of whist, unaware that Crazy Horse and about 750 warriors were approaching. Suddenly gunshots were heard. Crows and Shoshones rushed to meet the attack by a portion of the Lakota and Cheyenne force, succeeding in preventing the initial attack from over-running Crook's camp. As the attackers fell back, pursued by Crook's Indian allies, Crazy Horse, leading about 200 men, attacked east of the initial assault.

Captain Anson Mills' cavalry then succeeded in stopping Crazy Horse's attack, and the Oglala leader ordered his men to withdraw and move farther west. Near the site of the original engagement, Lieutenant Colonel William Royal led another cavalry charge, but Crazy Horse recognized that Royal had seriously extended the line of Crook's troops and had played into Crazy Horse's strategy of attacking and withdrawing so as to isolate segments of the enemy. Royal faced disaster, as Crook also recognized: He ordered two infantry companies to reinforce Royal.

Crook had sent Mills and his Third Cavalry, along with Captain Henry Noyes' Second Cavalry, to attack a village that, in fact, was not where Crook thought it was. With Crazy Horse's men threatening to encircle and wipe out Royal's five cavalry companies, Crook recalled Mills and Noyes. Royal ordered his men, who had dismounted to establish a defensive position, to remount. Crazy Horse's warriors charged, creating havoc among Royal's men. Supported by heavy infantry fire, however, Royal was able to break away.

It was then about 2:30 in the afternoon. Intensive fighting had been occur-ring for nearly six hours, and both sides were tired. Crook had lost 9 men, with more than 20 wounded; the Lakotas and Cheyennes had suffered perhaps 20 fatalities plus an unknown number of wounded.[14] The Lakota and Cheyenne losses may have been higher than these estimates, however, as Crazy Horse later put the number at 38.

The Lakota and Cheyenne forces withdrew, and Crook claimed victory as possessor of the battlefield. Nevertheless, the battle had neutralized him as an active participant in the three-pronged plan to subdue Sitting Bull and Crazy Horse. A little more than one week later, the U.S. military would suffer a his-toric loss at Little Bighorn; at that time, Crook, unbeknownst to Terry and Gibbon, would be far from the action near Tongue River in northern Wyoming awaiting reinforcements.

Crazy Horse, Sitting Bull, and their men had stopped Crook's advance, thereby keeping him away from their village, had withdrawn when they wished, and had driven Crook to the south. The Battle of the Rosebud had not been the backbreaking defeat for Crook that Crazy Horse had hoped for, but it was, at least from a tactical standpoint, a significant defeat for Crook.

The implications of Crook's failure to pursue his attackers for more than the seven miles that Bourke notes in his book became clear after Custer's defeat, leading Crook to react defensively regarding his decisions, especially in light of criticism from other officers. General Philip Sheridan, clearly critical, wrote in his official annual report to the Secretary of War, "The victory was barren of results, as . . . General Crook was unable to pursue the enemy . . . considering

The Fight Where the Girl Saved Her Brother

One of the heroes of the Battle of the Rosebud was Buffalo Calf Road Woman, sister of the Cheyenne chief Comes in Sight. Her brother's horse was shot, a hind leg broken, as he swung about after a charge against the infantry. A Cheyenne warrior, Little Hawk, later described in an interview how Buffalo Calf Road Woman saw her brother on foot with soldiers shooting at him and raced forward on her gray horse despite the shooting and the enemy scouts nearby. Comes in Sight jumped onto the horse in back of his sister, and they rode to safety, zigzagging to avoid being hit.

The Lakotas and Cheyennes immediately started chanting in response to this brave act. So impressed were they that the encounter usually referred to in historical writing as the Battle of the Rosebud was known to the Cheyennes as the Battle Where the Girl Saved Her Brother.

Little written documentation remains regarding the heroic sister, who also is reported to have fought at the Battle of the Little Bighorn. A recent fictional treatment of her story based on oral and written sources with fictional filling in of the gaps is Rosemary and Joseph Agonito's novel *Buffalo Calf Road Woman: The Story of a Warrior of the Little Bighorn* (2005).

himself too weak to make any movement until additional troops reached him." As Bill Yenne has argued in his *Indian Wars: The Campaign for the American West*, Crook "had suffered the worst defeat of his otherwise brilliant career as an Indian fighter."[15]

The Battle of the Rosebud, despite Crook's claim, would greatly enhance Crazy Horse's reputation as a military leader among both his own people and the U.S. military. A rumor began circulating among the latter that Crazy Horse, passing for white, had attended West Point, learning his military tactics there. The rumor, of course, expressed a common Euro-American assumption that a savage Indian could not possibly outthink U.S. forces without ultimately receiving his ideas from those same Euro-Americans.

Custer and Little Bighorn

In the middle of the afternoon of Sunday, June 25, Lieutenant Colonel George Armstrong Custer, leading the Seventh Cavalry, had his first clear look at a large Indian village across the Little Bighorn. Conservative estimates have fixed the size at more than 1,000 lodges with 7,000 inhabitants, including 2,000 males capable of military action. Still, Custer's primary fear seems to have been that the Indians would flee, depriving him of the victory he so desperately wanted.

Already, Custer had split his command, sending Captain Frederick Benteen with three companies and Captain Thomas McDougall with the pack train and another company south to explore for other hostile Indians. In addition, he sent Major Marcus Reno with three companies across the river to attack

Repeating Rifles

The Lakota and Cheyenne victory at Little Bighorn was the result of several factors, one of which was the repeating rifle. Kingsley Bray, author of *Crazy Horse: A Lakota Life*, has estimated that perhaps as many as 200 warriors had repeating rifles at the battle. That represents only 10 percent of the total number of American Indians who fought Custer, Reno, and the rest of the Seventh Cavalry, but is a large enough number to have had a major impact.

The guns that proved so effective were the Henry rifle, invented by Benjamin Tyler Henry in the late 1850s, and its successor, the Winchester, named after Oliver Winchester, majority owner of the company. After development of the Winchester in 1866, the owner also renamed the company after himself: from the New Haven Arms Company to the Winchester Repeating Arms Company. The 1873 Winchester became popularly known (from a Euro-American perspective) as "the gun that won the West."

A breech-loading, lever-action carbine with .44 caliber rimfire metallic cartridges and a magazine that could hold 16 cartridges, the Henry was a devastating weapon. The Winchesters were even better, especially given that they were less inclined to fire accidentally.

Crazy Horse apparently owned several Winchester rifles and used one at Little Bighorn. White Bull, Sitting Bull's nephew, also had a repeating rifle. Another nephew, One Bull, engaged in a ceremonial exchange of weapons with his uncle, giving Sitting Bull his Winchester in exchange for his shield, bow, and arrows as fighting began. Standard issue for the military remained the single-shot Springfield: This serviceable weapon could be quickly reloaded and had excellent range and accuracy, but was no match for the Winchester in close-up fighting. In an ironic twist, many of the men fighting Custer received their repeating rifles from the U.S. government through Indian agents, intended for use in hunting.

the village from the south. Custer's actions were in direct opposition to his orders, which were to move south along the Rosebud and then turn west to follow the Little Bighorn north on June 26, when Terry and Gibbon were expected to be reaching the Little Bighorn valley. Had Custer been patient, followed orders, and waited for the arrival of Terry and Gibbon, the outcome of the battle may have been much different. The results also might have been different had Custer not split his command. According to Bourke, who described the battle in his book *On the Border with Crook*, the consensus Indian judgment was that from the moment Custer divided his forces his defeat was inevitable.

Custer remained east of Little Bighorn with five companies, assuring Reno that he would support him, although he never did, perhaps because events moved so quickly once the first shots were fired. When Custer saw the size of the village, he quickly realized his error in sending Benteen and McDougall away and dispatched messengers to recall them. Neither, however, would return in time to save Custer and the men with him.

The villagers were no sooner warned of the approaching soldiers than Reno's men, drawn up in a skirmish line, opened fire. The time was about 3:00 P.M. according to John Gray, whose carefully reconstructed chronology in *Centennial Campaign: The Sioux War of 1876* is the basis for the times mentioned here. Crazy Horse applied his paint, fixed a single hawk feather in his hair, and grabbed a Winchester rifle and war club. He was determined to prepare properly for combat despite the attack, even consulting with a medicine man before entering the fray. According to a cousin, Standing Bear, Crazy Horse took so much time in preparations "that many of his warriors became impatient."[16]

By the time Crazy Horse entered the battle, Reno had realized that attacking the huge village was a suicidal act and ordered his men into a nearby timber to avoid being surrounded in the open. With their ammunition running out, Reno then ordered his men to mount and race for the river. According to Iron Hawk, a Hunkpapa, and Red Feather, an Oglala who was Crazy Horse's brother-in-law, this was the moment when Crazy Horse and his warriors arrived. Various reports have Crazy Horse killing two of the soldiers as they attempted to escape, although the accounts are impossible to verify. Bourke's book includes an account of Crazy Horse tossing aside his rifle, hitting a mounted soldier with his war club, and jumping on the fallen soldier's horse.

Reno's men charged for the Little Bighorn, with the survivors crossing back over the river and taking up a defensive position east of it on a bluff later named Reno Hill. The time was shortly after 4:00 P.M. From this position, they fended off the Indians' attacks, unaware of what was transpiring with Custer farther north. In fact, what probably saved them was that their opponents' attention quickly turned to Custer. Benteen arrived at Reno's position about 4:20 P.M., and the pack train followed an hour later.

Crazy Horse also had turned his attention to the soldiers farther north. Although warriors already were confronting Custer's men east of the river, Crazy Horse did not yet cross. Instead, he moved farther downstream (north of the village) to cross the water so that he would be positioned between Custer and the women, children, and other noncombatants and could prevent an attack on them. According to his cousin Flying Hawk, Crazy Horse started firing as soon as he crossed the Little Bighorn, hitting a soldier with each shot (likely something of an exaggeration on his cousin's part).[17]

At that point, Custer had reunited the five companies that he kept with him. As Crazy Horse employed a mixture of tactics—sometimes sending his men to infiltrate the enemy area, other times charging—Custer once again divided his force. The right wing under Captain Myles Keogh consisted of Companies C, I, and L; the left wing under Captain George Yates included Companies E and F, with Custer accompanying Yates. Custer apparently wanted to cross the river. Facing strong opposition, however, he turned north, perhaps looking for another place to ford the Little Bighorn. He left Keogh behind him to wait for Benteen and the pack train and provide a defense against the warriors massing from the village.

Company L under Lieutenant James Calhoun (Custer's brother-in-law) established a skirmish line on what would become known as Calhoun Hill, with Companies C and I kept in reserve. Company C charged south, but strong opposition forced it back to Calhoun's position. Crazy Horse, meanwhile, was flanking Calhoun, reaching a position several hundred yards northeast of him. Company L, joined by members of Company C, faced heavy fire from a variety of positions, including Crazy Horse's men. Then a charge led by Gall of the Hunkpapas overran the hill, with the survivors desperately trying to reach Company I. Crazy Horse and his warriors joined in pursuit.

Crazy Horse, in an act of great bravery, rode along Company I's line, urging his men on. He Dog recalled how Crazy Horse rode through the line, cutting it in two. Some of the soldiers raced for the river, only to be killed there. The rest were overrun, with some two dozen managing to make it to Custer for the final stand.

Custer and Yates reached Cemetery Ridge in what now is the Custer National Cemetery, then moved into a basin below Last Stand Hill (also known as Custer Hill). Faced with increasing numbers of Indians converging on them, they moved up onto Last Stand Hill. Approximately 100 men reached the hill, including the Keogh survivors. Then about 45 of them raced for the river, all of whom were killed immediately or shortly after taking refuge in Deep Ravine, which runs south and west of the current Visitor Center.

Crazy Horse realized that the final victory was at hand and raced his horse forward, circling the hill. Large numbers of his men rushed the remaining soldiers, and reportedly Crazy Horse pursued and killed a soldier who attempted to run away toward the east. The last man fell on Last Stand Hill about 4:45 P.M., with little more than an hour having passed since the first shots had been fired across the river at Custer's men. He Dog later affirmed that about two hours passed from Reno's first shots until the end. The Seventh Cavalry fatalities totaled 263 when fighting concluded the next day, 210 of them from the Custer–Yates–Keogh companies. Indian fatalities have been estimated at between 30 and 100.

Reno's men endured continued firing through the night and into the morning. When Terry and Gibbon were spotted approaching the next day, the fighting broke off. By evening, the Indian forces had departed.

CHANGING FORTUNES

Crazy Horse's Reputation

The U.S. military and general public now viewed Crazy Horse as at least the second most significant figure among the Plains Indians, after Sitting Bull, but perhaps superior to the great Hunkpapa leader as a military tactician. His performance first against Crook and then at Little Bighorn bred considerable respect for his ability to employ a variety of military tactics: isolating units, decoying them, infiltrating, using a frontal assault, altering strategy at precisely the right moment. He also was acclaimed for his personal bravery.

Among the Lakotas, Crazy Horse was clearly the principal war leader, second in stature to Sitting Bull, with whom the younger leader had developed a close and mutually respectful relationship. They formed a remarkable team: Perhaps the Indian Wars saw none better.

However, as the nonreservation groups faced increasingly difficult challenges on the battlefield and strong pressure to join their former allies at the Red Cloud and Spotted Tail Agencies in northwestern Nebraska, Crazy Horse steadily lost support for resisting the U.S. government. The next nine months presented Crazy Horse with dual adversaries—one external, the other internal: threats from the U.S. military and the desire of ever more Lakotas to leave their old ways and go into the agencies in hopes of realizing a peaceful existence. Before long, Crazy Horse would seem like a voice crying in the wilderness.

Slim Buttes

By September 8, General Crook, who after receiving reinforcements had taken the field again in August, was running seriously low on rations. Crook dispatched to Deadwood in present-day western South Dakota a pack train of mules, escorted by 150 men under the command of Captain Anson Mills. On September 8, near Slim Buttes, Mills, with Frank Grouard scouting, discovered a Lakota village consisting of 37 tipis. Early the next morning, Mills attacked. Many of the villagers managed to flee the 20 miles to Crazy Horse's camp. Crook soon arrived on the scene. Late in the afternoon, Crazy Horse and others from his camp arrived and began firing from the surrounding bluffs down onto the soldiers. The fighting continued into the evening when the Oglalas gradually withdrew, although sporadic fighting resumed the following morning. Crook lost three men at Slim Buttes while killing an indeterminate number of Indians, including women, children, and a prominent Lakota leader, Iron Plume (also known as American Horse). Enraged by the recent death of Custer and his men, the soldiers reportedly scalped some of the dead.

Crook moved out the next day, moving south to Deadwood in the Black Hills before heading to Camp Robinson in Nebraska. The battle signaled the Indians' loss of the Black Hills, less because of the outcome of the Slim Buttes conflict itself than because of the area's rapid settlement by miners and mining towns. In fact, almost at the same time as the victors of Little Bighorn were making their final military effort to retain the Black Hills, Lakota leaders at Pine Ridge Agency were signing over title to the sacred area.

Battle of Wolf Mountain

Throughout the fall of 1876 and into the winter, Crazy Horse tried to prevent defections to the agencies and attempted to gather sufficient forces to reclaim the military initiative. He turned his attention especially to General Nelson "Bear Coat" Miles, who had begun constructing a military base at the mouth of Tongue River in August 1876.

Crazy Horse planned to revisit the tactic he had used so effectively against Captain Fetterman 10 years earlier. A contingent of Oglala and Cheyenne warriors would serve as a decoy to lure Miles out of the Tongue River Cantonment, setting up an ambush that would wipe out his forces. The decoy group arrived at Miles' base in late December and stole about 150 head of cattle. Miles sent three infantry companies in pursuit, which recaptured about two-thirds of the cattle. Miles subsequently dispatched four additional companies and assumed command of the force, which numbered 436 men of the Fifth and Twenty-Second Infantry. He also had at his disposal two artillery pieces that he covered with canvas in wagon boxes to keep them hidden from Indian scouts.

As Miles approached Crazy Horse's village, the tipis were hurriedly taken down and the village started moving, drawing Miles forward up the Tongue River. Crazy Horse decided on an ambush from fixed positions as the best way to succeed against the oncoming infantry. By the morning of January 8, Cheyenne and Oglala warriors were positioned along bluffs at what was known as Wolf Mountain near present Birney, Montana, in the southeastern corner of the state.

The terrain was rugged, a foot of snow lay on the ground, and Miles's troops were 300 miles from the nearest settlement. Miles notes in his memoir, *Serving the Republic*, that he was acutely aware of the danger to his men, for "defeat would mean disaster and annihilation, and it would have been weeks before our fate would have been known." Miles, and certainly his men, were reminded of Custer's fate, with Miles stating that the attackers were determined to succeed in "another massacre" and noting that once the battle began they could be heard yelling to the infantrymen that "'you have had your last breakfast.'"[18]

The soldiers were, indeed, at breakfast when the Indians appeared on the bluffs. Miles' artillery opened fire from across the river, with one of the shells killing Crazy Horse's mount. Accounts are not definitive, but he may have had as many as nine horses shot out from under him over the years. Jumping onto another horse, the Oglala warrior led a charge across the river to the east side, taking up a position on Belly Butte.

Captain James Casey led a company of infantry up the ridge, and Crazy Horse and his men rushed to meet them, engaging briefly in hand-to-hand combat. The Cheyenne and Oglala force then withdrew to join other warriors farther south. As the battle reached noon, five hours after it had begun, and the weather worsened, turning into a blizzard, Crazy Horse and his men disengaged. Casey, along with Captain Edmond Butler and First Lieutenant Robert McDonald, received the Medal of Honor for bravery during the battle.

Miles could claim victory because he retained control of the battlefield, but that development, as with such engagements as the Battle at the Rosebud, was the result of differing strategies rather than an objective determinant of victory. In fact, the encounter was largely a standoff, with neither side achieving its overall objective of a decisive, war-ending battle.

End of a War

Sitting Bull and Crazy Horse reunited in the middle of January along the Tongue River. The meeting, however, was not a prelude to the great reunification of the Lakotas that Crazy Horse desired. In addition to growing sentiment against continued warfare, Sitting Bull was preparing to move toward Canada. After his departure, the Oglala leadership decided to send Red Sack to Red Cloud Agency to reopen dialogue with the agency Oglalas. Despite Crazy Horse's opposition, which included attempts to take the horses of the departing groups and physically intimidate them, Lakotas from several bands, including Oglalas, left in late January, as did a group of Cheyennes under Little Wolf. Others imitated Sitting Bull and started for Canada.

By early February, only 10 tipis of followers remained with Crazy Horse. His party included his wife, Black Shawl; his brother-in-law, Red Feather; his father, Worm; and his stepmothers. Black Shawl was in declining health, suffering from severe coughing; her ailment was later diagnosed as tuberculosis.

Representatives from General Miles arrived at the major Oglala–Cheyenne village near the Bighorn Mountains on February 1, resulting in a deputation from the village leaving for Miles' base to continue discussions. Meanwhile, a party from Red Cloud Agency led by Hunts the Enemy, a nephew of Red Cloud, had started north to meet with the nontreaty hunting bands. They were treated courteously by Crazy Horse at his camp on Powder River, but he made no specific commitments except to send them on to the main village with the promise that he would abide by what was decided there. After an Oglala consensus developed that further discussions should occur at Red Cloud Agency, Crazy Horse agreed, largely because he had little choice, and said that he would go in to the agency as well during the spring. For three weeks, Crazy Horse largely withdrew from society, apparently meditating on a future that must have looked increasingly bleak and likely seeking some sort of vision to give him hope. Whatever vision he received appears to have been directed especially toward healing his wife. He is reported to have appealed through his spiritual guardian, the red-tailed hawk, and received from the spotted eagle spiritual powers transmitted through later generations on Pine Ridge Reservation as a process of eagle doctoring to treat tuberculosis.

Crazy Horse's Surrender

On or around April 3, 1877, Crazy Horse reached Bear Butte, near Sturgis, South Dakota, where it is generally believed he had been born. He was surrounded by about 155 lodges, mainly occupied by Oglalas. The decision was made to go to the Oglala agency, and word was sent to Red Cloud, who at the time was on his way toward Bear Butte with a peace delegation. The Northerners (or Northerns), as they were called by government officials because of their desire to remain free in the north, began their trek on April 16 and about April 20 met Red Cloud and his delegation. Red Cloud promised that no arrests would take place but stated that the surrender would require the Northerners to relinquish their weapons.

Lieutenant J. Wesley Rosenquest left Camp Robinson near Red Cloud Agency in northwestern Nebraska on April 30 with 10 wagons of rations and a herd of beef cattle to meet the travelers, who had run out of food. Arriving the next day, Rosenquest was greeted politely by Crazy Horse. The trip resumed on May 3. On May 6, Crazy Horse and his companions, within a few miles of the agency, met a party headed by Lieutenant William P. Clark, military commander of the two agencies along the White River and an aide to General Crook. Crazy Horse shook hands with Clark, Rosenquest, and several others, declaring his commitment to peace.

Crazy Horse reached the agency about 2:00 P.M., leading his warriors but preceded by Red Cloud and the agency Indians who rode with Lieutenant Clark. As they arrived, Crazy Horse and his warriors sang a peace chant with the women and children coming in on the refrain. The women then started setting up camp while Crazy Horse and his men surrendered their horses. Then they started turning in their guns, with Crazy Horse leading the way by laying down a rifle. According to Bourke, some of the leaders placed small sticks on the ground to symbolize the number of guns they possessed and to indicate whether they were pistols or rifles to facilitate Clark's gathering of guns from the tipis, including three Winchester rifles from Crazy Horse.

That night Frank Grouard accepted his old friend's invitation to supper and took with him Lieutenant Bourke. As despondent as Crazy Horse surely must have felt, he conducted himself not only with dignity but also with courtesy and graciousness. In *On the Border with Crook*, Bourke offers a remarkable description of Crazy Horse, beginning with a visual depiction, then proceeding to Crazy Horse's apparent state of mind, and continuing to a broader view of the great war leader's values:

> I saw before me a man who looked quite young, not over thirty years old, five feet eight inches high, lithe and sinewy, with a scar in the face. The expression of his countenance was one of quiet dignity, but morose, dogged, tenacious, and melancholy. He behaved with stolidity, like a man who realized he had to give in to Fate, but would do so as sullenly as possible. . . . All Indians gave him a high reputation for courage and generosity. In advancing upon an enemy, none of his warriors were allowed to pass him. He had made hundreds of friends by his charity towards the poor, as it was a point of honor with him never to keep anything for himself, excepting weapons of war. I never heard an Indian mention his name save in terms of respect.[19]

LIFE IN CAPTIVITY

Political Jealousies

Crazy Horse could hardly have been expected to welcome what amounted to captivity or to quickly give over all hope of once again living in freedom. Yet he appears to have tried his best to maintain his commitment to live in peace. The greatest obstacle that he had to overcome at Red Cloud Agency turned out not to be mistreatment by the U.S. military but rather political jealousies within his own Oglala community. Such jealously especially emanated from

Red Cloud and other agency Indians who resented the great respect afforded Crazy Horse and perhaps feared repercussions to themselves from any "non-progressive" attitudes or behavior that he might manifest.

The military wanted to integrate Crazy Horse into reservation life as quickly and thoroughly as possible—a goal that Red Cloud apparently shared at first, until that integration threatened his own position of primacy among the Oglalas. Within days of Crazy Horse's surrender, both Lieutenant Charles Johnson, military agent at Red Cloud Agency, and Lieutenant Clark were urging him to become an army scout. Crazy Horse finally acceded to the request. He was formally accepted into the scouts on May 12 at Camp Robinson near the agency, becoming one of the three top sergeants among the scouts, along with Spotted Tail and Red Cloud.

On May 26, Lieutenant Colonel Luther P. Bradley became commander of Camp Robinson and the Black Hills, replacing Colonel Ranald S. Mackenzie, who was transferred to the southern plains. As the summer progressed, several important events were planned for the agencies: a series of Sun Dances, a buffalo hunt, and a trip to Washington, D.C., by a delegation of Indian leaders to meet with the new president, Rutherford B. Hayes. All of these events would affect Crazy Horse's life over the next few months.

The first Sun Dance may have occurred in late June (although the chronology of the Sun Dances that summer remains unclear) and included a reenactment of the Battle at Little Bighorn with northern village warriors (that is, the Northerners of Crazy Horse's village northeast of Red Cloud Agency) acting the part of the victors and the agency Indians performing as Custer's men. Given the tensions already existing between the two groups of Oglalas, that scenario seemed ready-made for trouble. Indeed, trouble did break out as the sides began to play their roles too realistically, until the action was broken up by Clark. At both this Sun Dance and the subsequent ones, Crazy Horse's importance was very much in evidence. In addition, the sacred Calf Pipe was transferred to Crazy Horse's village, angering Red Cloud and other reservation Oglalas.

In the 1960s, Alfred Ribman and James Chase in Morning, both elderly at that time, passed along accounts they had been told of the final Sun Dance. According to them, the Dance had especially honored Crazy Horse. It included five men sacrificing pieces of flesh for their revered leader and five large rocks arranged in a V with the opening facing the rising sun—also dedicated to Crazy Horse.

The army scouts at the agencies were reorganized in July, forming five companies but with northern and agency Indians integrated into the companies. Crazy Horse was made first sergeant of Company C. The sergeants under him included Little Big Man, who increasingly opposed Crazy Horse for leadership of the northern faction and who would play a leading role in the war leader's death. The reorganization emphasized Crazy Horse's status as at least an equal to Red Cloud.

Military authorities were anxious to have Crazy Horse travel to Washington, D.C., viewing the trip as a way to impress upon potentially resistant Indian leaders both the power and the fatherly affection of the U.S. government. As an inducement to complying with the request, Lieutenant Clark hinted that governmental authorities wanted to make Crazy Horse chief of all the Oglalas, a political carrot that held no sway with Crazy Horse, who was generally quite apolitical, and certainly won him no friends among the agency Indians.

Crazy Horse avoided committing to the trip until he was assured that the promised buffalo hunt would take place. General Crook, also pushing the Washington trip, hosted a council at Red Cloud Agency on July 27 and promised that the buffalo hunt would take place no later than August 5. Dr. James Irwin, recently installed as civilian agent at Red Cloud Agency, offered to provide three cattle and other provisions for the feast that customarily followed such a council. Young Man Afraid of His Horse proposed holding the feast at Crazy Horse's village, which greatly upset Red Cloud, who believed that the newcomers should come to him for the event. Red Cloud sent two messengers to make his case to Irwin and also to warn him that Crazy Horse wanted to use the buffalo hunt as a way to escape from the agency and return to war. Clearly, Red Cloud had embarked on a plan to marginalize Crazy Horse and sow seeds of deep distrust among the government officials toward him.

As the Washington trip moved forward slowly, the hunt was pushed back. Spotted Tail, among others, urged cancellation of the hunt, joining Red Cloud in warning that Crazy Horse intended to return to war or perhaps join Sitting Bull in Canada. Meanwhile, Crazy Horse had become convinced that the Washington trip was merely a ploy to isolate and imprison or kill him. He described to Frank Grouard a dream in which he stood on a mountain with an eagle soaring above him before it fell dead. The eagle, Crazy Horse believed, represented himself.

Nellie Larrabee

Amid the swirling currents of political intrigue, a personal relationship developed for Crazy Horse. It involved 18-year-old Helen Larrabee (also spelled Laravie), better known as Nellie, a daughter of a French trader, Joe Larrabee, and his Cheyenne wife. Little is known about the details of the relationship, although Nellie apparently had plenty of suitors, including an Oglala named Little Bear. Lieutenant Clark, according to translators Billy Garnett and Baptiste "Big Bat" Pourier, encouraged Crazy Horse, likely anticipating that a serious domestic relationship might make him more accepting of life at the agency.

Black Shawl, of whom Crazy Horse was consistently supportive, readily accepted the young woman, perhaps viewing her as a useful helpmate to Crazy Horse, especially in light of her own continuing medical problems. Black Shawl's ill health had persisted despite ongoing treatment by agency surgeon Valentine McGillycuddy. Consequently, Nellie moved in with Crazy Horse as his second wife—a marriage that would end 30 days later with the death of her husband.

Nellie came in for strong criticism from interpreter and guide Billy Garnett. In a 1907 interview conducted by Judge Eli Ricker, Garnett blamed "this insidious and evil woman" for sowing distrust in her husband toward government officials, especially concerning the Washington, D.C., trip, which she suggested was a trap.[20]

The Nez Perce and Frank Grouard's Mistranslation

As the summer of 1877 advanced, to the north the great Nez Perce leader Chief Joseph was accompanying his people on a desperate journey to reach Canada to avoid being forced onto an Idaho reservation. General Crook decided to use Lakota warriors against the Nez Perce. He naturally turned to the greatest of Lakota war leaders, Crazy Horse, for assistance. Lieutenant Clark conveyed the decision to Crazy Horse, and on August 31 the two men met to discuss the war leader's participation. Crazy Horse, accompanied by his close friend Touch the Clouds, High Bear, and about 20 warriors, entered Clark's quarters. Frank Grouard served as interpreter.

Crazy Horse clearly was reluctant, especially as military officials had not yet made good on their promised buffalo hunt. He explained that upon arriving at Red Cloud Agency, he had promised to remain peaceful. Yet despite his expressed misgivings, Crazy Horse finally yielded. According to Dr. McGillycuddy, who received reports of the proceedings from individuals who were in attendance (reportedly including the translator Louis Bordeaux), Crazy Horse stated that "we came in for peace, but now that the Great Father asks our help, we will go north and fight until there is not a Nez Perce left." According to McGillycuddy, Grouard misinterpreted Crazy Horse's words to say that "we will go north and fight until not a white man is left."[21]

The misinterpretation immediately sent the meeting into turmoil, with Clark and Crazy Horse growing increasingly angry at each other. Grouard, uncomfortable with the hostile environment, left the meeting. His replacement, Billy Garnett, was instructed by Clark to ask Crazy Horse once again whether he would fight against the Nez Perce. By this time, tempers had risen far enough that Crazy Horse was in no mood to accommodate Clark and flatly refused. Clark, in turn, informed Lieutenant Colonel Bradley that Crazy Horse, Touch the Clouds, and High Bear were planning to leave and resume their warfare.

The reasons for Grouard's distortion remain unclear. Incompetence as a translator is an unlikely possibility given Grouard's many years spent with the Lakotas. Bordeaux accused Grouard of deliberately distorting Crazy Horse's words. Grouard was viewed by many—including Sitting Bull, although apparently not by Crazy Horse—as untrustworthy after he joined the U.S. military in actions against men who had earlier befriended him. Bordeaux, as noted in E. A. Brininstool's lengthy article "How Crazy Horse Died" in the journal *Nebraska History*, argued that fear of possible future retribution led Grouard to try to get rid of Crazy Horse.

Woman Dress's Deception

General Crook ordered all loyal Oglalas to attend a council meeting on White Clay Creek south of Spotted Tail Agency on September 3; he also extended an invitation to Crazy Horse. Lieutenant Clark dispatched He Dog as an intermediary, and Crazy Horse's old friend had his wife prepare a feast to which he invited both Crazy Horse and officers from Camp Robinson. Crazy Horse, however, declined to engage in further talks. Crook persisted with a personal invitation, and Crazy Horse relented, informing Clark that he would attend. This change of heart was unwelcome news to those agency Indians who did not want the unpredictable and independent-minded war leader back in the good graces of U.S. officials so he could resume his earlier position of authority at the agencies.

As Crook and Clark were en route in an army ambulance, they met Garnett and Pourier talking with Woman Dress. Woman Dress, a cousin of Red Cloud and a Clark trustee who regularly spied on Crazy Horse for the officer, warned that Crazy Horse planned to pick a quarrel with Crook at the council and then stab him. Garnett and Pourier (the latter was related to Woman Dress through marriage) vouched for his truthfulness. Supposedly, Woman Dress had received the information from Lone Bear, whose brother, Little Wolf (both of them also Clark informers), had overheard Crazy Horse speaking of his plan in his tipi. The story, of course, was completely concocted. Nevertheless, Clark convinced Crook to return to Red Cloud Agency with the feigned excuse that he had been called back. Clark then sent Garnett to the council with orders to summon loyal chiefs to Camp Robinson.

That afternoon, the contingent, including Red Cloud, appeared at Colonel Bradley's headquarters to meet with Crook. Their conclusion was that Crazy Horse should be killed. According to Lieutenant Bourke, Crook rejected that proposal as murder, opting instead for having him arrested by loyal Indians.

After the meeting, a group led by Red Shirt that included Little Bear, the previous suitor of Nellie Larrabee, approached Crazy Horse's tipi and demanded that Nellie be given back to them. The visit apparently was an attempt to provoke a confrontation that might lead to killing Crazy Horse. However, Worm came out and informed the group that his son was not at home. The group then killed Crazy Horse's favorite horse and took Nellie with them, settling for a deeply humiliating insult to the absent Crazy Horse.

THE DEATH OF CRAZY HORSE

The Arrest

Colonel Bradley believed that the military should be involved in the arrest, and General Crook apparently acquiesced to his request. On the morning of September 4, after Crook had left to catch a train on his way to try capturing Chief Joseph, Bradley sent out a force of about 400 Indians and 8 companies of the Third Cavalry. Clarke led the Indian scouts, and Major Julius Mason commanded the cavalry.

Crazy Horse, informed of the threat by Red Feather and perhaps others, gathered his horses. With Black Shawl and two of his most loyal supporters, Kicking Bear and Shell Boy, he started toward Spotted Tail Agency. In the middle of the afternoon, they reached a small Oglala village near the agency, where Black Shawl's widowed mother and uncle lived. There Crazy Horse left his wife and continued. Increasing numbers of men joined the party, both supporters and opponents of Crazy Horse—a highly volatile mix that could lead to Crazy Horse's death at any moment. Afraid for the safety of his friend, Touch the Clouds hurried out from Spotted Tail Agency to ride beside him.

Camp Sheridan commander Captain Daniel Burke and Spotted Tail's military agent, Lieutenant Jesse Lee, asked Crazy Horse to go to Camp Sheridan with them. At the camp, Crazy Horse explained that he had left Red Cloud Agency to avoid trouble and expressed his wish to remain at Spotted Tail Agency. He also said that he had been willing to fight with the military against the Nez Perce despite his wish to live at peace.

A dispatch from Colonel Bradley then arrived ordering the arrest of Crazy Horse and his return to Camp Robinson. Burke and Lee, better understanding the tinderbox that could so easily be lit and perhaps sympathizing with Crazy Horse's position, tried to finesse the order by persuading Crazy Horse to return voluntarily to Camp Robinson. With promises to support his move to Spotted Tail and assurances that Agent Lee would accompany him to Camp Robinson, Crazy Horse agreed to make the journey the following morning. That night, perhaps sensing that his life was closing, Crazy Horse talked much of death with Touch the Clouds.

Early the following morning, September 5, another dispatch from Colonel Bradley arrived, again complicating matters. It required that Crazy Horse be brought in as a prisoner. Again Burke tried to balance obedience with prudence while attempting to keep his word to Crazy Horse. Burke responded that Crazy Horse would arrive in an ambulance with three scout sergeants: Swift Bear, High Bear, and Touch the Clouds.

As the party prepared to leave, Crazy Horse asked to ride a horse, as traveling in the ambulance would make him ill. Lee agreed, taking a considerable personal risk in deviating even more from Bradley's orders. The group also included the interpreter Bordeaux, supporters of Crazy Horse, and varying numbers of scouts to ensure Crazy Horse's compliance. According to Lee, Crazy Horse finally realized he was truly a prisoner when after lunch he went to relieve himself and discovered a scout following him.

At one point, Lee fell asleep, and on wakening discovered that Crazy Horse was gone. He sent scouts to catch up with him. In fact, Crazy Horse was just a short distance ahead watering his horse and talking with another group of Lakotas, from whom he probably received the revolver that he displayed later while resisting being jailed.

"It Is Good; He Has Looked for Death, and It Has Come."

Crazy Horse expected to meet with Colonel Bradley upon arriving at Camp Robinson, but that was not to be. Bradley ordered Officer of the Day Captain James Kennington to secure Crazy Horse in the guardhouse, with Lieutenant Henry Lemly's Company E assigned to guard the building. Then Bradley and Lieutenant Clark inexplicably retired to their own quarters.

Crazy Horse was escorted to the guardhouse with Little Big Man holding onto his sleeve. At that point, the war leader did not seem to know the sort of building that awaited him. Agent Lee tried hard to press the case for allowing Crazy Horse to speak with Bradley. Lee solicited permission from the adjutant, Lieutenant Fred Calhoun, to meet with Bradley, but Bradley refused Lee's petition.

Trying to put the best face on the situation and avoid a confrontation, Lee told Crazy Horse that it was too late in the evening for the meeting. He then relayed Bradley's promise that Crazy Horse would not be hurt if he went with Kennington. Kennington led Crazy Horse toward the guardhouse by his right hand with Little Big Man holding the prisoner's left arm. Around the guardhouse swarmed hundreds of Indians, both supporters of Crazy Horse and opponents.

Crazy Horse was expecting a building in which he could spend the night in reasonable comfort, but once inside the first room he could see the door leading into the jail area. Turning Bear, who just a moment before had offered to spend the night with Crazy Horse, now also realized the true nature of the building and raced outside yelling that it was a jail. Crazy Horse pulled his arms free and reached for his revolver. A scout, Plenty Wolves, grabbed the gun, at which point Crazy Horse pulled out a knife. He also snatched a knife from Little Big Man and raced for the door.

Little Big Man grabbed onto Crazy Horse from behind, receiving a cut on his left hand and another in his arm. Crazy Horse reached the outside running, with American Horse calling out to shoot him. Kennington also yelled out for the bystanders to kill Crazy Horse. Little Big Man again managed to take hold of Crazy Horse, but he broke free.

Accounts of what happened next differ. Some sources claim that Crazy Horse cut himself with his own knife, but it is now widely accepted based on first-hand accounts that a sentry twice struck Crazy Horse in the back with his bayonet. The sentry is usually identified as Private William Gentles. The severity of the first thrust may have been exacerbated by a sudden movement backward by Crazy Horse. The second thrust punctured his right lung.

As Crazy Horse lay on the ground mortally wounded, Touch the Clouds knelt beside him and tried to raise his head. He Dog covered Crazy Horse with a blanket, and Dr. McGillycuddy examined him, realizing that his condition was dire. Kennington, however, sought to carry out his original orders and have Crazy Horse carried into the guardhouse. His directive to that effect brought instant outcries from the surrounding Indians, who demanded that as an honored leader he not be imprisoned. Bat Pourier pleaded with Kennington to take Crazy Horse into the adjutant's office instead. After two trips by McGillycuddy to Bradley's quarters, the commander finally relented and permitted the dying Crazy Horse to be moved to the adjutant's office.

Throughout the following hours, Crazy Horse lay on blankets on the floor. Touch the Clouds, Bat Pourier, Louis Bordeaux, McGillycuddy, another surgeon named Charles Munn, Crazy Horse's father, Agent Lee, and a few other

Indians waited with him during part or all of the time that he lay dying. McGillycuddy administered morphine to reduce the pain, and Worm spoke about his son's greatness, blaming Red Cloud's and Spotted Tail's jealousy for what had befallen Crazy Horse.

At approximately 11:40 P.M., Crazy Horse, one of the greatest of Indian warriors, died. Touch the Clouds, looking down on his longtime friend, offered his own eulogy: "It is good; he has looked for death, and it has come."[22]

The Burial

The disposition of Crazy Horse's remains has been described in a multitude of ways, so that it is impossible to be certain of all the details. The body initially was transported to Worm's tipi so that he could perform the Ghost Owning ceremony, which included anointing Crazy Horse with red paint, cutting a lock of hair from his head (the lock was believed to contain a person's spirit), purifying the lock in smoke from burning sweet grass, and placing the hair within a Spirit Bundle. Some of Crazy Horse's supporters were distraught that in the turmoil of their leader's death, they had forgotten his admonition that if he were killed they should paint his body red and submerge him in water, which would bring him back to life. If they failed to do so, he had said, his bones would turn to stone.

What happened next has been variously reported. The most likely chain of events is that Worm then took his son to a site near Camp Sheridan where his remains, wrapped in a red blanket, were placed on a scaffold. As Lee records in his diary, after a few days, Worm expressed concern that cows might disturb his son's resting place, so the agent and a carpenter constructed a fence around the scaffold. According to Red Feather, an eagle visited the coffin each night, demonstrating that Crazy Horse's spiritual power remained with him in death. A less spiritual reason for the visit could be offered, of course: Eagles have long been associated with visiting fields of battle to eat the dead. A funeral reportedly was held on September 13, during which Crazy Horse was placed inside a coffin with a number of items, including a pipe, bow and arrows, guns, and foodstuffs. The coffin was placed on the scaffold, and a prized horse of Crazy Horse's was killed.

Other accounts have Worm performing the Ghost Owning ceremony with the body, which was then placed overnight on a platform in the branches of a "burial tree." Worm then supposedly took his son and buried him in a crack in a bluff, engineering a rock slide to hide the grave from view.

Alternative narratives have Worm taking Crazy Horse's remains with him on a travois when the agency Indians were forced to start their trek northward that would lead to permanent homes at Pine Ridge and Rosebud Reservations. That journey began for some of the agency Indians as early as October 25, although Worm apparently started his trek several days later. During the journey, by some accounts along Wounded Knee Creek (where a later, tragic battle effectively ended Lakota military action against the U.S. government), Worm may have given Crazy Horse his final burial.

Still other accounts posit multiple burials. Horn Chips claimed to have investigated the state of Crazy Horse's body and, having found it disturbed, reburied the body. In an interview in 1907, he told Ricker that he was the only person who knew where the Oglala leader was buried. Three years later, Horn Chips told Walter Mason Camp (a Chicago researcher on the Indian wars) that he participated in three burials of Crazy Horse. In contrast, Henry Standing Bear, son of Standing Bear and a maternal cousin of Crazy Horse, told Camp around 1910 that Worm buried his son by himself at night and told no one of the location of the grave.

Henry Standing Bear also offered what remains the most likely final word on whether Crazy Horse ever had his photograph taken, as some photographs allegedly of Crazy Horse have surfaced over the years. Henry Standing Bear asserted that Crazy Horse refused to have his "shadow" captured in photographs, an explanation reiterated by many others. The historical consensus remains that we have no visual image, photographic or otherwise, portraying the great war leader.

The Crazy Horse Memorial

One depiction of Crazy Horse continues to emerge out of a mountain in the Black Hills of South Dakota—the most impressive visual commemoration of any American Indian leader. Credit for this memorial belongs first of all to Henry Standing Bear, who as a Brulé chief welcomed the sculptor Korczak Ziolkowski to the Black Hills in 1940 to make the case for carving out a sculpture of Crazy Horse. At the time, Mount Rushmore was being adorned with the faces of several prominent figures in American history, and Henry Standing Bear and other Lakota leaders believed that there should be a memorial reminding people that American history also has included great Indian heroes.

Ziolkowski was seriously interested in the project and began to study the life of Crazy Horse in earnest. World War II interrupted his plans to create the memorial, however, as Ziolkowski volunteered and joined the military. He was wounded at Normandy in 1944. After the war, he turned down a request by the U.S. government to create war memorials in Europe and accepted the Crazy Horse project.

In 1946, Henry Standing Bear and Ziolkowski selected the 600-foot-high monolith that would become Crazy Horse's image, which the sculptor named Thunderhead Mountain. Ziolkowski purchased land nearby and created a model of the sculpture with Crazy Horse astride his horse and his left hand outstretched. Over the next few years, he continued his preparations for the massive project, which included building roads, erecting a studio home, constructing a 741-step staircase to the top of the mountain (6,740 feet above sea level), and establishing certain guiding principles (including rejection of both government funding and a personal salary).

The first blast occurred in 1948, and extensive work began the following year. Over the decades, the work progressed with Crazy Horse's visage slowly emerging from the stone. Ziolkowski died in 1982 at the age of 74, but his family continued, and still continues, his work and the great dream that he shared with generations of Lakotas, whose reverence for Crazy Horse's courage and leadership has endured.

Today visitors to the Black Hills can see the ongoing work on the Crazy Horse Memorial, visit the Indian Museum of North America and the Native American Educational and Cultural Center, and, if they wish, share in realizing the goals of Henry Standing Bear and Korczak Ziolkowski. Those goals include honoring the courage, generosity, leadership, and spirit of Crazy Horse; honoring the culture and heritage of North American Indians; and providing educational and cultural programs to improve harmony among all people.

A common question concerns the reason for Crazy Horse's outstretched arm, finger pointing forward over the horse's head. After Crazy Horse's surrender, a Euro-American is reputed to have mockingly inquired of the war leader, who tried so hard to protect his people's ancestral lands (especially the Black Hills), where his lands were now. Crazy Horse's response: "My lands are where my dead lie buried." According to Ziolkowski, the sculpture of Crazy Horse is pointing to those lands.[23]

NOTES

1. Charles M. Robinson III, *The Plains Wars 1757–1900* (Osceola, WI: Osprey, 2003) 35.

2. Mari Sandoz, *Crazy Horse: The Strange Man of the Oglalas* (1942; Lincoln: University of Nebraska Press, 1961) 69–70; Kingsley M. Bray, *Crazy Horse: A Lakota Life* (Norman: University of Oklahoma Press, 2006) 44–49, 408–09.

3. Sandoz 99; Bray 55.

4. Bray 412.

5. Sandoz 103–06; Larry McMurtry, *Crazy Horse* (New York: Lipper/Viking, 1999) 32–35.

6. Bray 65–67, 412–13.

7. Sandoz 163–66.

8. Bray 101.

9. Charles J. Kappler, ed., *Indian Affairs: Laws and Treaties*, 7 vols. (1904–41; Washington, DC: U.S. Government Printing Office, 1975–79) 2: 998–1007.

10. Eli R. Paul, "An Early Reference to Crazy Horse," *Nebraska History* 75.2 (Summer 1994): 189–90; speech quoted in Bray 137.

11. Joe DeBarthe, *The Life and Adventures of Frank Grouard*, ed. Edgar I. Stewart (Norman: University of Oklahoma Press, 1958) 181–82.

12. *Private Theodore Ewert's Diary of the Black Hills Expedition of 1874*, ed. John M. Carroll (Piscataway, NJ: Consultant Resources Incorporated, 1976) 57–58.

13. John G. Bourke, *On the Border with Crook* (1891; Lincoln: University of Nebraska Press, 1971) 300–18.

14. John S. Gray, *Centennial Campaign: The Sioux War of 1876* (Ft. Collins, CO: Old Army Press, 1976) 110–24.

15. Gray 124; Bill Yenne, *Indian Wars: The Campaign for the American West* (2006; Yardley, PA: Westholme, 2008) 187.

16. *Custer in 76: Walter Camp's Notes on the Custer Fight*, ed. Kenneth Hammer (Provo, UT: Brigham Young University Press, 1976) 215.

17. Lloyd E. McCreight, *Chief Flying Hawk's Tales: The True Story of Custer's Last Fight* (New York: Alliance, 1936) 28–29.

18. Nelson A. Miles, *Serving the Republic: Memoirs of the Civil and Military Life of Nelson A. Miles* (1911; Freeport, NY: Books for Libraries, 1971) 154–55.

19. Bourke 414–15.

20. Richard G. Hardorff, ed. *The Surrender and Death of Crazy Horse: A Source Book About a Tragic Episode in Lakota History* (Spokane: Arthur H. Clark, 1998) 25–58.

21. Bray 341.

22. Report from Lieutenant Colonel Bradley to the Adjutant General of the Department of the Platte, 7 Sept. 1877; in Hardorff 184.

23. Robb DeWall, *Sculptor Korczak Ziolkowski's Crazy Horse Memorial: Carving a Dream*, 10th rev. ed. (Crazy Horse, SD: Korczak's Heritage, 2003) 39.

RECOMMENDED READING

Ambrose, Stephen E. *Crazy Horse and Custer: The Parallel Lives of Two American Warriors*. 1975; New York: Anchor Books, 1996.

Bray, Kingsley M. *Crazy Horse: A Lakota Life*. Norman: University of Oklahoma Press, 2006.

Crazy Horse: The Last Warrior. Biography Series. A&E Television Networks, 1993. DVD.

Gray, John S. *Centennial Campaign: The Sioux War of 1876*. Ft. Collins, CO: Old Army Press, 1976.

Hardorff, Richard G., ed. *The Surrender and Death of Crazy Horse: A Source Book About a Tragic Episode in Lakota History*. Spokane: Arthur H. Clark, 1998.

Kadlecek, Edward, and Mabell Kadlecek. *To Kill an Eagle: Indian Views on the Last Days of Crazy Horse*. 1981; Boulder, CO: Johnson Books, 2008.

McMurtry, Larry. *Crazy Horse*. New York: Lipper/Viking, 1999.

Sajna, Mike. *Crazy Horse: The Life Behind the Legend*. 2000; Edison, NJ: Castle Books, 2005.

Sandoz, Mari. *Crazy Horse: The Strange Man of the Oglalas*. 1942; Lincoln: University of Nebraska Press, 1961.

Chief Joseph conveys pride and dignity in this photograph from around 1902, twenty-five years after leading his Nez Perce on the long trek to Canada that fell just miles short of his goal. (Library of Congress)

Chief Joseph (Hin-mah-too-yah-lat-kekht, Thunder Rising in the Mountains) 1840–1904

Hin-mah-too-yah-lat-kekht, whose name refers to thunder rising to the mountain heights but who was better known as Young Joseph and, later, Chief Joseph, was one of the best-known Indians of his time and the Indian leader probably most admired by Euro-Americans. That admiration was well deserved but partly based on misunderstanding his role during the long journey of his Nee-Me-Poo (usually referred to in historical accounts as Nez Perce) in 1877 as they attempted to evade U.S. military forces and make their way to Canada.

Both U.S. military opponents and the general public assumed that the Nez Perce successes against the U.S. army and their ability to outmaneuver their opponents over a stretch of some 1,800 miles must have been the work of a great military genius. That genius, they conjectured, was Chief Joseph because he was the Nez Perce leader they best knew and the most prominent leader to survive the long trek that ended just 40 miles short of the Canadian border. White Bird, a more war-like Nez Perce leader, was not killed in the final battle, but managed to make his way to Canada, evade capture, and largely escape the public eye. Thus Chief Joseph became the "Red Napoleon," even though one skill that he never consistently demonstrated was military leadership.

Chief Joseph's other attributes, however, were many. He was a deeply spiritual man who was committed both to traditional beliefs and to peace with Euro-Americans. A compassionate family man, he also cared deeply for the wider Nez Perce community, his strong sense of responsibility for their welfare ultimately playing a major role in his decision to surrender short of his Canadian goal. An able administrator, Chief Joseph coordinated camp movements during the long journey of 1877, oversaw handling of the large horse herd that numbered between 2,000 and 3,000 horses, and provided security for the Nez Perce families. He fought as a warrior, but he was not his people's war chief. Finally, after his surrender in 1877 and until his death in 1904, he lobbied consistently for the right of his people to return to their homeland. In that final effort, which ultimately proved unsuccessful, even his former military opponents joined his cause. Perhaps no American Indian in history brought so many Euro-Americans to sympathize with the history, struggles, and rights of Indians.

THE EDUCATION OF A CHIEF

The Nez Perce and Wallowa Valley

Joseph was born in the spring or summer of 1840 in eastern Oregon in the area known as the Columbia Plateau. The Nez Perce lands included what today are northeastern Oregon, southeastern Washington, and western Idaho, although Nez Perce also went as far as Montana to hunt the buffalo. Joseph's father was Tuekakas, head of the Wallowa band of the Nez Perce. When Tuekakas accepted Christianity, he also accepted the Christian name of Joseph. The son also was baptized and received the same name, with father and son later commonly referred to as Old Joseph and Young Joseph. Tuekakas had been born into the Cayuse tribe but married a Nez Perce and joined his wife's people. They also had a second son, Ollokot, about three years after Young Joseph's birth. Ollokot would become his people's war leader, while the elder son followed his father as civil leader of his band.

The heart of the Wallowa band was the Wallowa Valley within the Wallowa Mountains in northeastern Oregon, although they moved to lower ground during winter. The valley was especially dear to Tuekakas' heart, and his son inherited both his father's love for the area and an unyielding determination to maintain it as his people's homeland.

Coming of the Euro-Americans

By the time that Young Joseph was born, the Nez Perce had been acquainted with Euro-Americans for several decades. Their first significant encounter was with the members of the Lewis and Clark expedition, whom the Nez Perce welcomed as the explorers passed through on their way to the Pacific in the fall of 1805 and on their return during the following spring. These initial interactions were friendly, and before long other Euro-Americans arrived, including traders and missionaries. In the years preceding Young Joseph's birth, Presbyterian ministers Marcus Whitman (also a physician) and Henry Spalding came to the area. Whitman went on to work among the Cayuse to the southwest, but Spalding remained with the Nez Perce, for a time becoming a close friend of Tuekakas, who accepted the new religious teachings.

In 1843, Dr. Elijah White, subagent of Indian Affairs west of the Rockies, introduced a system of criminal laws to the Nez Perce, who also had been introduced to instructions in religion, farming, and traditional Euro-American education (reading, writing, and arithmetic) by Spalding. In an attempt to impose a Euro-American system of organizational hierarchy on the Nez Perce, White appointed a Nez Perce named Ellis as head chief, a decision thoroughly at odds with the local control and consensus-building approach natural to the Nez Perce and one roundly ridiculed by them. Tuekakas found White's actions offensive and began turning back toward his traditional beliefs. That movement accelerated as more settlers began establishing themselves on traditional Nez Perce land.

Then in 1847, the Cayuse, angered by Dr. Whitman's favoritism toward the settlers and fearful that his medicine was causing an illness (measles) that was killing especially the old and very young, turned on Whitman. Cayuse killed him, his wife, and 11 others, in addition to burning the mission and taking 47 captives. The Nez Perce had no involvement in the killings, but all Indians in the region suddenly became suspect. Even the Reverend Spalding and his family, escorted by 40 Nez Perce warriors, fled the area.

Subsequent peace talks occurred at the site of the former Whitman mission and included the Nez Perce. Despite the previous elevation of Ellis to head chief, the Nez Perce chose Tuekakas as their spokesman. He explicitly rejected war and refused to support those who committed the murders. Nonetheless, skirmishes between settlers and Indians continued until five Cayuse were apprehended. On June 3, 1850, they were hanged, temporarily bringing the crisis to a close.

In fact, changes were under way in the region that would increase tensions and lead to additional fighting. With the end of the gold boom of the late 1840s, growing numbers of Euro-American pioneers were looking to make their living by ranching and farming, and that pursuit took many to Cayuse and Nez Perce country. Other developments also were drawing settlers. The Oregon Compromise of 1846, which established the boundaries between Canada and the United States, had led to enactment of a law permitting each settler as well as his wife to claim 320 acres each in the northwest. In the near future, a gold rush into Nez Perce lands in 1860 and the Homestead Act of 1862 (which offered 160 acres to any homesteader who would live on and cultivate the land for five years) would place more Euro-Americans in close proximity to the Nez Perce.

The Treaty of 1855

The Nez Perce numbered only about 4,000 by the mid-1850s, but much of the land they occupied promised fertile fields for settlers' crops and fine grazing for their cattle. Isaac Stevens, governor of the Washington Territory, was determined to settle the tribes of the Columbia Plateau on reservations. To that end, in May 1855 he met with area tribes. Stevens made extensive promises, assuring the Nez Perce, for example, that they would be able to travel freely, even continuing their buffalo hunts on the Plains, if they would accept the land Stevens designated for them. As had been done with Ellis earlier, Stevens chose one individual to act as spokesman for the entire group to facilitate an agreement. That individual was Lawyer, a Christian and advocate for accommodating Euro-American wishes.

By this time, Tuekakas was convinced that he could not trust government representatives, although he still wished to live in peace. He had retreated into his traditional culture and had become a "Dreamer," one of those who accepted the vision of Smoholla, a Wanapam who had awakened from a three-day trance to share his vision of a revitalized Indian culture that included rejection of Euro-American ways. Farming was especially harmful, Smoholla taught, because it involved slicing into their mother, the earth, with which they should live in harmony.

After 18 days, all of the area tribes apparently agreed to something, although what they agreed to was (and remains) unclear. With all treaties, Indians were at a great disadvantage because they usually could neither read nor understand spoken English. Tuekakas understood the treaty not to affect his traditional homeland (which was included within the Nez Perce reservation), but did expect to receive money and goods from the U.S. authorities. Nothing was forthcoming, however, and Tuekakas soon grew even more wary of U.S. promises, including assurances that no additional settlers would move into their lands.

Smoholla

Smoholla (circa 1815–1895) was a dreamer-prophet of the Wanapum who was born in the current state of Washington. Suffering from a humpback, short legs, and an unusually large head, but eloquent of speech, he established a considerable reputation for himself as an important figure in the Indian revitalization movement. In the late 1850s, Smoholla disappeared for a time. When he returned, he claimed to have died and undergone a journey during which he was given divine powers and a vision of the future. The teachings that he conveyed he called Washani, which refers to Dancers. Those who followed him became known as the Dreamers.

According to Smoholla, Euro-Americans were evil and their manner of life should be rejected. In the spirit world, he had been taught certain rituals, among them the Washat, a dance accompanied by the ringing of bells. The number seven was supposedly sacred, and men knelt in rows of seven behind the prophet during singing. Smoholla was accompanied during the rituals by boys dressed in white, reminiscent of altar boys at Catholic mass. Indeed, Smoholla apparently borrowed some elements of his religion from Catholic rituals he had observed. He insisted that people should live naturally off what came from the earth, and stated that because the earth was their mother, no one should cut into it (as Euro-Americans did with the plow).

As with some of the other revitalization visions, Smoholla taught that the rituals and beliefs that he offered, if followed zealously, would bring back the Indians and the game that had disappeared from overhunting. In addition, Euro-Americans would be driven out. In short, the world would return to how it had been before the traders, settlers, and soldiers came.

Although Smoholla's vision did not come to pass, his descendants continued to practice the Washani way well into the twentieth century.

Congress did not ratify the treaty until 1859, when some of the promised payments began to arrive. Despite the long wait, the Christian "treaty" Nez Perce remained patiently accepting of their new way of life. By this time, a division was well under way between those Nez Perce who accepted Christianity and reservation life and the "nontreaty" Nez Perce.

The outbreak of the Civil War exacerbated tensions between the nontreaty Indians in the region and their Euro-American neighbors, who by 1862 numbered approximately 18,000.[1] In addition to farmers struggling to make a living for their families, the newcomers included criminals of many types who posed constant threats to the Indians, including their wives and daughters. Murder and rape were common dangers. From the viewpoint of U.S. officials, the tensions associated with the increased numbers of non-Indians required a simple (but not necessarily easy) solution: take more land from the tribes.

The Treaty of 1863 and the Splitting of the Nez Perce

Government representatives met at a council called by Stevens in 1863 and proposed that all Nez Perce move to a reservation near Lapwai in western Idaho, where each family would receive a small allotment of land and become farmers. The allotment approach was a common way for the government to secure additional land for settlers because it freed up most of the area in which Indians had traditionally lived and hunted. The payment for the land yielded would be the individual allotments near Lapwai. In other words, the Nez Perce would give up most of their land and be paid for what they had relinquished with a small percentage of the land that had also been theirs. The deal was analogous to asking someone to give up nine of ten dollars and be paid for the nine with the one dollar the person is permitted to keep.

The injustice of the plan was obvious to Tuekakas and his sons, who by now were fully grown men. Other Nez Perce apparently believed that they had no viable option or had so thoroughly accepted Euro-American ways, including Christianity, that they were prepared to accept the terms. Consequently, the Nez Perce decided to accept a reality that had been developing for years: a split between the treaty and nontreaty Nez Perce.

Lawyer (along with his son of the same name), Big Thunder, and their bands chose to accept reservation life near Lapwai, in part because their homes were already located within the reservation area. Other Nez Perce leaders, including Tuekakas, took their bands back home, resolving to stand together in defense of their traditional lands and way of life.

Lawyer, without authorization from the other Nez Perce, signed away five-sixths of his people's ancestral lands, including the Wallowa Valley. In an attempt to convey Nez Perce unanimity regarding the treaty, government officials arranged for 51 Indians to mark an X on the treaty—the same number who had marked the agreement of 1855. Four years later, President Andrew Johnson announced ratification of the treaty. After the council, Tuekakas returned to the Wallowa Valley and set up posts to mark his ancestral land, determined not to yield any of it.

A New Leader

Over the next few years, Tuekakas suffered from declining health and failing eyesight. He leaned more heavily on Joseph, who would succeed him as leader of the Wallowa band, which now numbered about 500. In an early biography of Joseph, Helen Addison Howard offers a vivid, if somewhat romanticized, description of the young man who was about to embark on his mission to lead the Wallowa Nez Perce:

> At full growth he possessed an athletic figure and a handsome, intelligent face. He stood six feet two inches in his moccasins, weighed two hundred pounds, and was broad of shoulder and deep of chest. With a square chin, finely shaped

features, and black piercing eyes he was an Indian Apollo. He had a dignified and quiet demeanor, and he clung to the aboriginal habit of wearing his hair in two long braids over his shoulders.[2]

As Tuekakas lay dying in 1871, he called for his elder son and imparted a message that would become Joseph's lifelong mission. On a trip to Washington, D.C., in 1879, Joseph recalled his father's words, although the prose cannot be assumed to be precisely Joseph's, as it went through translation and editing before being published in the *North American Review*. "Always remember," Tuekakas said, "that your father never sold his country. You must stop your ears whenever you are asked to sign a treaty selling your home. A few years more, and white men will be all around you. They have their eyes on this land. My son, never forget my dying words. This country holds your father's body. Never sell the bones of your father and your mother."

Joseph promised his father that he would protect his grave even with his own life and later carried out his father's wishes by burying him in his beloved valley. Joseph assured his Washington audience that he loved his homeland more than "all the rest of the world," and offered a fundamental principle by which he had tried to live: "A man who would not love his father's grave is worse than a wild animal."[3]

CHIEF OF THE WALLOWA NEZ PERCE

Settlers in the Wallowa Valley

Joseph had little time as leader of the Wallowa band before having to face new developments affecting his homeland. When he returned from the lowlands in the spring of 1872, he was surprised to find settlers occupying cabins along the creeks of the Wallowa Mountains. The settlers had arrived to find no one there and claimed the land as their own under the Treaty of 1863, which Lawyer had signed. Joseph, of course, had not signed the treaty and denied that Lawyer had any authority to transfer the Wallowa Valley to anyone.

Joseph and the settlers turned to the local Indian agent, John Monteith. Under President Ulysses S. Grant's Indian Policy, religious denominations were given jurisdiction over Indians in specific areas, which Grant thought would establish a more congenial form of control than that exercised by the government. Such policy also placed the financial responsibility for overseeing treaties and other Indian issues on the religions rather than on a country still strapped for cash after the Civil War.

However well meaning Monteith was, he had no natural inclination to side with Joseph. The Nez Perce who had converted to Christianity seemed content to accept the treaty and live in peace with the new arrivals. The most that Monteith was willing to push for was peaceful coexistence and a sharing of the valley.

General Oliver Otis Howard

With no definitive solution to the rising tensions between Joseph's band and the settlers, the government finally became involved in the person of General O. O. Howard, head of the Department of the Columbia. Howard had lost an arm in the Civil War and was a veteran Indian fighter who had brought about a peace agreement with Cochise's Chiricahua Apaches in the Southwest.

Known as "the Christian General," Howard was a staunch Presbyterian who saw himself as a man of peace and worked to assist the newly freed slaves during Reconstruction as head of the Freedman's Bureau. He also helped to establish Howard University in Washington, D.C., after the war to provide educational opportunities for African Americans and served as president of that institution from 1869 to 1874. Howard was no hater of Indians; instead, he viewed himself as a humanitarian. Nonetheless, he subscribed to the common belief that Indians—for their own good, as he saw it—must adopt the dominant values of the United States.

Diplomacy or War

Chief Joseph and General Howard first met in the spring of 1875, a meeting that Howard thought went well. He later wrote, "I think Joseph and I became then quite good friends."[4] Not long afterward, Joseph learned that President Grant, by issuing an executive order opening the Wallowa for new settlements, had withdrawn a concession he made in 1873 when he directed that parts of the Wallowa lands be removed from settlement and serve as a reservation for the Wallowa Nez Perce, with settlers to be compensated for the land that they had settled in the area. That earlier decision, however, had not led to evictions or the prevention of new arrivals.

Joseph responded by calling a council of nontreaty chiefs in the summer of 1875. The major leaders were Joseph, the younger Looking Glass, White Bird, Toohoolhoolzote, and Eagle from the Light. Among the five, only Joseph and Looking Glass argued against war, but the two succeeded in pushing for an attempt to reach a peaceful solution.

Then in the summer of 1876—the same summer when Sitting Bull, Crazy Horse, and their allies were defeating Custer at Little Bighorn—a friend of Joseph's, We-lot-yah, was apparently murdered by two settlers, Wells McNall and A. B. Findley, in a dispute over horses. Some Nez Perce were ready to meet the killing with violence, but Joseph again worked to keep the peace. Instead, he met with Howard's representatives and argued that the proper response to the killing of We-lot-yah, described by Joseph as a peaceful man, was to permit the Nez Perce to retain the Wallowa Valley that the death had rendered even more sacred. According to the *Report of the Secretary of War*, Joseph had argued

that the value of his life could not be estimated; nevertheless, that now, since the murder had been done, since his brother's life had been taken in Wallowa Valley, his body buried there, and the earth had drunk up his blood, that the valley was more sacred to him than ever before, and he would and did claim it for the life taken; that he should hold it for himself and his people from this time forward, forever; and that all the whites must be removed from the valley.[5]

What Joseph was offering, in the most high-minded of terms, was peace in exchange for the right to remain in the Wallowa Valley.

As much as Howard desired a peaceful resolution to the land issue, he would not (likely could not) agree to Joseph's offer. Howard, still impressed with Joseph, believed that he and his brother, Ollokot, were inclined to move to Lapwai. Working against these accommodations, he thought, were Smoholla and the Dreamers, and their insistence on keeping the land unmolested by cultivation while awaiting a return of their dead ancestors and the expulsion of the intruders.

Later in the summer, when Joseph threatened war if We-lot-yah's killers were not brought to justice, military officials assured him that the murderers would be dealt with. That justice proved elusive, however, as the two men were found not guilty when no sworn testimony contradicted their claims of self-defense. One explanation for this outcome is that the Nez Perce refused to testify against Findley, whom they liked. A more likely reason for the acquittal is that they were not familiar enough with the U.S. judicial system to use it as effectively as did the defendants, who were facing a jury of settlers, not a Nez Perce jury.

General Howard, meanwhile, became convinced that the only solution to the tensions between Euro-Americans and Nez Perce in the Wallowa Valley was to remove the latter to the Lapwai reservation. Howard summoned Joseph to a meeting at Lapwai in November 1876 and demanded that Joseph and his band accept a move to Lapwai. Not surprisingly, except perhaps to Howard, Joseph refused, declaring that he would never give up his land.

Unwilling to compromise in his determination to force the issue, Howard made plans over the winter to achieve his end by military force. The treaty Nez Perce, hoping to prevent armed conflict, sent a delegation to Joseph in the Imnaha Valley in the far northeastern corner of the current state of Oregon where the Wallowa band was wintering. The delegation unsuccessfully tried to convince Joseph to accept the Lapwai move. While preparing for military action if necessary, Howard also attempted to isolate Joseph by persuading other bands to accept relocation to the Lapwai reservation. These efforts proving largely unproductive, Howard once again planned to meet with Joseph.

Howard Shows the Rifle

Howard was determined to engage in no negotiations but rather to demand once and for all that Joseph yield and accept life at Lapwai. The Nez Perce arrived at Fort Lapwai, which consisted of several buildings surrounding a parade area rather than an enclosed stockade, for the meeting, which began

on Thursday, May 3, 1877. Toohoolhoolzote, an ardent Dreamer who har-
bored a strong distaste for the Euro-Americans, was chosen to act as spokesman for the nontreaty bands. Howard and Agent Monteith spoke on the first
day, and Toohoolhoolzote gave a lengthy speech on the second day about rev-
erencing the land. He also expressed anger about what he interpreted as a con-
descending attitude on the part of Howard.

Amid rising tensions that Joseph realized could escalate into violence, he
proposed a pause in the proceedings. Also sensing the growing hostility,
Howard concurred and suggested a weekend postponement. The delay, he
knew, would allow the additional troops whom he had requested to arrive.
The nontreaty Indians were heavily armed, but the weekend off from negotiations seemed to cool tempers temporarily. Sunday religious services helped,
according to Howard, as even the Dreamers engaged enthusiastically in the rituals and songs.

On the following Monday, May 7, Toohoolhoolzote resumed his speech
and Howard quickly lost patience. He upbraided the speaker for repeating
his comments about the land. The two engaged in an angry exchange, with
Toohoolhoolzote complaining that he was not being respected. Howard
offered an ultimatum, declaring that the Nez Perce would either accept the reservation or be forced onto it.

Howard then ordered Toohoolhoolzote arrested. When a soldier moved forward to execute the order, he—apparently unintentionally—caused Toohoolhoolzote to fall as he stepped back from the soldier. The incident almost led
to violence, but Joseph intervened once again to urge calm. The interruption,
threat, and arrest all were major violations of protocol from the Nez Perce perspective, because they occurred in a formal council meeting where they were
guests and consequently had left their weapons outside. Thus Howard's
actions amounted to the sort of infraction known as "showing the rifle."

The council broke up with no agreement. Toohoolhoolzote was released
from the guardhouse, and Joseph and White Bird managed to prevent attempts
at retribution. Howard, for his part, refused to compromise. He gave the nontreaty bands just 30 days to come into the reservation. Joseph explained that
30 days would not afford his people enough time to gather their horses and
cattle and move all of their possessions as well as the elderly, infirm, and
young. His remonstrance, however, fell on deaf ears.

THE NEZ PERCE AT WAR

A Revenge Killing

Joseph had vowed to his father to defend his homeland, but he also saw the situation with General Howard realistically. Not complying with Howard's
order would likely mean war, and war would mean many Nez Perce deaths,
including those of women and children, all of whom Joseph felt a solemn
responsibility to protect. In short, he faced two choices that involved his most

important obligations, yet he saw no way to meet one of the obligations without failing in the other. Consequently, he chose the one that involved protecting the living.

Meeting the 30-day deadline, however, could not be done efficiently. Most of the cattle were lost in hurried attempts to cross the Snake River. Rather than lose the rest crossing the Salmon River, Joseph left the cattle with the intention of returning later to butcher them. Complicating the arduous trek for Joseph personally was that Springtime, his wife, was in the final stage of pregnancy.

Joseph left his band in the Camas Prairie southeast of Fort Lapwai and returned with his men to butcher as many of the cattle as they could manage. Upon returning to his camp after accomplishing that task, he learned that some young men had turned to violence. Wahlitits, a member of White Bird's band, had engaged in a minor altercation with Yellow Grizzly Bear after accidentally damaging some kouse roots that Yellow Grizzly Bear's wife was drying. Told that he should avenge the killer of his father, Eagle Robe, rather than interfering with a woman's hard work, Wahlitits (who had surely been longing for justice for his father anyway) took off with two cousins to locate the object of his anger, Lawrence Ott. They missed Ott but found a retired sailor named Richard Devine and killed him. Other attacks on settlers followed, and soon Joseph and the rest of the Nez Perce leaders realized that they were enmeshed in a war that few of their people wanted.

Battle of White Bird Canyon

Most of the Nez Perce moved to White Bird Canyon near the Salmon River southeast of Lapwai, which they believed could be defended effectively if the soldiers attacked. Looking Glass, however, took his band back to his village along the Clearwater River, north of Fort Lapwai. The Nez Perce at White Bird Canyon were led by Joseph, White Bird, and Toohoolhoolzote; Hahtalekin and Husis Kute led two bands of Palouse from southeastern Washington.

Howard dispatched Companies F and H of the First Cavalry, totaling 103 men, under Captain David Perry to end the crisis, either by negotiation or force. Later, 11 settlers joined Perry as guides. When Perry arrived at White Bird Canyon on June 17, 6 warriors rode out under a white flag of truce to meet them. One of the settlers opened fire, and the battle was on.

The Indians were reasonably well armed with an assortment of repeating and muzzle-loading rifles, muskets, pistols, and bows and arrows. At the first shots, Captain Perry brought both companies forward, with the volunteers forming the left flank, leaving no men in reserve. The defenders shot from the front, rear, and left, shooting the bugler and aiming for officers in an attempt to disrupt the chain of command. The cavalry tried to retreat, but the effort at times dissolved into panicked disorder, with the battle quickly turning into a rout. Thirty-four soldiers, were killed, including Lieutenant Edward Theller, Perry's subordinate officer in Company F, which Perry personally led.

Joseph was not the leader of this battle, nor did he serve as a war leader in later engagements with the army. He did participate in the fighting, undoubtedly concerned as he did so about the welfare of his newly born daughter.

After their victory, the Nez Perce leaders decided to cross back over the Salmon River in an effort to lure Howard's forces across the river as well. The bands would then move north, recross, and hurry eastward where they hoped to meet up with the Flatheads, with whom the Nez Perce had long been friendly and whom they saw as likely allies. A rearguard would delay the troops' crossing to give the rest time to push far ahead of Howard. For four days, Howard attempted to cross to the west bank of the river, but each time faced fire from the warriors who had been left behind. Once he was able to cross and discovered the stratagem, he had to recross yet again.

As the Indians moved east, Joseph, helped by White Bird, exercised the role that he would maintain over the long journey that was starting: watching over the people and organizing the logistics of the journey, such as setting up and dismantling camp.

Looking Glass's Return

Looking Glass's men had played no part in the outbreak of violence, and he had no wish to fight the soldiers. Even so, Howard feared that Looking Glass might move to join Joseph. He sent two companies (E and L) along with 20 civilian volunteers to ensure that his people not become part of the fighting. Howard further ordered his commander, Captain Stephen Whipple, to arrest Looking Glass.

Looking Glass had every intention of avoiding war. Thus, when the soldiers arrived on July 1, 1877, he hoisted a white flag and sent a messenger out to meet them. According to one account, Whipple and a small group of his men rode toward the village demanding to see Looking Glass, but as they approached someone fired and hit a villager. The soldiers rode into the village shooting as the villagers fled. They trampled gardens, set fire to tipis, and engaged in wanton looting and destruction. The result was precisely the opposite of what Howard wanted: Two days later, Looking Glass rode into the nontreaty Indians' camp and declared that he was ready for war.

Battle at Clearwater River

Howard continued his pursuit of the main body of nontreaty Nez Perce. A battalion of volunteers under Colonel Edward McConville caught up with them on July 8 along the south fork of the Clearwater River. In the previous days, there had been short but deadly encounters between the two sides. Along Cottonwood Creek on July 3, for example, an advance party consisting of 10 soldiers and the scout William Foster, led by Lieutenant Sevier Rains, was ambushed and completely wiped out.

McConville's men decided to wait for Howard's arrival, but the following morning they were surrounded by Nez Perce warriors. They took refuge on top of a hill that became known as Misery Hill because of the danger they constantly faced. A party of volunteer reinforcements arrived on July 10. The next day, McConville was able to lead his men off the hill but consequently was unable to coordinate efforts with Howard, who reached the area later that day.

Joseph and the others in the village were unaware of Howard's approach. The general positioned his men on a high bluff and attempted to train howitzers on the village, although the guns could not be positioned to shoot downward at the angle necessary to hit the village.

The Nez Perce surrounding the bluff mounted attacks against the soldiers' position. The battle continued into the next day, July 12, but the Indians had little experience of or enthusiasm for a siege. In addition, the howitzers and Gatling guns were now taking a toll on the warriors. They retreated, and the entire group headed north for Kamiah where there was a Christian Nez Perce settlement. Kamiah also was the place where the Nez Perce believed their original ancestors had been created. Howard's men were delayed in crossing the Clearwater, and their pursuit was temporarily halted while the cavalry helped ferry the infantry across the river.

Howard's forces suffered 15 fatalities in the battle. The casualties included a heavy proportion of officers and buglers, testament not only to their great visibility but also to the deliberate strategy of targeting them. Howard reported 23 Indian fatalities, but as Jerome Greene points out in *Nez Perce Summer, 1877*, the actual number of casualties was much lower, about 4 killed and 6 wounded.

Howard labeled the battle a tremendous victory, with the Indians "completely routed." History has judged the battle differently. In Greene's words, "By not pressing them in their retreat from their village, General Howard lost both the initiative and an opportunity to finally curb the nontreaty Nez Perces and end the war."[6]

Kent Nerburn notes the battle also served as a watershed event in that both Howard and Chief Joseph were increasingly receiving much public attention, not to the general's credit. Howard believed that Joseph was firmly in charge of the entire group and dictating strategy, a position that he made clear even four years later in his book *Nez Perce Joseph*. That view of Joseph was popularized in the war dispatches emanating from the battlefield pen of Thomas Sutherland. Increasingly, the press was portraying Joseph as a brilliant strategist and leader whose military acumen far outstripped that of the bumbling Howard; the latter was portrayed almost as a comic figure vainly pursuing the Nez Perce.

Kamiah

Joseph and the Nez Perce, after following the Clearwater north, received little help from their Christian brothers, who refused them their boats for crossing the river. Instead, Joseph and his nontreaty Indians built buffalo skin boats to cross the river. They then moved into the Bitterroot Mountain foothills, waiting to attack their pursuers when they crossed the Clearwater once again in pursuit.

Howard had a trick up his sleeve as well. He took his cavalry north rather than crossing the river, hoping to mislead the Nez Perce into believing that he had given up the pursuit. Instead of falling for the ploy, however, the Nez Perce sent a contingent north to where the ferry that Howard intended to use was kept. They cut the rope used to pull the ferry, rendering it useless and giving themselves some breathing room.

The Nez Perce, now in the Weippe Prairie, considered whether they should follow the Lolo Trail east to meet up with the Flatheads or Crows in Montana, move north toward Canada to join Sitting Bull and the Lakotas, or return to Lapwai. Joseph favored none of these choices, instead preferring to move back to his homeland and die if necessary fighting to protect his home. The majority opinion disagreed with his choice, and Looking Glass was named to lead the continued exodus over the Bitterroot Mountains. Despite Joseph's important administrative function on the journey, he actually had little impact on strategy during most of it, as he had no input into the pivotal decision taken in the Weippe Prairie to continue toward Montana.

On July 16, 1877, the nontreaty group—consisting of 800 men, women, and children, plus 3,000 horses—continued its fateful journey.

THE JOURNEY EAST

The Lolo Trail

Chief Joseph and his nontreaty Nez Perce took the most northerly route across the Bitterroot Mountains. This passage, known as the Lolo Trail, ran from the Idaho Territory through the mountains to the Bitterroot Valley in Montana Territory. From Kamiah, it was approximately 100 miles in length and included the Lolo Pass where the Clearwater Mountains of Idaho met the Bitterroot Mountains. Indians had used the trail for generations despite its difficult terrain, Lewis and Clark had traversed portions of it in 1805 and 1806, and in the 1860s a federally funded attempt to build a wagon road along the trail had begun.

By this time, General Howard was inclined to abandon the pursuit of Joseph in favor of establishing security for the settlers residing on Nez Perce lands, who feared continued Indian attacks. Commanding General William Sherman, however, ordered Howard to continue on his present course irrespective of jurisdictional boundaries. A combination of factors put Howard well behind Joseph and the main body of fleeing Indians. He waited for reinforcements who would handle security in Idaho and was still dealing with raids that, unknown to him, were actually conducted by small groups of rearguard Nez Perce seeking horses and supplies while the main body moved steadily eastward.

By the time Howard began to follow the fleeing Indians along the Lolo Trail, the main body of Nez Perce had reached Montana. Confident that they had escaped Howard, Looking Glass concluded that the war was over and directed his warriors not to harm settlers.

Then the Nez Perce learned that soldiers were constructing a fort ahead of them at Missoula. Captain Charles Rawn had been ordered to stop the Nez Perce at the other end of the Lolo Trail, but his force was small, consisting of only 30 regulars plus volunteers who expanded the force to about 200. Also in support of Rawn were Flatheads, longtime allies of the Nez Perce, who promised to supply information about the Nez Perce but remain neutral in any fighting.

Captain Rawn met with Looking Glass, White Bird, and Joseph on July 26 and demanded that the Nez Perce surrender their guns and horses. Joseph and Looking Glass met with Rawn again the next day, along with Chief Charlo of the Flatheads. At this meeting, the Nez Perce put forth their own offer. They would surrender ammunition but no guns in exchange for safe passage. Rawn refused, and Looking Glass told him that he would have to consult his people about Rawn's demands.

Rawn and his mixed contingent prepared for battle behind hastily constructed breastworks of logs. The positioning of the barricades on a valley floor put the soldiers and volunteers in jeopardy from forces firing on them from above. This risk, coupled with the Nez Perce's promise to move by without harming any of the settlers, induced many of the volunteers to leave Rawn. Throughout the night of July 27–28, the remaining force, numbering about 30 regulars, 30 volunteers, and 21 Flatheads, awaited an attack.[7] Instead, the Nez Perce passed silently and peacefully by the small, outmanned force.

Captain Rawn incurred considerable criticism for not having made a more concerted effort to stop the Nez Perce, with his makeshift fort being mockingly dubbed "Fort Fizzle." Although unproven, it has long been conjectured that Rawn and Montana Territory Governor Benjamin Potts may have secretly finalized an agreement with the Nez Perce to allow them to pass through so as to avoid a battle involving Rawn's small and vulnerable party.

The Big Hole

The next significant military encounter for Joseph and the Nez Perce was in an area known as the Big Hole, a Montana prairie surrounded by mountains. It was a traditional resting place for the Nez Perce on their way east to hunt the buffalo.

Joseph, as usual, oversaw the setting up of the camp on August 8 and made sure that the horses were well tended to. Some warriors wanted to scout the back trail to ensure they were not being followed, but Looking Glass insisted that there was no cause for alarm.

General Howard was, in fact, far in the rear. Nevertheless, unknown to Looking Glass and the rest of the Nez Perce, Colonel John Gibbon, commander of the

District of Western Montana, was preparing to attack. He had a total force of 15 officers and 146 men, including two companies under Captain Rawn. About 4:00 A.M. on August 9, Gibbon ordered an advance.

Hahtalekin had risen early and gone out to tend his horses. The first shots killed him. Heavy gunfire then swept the village. Men searched in the dark for their weapons. Women grabbed their children and ran, seeking a nearby creek or any spot that might offer some protection. The tipis quickly were ignited by the attacking soldiers and lit up the sky, burning to death children who had not been able to escape.

Seventy-year-old White Bird rallied the warriors, and they fought back ferociously. Joseph held his infant daughter and called for a gun. As the Nez Perce drove the soldiers back, Joseph organized a group of young boys to protect the horse herd and pack animals. As the fighting subsided, Joseph helped to bury the dead and care for the wounded.

The warriors gathered the following morning after spending the day and night shooting at the soldiers, who were pinned down on a hillside. After the early onslaught by Gibbon, the Nez Perce had responded vigorously, securing a victory, albeit at a great cost. Losses were high on both sides. Gibbon suffered 69 casualties, including 29 fatalities in the battle plus 2 men who died later of their wounds. Among the dead was First Lieutenant James H. Bradley, an accomplished officer and widely published author who was writing a book about the Sioux wars of 1876. He was considered one of the most promising young officers in the army.

Despite the victory, Joseph had much reason to mourn. His wife had been wounded. His brother Ollokot's wife was killed in the battle. A number of prominent Nez Perce warriors died, as did the Palouse leader Hahtalekin. Somewhere between 60 and 90 men, women, and children died. Gibbon claimed 89 deaths in his report, without mentioning that the majority were women and children. Others who had been wounded succumbed later on the journey.

The Nez Perce disengaged on August 10, and Gibbon sent soldiers to bring in the supply train, which had not been captured. His howitzer had been destroyed and a large supply of ammunition taken. Despite the failure to stop the Nez Perce and the very real danger of annihilation that Gibbon's men faced, the army and the newspapers portrayed the battle as a victory. Six enlisted men were awarded the Medal of Honor for their roles in the fighting.

New Leadership

There was much anger as well as grief among the Nez Perce in the wake of Gibbon's attack. Clearly, the assumption that war was behind them was terribly wrong, and all now understood that they faced a constant danger of attack. Looking Glass was roundly blamed for not heeding the call to send out scouts, who might have discovered the soldiers before they could attack. The leaders decided to replace Looking Glass with Poker Joe, who immediately established a pattern of surrounding the main body with groups of scouts and placing the women and children in front to protect them. Caring for the wounded fell to Joseph, as did providing for children who had lost parents.

Joseph's military role continued to be lauded in the media and in the minds of the military and general public, but did not reflect reality. Joseph kept doing what he had been doing while Euro-Americans chose up sides regarding him; meanwhile, the pendulum of popular opinion, especially in the East, increasingly swung in favor of Joseph as the "Red Napoleon" bravely and honorably leading his people on a gallant race to avoid confinement on a reservation.

HOWARD'S PURSUIT

Camas Meadows

Joseph and the Nez Perce moved southeast from Big Hole, reaching Camas Meadows in Idaho Territory near the northwest corner of Wyoming Territory by August 19. Howard was close behind but seemed reluctant to attack the Indian village. He believed that the Nez Perce were moving into Yellowstone National Park, and his strategy was to send about 40 soldiers to get ahead of them so he could catch the fleeing Indians between the two forces as they approached the park.

The Nez Perce decided to take the offensive. Approximately 30 of their top warriors, including Ollokot, Looking Glass, and Toohoolhoolzote, moved back to Howard's camp under cover of night and prepared to attack. Unfortunately for the Nez Perce, one of their warriors fired his gun in the predawn hours of August 20, precipitating frenzied action on both sides.

The Nez Perce attempted to drive off the soldiers' horses but ended up mainly with their mules instead. A rearguard of warriors fought with the soldiers for several hours, while others drove the mules to the Nez Perce camp. Although less valued than the horses, the mules actually were an important acquisition because they deprived Howard of much of his pack train while offering considerable assistance to the Nez Perce families on their continued migration.

Howard, without his pack mules, fell farther behind Joseph and the Nez Perce, and the soldiers who were to initiate an ambush at the entrance to the park withdrew before their intended quarry arrived. As Howard's scouts from the Bannock tribe came upon any wounded, elderly, or ill Nez Perce left behind along the trail, they methodically killed them. In the newspapers, meanwhile, the loss of Howard's mules provided additional grist for stories mocking the general's seemingly bumbling pursuit of Chief Joseph.

Yellowstone National Park

The Nez Perce entered Yellowstone National Park on August 22. The area had been designated a national park in 1872, and some tourists happened to be visiting the park even as Joseph and his party moved through it.

One group of seven men and two women were enjoying some music in their camp when they were discovered by Nez Perce scouts. Some young warriors wanted to kill them, but the leaders refused. Yellow Horse in his memoir recalled approaching and shaking hands with one of the men, an act that erased his previous violent thoughts. The visitors had heard about the journey of the Nez Perce and asked to see Joseph.

Some young warriors persisted in threatening the nine, even shooting and wounding one of the men before other Nez Perce intervened. Three of the seven men escaped, and Joseph and his wife treated the remaining prisoners well, giving them shelter, food, and blankets. Finally, Poker Joe gave them horses so that they could leave.

Having been rejected by their former allies the Flatheads, the Nez Perce now hoped that they might receive assistance from the Crows, whom they had helped in battles against the Lakotas. Looking Glass went ahead to meet some Crow friends, while Poker Joe continued to lead the group across Yellowstone National Park.

The Nez Perce realized that Howard's approach was to split his forces, with some soldiers getting ahead of the party and waiting to ambush the Nez Perce. The ideal trap likely would be laid at the end of a canyon, where the Indians could be caught in close quarters. Poker Joe devised a plan to outwit any soldiers who might be waiting ahead. He would lead his people through one canyon but then turn north to another canyon, while a group of warriors rode in circles with the horses and mules. The goal of the warriors was to raise such a large amount of dust that the soldiers would believe the entire group was coming that way.

At this point, approximately 150 of the Nez Perce had died during the journey, and Joseph realized that additional fighting would add greatly to that toll. Kent Nerburn estimates that only 100 able-bodied warriors remained as part of the group.[8] Nonetheless, there was little sentiment for surrendering.

Waiting at what turned out to be the wrong canyon was Colonel Samuel Sturgis. Colonel Nelson Miles, commander of the District of the Yellowstone, had ordered Sturgis to try to prevent Joseph, whom Miles also viewed as the leader of the Nez Perce, from joining forces with Sitting Bull. Sitting Bull had been demonized by the U.S. military and the press as the conqueror of Colonel Custer at Little Bighorn and was viewed as a constant threat to descend from Canada and resume fighting. Sturgis was determined to blockade the Nez Perce in Yellowstone, although he was uncertain as to which route they would be taking. He arrived at Clark's Fork Canyon on September 5. Upon being told that the route through the canyon was impassable, he moved on September 8 to the Stinking Water Canyon, so-called because of the sulfur beds nearby.

Apparently contributing to Sturgis's decision was intelligence he received regarding dust clouds being sighted in the vicinity of Stinking Water. The clouds, however, were Poker Joe's diversion created by the horses and mules. About the time that Sturgis departed Clark's Fork, the main body of Indians passed safely through the canyon. The good news of this successful stratagem was tempered by the return of Looking Glass, who had failed to enlist Crow support. The Crows did not want to antagonize the U.S. soldiers; in fact, some Crows already were scouting for the soldiers.

Having been betrayed by both the Flatheads and the Crows, the Nez Perce now pinned their hopes on reaching Canada. Their only chance to avoid either surrendering or being annihilated in combat appeared to lie with Sitting Bull. The Nez Perce and Lakotas had once been enemies, but they had since made peace. Perhaps, they thought, the Lakotas would offer the support and security that the Flatheads and Crows had refused.

Nelson Miles

General Howard sent 50 of his own men with Colonel Sturgis's command in pursuit of Joseph and the Nez Perce while he followed more slowly, allowing his tired soldiers to recover from the already long trek. Sturgis was determined to catch up with Joseph. In addition to having been outmaneuvered by the Nez Perce, Sturgis could not forget the death of his son, Second Lieutenant James Sturgis, who had fallen at Little Bighorn. The younger Sturgis's body had been so badly mutilated by the victors that he had been identified only by the bloody underwear he was wearing.

On September 13, the Nez Perce camped along Canyon Creek near the Yellowstone River, a few miles south of where Clark's Fork met the Yellowstone. They knew that Howard was far behind but were unaware that Sturgis was close. Some young warriors discovered a stagecoach, set the building near it on fire, and drove the stage back toward their camp. Sturgis's scouts saw smoke rising from the burning building and located in the distance the main body of Nez Perce.

At this point, the Nez Perce also saw Sturgis's men and hurried to move through the canyon. Joseph tried to keep both the people and the horses in order and leave no one behind while the party moved as fast as possible. Hoping to safeguard the women and children, warriors rode their horses to the top of a mesa in the canyon and prepared to fire down on the soldiers.

As Sturgis's command approached, the Nez Perce fired, shooting soldiers off their horses. The cavalry dismounted and formed a skirmish line. A rearguard body of warriors slowed down the soldiers while other warriors caught up with the main body of Nez Perce. Another group of cavalry attempted to ride along a bluff to reach the canyon mouth before the Nez Perce could escape, but to no avail. Sturgis recalled his men and halted.

Sturgis's losses included 3 dead and 11 wounded at what has usually been called the Battle of Canyon Creek, although historians usually acknowledge that it was more of a skirmish than a battle. Sturgis claimed that 21 Nez Perce were killed, a claim that Elliott West labels "a ridiculous inflation that his [Sturgis's] own scout rejected." West similarly debunks the colonel's claim to have captured between 900 and 1,000 ponies, noting that the only horses claimed by Sturgis were some worn-out ones left behind by the Nez Perce.[9]

For several days, though, the Nez Perce had to contend with raids by Crows and Bannocks, who stole horses and, according to Yellow Wolf, killed three Nez Perce.

Howard and Sturgis now were both far behind, but the Nez Perce did not realize that another military force was about to enter the picture. Believing that the primary threat was in the rear, they thought that they needed to move only fast enough to keep Howard and Sturgis at a distance. Moving slowly at times, therefore, became a useful tactic for Howard because he realized that it would induce the Nez Perce to slow down, leaving Colonel Miles to get in place to stop Joseph. As Howard wrote in his memoirs, *My Life and Personal Experiences Among Our Hostile Indians*, "My only hope of striking the Indians lay in apprising Colonel Miles ... of the situation, and asking him to make a diagonal march across our front and take Joseph unawares." Consequently, Howard added, "Sturgis and I slowed our marches for fear of causing the Indians to hasten too rapidly ...."[10]

At this point, Colonel Miles was moving to cut off Joseph. Miles's primary concern had been, and remained, Sitting Bull. However, he now considered the real possibility that Joseph, whom Miles considered to be a lesser threat, might reach Canada and join forces with the Lakota leader—an alliance that Miles believed could have disastrous consequences.

By early in the morning of September 18, only hours after hearing from Howard regarding Joseph's continued progress, Miles had his force of about 500 men (six companies each of cavalry and mounted infantry), along with wagons, artillery, and a pack train, ready to move northwest from the Tongue River cantonment in Montana.

Cow Island

As Joseph continued to oversee the welfare of the Nez Perce, especially the young and elderly, and help keep the whole party functioning as efficiently as possible, the group prepared to cross the Missouri River at the traditional Nez Perce crossing point on their buffalo hunts: Cow Island. The river was usually shallow enough there to cross on foot, and several small tree-covered islands provided shade.

The crossing also was popular with Euro-Americans. When the Nez Perce reached it on September 23, they found soldiers guarding a large pile of goods on the north bank of the river deposited by a train of 15 wagons that was making its way from the river toward the plains. The Nez Perce crossed the Missouri farther upriver and started up Cow Creek, a tributary of the Missouri.

A delegation of Nez Perce led probably by Poker Joe asked Sergeant William Moelchert for some supplies. Rebuffed, they then offered to buy supplies. Finally, Moelchert handed over a side of bacon and a sack of hardtack. Angered by the perceived lack of generosity, a group of young warriors started firing at the soldiers. The supplies were stacked between the soldiers' trenches and the Nez Perce, so while firing kept the soldiers pinned down, the Indian women ran back and forth to the supplies, carrying off a variety of foodstuffs as well as pans and other household goods. The food provided a welcome dinner for the hungry Nez Perce.

The following morning the Nez Perce began to move away from the river. In the afternoon they found the bull train from Cow Island. With his people much in need of ammunition, Poker Joe tried to obtain additional supplies yet prevent a battle. He informed the drivers that he had recently seen a band of Sioux and suggested that the drivers leave the wagons and hide. The sighting was not true, but the drivers could not be sure, and the idea of facing two large groups of potentially hostile Indians was frightening. Even so, it took a direct attack by some of the warriors the following morning, September 25, which killed one of the drivers, to send the rest fleeing. The subsequent confiscation of goods from the wagons went on successfully despite the approach of a small contingent of volunteers under Major Guido Ilges, who ultimately chose not to take on the much larger group of Nez Perce directly. When he tried to lure the Nez Perce into an ambush, warriors climbed surrounding hills and fired down on Ilges's men, killing one. After a few hours, the Nez Perce withdrew, leaving Ilges to return to Cow Island.

Two days earlier, on September 23, Miles had approached within 6 miles of the Missouri River in preparation for a crossing. The next morning, Miles learned that the Nez Perce had crossed the Missouri at Cow Island, 40 miles west of Miles's position. Managing to recall a steamboat that had passed not long before, Miles arranged to have those of his men who had not previously crossed ferried across the river.

A Fateful Decision

With the Nez Perce having outpaced Howard and with seemingly only prairie land between them and Canada, sentiment turned against Poker Joe's hard driving. Looking Glass believed that it was time to slow down and permit the tired to rest. Many agreed with him. In a fateful decision, leadership was returned to Looking Glass, whose foresight would be no better now than at Big Hole. This time, complacency would prove disastrous.

Many Wounds later recalled the exchange between Looking Glass and Poker Joe. Poker Joe accepted the change but issued a prescient warning. "All right, Looking Glass," he said, "you can lead. I am trying to save the people, doing my best to cross into Canada before the soldiers find us. You can take command, but I think we will be caught and killed."[11]

Looking Glass, of course, did not know that Miles was moving rapidly to cut off the Nez Perce. Miles's intelligence was good enough to ascertain the speed with which his quarry was moving, and he was confident that he could intercept Joseph's band so long as the group did not increase its speed—which it would do if Nez Perce scouts discovered Miles's men. For this reason, Miles tried to maintain invisibility by keeping a mountain range known as the Little Rockies between him and the Nez Perce until he was close enough to attack.

Legends of American Indian Resistance

"FROM WHERE THE SUN NOW STANDS, I WILL FIGHT NO MORE FOREVER"

Place of the Manure Fires

Looking Glass decided to establish camp in a hollow known as the Place of the Manure Fires. To the north, just within sight, stood the hills called the Bear's Paw (or, alternatively, the Wolf's Paw). The battle that would soon ensue would come to be known as the Battle of Bear's Paw. Still farther northward loomed the mountains that marked the border between the United States and safety in Canada. The day grew colder as the Nez Perce set up camp, and rain turned into snow. Joseph, as usual, oversaw the work and made sure that the horses were secured.

Looking Glass rejected the plea by some warriors to scout backward to make sure that no soldiers were following. Joseph, focused on caring for the elderly, sick, and young, supported Looking Glass's decision. The location of the camp was low and out of the wind. Nearby were water and plenty of buffalo chips with which to make fires to warm those who were cold—the characteristic of the location that gave the site its name. It was the evening of September 29. Fifteen miles away Colonel Miles and his men attempted to sleep through the cold night, unable to build effective fires with the buffalo chips.

Miles had his men up by 2:00 A.M. By 4:30, they were on the march again. Then came a Cheyenne scout to report that he had discovered Joseph's camp.

Meanwhile, Joseph had gone with his daughter Noise of Running Feet to see to the horse herd. Two scouts raced into camp to report that soldiers were approaching, and on a nearby hill another scout rode in circles waving a blanket and firing his rifle to signal the danger.

As the Nez Perce warriors raced to grab their weapons, Joseph instructed Noise of Running Feet to grab a horse and flee north toward Canada, as many women and children were doing. She would escape the battle, but her father would never see her again.

Joseph leaped onto a horse and dashed for his wife and infant daughter. A bullet struck his horse, but the animal stayed on its feet. Reaching the shelter where his family had spent the night, Joseph took the rifle his wife handed him and hurried to enter the fight.

The Nez Perce drove the soldiers back, but the camp was badly damaged by the attack. The soldiers, although unable to achieve the quick victory they wanted, had taken cover on surrounding bluffs, from which they could keep the Nez Perce pinned down. Heavy fire soon commenced, and the warriors withdrew from the original campsite to a draw where women and children who had not fled north had taken refuge.

The situation clearly was dire. The initial onslaught and counterattack had cost the Nez Perce dearly. Joseph's brother, Ollokot, was dead. So was Toohoolhoolzote. Husis Kute had accidentally killed Lone Bird. Poker Joe also had fallen to friendly fire. Altogether, about 20 Nez Perce had died. Four band leaders—Joseph, Looking Glass, White Bird, and Husis Kute—remained alive.

Casualties also were high on the other side. Although Miles had superior forces and the element of surprise, his men had been outfought. Only a single officer of the Seventh Cavalry remained alive and unharmed. The three first sergeants of the Seventh were dead. Miles noted that 22 of his men were killed and 42 wounded, with "the line encircling the camp ... dotted with dead and wounded soldiers and horses."[12]

Under Siege

The Nez Perce had withstood the initial onslaught, but their prospects for escape were bleak. They had lost most of their horses. Families were split, with many members having fled, although those left behind could not know whether their kinsmen had been successful in escaping the attack or were killed or captured by the soldiers. Now those who remained were surrounded. The situation would become even worse when General Howard arrived.

Joseph and the other leaders debated what to do. They could stay and fight, surrender, or try to sneak away under cover of darkness. For Joseph, the long struggle to reach Canada had come to an end. As he looked at the elderly, the women and children, and the wounded, he knew that they could neither fight nor flee. Yet White Bird and Looking Glass wanted to wait. They sent six men as messengers to Sitting Bull. Perhaps if he came, together they could repel the soldiers and still reach their destination.

The situation also was uncertain for Miles and his men. They had endured heavy casualties, and the wounded were suffering mightily in the cold. During the afternoon, a brisk north wind rose and snow started falling, with 5 inches piling up by morning. They still had not succeeded in defeating Joseph, and they also realized that Sitting Bull might appear. After all, he was only 80 miles away. If his forces arrived to defend the Nez Perce, Miles's men knew well that they might be facing another Little Bighorn. Time might actually be on the side of the Nez Perce, Miles realized, so he decided to apply pressure to force a surrender.

The following morning, October 1, the Nez Perce found themselves under fire, not from rifles, but from the army's Hotchkiss guns. In reality, these guns were hard to position so that they could hit the Indians below, but the pounding reverberations of the shells were at least unsettling and a sharp reminder to Joseph and the rest of the Nez Perce huddled in the draw that they were surrounded. The concussion from shells also threatened to cause the pits in which women and children were hiding to collapse, potentially burying them alive.

Miles had his men stay alert but hold their rifle fire unless they had a clear target. Such a target presented itself when Looking Glass saw a figure in the distance. He thought that it might be one of Sitting Bull's men, so he stretched up to get a better look. Among the bad decisions that Looking Glass made on the trek toward Canada, this one was the worst for him personally: A sharp-eyed soldier snapped off a shot and hit Looking Glass in the forehead, killing him.

Joseph and Miles

In the morning of October 1, discussions began between the Nez Perce and Colonel Miles. Yellow Bull was sent to meet an emissary from Miles, who entered the camp under a flag of truce. Miles was requesting a meeting with Joseph. Joseph, acutely concerned about the welfare of his people, was willing to talk with Miles, but White Bird opposed any discussion between the two. Joseph promised that he would enter into no agreement, but merely hear what Miles had to say and then report back to the Nez Perce.

Tom Hill, a part Nez Perce and part Delaware warrior who spoke English, was sent to Miles to arrange the meeting. After discussing the arrangements, Hill and Miles walked partway toward the Nez Perce, and Hill called for Joseph to join them. Miles still considered Joseph the primary leader and strategist of the Nez Perce, the individual responsible for both the military victories by the Nez Perce over the summer and their until now successful flight toward Canada.

Joseph and Miles shook hands and walked together to the colonel's tent. Miles promised Joseph that the Nez Perce could return to their homeland in the spring; until then, he said, they would stay in the Yellowstone area. He insisted that they give up their weapons, however—a demand that drew Joseph's quick opposition for both philosophical and practical reasons. Joseph was prepared to stop fighting, but he was not prepared to surrender. In addition, the weapons were needed for hunting so that the Nez Perce could feed themselves.

As Joseph started to leave, soldiers blocked his departure, forcing his return to Miles's tent. Tom Hill relayed the bitter news to the Nez Perce that despite the white flag of truce, Joseph had been taken prisoner. Fortunately for Joseph, Lieutenant Lovell Jerome, who had been sent by Miles to observe what the Nez Perce were doing, rode so close that he was easily captured. The next day, Joseph was freed in exchange for Jerome.

White Bird argued that the Nez Perce should attempt to escape. He was confident that at night they could secretly kill enough soldiers to open a gap in the lines large enough to allow their exodus. Relying on justice from the soldiers, White Bird contended, was foolish. Joseph, as always, was concerned about those who were most vulnerable. He knew that women, children, and the elderly could not move rapidly enough to escape the soldiers; moreover, he did not want to leave his dead unburied.

Resumption of shelling on October 3 helped push the Nez Perce closer to a decision. Yet there was no good option unless Sitting Bull appeared, so Joseph and White Bird decided to wait another day and hope for what must increasingly have seemed like a desperately unlikely miracle.

The End of the Fighting

General Howard finally arrived on October 4. He had with him two treaty Nez Perce, Jokais and Meopkowit, known to the soldiers as Captain John and Old George, respectively. Both of the Indians had daughters among those holding out with Joseph. The following day, Howard sent them as emissaries to Joseph. Although the two were welcomed, the Nez Perce found it difficult to trust either them or Howard.

Joseph wanted the fighting to stop, but he was not willing to surrender. Peace for him meant a ceasefire and an agreement that would permit his people to return home. With that message, Captain John and Old George were sent back to Miles. Before long, the two returned, carrying Miles's invitation to Joseph to confer personally with him and an assurance from Miles and Howard that they did not want any more fighting.

At that point, Joseph made the remarks that have come down through history as one of the most famous and poignant speeches ever made within the history of the Indian wars. History generally has misrepresented the remarks, in large part because of the translation and editorial commentary by Howard's aide, Lieutenant Charles Erskine Scott Wood. After Captain John relayed the remarks, Wood turned them from a conclusion shared with fellow Nez Perce to a surrender speech directed toward Miles and Howard. According to Kent Nerburn, Joseph addressed his comments initially to Old John and Captain George and then turned to White Bird, Yellow Bull, and Husis Kute:

> Tell General Howard that I know his heart. What he told me before, I have in my heart. I am tired of fighting. Our chiefs are killed. Looking Glass is dead. Too-hoolhoolzote is dead. The old men are all dead. It is the young men who say yes or no. He who led on the young men [Joseph's brother, Ollokot] is dead. It is cold and we have no blankets. The little children are freezing to death. My people, some of them, have run away to the hills and have no blankets, no food; no one knows where they are—perhaps freezing to death. I want to have time to look for my children and see how many of them I can find. Maybe I shall find them among the dead. Hear me, my chiefs. I am tired; my heart is sick and sad. From where the sun now stands I will fight no more forever.[13]

As eloquent as Joseph was (although the words attributed to him may, in fact, have been only somewhat his), not everyone was convinced. White Bird disagreed strongly, arguing that Joseph was foolish to trust the army and expressing his continued determination not to give up.

The subsequent meeting between Joseph and the army officers involved two translators: Tom Hill for Joseph and Ad Chapman for Howard and Miles. Miles agreed that Joseph and his people would be able to return home in the spring. The coming winter they would spend in a safe location. Joseph negotiated a gradual turning over of his people but, of course, did not admit his reason—that it would give White Bird and others who wished to do so an opportunity to escape.

Joseph gave up his rifle to Miles, and the two men shook hands. Then other soldiers also shook hands with Joseph. Howard charged Lieutenant Wood with seeing to Joseph as a prisoner but one who was to be treated well. During the night, a group led by White Bird carefully made their way through the army lines and on toward Canada.

JOSEPH'S LONG STRUGGLE TO RETURN HOME

Promises

The future looked hopeful for Joseph. The fighting and dying appeared to be at an end. He had a promise from General Howard and Colonel Miles that the fighting was over and a promise from Miles that when the spring came he and his people could return to their homeland. During the winter, they would be safe and secure, free from hunger and the threat of freezing temperatures taking the lives of the young, ill, and elderly.

Unfortunately, even sincerely made promises—and there is every indication that Miles was sincere in his promise to allow Joseph to return—sometimes are not kept. Related to these failed promises was a root problem endemic to Indian–Euro-American relations: Neither adequately understood how the other was organized in terms of responsibility and leadership. The U.S. military kept assuming the existence of an Indian organizational structure similar to its own, with established hierarchies and chains of command, and always someone in charge able to give orders that all would follow. Such a structure was never truly natural to a people who relied on discussion, consensus, and persuasion, and who demonstrated tolerance for dissent in both word and deed. Typical of this military assumption was the false conclusion that Joseph was such an absolute commander when, in fact, he had little impact on decisions involving war strategy until the end, when most Nez Perce war leaders were dead. Even then, White Bird refused to go along with his decision.

Indian leaders also misunderstood the structural authority of U.S. military leaders. Joseph assumed that when Howard and Miles gave their word, they were personally committed to following through and would do so regardless of what other men did. After all, they were leaders, chiefs, the men in charge. They might not be able to dictate everyone else's actions, but they themselves could do what they said they would do. Thus, when Howard and Miles promised Joseph that he would be able to return to his home, Joseph believed them. He did not realize that the chain of command went above both officers, that military and political superiors could countermand their assurances. That, of course, is what happened.

The remainder of Joseph's life would be one long attempt to return to the Wallowa Valley. Joseph understood the necessity of compromise, and from time to time he did compromise, but always with the hope that he and his people, even if only gradually and step by step, would be able to return home someday.

Disappointments

As Howard and Miles took stock of the group of tired and hungry men, women, and children who came forward, they found that the original number of about 800 people in the group with Joseph had been cut almost in half—to

418, including more than 300 women and children. The number who escaped to Canada remains uncertain, with estimates ranging from a handful (according to Miles and Howard, a low figure that may be self-serving by officers not wanting to admit that a large number escaped from their control) to more than 230 (the number cited by the Nez Perce Black Eagle, a figure likely far too high). For those 418 Nez Perce who surrendered, the long flight to Canada was over, having covered some 1,800 miles, counting the backtracking and circumlocutions required to evade their pursuers.[14]

Now the remnant of the Nez Perce were to begin another long, torturous journey that would cover many years. It began shortly after the surrender that Joseph continued to believe in his heart was never truly a surrender.

The first disappointment for Joseph related to the location of their winter home. Howard and Miles had settled on the Tongue River Cantonment (renamed Fort Keogh the next year) near the confluence of the Tongue and Yellowstone Rivers in southeast Montana. Howard left Miles on October 7, and Miles departed with the Nez Perce the same day for Tongue River, soon meeting Sturgis, who had been looking for any excursion south by Sitting Bull.

Joseph rode with Miles at the head of the party on the 65-mile trek to the Missouri River, with Ad Chapman riding between the two to translate. At the Missouri, Howard returned to confer with Miles before taking a steamer for St. Louis. Miles sent wounded soldiers and Indians by boat to the nearest hospital, and the rest of the Nez Perce and Miles's men continued overland to the Yellowstone River.

The 500-mile journey to the Tongue River Cantonment allowed ample time for Joseph and Miles to get to know each other well. Miles quickly came to respect Joseph and determined that he should do all he could to help Joseph return to his home region. Miles later wrote of his Nez Perce friend that "Chief Joseph was the highest type of the Indian I have ever known, very handsome, kind, and brave."[15]

Further orders then arrived from General Philip Sheridan, commander of the Division of the Missouri, ordering that Joseph and the Nez Perce be sent farther east to Fort Abraham Lincoln near Bismarck, a new town in what is now North Dakota. The location was the meeting point for the Northern Pacific Railroad and the Missouri River, making supplying the captives less expensive. Miles objected but to no avail, and assured Joseph that he had tried to keep his promise.

Miles sent the wounded, elderly, and young by boat on the Yellowstone (continuing on the Missouri) while the rest of the party continued overland in wagons. Along the way, they stopped at Fort Buford in the northwestern corner of Dakota Territory, continued on to Fort Berthold, and finally arrived at Bismarck on November 19.

At Bismarck, Joseph was treated like a conquering hero. He and Miles were met by the mayor, serenaded with the "Star-Spangled Banner," and applauded by many of the townspeople. Miles was feted at a banquet held at the Sheridan House Hotel, during which he spoke movingly about Joseph's desire for peace,

Indian Territory

The area of the United States west of the Mississippi River comprising present-day Kansas, Nebraska, Oklahoma, and part of Iowa was designated "Indian country" in 1825, with general borders established by the Indian Intercourse Act of 1834. Indians were moved to this region starting in the early nineteenth century as part of the Indian Removal Policy of the U.S. government. The Indian Removal Act of 1830 accelerated that process, permitting the President to require tribes to move beyond the Mississippi—a position strongly advocated by President Andrew Jackson.

Portions of that area were gradually removed from its intended use—for tribes originally living in the eastern half of the country—as territories and later states were carved out of the region. After the Civil War, the remaining portion roughly approximated the later state of Oklahoma. In addition, western peoples, including the Nez Perce, were sent to Indian Territory.

Indian Territory, however, was never officially a territory, which made it relatively easy for the federal government to shift its boundaries. A federal court system was finally established in the unofficial territory in 1889; in the same year, firm boundaries for the area were established. Nonetheless, those boundaries were changed again in 1890 when Oklahoma Territory was carved out of the area, with Indian Territory comprising about the eastern half of the current state of Oklahoma.

Efforts by Indian leaders early in the twentieth century to receive statehood for the region as the state of Sequoyah failed. In 1907, Oklahoma Territory and Indian Territory were joined as the state of Oklahoma. At that point, Indian Territory ceased to exist.

his unjust sufferings, and his kindness toward wounded soldiers who had been captured. An enthusiastic Bismarck citizenry then threw another gala at the Sheridan for Joseph, who was accompanied by several other Nez Perce, including Husis Kute and Yellow Bull.

Before Joseph's banquet, Miles departed for St. Paul without having the heart to tell his friend that additional orders had come through requiring the Nez Perce to be transported by train to Fort Leavenworth, Kansas. There they would await a final decision regarding their permanent home, which would probably be in Indian Territory (the future state of Oklahoma), far from the Wallowa Valley. Having come so far since the Bear's Paw, Joseph and the Nez Perce were pleased with the reception they were given in Bismarck and wanted to spend the winter there. However, that was not to be.

Yet another indignity awaited Joseph before he boarded the train to Fort Leavenworth: He had to sell his horse that he had ridden for so many miles. The money he received from the forced sale was $35.

Indian Territory

The train made its way through the city of St. Paul, where Joseph was disappointed that he did not see Colonel Miles. As the train made its stops, people crowded around to see the famous "Red Napoleon," and Joseph responded graciously, moving out onto the rear platform to greet the onlookers.

The train arrived at Fort Leavenworth on November 27, 1877. Again Joseph proved an immensely popular draw, with people traveling even from other states to see him. Joseph willingly signed autographs, spelling out "Young Joseph" (which he had been taught to write years earlier at the Spaldings' mission) as well as he could.

By summer of 1878, the living conditions for the Nez Perce had deteriorated badly at their riverside camp. The water was polluted by sewage from the city of Leavenworth, the high temperatures spoiled their food, and increasing numbers of Joseph's people fell ill and died. On July 21, the Nez Perce were again herded onto a train, their destination this time Indian Territory.

That evening the train chugged into Baxter Springs at the southern edge of Kansas, and the Nez Perce boarded wagons brought by Modoc drivers. In charge of the Nez Perce was a Quaker agent named Hiram Jones. Quakers, under President Grant's Peace Policy, were given charge of Joseph's people. Unfortunately, Jones was a thoroughly corrupt individual whose personal morality was sharply at odds with Quaker principles. Jones, while in charge of Quapaw Agency in the northern stretch of Indian Territory, skimmed off much of the money allotted to him for his Indian charges and cheated them on rations.

Several tribes, most of them consisting of small remnants of their people (including the Peoria, Miami, Shawnee, Seneca, Wyandot, Ottawa, and Quapaw), had been moved to Indian Territory from the Midwest and East. From the West came the Modocs and now the Nez Perce. It was among the Modocs that the Nez Perce were initially settled.

The Nez Perce arrived at the agency virtually destitute of the possessions necessary to survive, including clothing and materials for shelter. They also lacked food, and sickness spread rapidly among the group, especially killing children. The new arrivals' condition alarmed government visitors who came to help Joseph choose a site for the Nez Perce to live. In addition to their deplorable physical condition, they seemed to have given up. Yet, Joseph, despite his people's current condition, balked at another move short of a return to their original home.

The government representatives contacted the Commissioner of Indian Affairs, A. E. Hayt. Hayt informed Joseph that his people would not be permitted to return to the Wallowa Valley and would have to accept permanent residence in Indian Territory. According to Nerburn, this was the first time that Joseph had definitively been told that he would not be permitted to take his people back home.[16]

Joseph did not give up his quest. During the following years, he struggled to make his case for a return to the Wallowa Valley. Assisting him was Ad Chapman, paid by the government to serve as interpreter but increasingly a passionate advocate for the Nez Perce. Joseph and Chapman used tools previously unknown to Joseph, such as the newspaper and the telegraph, to raise public awareness of their plight. Chapman wrote letters reporting on the actions of Agent Jones. They gave interviews to reporters, appealed to Congress, and visited Washington, D.C. On January 17, 1879, Joseph, wearing traditional Nez Perce dress of a blanket coat of skins and furs and beaded moccasins, and with his forelock flipped backward and braids hanging down the sides of his face, spoke to a large and responsive audience in Lincoln Hall in the nation's capital. Accompanied by Yellow Bull and with Chapman translating, Joseph told his story. An English-language version of Joseph's speech was soon published in a respected journal, *North American Review*, contributing further to his fame. Before leaving Washington, he met with President Rutherford B. Hayes. Joseph was a great hit, but, unfortunately, nothing changed for his people.

Back at Qualpaw Agency, Jones attempted to counter attacks on him by bringing in several treaty Nez Perce who had converted to Christianity. James Reuben, a former scout for General Howard, served as interpreter. Archie Lawyer, a schoolteacher and minister, and Mark Williams, who had become an accomplished farmer, were among the group. They were good and decent men who sincerely believed that the nontreaty Nez Perce should accept Christianity and the white man's ways, but they offered yet another obstacle for Joseph. He now not only had to persuade the U.S. government to honor the promises made by Colonel Miles, but also had to contend with an increasing division within his own people.

Over the next six years, Joseph continued his campaign to move his people back west. During those years, Jones was removed as Quapaw agent, but illness and suffering continued to afflict the Nez Perce. Among those who died was Joseph's young daughter, who had been born as the Nez Perce were starting their journey to the northeast in 1877. Still, success was coming gradually. Miles and Howard, Joseph's old adversaries, lobbied in support of Joseph's requests. Reuben and Lawyer expanded their religious contacts, especially among Presbyterians, to gain support from religious communities. Although far from Joseph on spiritual issues, they shared his goal of returning to the homeland.

A group of about three dozen Nez Perce, mainly widows and orphans, was permitted to leave in June 1883 under the direction of James Reuben. During the following year, a number of Presbyterian congregations petitioned Congress to permit the relocation of all the Nez Perce. Miles, now a general and commanding officer of the Department of the Columbia, continued to make his pleas, still trying to honor his promise made years before.

Finally, in July 1884, Congress acted, authorizing the return of the Nez Perce to their home in the West. Immediately, opposition arose to allowing Joseph to return, as his fame now became a double-edged sword. In the East, he was a hero; in the West, he was held accountable for violence that he had never wanted and had vehemently opposed. Warrants were still outstanding on some of the Nez Perce, including Joseph. For the sake of his people, he agreed to a division of the Nez Perce into two groups. Joseph and those who chose to follow him would join Chief Moses of the Columbias (also known as the Sinkquaius) at Colville Reservation 200 miles north of Lapwai in Washington Territory, not far from the Canadian border. The rest of the Nez Perce would return to Lapwai.

Return to the Northwest

On May 21, 1885, the Nez Perce started for the railroad station at Arkansas City. Only 268 of the original number of about 800 remained. About 100 had died since arriving at Indian Territory. Ultimately, 118 chose Lapwai as their destination; 150, including Joseph, went on to Colville. In 1890, those who wished to do so were permitted to leave Colville for Lapwai, but only a few—among them Yellow Wolf—made the move.

Joseph, who had moved with his Nez Perce group farther west on the reservation to Nespelem Valley to live with the Columbias shortly after arriving, did not view Lapwai as his home. He continued to wait, hoping that eventually he would be permitted to return to the Wallowa Valley. He rejected an allotment of land under the Dawes Act of 1887 (authored by Senator Henry Dawes of Massachusetts). Also known as the General Allotment Act, it divided reservations into small parcels of land that were given to individuals and families. The same legislation also reclaimed substantial amounts of reservation land that could then be made available to settlers. Joseph believed that to accept such an offer would mean that he was relinquishing his right to his native land in the Wallowa.

Joseph resumed his journeys to Washington, D.C., meeting with officials, including the president. On an 1897 trip, he was invited to visit New York City. There he joined in a parade and participated in dedicating Ulysses Grant's tomb. He also attended Buffalo Bill's Wild West show at Madison Square Garden and was visited during the show by Generals Howard and Miles, who were in the audience.

James McLaughlin, who served as the agent in charge of Standing Rock Reservation, where Sitting Bull spent the final years of his life, was charged with preparing a report and recommendation regarding Joseph's potential return to the Wallowa Valley. Together Joseph and McLaughlin traveled to the Wallowa Valley in the summer of 1900. Joseph visited the graves of his father and mother, finding that someone had put up a fence around the site to protect it. McLaughlin

From the Dawes Act (1887)

Be it enacted by the Senate and House of Representatives of the United States of America in Congress assembled, That in all cases where any tribe or band of Indians has been, or shall hereafter be, located upon any reservation created for their use ... the President of the United States be, and he hereby is, authorized, whenever in his opinion any reservation or any part thereof of such Indians is advantageous for agricultural and grazing purposes ... to allot the lands in said reservation in severalty to any Indian located thereon in quantities as follows:

To each head of a family, one-quarter of a section;
To each single person over eighteen years of age, one-eighth of a section;
To each orphan child under eighteen years of age, one-eighth of a section; and
To each other single person under eighteen years now living, or who may be born prior to the date of the order of the President directing an allotment of the lands embraced in any reservation, one-sixteenth of a section . . ..

[A]t any time after lands have been allotted to all the Indians of any tribe as herein provided, or sooner if in the opinion of the President it shall be for the best interests of said tribe, it shall be lawful for the Secretary of the Interior to negotiate with such Indian tribe for the purchase and release by said tribe ... of such portions of its reservation not allotted ... Provided however, That all lands ... so sold or released to the United States by any Indian tribe shall be held by the United States for the sole purpose of securing homes to actual settlers . . ..

eventually recommended that Joseph stay at Colville, and the Indian Commission agreed, effectively ending Joseph's final real chance for a permanent return.

Joseph returned to Colville but continued to remain loyal to the old ways. He lived in a tipi, rejecting the wooden house built for him. He opposed sending his people's children to boarding schools, encouraged traditional spiritual beliefs, and generally used his Nez Perce name—Hin-mah-too-yah-lat-kekht. In 1903, he traveled to Washington yet again, meeting with President Theodore Roosevelt. On the trip back, he visited with General Howard when the two spoke at an event at the Carlisle Indian Industrial School in Carlisle, Pennsylvania.

Joseph died on September 21, 1904. Sensing death's approach, he asked his wife to get his headdress so that he could die looking like a leader, but he died before she returned with it. Joseph was buried in the Nespelem Valley, preceded in death by all nine of his children. His daughter Noise of Running Feet (also known as Sarah Moses) was never reunited with the father who had sent her off, he hoped to safety, during the final Nez Perce battle.

To the very end, Joseph had refused to accept a U.S. takeover of his homeland. Ironically, this man of peace had persisted perhaps more consistently than any other Indian leader, including the great war leaders, in resisting pressure to submit to the wishes of the U.S. government.

NOTES

1. Kent Nerburn, *Chief Joseph and the Flight of the Nez Perce: The Untold Story of an American Tragedy* (New York: HarperSanFrancisco, 2005) 55.
2. Helen Addison Howard, *Saga of Chief Joseph* (1941; Lincoln: University of Nebraska Press, 1978) 81.
3. Chief Joseph, "An American Indian's View of Indian Affairs," *North American Review* (April 1879); reprinted in *Chief Joseph's Own Story* (St. Paul: Great Northern Railway, 1925) 15.
4. O. O. Howard, *Nez Perce Joseph: An Account of His Ancestors, His Lands, His Confederates, His Enemies, His Murders, His War, His Pursuit and Capture* (1881; New York: Da Capo Press, 1972) 29; O. O. Howard, *My Life and Experiences Among Our Hostile Indians* (1907; New York: Da Capo Press, 1972) 239.
5. Helen Addison Howard 106.
6. O. O. Howard, *Nez Perce Joseph* 164; Jerome A. Greene, *Nez Perce Summer, 1877: The U.S. Army and the Nee-Me-Poo Crisis* (Helena: Montana Historical Society Press, 2000) 97.
7. Greene 111.
8. Nerburn 181, 187.
9. Elliott West, *The Last Indian War: The Nez Perce Story* (New York: Oxford University Press, 2009) 248.
10. O. O. Howard, *My Life and Personal Experiences Among Our Hostile Indians* 297.
11. Lucullus Virgil, *Hear Me, My Chiefs*, ed. Ruth Bordin (Caldwell, ID: Caxton Printers, 1952) 473–74.
12. Nelson A. Miles, *Personal Recollections and Observations of General Nelson A. Miles* (1896; New York: Da Capo Press, 1969) 272–73.
13. Nerburn 267–68; "Howard's Official Report, December 27, 1877," *Report of the Secretary of War*, 1877, I, 630.
14. Helen Addison Howard 333; West 181–82.
15. Nelson A. Miles, *Serving the Republic: Memoirs of the Civil and Military Life of Nelson A. Miles* (1911; Freeport, NY: Books for Libraries Press, 1971) 181.
16. Nerburn 336.

RECOMMENDED READING

Chief Joseph. *Chief Joseph's Own Story*. St. Paul: Great Northern Railway, 1925.
Greene, Jerome A. *Nez Perce Summer, 1877: The U.S. Army and the Nee-Me-Poo Crisis*. Helena: Montana Historical Society Press, 2000.
Howard, Helen Addison. *Saga of Chief Joseph*. 1941. Lincoln: University of Nebraska Press, 1978.
Howard, Oliver O. *Nez Perce Joseph: An Account of His Ancestors, His Lands, His Confederates, His Enemies, His Murders, His War, His Pursuit and Capture*. 1881; New York: Da Capo Press, 1972.
Josephy, Alvin M., Jr. *The Nez Perce Indians and the Opening of the Northwest*. New Haven: Yale University Press, 1965.
McWhorter, Lucullus Virgil. *Yellow Wolf: His Own Story*. 1940. Caldwell, ID: Caxton Printers, 1948.

Miles, Nelson A. *Personal Recollections and Observations of General Nelson A. Miles.* 1896. New York: Da Capo Press, 1969.

Miles, Nelson A. *Serving the Republic: Memoirs of the Civil and Military Life of Nelson A. Miles.* 1911. Freeport, NY: Books for Libraries Press, 1971.

Nerburn, Kent. *Chief Joseph and the Flight of the Nez Perce: The Untold Story of an American Tragedy.* New York: HarperSanFrancisco, 2005.

West, Elliott. *The Last Indian War: The Nez Perce Story.* New York: Oxford University Press, 2009.

Geronimo appears still ready to fight for his freedom shortly before surrendering to General Crook in 1886. (Library of Congress)

Geronimo (Goyahkla) 1829–1909

Geronimo, named Goyahkla by his parents, remains one of the best-known American Indian leaders. That fame continues to rest almost entirely on his reputation as a warrior. His military exploits struck fear into the hearts of settlers throughout the Southwest and of Mexicans south of the U.S. border. Reviled in his lifetime by Euro-Americans, and even by some fellow Apaches who blamed him for continuing to fight after resistance seemed hopeless, Geronimo lacked the multidimensional qualities that characterized such figures as Sitting Bull and Chief Joseph. His primary endeavor was war, with his dedication to combat embedded in him not only by historical circumstance but also by personal tragedy.

Such was the identification of the name "Geronimo" with daring, often violent action that U.S. paratroopers in World War II would shout it out as they leapt from planes. Euro-American children growing up in the decades following Geronimo's death would call out his name as they jumped from a swing or engaged in some other type of derring-do.

Even as the twenty-first century dawned, Geronimo was to be found in news accounts amid the resurfacing of old rumors concerning his remains and the secret Yale fraternity, Skull and Bones, that includes such famous political figures as President George W. Bush and Massachusetts Senator John Kerry. According to the story, the President's grandfather was stationed as a young soldier at Fort Sill, Oklahoma, in 1918, where the Apache leader had been buried less than a decade earlier. Prescott Bush and other youthful fraternity brothers supposedly dug up the grave and stole Geronimo's skull and an assortment of bones for use in the fraternity's exotic rituals. History tends not to give much credence to the story. Some of Geronimo's descendants, however, believe that the theft did take place. They sued Skull and Bones (along with Yale University and the U.S. government) over the matter, filing their lawsuit in Washington, D.C., on February 17, 2009—the one hundredth anniversary of the war leader's death. They demanded that the remains be returned for proper burial near Geronimo's birthplace in New Mexico. If successful, the lawsuit would achieve what Geronimo had wanted for so long after his final surrender: to return home.

THE WARRIOR'S CALLING

Early Years

Goyahkla (also spelled Goyathlay and meaning "one who yawns"), later to be known more famously as Geronimo, was born in 1829, apparently in what is now known as the Gila National Forest in southwestern New Mexico. In his autobiography, published in 1906, Geronimo names Arizona as his birthplace, but historians and tribal sources generally prefer New Mexico, recognizing that when Geronimo was born neither state existed and most of the land later incorporated into the states (plus western Texas and northern Mexico) was

Apache territory. He was born into the Bedonkohe, one of several bands of the Chiricahua Apaches—along with the Chokonen, Nednai, and Chihenne (Mimbreno). Both the number and identification of the Chiricahua bands, however, have been subject to various interpretations, and the spelling of their names varies considerably from source to source. One of the most helpful summaries of the Chiricahua band structure appears in Edwin R. Sweeney's biography *Mangas Coloradas: Chief of the Chiricahua Apaches.*[1]

Goyahkla's father was Taklishim, son of the revered chief Mahko of the Bedonkohe. His mother was Juana (or Juanita). He had seven siblings—three brothers and four sisters. Little is known specifically about Goyahkla's childhood, but the autobiography indicates a normal Chiricahua upbringing that included helping with crops, playing war games, and practicing skills such as horseback riding and shooting with bows and arrows. Much of his childhood, like that of other Apache boys, served as preparation for his adult roles as a hunter and a warrior.

Goyahkla had to assume adult responsibilities even sooner than did many of his childhood friends. Taklishim died after a lengthy illness around 1844, and the son notes in his autobiography that he assumed the role of protector of his mother, who did not remarry and lived the rest of her life with (or at least near) Goyahkla. By the age of 17, the son was also accepted as a warrior. At that point, he was, by every standard of his people, an adult.

The Turning Point

Goyahkla, having reached adulthood, took an attractive young Nednai woman named Alope as his wife. Her father, Noposo, required several ponies for her, a price Goyahkla paid without complaint. Many years later, Goyahkla noted that she had been a good wife and had borne three children but was never strong. After the marriage, he set up a tipi for her near his mother's.

The Apaches had alternately traded with and fought the Mexicans, and Goyahkla entered into this dual relationship as soon as he qualified to be called a warrior. It all seemed natural enough and not particularly threatening to the young husband and father when around 1850 he made another trip south of the border. His Bedonkohe Apaches along with Chihennes, both under the leadership of Mangas Coloradas, traveled through Sonora, making their way toward Casas Grandes. On the way they camped at the town they called Kaskiyeh, generally believed to be Janos, going daily into town to trade.

As a group of Apache men, including Goyahkla, were returning one afternoon, they were met by women and children fleeing the camp. The news was horrifying: A group of Mexican soldiers had attacked the camp, killed the warriors who had remained in camp, captured the ponies and supplies, and murdered many of the women and children.

The leader of the troops, General José María Carrasco, commander of the Mexican forces in Sonora, had decided to end the practice of Apaches raiding towns in one state to gain goods with which to trade in another. Consequently,

Carrasco had led his men into the neighboring state of Chihuahua despite having no jurisdiction there and attacked the Chiricahua camp.

Among the dead were Goyahkla's mother, Juana; his wife, Alope; and his three children. The loss would stay with Goyahkla long after he became the famous Geronimo. In his autobiography decades later, he recalled his emotional reaction to his tragic discovery: "I did not pray, nor did I resolve to do anything in particular, for I had no purpose left. I finally followed the tribe silently, keeping just within hearing distance of the soft noise of the feet of the retreating Apaches."[2]

After returning to the Chiricahua camp in Arizona, Goyahkla, following Apache tradition, burned his mother's tipi and possessions. Although he was entitled to retain his own tipi, he also burned it, along with his family possessions. He specifically cited his children's playthings as among the objects he burned. "I was never again contented in our quiet home," he said, adding that whenever he approached his father's grave or was reminded of his happy family life, his "heart would ache for revenge upon Mexico."[3] Goyahkla would marry several more times and have other children, but they would not wipe away the traumatic impact of his losing his first family. From that time forward, his mission was clear: He would fight, first against the Mexicans who had destroyed his family, and later against the soldiers and settlers of the United States.

Now Geronimo

Goyahkla would begin seeking his revenge about a year later, probably in 1851, although his autobiography, apparently erroneously, assigns the massacre and revenge battle to 1858 and 1859. Before then, the grieving widower underwent a spiritual experience that would help direct his life. According to his biographer Angie Debo, Goyahkla was sitting alone crying when he heard a voice calling his name. The voice called out four times (a spiritually significant number for the Apaches), and then pronounced that no gun would ever kill him and that the power speaking to him would guide his arrows. Such power, whatever its specific source, transformed the recipient into a *diyin*, a term sometimes translated as a shaman or medicine man, although like most such translations the English word does not adequately convey the precise essence of the spiritual capacity that the individual possesses.

There is no reference to this incident in Geronimo's autobiography, although Sam Haozous, grandson of Mangas Coloradas, testified to its occurrence in an interview with Debo in 1955. It is possible that the aging Geronimo considered the incident too personal or its spiritual nature inappropriate to share with Euro-Americans. The incident is usually believed to have occurred between the massacre at Janos and the retributive raid into Mexico.

Mangas Coloradas would lead the raid, but he appointed Goyahkla to solicit support from Cochise, leader of the Chokonen Apaches. Goyahkla then traveled to the Nednai led by Chief Juh (also spelled Whoa, in either case pronounced "Who"). Juh was married to Ishton, a favorite cousin of Goyahkla's often referred to as his sister, not only because of the family closeness common in Apache culture but also because the two were particularly close. The marriage helped greatly to strengthen the bond between Goyahkla and Juh.

The Bedonkohe, Chokonen, and Nednai Apaches, according to Goyahkla, traveled in three divisions, with Goyahkla as guide. The warriors marched on foot, covering about 40 to 45 miles per day. When they reached Arizpe in Sonora, which the Apaches identified, quite possibly correctly, as the town from which the soldiers had come the previous year, they camped. Eight men from the town came out to talk with the Apaches and were killed, a ploy to draw troops into the action. The following day the Apaches fought skirmishes with the troops and captured a supply train.

Because Goyahkla had lost so much in the massacre, he was given the honor of directing the battle the next day when a large Mexican force arrived. He arranged his men in a circle within the woods near a river. When the Mexicans advanced, Goyahkla led a charge from the front while directing other warriors toward the rear of the Mexicans. At one point, he and three other warriors became isolated from the rest, and only Goyahkla among the four managed to survive and reach the rest of the Apaches.

It was during this battle that Mexican soldiers were reported to have started calling out the name Geronimo, although why they did so remains uncertain. Theories include a mispronunciation of his name or the possibility that the soldiers were actually calling upon Saint Jerome for protection. The latter, if correct, might identify the date of the battle as September 30, the saint's feast day, although Geronimo stated in his autobiography that the expedition into Mexico occurred in the summer.

During the conflict, Goyahkla, by his own account, struck down many Mexicans. He had helped to secure an impressive victory and revenged himself on the Mexicans for their destroying his family. He also had a new name—one that would stay with him long after his deeds had become part of history.

DUAL ENEMIES

Mexicans

In the years leading up to the Civil War, Geronimo continued fighting against forces from Mexico but would encounter another enemy as well, in the form of the United States. In his autobiography, Geronimo recounts a long succession of excursions into Mexico—some successful, some not. Although his recollection of dates is sometimes faulty, he seems thoroughly willing to note both the battles that brought him praise and those that elicited blame.

After the successful revenge expedition under Mangas Coloradas, Geronimo persuaded two other warriors to return to Mexico with him. Unfortunately, the raid proved disastrous, and Geronimo's companions were killed. When Geronimo returned to his camp in Arizona, he was much blamed for the failure. A raid that Geronimo assigns to 1860 was much more successful. A party of 25 warriors ambushed Mexican troops and wiped out the entire contingent. Geronimo, however, was hit in the head with a gun and knocked unconscious, bearing a scar for the rest of his life after a convalescence of several months. Other raids were notable for the booty captured, such as a pack train taken in 1861. On the way home, though, Mexican troops caught up with the Apaches. A bullet struck Geronimo near his left eye, and after he recovered consciousness he was shot again, this time receiving a slight wound to his side.

Not long after returning home from that raid, Geronimo, his left eye still swollen shut, was at his camp when Mexican troops attacked. The soldiers killed primarily women and children (many of the men were absent on a hunt), burned tipis, and stole ponies and supplies. With winter approaching, the successful surprise attack proved especially difficult for the Apaches, as it deprived them of many of their provisions.

Usually the Mexicans did not pursue their quarry north of the border, a stratagem that could prove disastrous if they lost the element of surprise. In 1862, according to Geronimo, troops again came north, but this time they were spotted. Geronimo and Mangas Coloradas led two groups of warriors against the Mexicans, killed several of the soldiers, and drove the rest south of the border.

Geronimo's battles with Mexicans continued into the 1880s. A trading mission led by Geronimo and Juh at Casas Grandes that Geronimo dated to the early 1880s was followed by a serious binge on mescal. While many of the Apaches were intoxicated in their camp near Casas Grandes, troops attacked. Geronimo and Juh escaped, but 20 (according to Geronimo) were killed and 35 captured. Among those taken captive by the Mexicans was Cheehashkish, a wife of Geronimo, whom he never saw again.

What Geronimo called his final battle with Mexicans occurred in 1882, although he dated it later. The battle is discussed later in this chapter. It appears, however, that this conflict actually preceded the Casas Grandes attack, still another sign of problems with chronology in Geronimo's autobiography.

U.S. Forces in Apache Land

Until the 1850s, Apaches viewed the Mexicans alternately as trading partners and enemies, a split vision made possible by their inability fully to appreciate the reality of a Mexican nation. One village or region, from the Apache perspective, could be approached as friends, another perceived as enemies. Sometimes that worked, sometimes not. Nonetheless, the Apaches' Euro-American enemies resided primarily to their south. That situation changed, however, after the Mexican–American War.

Initially, the Apaches hoped that the conflict would benefit them, perhaps even establishing the Euro-Americans from the north, with whom they had experienced little interaction, as allies against the Mexicans. Historical forces would soon put that hope to rest.

The U.S. victory in 1848 forced terms on Mexico that included ceding to the victor northern California as far north as Oregon and accepting the Rio Grande as the boundary between Texas and Mexico. Most importantly for the Apaches, Mexico also ceded New Mexico to the U.S. government. Then in 1853, the United States, wanting to ensure access for a railway to the Pacific as well as to clarify its southern border, purchased from Mexico a strip of land across the southern portions of the current states of New Mexico and Arizona. This transaction is known as the Gadsden Purchase after the prominent railroad man and former soldier, James Gadsden, who as U.S. minister to Mexico negotiated the deal. The area that was added through Gadsden's efforts stretched from the Rio Grande on the east westward to the Colorado River and northward to the Gila River.

Posing additional dangers for the Apache residents of Arizona, New Mexico, and northern Mexico was the spread of mining into the area. Copper mines were established by the early 1850s, and gold was discovered in New Mexico in 1859, with the town of Pinos Altos quickly taking shape nearby.

It may have been an incident at Pinos Altos that set the Apaches and the U.S. military on a path that would make Geronimo one of the most famous, feared, and despised Indians from the perspective of the United States. The central figure in this pivotal incident, however, was not Geronimo but Mangas Coloradas, chief of the Chihenne Chiricahuas, if the incident actually occurred.

Mangas Coloradas was a huge figure, in terms of both his physical stature and the respect that he enjoyed from other Apaches. He stood about six feet four inches at least, possibly taller, and was noted for his generosity and spirituality as well as his bravery. He also possessed no animosity toward the northern Euro-Americans. Many historians have perpetuated a story, typically set in the spring or summer of 1860, in which Mangas Coloradas decided to visit the miners at Pinos Altos to reduce tensions between his people and the new arrivals, who were not only ripping up the earth but also cutting down trees and killing game that the Apaches needed. The miners supposedly tied the chief, by then approximately 70 years old, to a tree and whipped him. Afterward, he turned to his son-in-law, the Chokonen leader Cochise, and together they went to war against the intruders, primarily in the current state of New Mexico. Mangas Coloradas' biographer, Edwin Sweeney, remains skeptical about the incident ever having taken place. He sees the cause of war not in a personal humiliation of Mangas Coloradas but in broader actions: "the miners' assault at the Mimbres River and Bascom's actions at Apache Pass."[4]

THE COCHISE WARS

Early Conflicts

The first of the events referred to by Sweeney occurred on the morning of December 4, 1860, along the Mimbres River in southeastern New Mexico. Approximately 30 miners attacked a Chihenne camp, killing 4 people and capturing 13 women and children. Among the dead was Chief Elias. The prisoners were eventually turned over to the military, but the miners were never punished for their actions.

The second incident took place at Apache Pass in southeastern Arizona in January 1861. Second Lieutenant George Bascom was sent to recover a boy who had been kidnapped. Cochise, who had been trying to live peacefully with the settlers and miners, arrived delivering wood, accompanied by his wife, a son, a brother, and other relatives. While Cochise and his party were inside a military tent, Lieutenant Bascom demanded return of the boy. Cochise had not been involved in the abduction and knew nothing of the affair but offered to try to locate the missing boy.

Bascom refused to allow the party to leave, declaring that they would be held prisoner until the boy was returned. Cochise pulled out a knife and slashed the tent, escaping. He then captured three men and offered to trade them for his relatives. Bascom refused the deal, demanding that Cochise return the boy—a demand that Cochise was clearly unable to fulfill. Cochise then killed his three prisoners, and the soldiers did the same to theirs, hanging their bodies in Apache Pass. Cochise responded by making war on the Euro-Americans: attacking stagecoaches and forts, and spreading fear throughout the area. During these battles, Geronimo was very much involved.

Battle of Apache Pass

The first major battle of the Cochise Wars occurred at Apache Pass, near the present town of Bowie, in the summer of 1862. Geronimo does not mention the battle in his autobiography, but Peter Aleshire in *The Fox and the Whirlwind: General George Crook and Geronimo: A Paired Biography* notes that it is most unlikely that he would not have been part of the battle.[5] This conflict, after all, involved Cochise, Mangas Coloradas, and some 400 to 700 warriors, perhaps the largest Apache force ever.[6]

The encounter between the Chiricahuas and the U.S. military took place within the context of the Civil War. With the Union and Confederate military forces largely concerned with each other, the Apaches had been able to oppose the Euro-American intruders with minimal resistance. Confederate Colonel John B. Baylor proclaimed himself governor of the Territory of Arizona in 1861. The following year, angered by Apache war making, he ordered that Apache adults be killed and their children sold into slavery to raise money for the Confederate cause. Confederate President Jefferson Davis, however, repudiated Baylor's bloodthirsty policy.

Meanwhile, the tide was beginning to turn against the South in the region. A small Confederate detachment pulled out of Tucson and retreated eastward. At Dragoon Springs west of Apache Pass, Apaches attacked them, killing three soldiers and capturing supplies and livestock. At the same time, a Union force of about 1,800 men under General James H. Carleton was moving east from California. As the Union force reached Tucson, Cochise became concerned about the large number of soldiers. With Mangas Coloradas and quite possibly Geronimo, he prepared to contest the troops' movement eastward.

On June 20, soldiers under Lieutenant Colonel E. E. Eyre arrived at Apache Pass. Some Apaches initially parleyed with Eyre, but another group killed three soldiers who had wandered off by themselves. Eyre, keeping his focus on his principal enemy, the Confederates, tried to avoid a major confrontation with the Apaches. When no attack followed, he led his men east.

A few weeks later, 13 miners from Pinos Altos, New Mexico, arrived from the east and were attacked. Not a single miner survived.

Next to arrive were General Carleton's troops, with the advance detachment being led by Captain Thomas L. Roberts. The party included 126 soldiers and 26 wagons. Captain John C. Cremony commanded the wagon train. Roberts led part of his command to Dragoon Springs, leaving Cremony and the wagons behind until Roberts discovered whether there was sufficient water at Dragoon Springs for the whole command. Cochise and Mangas Coloradas concentrated their men on the spring at Apache Pass, waiting to ambush the soldiers when they approached to replenish their water supply there. Ultimately, Cremony joined Roberts at Dragoon Springs, from which point Roberts—with 60 infantrymen, 7 cavalrymen, and 2 howitzers—continued toward Apache Pass, leaving Cremony temporarily behind.

Roberts and his men ascended the pass on July 15. As Roberts reached the summit and headed through a narrow canyon leading to a station house, the Apaches opened fire. Roberts ordered his men back to the summit and then, braving the fire, led his men to the station house. What Cochise counted on was the stretch of several hundred yards from the building to the spring, a stretch that promised a high level of fatalities when the soldiers tried to reach the spring, as they must to obtain water. However, Roberts ordered the howitzers into action, and the shelling wreaked such destruction on the Apaches that the soldiers were able to reach the spring, collect the water they needed, and return to the station house.

Roberts, who was concerned that the wagon train might be ambushed as it made its way toward Apache Pass, sent messengers to warn Cremony. Five of the six men whom Roberts sent outraced their Apache pursuers. The sixth, a cavalryman named John Teal, was separated from the other messengers and surrounded by Apaches. However, his repeating rifle surprised his attackers with its firepower, and Mangas Coloradas decided to wait to kill him until he ran out of ammunition. Unfortunately for Mangas Coloradas, his height and his sense of command made him stand out above the other Apaches, and Teal took careful aim at him. The bullet flew true, striking the chief in his chest. The wound was serious, although not fatal. Shocked at their leader's plight, the warriors forgot about Teal, who escaped.

Under cover of darkness, Roberts led his men out of the station and back to Cremony and the wagon train. The entire command then made its way back to the station at Apache Pass. By the morning of July 17, with both men and animals desperate for water, Roberts mounted an attack on the Apaches who were waiting on the slopes surrounding the spring. The combination of howitzer shells and repeating rifles soon routed the Apaches.

When General Carleton arrived with an even larger contingent of troops, Cochise made no attempt to stop him from moving through the pass. Further dismaying the Apaches, Carleton assigned Major T. A. Coult with 100 men to build a fort nearby. Soon Fort Bowie provided a U.S. military presence to control movement through the strategically important pass.

Death of Mangas Coloradas

Geronimo needed no further evidence of the treachery that Euro-Americans were capable of perpetrating. He had lost his beloved first wife and three children to a Mexican massacre. Cochise had been falsely accused by supposedly friendly "white eyes," who had then killed several members of his family, including his wife. So when Mangas Coloradas informed other Apache leaders that miners and soldiers at Pinos Altos desired peace and had promised food and provisions for the Chihennes and Bedonkohes, Geronimo urged him not to return there. Other leaders, including the Chihennes Victorio and Nana, also expressed their distrust of the offer. Mangas, however, was an idealist who believed that Euro-Americans in general were trustworthy, and he resolved to proceed under this assumption.

On January 17, 1863, Mangas approached Pinos Altos. Jack Swilling, whom the Chihenne leader knew, went to meet him. Other members of Swilling's party aimed their guns at the Apaches. Mangas told his bodyguards to leave and continued onward with Swilling.

Swilling and others, including soldiers who had been at Pinos Altos, took Mangas the following day to Fort McLane, known to Apaches as Apache Tejo (the name Geronimo uses in his autobiography). There Swilling turned Mangas over to Brigadier General Joseph Rodman West. General Carleton had earlier ordered a campaign against Mangas Coloradas's Apaches, and both Carleton and West held him responsible for much of the violence perpetrated against settlers and miners in the region, following the common Euro-American practice of assuming a level of generalship in one Indian leader that never existed. In fact, Mangas had long been quite willing to make peace.

West had Mangas confined to an open adobe room, the only building even partly remaining at the abandoned fort. He warned his prisoner against attempting an escape and then told the guards to kill the chief. Private Clark Stocking, who was present, said that he heard West saying, "Men, that old murderer has got away from every soldier command and has left a trail of blood for 500 miles on the old stage line. I want him dead or alive tomorrow morning, do you understand? I want him dead."[7]

While Mangas Coloradas lay on the ground with a single blanket to ward off the cold, the guards tortured him by heating their bayonets in a fire and sticking his feet with the hot points. When Mangas propped himself up on an elbow to complain that he was no child to be treated this way, the guards, Privates James Colyer and John Mead, as reported by another observer, Daniel Ellis Conner, shot him with their muskets. Apparently Sergeant Henry Foljaine then shot him in the head. The execution occurred about 1:00 A.M. on January 19. Later that morning, another soldier, John T. Wright, scalped Mangas. A group of the chief's relatives and friends, unaware of his fate, were attacked. Eleven, including a son of Mangas, were killed, and the dead leader's wife was wounded.

A few days later, the army surgeon David Sturgeon and some soldiers decapitated Mangas Coloradas and boiled the head to remove the flesh. Sturgeon took the skull with him to Toledo, Ohio, after he resigned from the army in 1864. A phrenologist, Orson Squire Fowler, carefully examined the skull and published the results in his book *Human Science or Phrenology*. There have been reports—apparently untrue—that the skull ultimately made its way to the Smithsonian Institution. No Smithsonian record of the skull exists, although Fowler did put it on display in his New York museum, the Phrenological Cabinet.

Geronimo had been left in charge of the Apaches who remained in Arizona. When he heard of Mangas Coloradas' death, Geronimo led his people into the mountains near Apache Pass. A few weeks later, they discovered four men herding cattle and killed all four, after which they drove the cattle back to their camp and began to butcher them. Before completing their work, they were surprised by the arrival of U.S. troops. Having given most of their weapons to Mangas Coloradas and the Apaches who went to New Mexico, Geronimo's warriors had to fight the troops with spears, bows, and arrows. The contest, according to Geronimo, was especially disadvantageous to the Apaches, who lost one warrior, three women, and three children before they could scatter into the mountains.

Troops attacked Geronimo's new camp about 10 days later, with the fighting lasting all day. Geronimo and his warriors exhausted their supply of arrows and were reduced to fighting with rocks and clubs. During the night, they were able to withdraw. The arrival of Cochise and Chokonen warriors did not prevent yet another army attack, and again the Apaches, at a severe disadvantage, had to withdraw. Geronimo seems to imply in his autobiography that confirmation of Mangas Coloradas's death did not arrive until after this series of encounters with the U.S. military, although the challenges of memory and translation raise questions about the chronology of events here, as elsewhere in his autobiography.

A Fragile Peace

Over the next few years, Geronimo made repeated raids into Mexico. His autobiography mentions a number of conflicts with Mexicans but passes quickly over this period north of the border. He spent some time in New Mexico with Victorio, the greatest of the Chihenne leaders after the death of Mangas Coloradas. Geronimo points out in his autobiography, "No one ever treated our tribe more kindly than Victorio and his band. We are still proud to say that he and his people were our friends."[8]

At other times, Geronimo stayed with Cochise. Despite his reluctance in the autobiography to discuss the continuing engagements with U.S. settlers and soldiers, he undoubtedly played a role in the attacks that disrupted the stage line, endangered miners, captured horses from military posts, and frightened the new inhabitants of the region. In 1863, this area was split between the territories of New Mexico and Arizona, creating the boundaries of what would become the two states in 1912.

By 1870, efforts were under way from both sides to explore the possibility of peace. Cochise, Victorio, and Loco, also a Chihenne leader, made overtures to the U.S. military. In that same year, Arizona was made a department in the Military Division of the Pacific, with Major General George Stoneman established as the department's commander. Stoneman set up stations at forts to distribute food in an effort to advance peace efforts.

Mob action led by a group of Tucson citizens, however, almost derailed the movement toward peace. On April 30, 1871, some of Tucson's most prominent citizens, augmented by Mexicans and Papago Indians (who were traditional enemies of the Apaches) attacked an Aravaipa Apache ranchería (a small, semi-permanent community). They killed about 150 people and kidnapped approximately 28 children, whom they sold to farmers in Arizona and Mexico. President Ulysses Grant, deeply concerned by the violence, sent Secretary of the Board of Indian Commissioners Vincent Colyer to try to make peace. Grant also directed Colyer to establish temporary reservations.

Grant dispatched General Oliver O. Howard to the region in the spring of 1872 to continue implementation of his "Peace Policy," which included establishing reservations and soliciting Indian agents from various religious denominations. Howard, a devout Christian who also had (at least by Euro-American standards) sympathy for the Indians whom he sometimes had to fight, listened attentively to the Aravaipa chief Eskiminzin plead for the return of the children. Despite opposition from local authorities and General Crook, who had replaced Stoneman, Howard prevailed in returning the children to their families.

Howard was helped in his peace effort by Thomas Jeffords, formerly superintendent of the mail route between Tucson and Fort Bowie. Despite being wounded himself and losing many drivers to Indian attacks, Jeffords had become friendly with Cochise and earned his trust. Cochise, Geronimo, and Cochise's sons, Naiche and Taza, met with General Howard and Jeffords.

Discussions lasted for 11 days, with Cochise finally agreeing to the peace so long as he could stay in the Dragoon Mountains and have Jeffords designated as the military's representative.

Howard established a reservation in the Dragoon and Chiricahua Mountains in southeastern Arizona Territory with Jeffords in charge. At the Chiricahua (also known as the Fort Bowie) Reservation, Jeffords worked hard to maintain the peace and operate the reservation as fairly as possible. Geronimo also made the peace with Howard and lived near Cochise while continuing to make raids into Mexico. Geronimo has high praise for Howard in his autobiography:

> He [Howard] always kept his word with us and treated us as brothers. We never had so good a friend among the United States officers as General Howard. We could have lived forever at peace with him. If there is any pure, honest white man in the United States army, that man is General Howard.[9]

Raids into Mexico continued, of course, and Jeffords was largely powerless to prevent them. Then, in 1874, the great Cochise died. Cochise had prepared Taza to assume leadership, but the Chiricahuas who had followed Cochise's lead began to form various splinter groups. The brothers Skinya and Poinsenay refused to follow Taza, and Geronimo and his cousin Juh believed that Taza was too trusting of the U.S. representatives. In a dispute that grew out of the refusal by the manager of a stagecoach station to continue selling Skinya and Poinsenay whiskey, the two murdered the man and his cook. This incident, which occurred in April 1876, led to demands from local leaders, including Arizona's Governor Safford, that the reservation be closed and the Chiricahuas relocated.

Finances also factored into the dispute, with the U.S. government wanting to save money by concentrating the Apaches on the San Carlos Reservation farther north on the Gila River, where John Clum had become the agent in August 1874. San Carlos was also readily accessible to contractors at Tucson, the territorial capital. The concentration of tribes, both Apache and non-Apache, had begun in February 1875, and the 1876 killings reinforced the decision to shift reservation policy in this direction.

The effort to relocate all Chiricahuas and other area Indians to San Carlos precipitated considerable tension and even violence. In one clash, Cochise's sons Taza and Naiche killed Skinya and wounded Poinsenay. When Clum met with a group headed by Geronimo in June 1876, Geronimo said that he would go to San Carlos but stated that he needed time to gather the rest of his people. Geronimo and Juh then returned to their camp, killed their dogs so that they would not give away their movements, and traveling as lightly as possible, fled.

Clum made the bizarre decision to raise money for his marriage to a young woman from Ohio by taking a group of Indians east as a sort of show-business venture. The group visited the Centennial Exposition in Philadelphia and toured Washington, D.C. In Washington, Taza became ill with pneumonia and died. Clum put on an elaborate funeral with General Howard attending but ran out of money for the return trip. The Commissioner of Indian Affairs paid the group's way back to Arizona. Naiche, who had not gone on the excursion, believed that Clum had poisoned his brother. Naiche became the new successor to Cochise. Although respected as a warrior, he never developed the leadership skills that his father and even his brother had possessed.

SAN CARLOS RESERVATION

Captured

In the immediate aftermath of the Chiricahua Reservation's closing, prominent Apache leaders were widely scattered. Juh escaped from Clum with Geronimo but went down into the Sierra Madre Mountains in northwest Mexico. Naiche remained at San Carlos. Geronimo, with about 40 warriors, visited Victorio in New Mexico at the Warm Springs (Ojo Caliente) Reservation.

John Clum arrived at Warm Springs with a large body of Indian police and asked to speak with Geronimo. On April 21, 1877, Geronimo, along with six other men, went to see Clum. They found him with about a half-dozen police on the porch of an agency building. Geronimo stated his refusal to go to San Carlos and threatened Crum. At that point, approximately 80 armed police burst out of the commissary building. Geronimo and seven other leaders were chained and, for want of a guardhouse, held in a corral. They soon were transported to San Carlos. Victorio was allowed to remain temporarily at Ojo Caliente. The rest of Geronimo's group also was taken to the Arizona reservation, where Geronimo and the other shackled leaders were kept in the guardhouse.

Clum wanted Geronimo to be hanged, but ultimately quit his position at San Carlos after disputes with the army that included a demand for increased pay. His successor, Henry Lyman Hart, freed Geronimo, who had been imprisoned for four months. Clum's attitude toward giving Geronimo his freedom was reflected in his son's later assertion that "they [his leg irons] never should have been removed, except to permit him to walk untrammeled to the scaffold."[10] Geronimo states in his autobiography that after being released, he was allowed to live near San Carlos at a place named after him. He added, "All went well here for a period of two years, but we were not satisfied."[11]

Death of Victorio

During this time of relative peace for Geronimo, Victorio was arguing to stay at Ojo Caliente. In 1878, his Chihennes were ordered to San Carlos, but Victorio and 50 warriors took to the hills. By January of the following year, Victorio was negotiating with the government about some possibility of his staying with the Mescaleros on their reservation in New Mexico or even returning to Ojo Caliente. By summer the prospects looked good for the Chihennes' being permitted to reside on the Mescalero Reservation.

Unfortunately, Victorio learned that Grant County had handed down indictments against him for murder and horse stealing—actions apparently committed by Poinsenay. On August 21, 1879, a group of men from Silver City, including the judge and district attorney, arrived at the Mescalero Reservation. Although they were actually on a hunting and fishing outing, Victorio assumed that they had come to arrest him and fled with about 80 warriors into Mexico.

For the next two years, Victorio and his band outran and outfought their adversaries both north and south of the border, causing many deaths. On October 14, 1880, however, a Mexican force under Colonel Joaquin Terrazas caught up with Victorio. Taking the Apaches by surprise at a place called Tres Castillos, Terrazas and his men killed 78, including 62 warriors (all of whom they scalped for the bounty on Apache scalps), and took 68 women and children captive. Just 17 Apaches escaped, including Nana and Victorio's son-in-law, Mangus. Among the dead was Victorio. Terrazas' army suffered only 3 fatalities. The Mexican troops rode triumphantly into the city of Chihuahua with the 78 scalps borne aloft on poles. The collective bounty on the scalps reportedly came to $50,000.[12]

Troubles at San Carlos

Geronimo recalled that his life at San Carlos was largely uneventful for about two years. Those times, however, were not without problems. The close proximity of a variety of tribes and bands led to tensions that sometimes escalated into violence. Poinsenay, for example, returned from raids into Mexico to brag about his accomplishments and recruit young men to go with him. Juh also dispatched warriors to San Carlos to seek recruits. Yet even when Victorio and Nana headed toward Mexico, Geronimo, along with Naiche, remained at San Carlos.

With conflict mounting on the reservation, Geronimo became increasingly dissatisfied and considered leaving. A cousin of Geronimo, Jason Betzinez, who wrote an autobiography called *I Fought with Geronimo*, recalled an incident that may have played a role in convincing Geronimo to leave. According to Betzinez, Geronimo, who had been drinking, scolded his nephew, so humiliating the young man that he committed suicide. The nephew was the son of Geronimo's sister, Nahdoste, and Nana. Betzinez adds that "Geronimo, blaming himself for his nephew's death, left the reservation and joined Juh's group which intended to flee to Mexico."[13] Leaving in early April 1878, he took with him his wives Cheehaskish and Shegha, his two children, and other members of his family. In contrast, Betzinez remained at San Carlos with his mother and sister.

San Carlos and the Prophet Nochaydelklinne

Geronimo and Juh, from their camp in the Guadalupe Mountains just north of the Mexican border near the Arizona–New Mexico line, sent word that they were interested in returning to San Carlos. In the fall of 1879, Captain Harry L. Haskell, accompanied by an interpreter, possibly Thomas Jeffords, visited the camp. Summoned back the next day, Haskell went with Jeffords and Archie McIntosh, a scout for General Crook. The negotiations concluded, with Geronimo returning to San Carlos around the end of the year.

By now Geronimo had taken a third wife, Shtshashe. Apparently about the same time, Geronimo's daughter Dohnsay was honored as one of the three outstanding women in their band, although the reasons for this honor remain unknown. In addition to his family, Geronimo busied himself with planting crops, determined to live a peaceful life. That, however, was not to be.

Geronimo learned of a man named Nochaydelklinne who had begun to hold mystical circle dances and who claimed that he had received a vision of a future in which the Apache dead would return to life and the Euro-Americans vanish from their land. Known as the Prophet, he believed that he was impervious to enemy bullets. Like other revitalization messages that occurred periodically throughout other Indian cultures (including Wovoka's vision among the Paiutes), Nochaydelklinne's approach was essentially non-violent. However, given the Euro-Americans' fear of any message that offered Indians hope while prophesying their own removal, these revitalization movements usually ended violently. For example, Euro-American hostility to the Ghost Dance, a pivotal revitalization ritual for the Lakota, led to the death of Sitting Bull and precipitated the massacre at Wounded Knee.

In late August 1881, a large group of Apaches gathered for one of the Prophet's dances at Cibecue Creek near Fort Apache. This area was under the authority of the San Carlos agent, Joseph Tiffany, despite its not actually being part of the San Carlos Reservation. The commander of Fort Apache was Colonel Eugene Asa Carr. Tiffany urged Carr either to arrest or to kill Nochaydelklinne.

On August 29, Carr left Fort Apache with 117 soldiers and 23 Indian scouts for Cibecue Creek. Warriors gathered around the Prophet to protect him. When Nochaydelklinne promised to go with the soldiers as soon as he had his lunch, Carr agreed to those terms. Carr directed some of his soldiers and scouts to bring him in, but they grew tired of waiting and pulled Nochaydelklinne to his feet. Firing began, but the Prophet restored calm. As tension again escalated between the soldiers and warriors, firing resumed.

Believing that he could not be killed, Nochaydelklinne refused to flee, but his wife was killed trying to protect him, as was his son. After being wounded several times, the Prophet was eventually killed when a soldier hit him in the head with an ax.

The resulting battle lasted much of the day. Most of the scouts turned against the soldiers and fought beside Nochaydelklinne's followers. It was perhaps the only time in all of the Indian wars that Indian scouts turned on the soldiers whom they had committed to support. In addition to the Prophet, approximately 18 Indians were killed, along with 8 soldiers. Carr and his men were in serious jeopardy, but under cover of darkness they withdrew and returned to Fort Apache. The Apaches then moved on the fort, attacking it unsuccessfully.

Whether Geronimo participated in this battle is unknown. He does not mention it in his autobiography, but that omission is not proof of his lack of participation. Indian autobiographies tend to downplay battles against U.S. soldiers and civilians because they inevitably are composed after the authors are no longer waging war and instead are living under the control of U.S. authorities.

Major General Orlando Willcox, commander of the Department of Arizona, brought in military reinforcements from other parts of Arizona and from New Mexico and California. Rumors circulated that Apache leaders were to be arrested. Geronimo cites this rumor as occurring in 1883 in his autobiography, but he is clearly mistaken in the year. Given earlier incidents of betrayal, Geronimo understandably feared treachery when in late September 1881 he and other leaders were invited to attend a council at Fort Thomas.

Determined to die fighting rather than succumb to death in a prison, Geronimo led about 250 Indians, mainly Bedonkohe and Nednai Apaches, off the reservation. The group included Victorio's son, Naiche, and Juh. Among those who remained at San Carlos was the Chihenne leader Loco.

THE APACHE CAMPAIGN

Strategies

As Geronimo headed toward Mexico, his band raided camps and attacked a wagon train (killing seven) to get horses, ammunition, and supplies. They also successfully resisted an attack by U.S. troops. Among those accompanying Geronimo were his cousins Perico and Fun, both courageous and able allies. Juh had separated from Geronimo, but once in the Sierra Madre Mountains they reunited.

Geronimo recognized that he did not have enough warriors with him to both resist Mexican forces and successfully carry out the raids necessary to maintain the supplies they needed to remain free. He decided on a plan to address that need. Having failed through messengers to induce Loco to join him in Mexico, he would lead an expedition back to San Carlos and persuade or compel Loco and his people to leave with them.

This undertaking was perilous, as it required retracing their steps back to the reservation, where they could be discovered at any moment. Nonetheless, Geronimo and Naiche, accompanied by Chihuahua, led a body of about 60 warriors across the border into Arizona. Juh also may have been a member of the party. Along the way, two warriors headed off by themselves to steal horses and were captured by the Mexican army. Threatened with death, they reported on Geronimo's mission and when he would likely be returning to Mexico. The Mexicans were determined to use this intelligence to attack the Apaches as they returned.

As Geronimo neared the reservation, he stopped at a sheep ranch owned by George Stevens, the Graham County sheriff. The primary sheepherder there was a Mexican named Victoriano Mestas, also known as Besdas, whom Geronimo had captured years before and reared, later trading him to a rancher. Despite the close connection, Geronimo ordered Besdas and the other Mexican males killed. Naiche is reported to have intervened to save Besdas's nine-year-old son. Geronimo left warriors to guard the Apache women who had been working at the camp, his motivation behind the killings apparently a desire to ensure that no one would report his whereabouts before he could carry out his plan to bring Loco's people out of the reservation.

Early in the morning of April 19, 1882, Geronimo, having sent out warriors to cut telegraph lines, approached Loco's camp. He warned that anyone who did not leave with him would be shot. Loco, certain that his people would suffer greatly in a confrontation with the U.S. military but also unhappy with life at San Carlos, did not put up much resistance. As the large group moved south, Geronimo left a rearguard force to protect against anyone following them. When the head of the Indian police, Albert Sterling, and an Apache policeman arrived to see what was happening, they were both shot to death.

Geronimo's raiding parties struck widely during the flight from San Carlos. The goal was to capture guns, ammunition, horses, and supplies. To obtain these items, the raiders killed approximately 50 Euro-Americans, including wagon drivers, ranchers, and, in short, anyone they encountered.

Colonel Forsyth's Pursuit

Following Geronimo were six companies of cavalry under the command of Lieutenant Colonel George Forsyth. The first encounter with Forsyth's forces was an Apache ambush of some of his scouts who had moved well ahead of the cavalry. Four scouts were killed. Before long, the cavalry arrived, and the warriors took up positions between the soldiers and the Apache women and children. Fighting fiercely, Geronimo's men drove off their pursuers.

Moving swiftly at night, the Apaches continued toward Mexico. Despite having no authority to cross the border, Forsyth continued into Mexico in pursuit of Geronimo. He kept his force of approximately 400 soldiers and 50 scouts at a safe distance to avoid discovery, while Captain Tullius Tupper with 39 soldiers and 37 Apache scouts led by Al Sieber moved ahead. Sieber had served as chief of scouts under General Crook, who devised the effective strategy of using Apache scouts to track down other Apaches.

During the night of April 27, 1882, Sieber's scouts detected Geronimo's campfires. Tupper arrived before dawn, and the scouts took up position on a ridge overlooking the camp while Tupper positioned his soldiers on the opposite plain. Four Apaches, including two girls, approached the ridge; fearing discovery, the scouts opened fire, killing the two girls. The troopers then attacked from the other side.

The Apache band took cover on a hill, and the fighting continued into the afternoon. At that point, four warriors managed to get behind the ridge and open fire on the army scouts, who withdrew to the plain. Their retreat gave the Apaches an opening to escape into the nearby hills. Tupper, his men exhausted and almost out of ammunition, withdrew to where he had camped the previous night. Soon Forsyth arrived with the rest of his force. Although Geronimo and his group had managed to escape, they had lost 14 warriors and most of their supplies and horses.

The Mexican Block

Geronimo was concerned that the cavalry might continue to pursue him, but the next threat came instead from a Mexican force under the command of Colonel Lorenzo García that was waiting in a ravine to block the Apaches' movement south. García apparently had learned of Geronimo's probable path from the two warriors captured earlier.

The Mexican ambush occurred the day after the battle with the U.S. cavalry. The Mexicans started shooting and rode in among the Apache women and children, killing many of them. Geronimo called to his warriors to join him in protecting the women and children. Geronimo, about 30 warriors, and a few women and children later took refuge in a dry creek bed. Several times the Mexicans, who knew well that Geronimo was their target, attacked. Geronimo records in his autobiography that he could hear the soldiers calling his name and urging their comrades to kill him. Geronimo mentions that he was close enough to see an officer (he refers to a general but the officer was certainly of lower rank), take aim, and shoot him.

When dark fell, someone set the grass on fire. Different accounts credit the diversion alternately to the Apaches and the Mexicans, although Geronimo says that the Apaches were responsible. The fire gave them cover to escape.

When Forsyth arrived the next morning, he met with García. The Mexican officer showed his U.S. counterpart the battlefield where lay the bodies of 19 Mexican soldiers, 3 officers (apparently including the one whom Geronimo had shot), and 78 Indians, only 11 of whom were warriors. The Mexicans also had captured 33 women and children.[14]

By the time Geronimo's party arrived at Juh's Nednai camp, Geronimo had lost 26 of the approximately 100 warriors who had left San Carlos with him. Nonetheless, Jason Betzinez noted that the several hundred Apaches who gathered together at this site represented "the largest number of Apaches that had come together in many years."[15]

In the Sierra Madre

Geronimo's time in the mountains of Mexico included the massacre at Casas Grandes discussed earlier, a catastrophe that resulted in 20 dead and 35 taken captive, including Geronimo's wife Cheehaskish. Afterward, Geronimo took yet another wife, Ziyeh, daughter of a Nednai mother and a Euro-American father.

Geronimo continued raiding in Mexico and north in Arizona. He also led a successful attack on Mexican troops that netted his group both horses and supplies. At the instigation of Nana, Geronimo and a band of warriors went to Galeana to seek revenge on the soldiers who had attacked at Casas Grandes. At Galeana, a few warriors induced soldiers to pursue them, leading the Mexicans into an ambush. Among the 22 Mexicans who died was Juan Mata Ortiz, who had participated in the battle that resulted in Victorio's death. Two Apache warriors also died.

Juh then led his Nednais and some Chihennes away from the rest. However, Mexicans launched a surprise attack on Juh's camp and killed many in his group, including Geronimo's sister Ishton. Juh then led the survivors back to Geronimo. Approximately 100 warriors now accompanied Geronimo, who shared leadership roles with Naiche, Chihuahua, Juh, Nana, Kaytennae, and the fierce warrior Chato (also spelled Chatto). Chato led a party into Arizona in March 1883, where they killed a federal judge named H. C. McComas and the judge's wife, and kidnapped their son, Charlie. The attack engendered considerable outrage among the citizens of Arizona, and rescuing the missing boy became a cause célèbre. He was never found, and different stories of his death have been reported. There was even a news account in 1938 that a lost Apache tribe had been discovered in Mexico led by a red-haired individual who supposedly was Charlie McComas.[16]

On April 25, 1883, Geronimo succeeded in ambushing Mexican troops as they were ascending out of a canyon. The Apaches not only shot at the soldiers, but also rolled boulders down on top of them, killing a large number and sending the rest fleeing.

THE GRAY FOX AND GERONIMO

Return to Arizona

General Crook, known to the Apaches as the Gray Fox, returned to the Department of Arizona in early September 1882. He set about meeting with Apaches on the reservation and examining the situation carefully. A usually fair and honest man, Crook understood that the Apaches had genuine grievances. The size of the reservation, for example, had been reduced five times, primarily to make way for silver and copper mines. Crook gave the reservation Apaches considerable latitude to move their camps to more desirable locations and established an Indian judicial system on the reservation with Indian judges, juries, and police. At the same time, he was deeply concerned about the violence occurring in connection with the bands that had left San Carlos for Mexico.

Consequently, Crook sought and received permission from both U.S. and Mexican officials to go into Mexico after Geronimo and the other Apaches who had taken refuge there. On May 1, 1883, he crossed the border with a contingent that included 9 officers, 42 enlisted men, 193 Apache scouts, and 5 pack trains with 76 packers. Captain John G. Bourke, who recorded his experiences with his commander in *On the Border with Crook*, accompanied Crook. Al Sieber was chief of scouts, assisted by Archie McIntosh and Sam Bowman. Captain Emmet Crawford commanded the troops, aided by Second Lieutenant Charles Gatewood. Mickey Free was one of the interpreters. Both Bourke and John Rope, a White Mountain Apache scout, have left first-hand accounts of the mission.

In Pursuit

Crook, realizing that he could not move fast enough with the pack trains, sent 150 Apache scouts ahead with Crawford and Sieber. On May 15, 1883, the scouts attacked the Apaches' main camp. Nine Apaches were killed, but most of the warriors from the various bands were away hunting. Crook brought the rest of his force forward to the camp and set up his field headquarters there.

As women and children gradually made their way into the camp, the general gave them food, treated them kindly, and, rather than holding the returned Apaches prisoner, urged them to return to their warriors and encourage them to come in as well. Some, including Chihuahua, did exactly that.

When Geronimo arrived on the night of May 19, his men took up positions overlooking the camp. The next morning he sent two emissaries to confer with Crook. Determined to appear casual regarding whether Geronimo came in or not, Crook took his shotgun and strolled away by himself as if he were on a private hunting expedition. Geronimo and several of his warriors surrounded Crook, who sat down and started talking with Geronimo. He assured the Apaches that if they did not return to San Carlos, he would come back with a large force and, in partnership with Mexican troops, hunt down all of them.

As more Apaches decided to return to the reservation, Geronimo engaged in several talks with Crook over the next few days. Finally, Geronimo agreed to return but requested a week to find all of his people. Crook, who was running short of supplies, said that he had to leave soon but that Geronimo could catch up with him. On May 24, 1883, Crook began his return journey to San Carlos with 52 warriors and 273 women, a party that included Loco, Nana, and Kaytennae. Geronimo promised to arrive within two months. Only Juh, among the Apache leaders, had not agreed to return.

Crook reached Arizona in June. Gradually leaders who had promised to arrive did so, including Naiche, Chihuahua, Mangus, and Chato.

Geronimo's Return

Geronimo did not make his two-month deadline, but he did return, arriving in late February 1884. The journey had not been easy for Geronimo: One of his sons died on the way. In addition, Geronimo's brother-in-law Juh had died after a fall from his horse.

Lieutenant Britton Davis met Geronimo at the border but angered the war leader by implying that he could not be trusted to keep his word. Britton explained, however, that he was there to protect Geronimo from people who would like to do him harm. While they were resting in camp, two men arrived. One said that he was a U.S. marshal, the other that he was a customs agent from the border town of Nogales, Arizona. They informed Davis of their plan to arrest Geronimo and the other Indians and confiscate the herd of some 350 cattle that Geronimo had brought with him. The marshal deputized Davis and ordered him to assist in the arrest. That action put the officer in a difficult position, as he had been ordered by General Crook to deliver Geronimo to the reservation.

Fortunately, a friend of Davis's, Second Lieutenant J. Y. F. Blake, arrived. The two hit upon a way to get Geronimo to Crook without Davis running the risk of defying the marshal. Davis woke up Geronimo and told him about the plan to take his cattle but not about the intended arrest, fearing that if he did so Geronimo might flee back into Mexico.

Davis then suggested that it would be quite a joke on the two visitors if Geronimo could lead his cattle away while they slept off the heavy drinking bout they had engaged in throughout the evening. Geronimo concurred and, while the two slept, led his cattle and the approximately 100 Apaches in his party, accompanied by Blake, toward the reservation. Davis stayed behind to feign surprise the following morning at Geronimo's absence.

Geronimo and his party arrived safely at San Carlos and were met by Captain Emmett Crawford, who was in charge at the reservation. Crook took the cattle from Geronimo, however, as he assumed the animals had been stolen. Geronimo was also disappointed to find that he must live at Turkey Creek rather than farther away from other reservation tribes at Eagle Creek. Eagle Creek, Crook explained, had been removed from the reservation and was now occupied by settlers.

Archie McIntosh, a scout married to an Apache woman, was in charge of distributing supplies to Geronimo's people, including the wagons, plows, and ponies necessary for farming. Although well liked by the Apaches, McIntosh was found to have been shortchanging reservation Indians on supplies and was discharged. Lieutenant Davis, with whom Geronimo was now quite familiar, was put in charge of Geronimo and the others at Turkey Creek. Both Davis and Crawford supported Geronimo's desire to raise cattle and sheep rather than farm, but Washington policy decreed otherwise.

THE FINAL BREAKOUT

Tensions at Turkey Creek

For a time, reservation life was peaceful for Geronimo, but soon tensions began to arise. Mickey Free was chosen by Lieutenant Davis to serve as his primary translator, but Apaches well remembered Free as the boy whose abduction years earlier had precipitated the conflict between Cochise and the U.S. military, and that association engendered considerable animosity toward him. In addition, Chato, who had fought alongside Geronimo against the military, was now a prominent scout for Davis. Adding to Apache resentment were orders from Crook forbidding the making of tizwin (a fermented drink made from corn) and a man physically punishing his wife, both of which appeared to be unwarranted intrusions into their lives.

Arrests also began to occur. Kaytennae was accused of planning a breakout, arrested, and imprisoned at the military prison on Alcatraz. Others were arrested for violating the bans against manufacturing tizwin or beating a wife. Rumors circulated that Crook planned to arrest Geronimo and other leaders. Then Crawford, at his request, was transferred back to his regiment and replaced by Captain Francis Pierce. The change troubled members of Geronimo's band, who had reached at least a modest level of accommodation with Crawford.

By the middle of May 1885, Geronimo was determined to leave San Carlos, but many others were reluctant to resume warfare and the hardships that it inevitably would bring. Geronimo needed a way to convince other prominent Apache leaders to join him, so he devised a plan to win their support. If some deceit in a worthy cause was needed, so be it. Geronimo told a number of leaders—including Naiche, Chihuahua, Mangus, and Nana—that his son Chappo had killed Lieutenant Davis and Chato, and as a result soldiers were coming for all of them. Believing that they had to flee or suffer severe punishment, these leaders left the reservation with about 150 others, including 35 warriors.

When Perico and Chappo joined Geronimo, the rest of the group learned that Davis and Chato had not been killed. It remains uncertain whether Geronimo had actually directed his son and his cousin to kill the two men and they did not have an opportunity to do so, or whether he had completely manufactured the story as a trick to induce others to leave San Carlos with him. At least some of those who had accompanied Geronimo, including Chihuahua and Naiche, reportedly believed that they had been tricked and were outraged by the deceit. Geronimo does not mention the incident in his autobiography, but Apaches who remained at San Carlos related this story to Davis, adding that Mangus was in on the plot. Geronimo's biographer Angie Debo notes that "it is impossible now to determine the truth of the story Davis heard of conflict among the leaders."[17] That the group soon split into several units lends credence to reports of discord among those who fled. However, except for Mangus, the others soon reunited, so the split may have been a maneuver to throw off any pursuers.

Considerable violence followed in the wake of the flight by Geronimo and the others toward Mexico. By June 10, most of the Apaches had reached the border, leaving at least 17 dead civilians behind.

The Pursuit of Geronimo

The U.S. military was quick to pursue the fleeing Apaches and did not hesitate at the border. Captain Crawford crossed into Mexico by June 11, Captain Wirt Davis led another force into Mexico on July 13, and General Crook stationed troops at the border. Assisting the military were Apache scouts, including Chato. On June 23, the scouts found Chihuahua's camp and attacked, capturing about 15 women and children. On August 7, the scouts, who knew the likely routes and campsites that Geronimo and the other leaders would use, struck Geronimo's camp. Almost 80 scouts succeeded in taking many prisoners, primarily women and children, including Geronimo's wives Ziyeh and Shegha and five of his children.

The following month, Geronimo led a small party back to San Carlos to reclaim at least some of those who had been captured, including Shegha and a young daughter. On the way back to Mexico, they discovered some Mescalero women, one of whom, Ihtedda, Geronimo apparently took as yet another wife.

Consistently faced with a shortage of supplies, the Apache leaders sent Ulzana (also known as Jolsanny), a brother of Chihuahua, to get ammunition and supplies. In November, Ulzana led 10 warriors into New Mexico and then to the reservation in Arizona. The band killed as they went, and at San Carlos exacted revenge against the families of Apache scouts, killing approximately 20 people, most of them women and children.

Geronimo, meanwhile, was having difficulty eluding Crawford's scouts, who hit his camp again. Geronimo had sufficient warning so that his people could get away, but they lost their horses and supplies in the flight. Crook's decision to use Apaches to hunt down other Apaches was proving remarkably successful, and Geronimo accepted Naiche's advice to talk with the soldiers. Geronimo sent a woman as emissary, perhaps the acclaimed woman warrior Lozen, a sister of Victorio, to meet with Crawford.

The Apache leaders, minus Mangus, who was not with the party at that time, agreed to meet with Crawford on January 11, 1886. As the Apaches watched from a hill overlooking Crawford's camp to see if the officer planned any trickery, they observed a Mexican force approach. Some shots rang out as the Mexicans apparently mistook Crawford's scouts for a hostile band of Apaches. Crawford mounted a large rock to signal to the Mexicans that he was an American soldier but was struck by a bullet and killed.

A few days later, Geronimo, Naiche, Nana, Chihuahua, and 14 other men met with the officer who had assumed command since Crawford's death,

Lozen

Little written information exists concerning Lozen (circa 1840–circa 1890), but oral tradition has marked her as a true Apache heroine. A sister to Victorio, Lozen was renowned as both a great warrior and a possessor of unusual spiritual gifts.

Tradition places Lozen as Victorio's close confidant, military strategist, and prophet. Lauded for her bravery and daring, she risked her life many times in battle and to save the lives of other Apaches, especially women and children.

After learning of her brother's death in October 1880, Lozen set off alone from the Mescalero reservation in New Mexico, crossing the border despite the presence of both U.S. and Mexican troops. She undoubtedly hoped that the news was not true but knew that if it were, she would be needed even more by Victorio's Chihenne survivors. She apparently fought alongside the elderly Nana, who led the survivors of the attack that had killed Victorio. Lozen later fought beside Geronimo, finally surrendering when he did, in 1886.

Lozen, tradition notes, was able after ritualistic prayer to Usen (recognized by Apaches as the creative spirit) to determine an enemy's location. She also was believed to have the power to heal wounds and was greatly skilled at horseback riding. Although Apache women underwent rigorous physical training, they usually did not engage in combat. Lozen, however, was as great a warrior as almost any male Apache. She never married, instead devoting her life to helping Victorio and their people defend their land and their way of life. Such was the respect accorded her that she participated in war councils.

Lozen was sent south with the other Chiricahua Apache prisoners after the 1886 surrender. She died in Alabama sometime around the end of the decade, from an enemy she could neither outfight nor outride—an illness thought to be tuberculosis.

Lieutenant Marion Maus. At that January 15 meeting, Geronimo agreed to talk with Crook near the border in two months. As a guarantor of his sincerity, Geronimo sent 9 Apaches as essentially hostages, including Nana, Nana's wife (Geronimo's sister), and Ihtedda. Maus took his hostages to Fort Bowie and then crossed back into Mexico, establishing a camp about 10 miles south of the Arizona line.

Surrender

Geronimo arrived at the Canyon de los Embudos (the Canyon of the Funnels) and awaited Crook's arrival from Fort Bowie. Accompanying Crook were Kaytennae, who had been released from Alcatraz and given a tour of San Francisco to acquaint him with the power of the United States, and a scout named Alchise. As usual, Bourke was the general's aide and kept a detailed transcript of conversations. Crook stopped at Maus's camp about one-half mile from where the Apaches were camped.

Geronimo, Naiche, and Chihuahua were among those who arrived at Crook's camp on March 25. Mangus was not present, having taken his small band away several months earlier. Geronimo gave a lengthy defense of himself, explaining that he had lived peacefully at San Carlos, killing no one. He explained that only when he learned soldiers were planning to arrest and kill him did he leave the reservation. Crook listened patiently and then denied that any orders had been given to arrest him. Geronimo, in turn, denied that he had sent anyone to kill Davis and Chato.

The Apaches withdrew to consider their next course of action. Kaytennae and Alchise circulated among them, encouraging surrender. The offer from Crook consisted of unconditional surrender, to be followed by two years in the East with their families and then a return to the reservation. On March 27, word arrived at Crook's camp that the leaders wanted to talk with him.

Chihuahua was the first to give his surrender speech, followed by Naiche. Geronimo, who had been the last holdout, agreeing to surrender only when it became clear that everyone else had decided on that course of action, spoke last. He had less to say than the others. Poignantly, he remarked, "Once I moved about like the wind. Now I surrender to you and that is all."[18] Geronimo then stepped forward and shook the general's hand. He added his hope that his wife and daughter would be permitted to join him at Fort Bowie or Silver Creek, perhaps referring to Ziyeh and his adult daughter, Dohnsay.

Second Thoughts

That night, however, Geronimo and many others of the Apaches imbibed considerable alcohol. It had been supplied by a notorious trader named Tribolett, who specialized in smuggling and was among the class of traders who did not want peace because it would deprive them of a major market among the Indians. Tribolett was the source of not only the alcohol with which Geronimo could try to ease his sorrow over surrendering, but also the rumor that U.S. authorities planned to hang Geronimo once they had him back within the United States.

The following day, March 28, General Crook left for Fort Bowie, leaving Lieutenant Maus to escort the Apaches back to Arizona. Given the heavy drinking of the night before, they were in poor shape for heavy traveling and made limited progress. During the night, Geronimo and Naiche led a group of about 40 away from the camp, including Geronimo's son Chappo and his cousins Fun and Perico. Maus sent Nana and Chihuahua to try to persuade them to return, but Geronimo had made his decision to continue fighting—a course that he surely knew could not end happily. He was determined at least to die free.

Geronimo and Naiche well recognized their precarious position and knew that almost anyone whom they met could end their lives by informing on them. Consequently, they tried to leave no witnesses among anyone they encountered.

General Miles

Crook returned to Fort Bowie on March 29 and sent off a telegram to General Philip Sheridan, Commanding General of the U.S. Army, informing him of the surrender and of the terms that he had offered: that the prisoners would be sent to Florida to be with their families for no more than two years before being returned to the reservation. Sheridan's quick response rejected the terms on authority of President Grover Cleveland, agreeing to only one promise—that those who surrendered would not be killed.

The following day, Crook learned from Maus that Geronimo and Naiche had escaped. After another exchange of telegrams with Sheridan, Crook asked to be transferred. Sheridan complied in a message of April 2, shifting Crook to the Department of the Platte and replacing him with Brigadier General Nelson A. Miles.

Miles did not trust the Apache scouts despite their almost unbroken record of loyalty, and abandoned Crook's innovative and successful strategy of using them to track down other Apaches. Instead, he relied on cavalry to pursue the escapees, but the horses had little ability to scale the mountains in which Geronimo and his band took refuge. On foot, the soldiers were not much better than the horses at following Geronimo, as they lacked the stamina in rugged terrain that even the Apache women and children possessed. Heliograph messages from mountain to mountain were effective only if the military actually had something to report.

Geronimo raided seemingly at will on both sides of the border, leaving few witnesses alive to report on his whereabouts. Meanwhile, Miles achieved no successes, failing to capture or kill any of Geronimo's band. On the San Carlos Reservation and nearby, hatred was growing toward the Apaches, on the part of both other tribes on the reservation and the area settlers and townspeople. Miles suggested to Sheridan that the reservation Apaches be relocated to Indian Territory in present-day Oklahoma or in Kansas. The government agency decided instead to send them to Fort Marion at St. Augustine, Florida.

Miles sent Lieutenant Charles Gatewood to try to make contact with Geronimo. Gatewood was accompanied by a Nednai named Martine; Kayihtah, a brother of Yahnozha, one of Geronimo's warriors; a translator named George Wratten; and a packer. Gatewood may not have needed the translator, as he knew the Apache language and was respected by the Apaches. He was authorized to seek assistance from any military force and joined the command of Captain Henry Lawton. When Gatewood learned that Geronimo had sent two women on an exploratory peace mission to Mexican officials at Fronteras, 30 miles south of the U.S. border, he hurriedly moved to pick up the women's trail as they returned to Geronimo.

The Final Surrender

On August 24, 1886, the Apaches saw the Gatewood party approaching under a white flag. They recognized Martine, Kayihtah, Gatewood, and Wratten, the last of whom was married to an Apache. Geronimo wanted to shoot them, but others in the party refused, threatening to kill anyone—even Geronimo—who attempted to harm Gatewood and his companions. At a council the following day, Gatewood told Geronimo that the group's families had been sent to Florida (although Gatewood knew that they had not actually been transported yet) and that Geronimo and his group would join them in Florida if they surrendered. By August 26, Geronimo was ready to turn himself in to Miles. The party, about 28 strong, including 18 warriors, then began the journey back to the United States with Gatewood, Lawton, and Lawton's troops.

Geronimo may not have fully understood the depth of hatred that many felt toward him. Even President Cleveland had telegraphed the War Department, saying, "I hope nothing will be done with Geronimo which will prevent our treating him as a prisoner of war, if we cannot hang him, which I would much prefer."[19]

Miles waited to meet with Geronimo and Naiche, and also delayed informing Sheridan of their surrender, until he was certain there would be no turning back or slip-up of any sort. Finally, Miles set out for the designated meeting place, Skeleton Canyon in southern Arizona. The group arrived there on September 3.

When the translator told Geronimo that General Miles was his friend, Geronimo said, "I never saw him, but I have been in need of friends. Why has he not been with me?"[20] The response elicited laughter from the other officers, although Geronimo seemed to be quite serious in his statement. Miles explained the terms of the surrender. Geronimo would accompany Miles to Fort Bowie and then travel on to Florida to be reunited with his family. There Geronimo and the other Apaches would receive cattle and implements for farming. Geronimo describes Miles's symbolic actions in specific detail in his autobiography:

> We stood between his troopers and my warriors. We placed a large stone on the blanket before us. Our treaty was made by this stone, and it was to last until the stone should crumble to dust; so we made the treaty, and bound each other with an oath.... Then General Miles swept a spot of ground clear with his hand, and said: "Your past deeds shall be wiped out like this and you will start a new life."[21]

Geronimo says in the autobiography regarding this agreement, from the vantage point of about 20 years later, "I do not believe that I have ever violated that treaty; but General Miles never fulfilled his promises."[22]

Geronimo and his band then rode back to Fort Bowie with Miles. The vanquished were put on a train at Bowie Station to the sarcastic playing of "Auld Lang Syne" by the military band. The prisoners from the reservation, almost 400 of them, arrived at Fort Marion on September 20. Geronimo, Naiche, and their associates, however, were stopped at San Antonio, Texas, on September 10 on orders of the War Department, where they were held in a prison. Brigadier General D. S. Stanley, commander of the Department of Texas, was ordered to question the prisoners and report on their character as he awaited further orders.

Considerable sentiment existed for trying and executing Geronimo and the other leaders. President Cleveland decided instead that Miles's agreement with the Apaches must be supported, at least insofar as he had promised that they would not be killed. In the end, Geronimo and the others with him were put onboard another train and sent on to Fort Pickens near Pensacola, Florida. They arrived on October 25. The president's decision was received enthusiastically at Pensacola, where more prisoners meant more financial opportunities for area merchants.

Just a few days before Geronimo left Texas, the last of the Apache holdouts—Mangus, and his party of two warriors, three women, and five children—surrendered. They arrived at Fort Pickens on November 6.

ON THE RESERVATION

Longing to Go Home

Like so many Indians who were consigned to reservations far from their native lands, Geronimo longed to go home. And like so many others, he would never do so. Geronimo and the rest of the Chiricahuas were reunited by May 1888, but near Mobile, Alabama, far from their homeland. By 1890, approximately 120 of those who had been transported to Florida were dead. That number included 30 children who had been sent to the Carlisle Indian Industrial School, a boarding school intended to educate young Indians and transform them essentially into imitation Euro-Americans. Diseases such as malaria and tuberculosis, exacerbated by an unfamiliar climate and a strong portion of despair, contributed greatly to the high mortality rate.

Ironically, among the strongest advocates for a more humane treatment of the Chiricahuas were two men who had spent much time as opponents of Geronimo—Generals Howard and Crook—although the former had won the war leader's enduring respect. They urged removal of the refugees to a healthy climate, although the best that they could come up with was Fort Sill, Oklahoma, then part of Indian Territory. The exiles arrived at this location, which was closer to home but still not there, in the fall of 1894.

Geronimo became a competent farmer, but the soldiers had not forgotten his past deeds and regularly insulted him—for example, calling him "Gerry," a name that he despised. He also became a celebrity as the United States, having defeated the last of the great Indian resistance leaders, now embarked on the mythologizing of the Indian wars that rendered history both more palatable and less true.

Geronimo became a popular subject of photographers and took to selling souvenirs, such as buttons and signed photographs. He attended the Trans-Mississippi and International Exposition at Omaha, Nebraska, in 1898; the

Pan-American Exposition in Buffalo, New York, in 1901; and the St. Louis World's Fair in 1904. In 1905, he was a guest at the inauguration of President Theodore Roosevelt, riding in the inaugural parade with the president and another prominent Indian war leader, Quanah Parker. Onlookers along Pennsylvania Avenue cheered loudly for Geronimo, the man who had spread fear throughout the Southeast.

The end came for Geronimo on February 17, 1909. He had gone to the town of Lawton to sell a bow he had made and then spent the money drinking. He had a long history of what now is called binge drinking, surely a way to help temporarily erase some of the memories of relatives and friends he had lost and the way of life that had been taken from his people. On his way home, he fell from his horse and lay in the road during a freezing rain. When he

Quanah Parker

Quanah Parker (circa 1852–1911) was a powerful war leader who mightily resisted Euro-American intruders into the southern plains. Emblematic of the intruders were the buffalo hunters, men who could kill the buffalos from a great distance with their Sharp's .50-caliber rifles, leaving the carcasses to rot while they hauled away the hides.

In the early morning of June 27, 1874, Quanah helped lead a large war party of Cheyenne, Kiowa, and Comanche warriors (including Quanah's own Quahada Comanches) against a small trading settlement known as Adobe Walls in the northern panhandle of Texas north of the Canadian River, near present-day Borger. Warned of an impending attack, the Adobe Walls saloon-keeper managed to awaken a number of men to prevent their being overrun in their sleep. Behind thick adobe walls and with their heavy guns, the 28 men (most of them buffalo hunters) and 1 woman managed to survive with just 3 fatalities.

Quanah continued to wage war, but by 1875 he knew that war was futile. Ultimately, he helped his people to settle on a reservation in Indian Territory and learn how to live as farmers and ranchers. Shortly after the Quahadas' surrender, General Ranald Mackenzie appointed him chief of the Comanches. Quanah established good relations with the family of his Euro-American mother, Cynthia Parker, taking the Parker surname. He also developed a keen financial sense, arranging leasing arrangements with area ranchers to graze cattle on reservation land as a source of revenue for the Comanches.

Quanah himself became a successful rancher, helped to establish the Native American Church, and numbered among his many prominent friends President Theodore Roosevelt. In fact, he rode in the president's inaugural parade in 1905 and accompanied him on a wolf hunt. Upon Quanah's death, a funeral procession about two miles long attended his burial.

Cynthia Ann Parker

Cynthia Ann Parker (circa 1825–1871) moved with her family from Illinois to Texas around 1835. There, the family built a community known as Fort Parker around an uncle's Baptist church. On May 19, 1836, a group of Quahada Comanche warriors raided the community and took five captives, including Cynthia. Ultimately, all of the captives except Cynthia were returned.

Cynthia was reared by a Comanche couple who loved her very much. Eventually, she married Peta Nocona, a Quahada chief. She bore him two sons, Quanah and Pecos, and a daughter, Topsana (Toh-Tsee-ah, or Prairie Flower). Cynthia repeatedly refused opportunities to return to her original family, explaining that she loved her husband and children too much.

Texas Rangers attacked Peta's camp on December 18, 1860, wounding Peta and capturing Cynthia and her infant daughter. Cynthia was returned to her Parker family, and the Texas legislature allotted her both land and an annuity of $100 per year. She was never reconciled to life with the Parkers, however, and longed to return to the Comanches, several times trying unsuccessfully to escape from the Parkers. In 1863, Cynthia learned that Pecos had died; a few months later, her daughter also died. Gradually drawing into herself and often refusing to eat, Cynthia followed them in death in 1870.

Quanah's devotion to his mother never wavered over the years. Shortly before his own death, he succeeded in having her remains and those of his sister moved to a nearby cemetery near Cache, Oklahoma. Just two weeks before he died, a large marble monument that he had requested was erected over her grave. In 1957, all three were reburied in the Fort Sill cemetery in Oklahoma.

was found the following day, he was taken to the military hospital at Fort Sill. He died there, not from the bullets that could never kill him, but from an equally deadly weapon, and while still a prisoner.

Four years later, approximately 260 of the Chiricahuas were allowed to return to the Southwest, to live among the Mescalero Apaches in New Mexico. It was not quite home, but it probably would have been close enough for Geronimo.

Geronimo's Autobiography

Stephen M. Barrett was superintendent of schools in Lawton, Oklahoma, in 1905, when he sought permission from the military to tell the story of Geronimo. Rebuffed by local officers (a Lieutenant Purington, for example, said that Geronimo should be hanged rather than given so much public attention), Barrett wrote to President Roosevelt. The president was more accommodating and granted permission. Barrett then arranged for a translator to work with him as he interviewed Geronimo. The translator was Asa Daklugie, a son of Juh and a recent student at the Carlisle Indian Industrial School.

The interviews began in the fall of 1905. Geronimo told his story, sometimes at his own tipi, sometimes at Asa Daklugie's house, or even while riding. He declined to stop for note taking or corrections, preferring to return on another day to listen to the transcription and make changes.

Barrett submitted the manuscript to Major Charles Taylor, commander of Fort Sill, for approval, who suggested additional questions to ask Geronimo. When Barrett concluded that the autobiography was complete, he sent it to President Roosevelt, who suggested that Barrett include disclaimers to the effect that controversial statements and conclusions potentially offensive to readers were Geronimo's and not the editor's. The final manuscript went to the War Department in June 1906, which declined formal approval but did not attempt to stop Barrett from proceeding with the book's publication. Later that year, the book was published.

The autobiography offers much information about Geronimo and his people, although it is far more forthcoming about battles against Mexicans than against the U.S. military. That Geronimo remained a prisoner of war certainly led him to deemphasize his conflicts with the United States. David Roberts, author of *Once They Moved Like the Wind: Cochise, Geronimo, and the Apache Wars*, refers to Asa Daklugie's acknowledgment years later that Geronimo feared an effort by Barrett to lead him into incriminating himself and thus incurring additional punishment.[23]

Above all, the autobiography is a plea that President Roosevelt allow him to return home, where, Geronimo wrote, "I could forget all the wrongs that I have ever received, and die a contented and happy old man."[24] Roosevelt sympathized but feared there was still too much hatred against Geronimo in Arizona. He decided instead that Geronimo should remain where he was.

NOTES

1. Edwin R. Sweeney, *Mangas Coloradas: Chief of the Chiricahua Apaches* (Norman: University of Oklahoma Press, 1998) 5–10.

2. *Geronimo: His Own Story*. Ed. S. M. Barrett. Newly edited with Introduction and Notes by Frederick Turner (1970; New York: Meridian, 1996) 77–78.

3. *Geronimo: His Own Story* 78.

4. Sweeney 406.

5. Peter Aleshire, *The Fox and the Whirlwind: General George Crook and Geronimo: A Paired Biography* (2000; Hoboken, NJ: Castle Books, 2005) 335.

6. Alexander B. Adams, *Geronimo: A Biography* (New York: G. P. Putnam's Sons, 1971) 126.

7. Sweeney 455.

8. *Geronimo: His Own Story* 124.

9. *Geronimo: His Own Story* 124.

10. Woodworth Clum, *Apache Agent: The Story of John P. Clum* (1936; Lincoln: University of Nebraska Press, 1978) 228.

11. *Geronimo: His Own Story* 127.

12. Angie Debo, *Geronimo: The Man, His Time, His Place* (Norman: University of Oklahoma Press, 1976) 124.

13. Jason Betzinez, with Wilbur Sturtevant Nye, *I Fought with Geronimo* (Harrisburg, PA: Stackpole Company, 1959) 47.

14. Debo 153.

15. Betzinez 77.

16. Federal Writers' Program, *New Mexico: A Guide to the Colorful State* (New York: Hastings House, 1953) 417–18.

17. Debo 241.

18. Debo 262.

19. David Roberts, *Once They Moved Like the Wind: Cochise, Geronimo, and the Apache Wars* (New York: Simon and Schuster, 1993) 297.

20. Debo 291.

21. *Geronimo: His Own Story* 136–38.

22. *Geronimo: His Own Story* 138.

23. Roberts 311.

24. *Geronimo: His Own Story* 169.

RECOMMENDED READING

Adams, Alexander B. *Geronimo: A Biography*. New York: G. P. Putnam's Sons, 1971.

Betzinez, Jason, with Wilbur Sturtevant Nye. *I Fought with Geronimo*. Harrisburg, PA: Stackpole, 1959.

Clum, Woodworth. *Apache Agent: The Story of John P. Clum*. 1936. Lincoln: University of Nebraska Press, 1978.

Debo, Angie. *Geronimo: The Man, His Time, His Place*. Norman: University of Oklahoma Press, 1976.

Faulk, Odie B. *The Geronimo Campaign*. New York: Oxford University Press, 1969.

Gatewood, Charles B. *Lt. Charles Gatewood and His Apache Wars Memoir*. Ed. Louis Kraft. Lincoln: University of Nebraska Press, 2005.

Geronimo. *Geronimo: His Own Story*. Ed. S. M. Barrett. Newly edited with Introduction and Notes by Frederick Turner. 1970. New York: Meridian, 1996.

Geronimo: The Last Renegade. Executive Producers Craig Haffner and Donna E. Lusitana. A&E Television Networks, 1996.

Howard, Oliver O. *My Life and Experiences Among Our Hostile Indians*. 1907. New York: Da Capo Press, 1972.

Sweeney, Edwin R. *Mangas Coloradas: Chief of the Chiricahua Apaches*. Norman: University of Oklahoma Press, 1998.

Dennis Banks holds aloft a burning paper containing a government offer to allow Indians to leave Wounded Knee during the 1973 occupation. Russell Means looks on approvingly. (AP Photo)

Dennis James Banks (born 1937)

Dennis Banks, an Ojibwa from Minnesota, became one of this country's most influential American Indian leaders of the twentieth century. He co-founded the American Indian Movement (AIM) in 1968 and participated in a wide range of efforts designed to bring to the nation's attention the injustice and lack of opportunities that constituted the basic condition for a huge percentage of Indians throughout the country.

During the 1970s, Banks participated in the occupation of Alcatraz Island, protests at Mount Rushmore and Plymouth Rock, efforts to gain justice for murder victims Raymond Yellow Thunder and Wesley Bad Heart Bull, the Trail of Broken Treaties, and the occupation of Wounded Knee. His actions at Wounded Knee and Custer, South Dakota—the latter concerned with bringing the killer of Wesley Bad Heart Bull to justice—led to criminal charges against Banks.

In the Custer case, Banks was convicted of assault and incitement to rioting but refused to turn himself in to begin serving his prison term. He remained a fugitive for almost a decade before surrendering in 1985. Upon his release, Banks continued his efforts to improve the quality of life for Indians. He also began acting in films and recording American Indian songs.

BEFORE THE AMERICAN INDIAN MOVEMENT

Leech Lake Reservation

Dennis Banks was born on April 12, 1937, on the Leech Lake Chippewa Reservation in central Minnesota, about one-third of the way from the northern border of the state. The area was the site of the last battle between Ojibwas (also known as Chippewas) and the U.S. army, which occurred in 1898. Banks's birth took place in the home of his maternal grandparents, Jenny and Josh Drumbeater. The small Drumbeater house, which lacked both electricity and indoor plumbing, also provided shelter for Banks's older siblings, Mark and Audrey. He later would have a younger sister, Charolette, as well. The father, Walter Chase, entered the military and then built a new life for himself, establishing a second family and having little contact with Dennis and his siblings.

Banks received his Ojibwa name, Nowa-Cumig, from a dream his grandfather had. The name means "at the center of the universe" and would prove apt by the 1970s, when Banks became pivotal, if not at the center of the entire universe, then at least at the center of the American Indian universe. Banks, along with many Ojibwas, prefers to call himself an Anishinabe, a name that means "first peoples."

Banks spent the early part of his childhood with his mother, grandparents, brother, and sister at Headquarters Bay. As he reached school age, the local school moved from the village of Federal Dam near Headquarters Bay to the town of Walker west of Leech Lake. Consequently, Banks's mother moved with the children to Old Agency, a settlement near Walker. As Banks notes in his memoir, *Ojibwa Warrior*, which he co-wrote with Richard Erdoes, he mainly spoke English as a child, although he was able to speak Ojibwa to some extent, and his grandparents spoke the native language. His mother, who had attended an Indian boarding school, spoke English with the children, having been permanently influenced by common boarding-school efforts to convert students to Euro-American culture, including use of the English language.

By 1942, Banks was experiencing a growing isolation that he would not overcome until years later. His mother was growing distant and eventually remarried. In addition, all three of the school-age children were bused off to boarding school at Pipestone in the southwestern corner of the state. As was common in boarding schools run for Indian students, young Dennis had his long hair cut short and his clothes replaced by a school uniform complete with black shoes. During his time at Pipestone, his mother never visited, although the journey would have been long and difficult for her. She wrote, however—letters read to Dennis by his brother and sister. During the summer, when most students were able to go home, the Banks children stayed at Pipestone. The ongoing effort to transform students there into imitation Euro-Americans worked well, as Banks describes in *Ojibwa Warrior*:

> Their efforts to acculturate us extended even as far as our history books, which depicted Native people as murderous, mindless savages .... I began to hate myself for being Indian, and made myself believe that I was really a white boy. My white teachers and their books taught me to despise my own people. White history became my history because there was no other. When they took us once a week to the movies—the twelve-cent matinee—I cheered for Davy Crockett, Daniel Boone, and General Custer. I sided with the cavalry cutting down Indians. In my fantasies I was John Wayne rescuing the settlers from "red fiends." I dreamed of being a cowboy. My teachers had done a great job of brainwashing me. They had made me into an "apple"—red outside but white inside.[1]

Finally, his grandparents came for a visit. The result was to revive Banks's memories of his early years at Leech Lake rather than to ease the pain of his long separation from Leech Lake. After they left, he tried to run away but was captured and brought back.

Banks was sent to Wahpeton, North Dakota, for his seventh and eighth grades. He spent ninth grade at Flandreau, South Dakota. By the age of 16, Banks had all that he could take of the boarding schools: He walked 18 miles to Pipestone, Minnesota, where he caught a freight train part of the way home, hitchhiking the rest of the way to Leech Lake.

Back home, Banks attended high school at Walker. Finally, he was not in an institution run by the Bureau of Indian Affairs (BIA). That offered new possibilities and new challenges. He was mainly in school with white children, but he was able to reclaim something of traditional Ojibwa life. He also had the freedom to hitchhike to Minneapolis to visit his sister. Still, he had to find a future, and the reservation offered few paths forward.

The Air Force

Dennis Banks's choice of a path into the future was the U.S. Air Force. Before he left to join the military, an uncle gave him a small medicine bundle to wear around his neck. With his protective medicine, he entered the Air Force in April 1954 and trained as an aerial photographer. The FBI conducted a background check of Banks, and he received top-secret clearance to work with secret material, principally aerial photographs of China, Korea, and the Soviet Union.

Banks was sent abroad to Japan and initially stationed at Itami Air Base in Osaka. He came to love Japan as well as a young Japanese woman whom he met there. He found himself recognized as an American Indian but also accepted as a human being. At a bar named The Top Hat, he met a bartender named Machiko. She was only 16, a year younger than Banks, but they quickly fell in love. When Banks's unit was transferred to Yokota Air Base, operated by the Strategic Air Command near Tokyo, Machiko went with him. The young couple shared a house with another soldier and his girlfriend, spending the next three years together.

Banks and Machiko had a daughter, Michiko, and decided to marry. The ceremony was performed by a Shinto priest, but when Banks applied for permission to also have a civil ceremony, the Air Force refused, citing a policy against U.S. servicemen marrying Japanese women. Nor would Air Force officials recognize the Shinto marriage. Banks was later informed that Machiko's family was suspected of being communists; as a consequence, his security clearance was withdrawn.

Angered by the military's response to his marriage, Banks went AWOL with his wife and daughter. Tracked down, he was arrested, court-martialed, and jailed for 30 days. After being released, Banks tried again to get away with his family but was once more apprehended. He was sent back to the United States, while being forced to leave his wife and baby behind. An escape attempt when the plane stopped at the Midway Islands failed, and he was forced to continue to the United States.

Banks's intention was to save enough money to bring Machiko and Michiko to the United States. He had little success in raising the necessary money, and his steady descent into heavy drinking further blocked that effort. Banks's memoir, published in 2004, recounts efforts that he made over the years to try to find his Japanese family, including many trips back to Japan. At the time when his memoir was published, he had not been able to locate either wife or daughter. He writes of these trips: "Every now and then a young girl will come up to me and say, 'My father is an American Indian.' Shivers run through my whole body. But then she is not Michiko at all, but someone else's child."[2]

Incarceration

The early 1960s found Dennis Banks back in Minnesota, living in Minneapolis with friends from military days. Banks spent a great deal of time hanging out in bars and was repeatedly arrested—he mentions 25 times in his memoir—for being drunk and disorderly, or just for being Indian.

Becoming familiar with jails, Banks also learned that American Indians made up a sizable percentage of the jail population in Minnesota—approximately one-third. The climax of these arrests came in 1966 when, now married to an Indian woman named Jeanette, and with eight children (four from her previous marriage and four from his marriage with her), he stole 16 bags of groceries to try to feed his large family.

Another man, Bill, was also arrested for the burglary. Bill, a white man, had an attorney and received probation; Banks, without an attorney and of Indian heritage, was sentenced to five years in prison. Banks served about two years at Stillwater Prison in Minnesota before being released in May 1968. During this time in prison, he began to read about Indian history and became increasingly political. A book that especially affected Banks was *Black Elk Speaks*, which encapsulated the wisdom of the Oglala spiritual leader Black Elk as recorded by John Niehardt.

By the time Banks was released from prison, Jeanette had left. With no one specific to be responsible for, Banks began traveling down a long path of becoming responsible, in a sense, for all Indians. He contacted an old boarding-school friend, George Mitchell, and set up a meeting to begin organizing for the cause of Indian civil rights.

THE AMERICAN INDIAN MOVEMENT

The Beginning

The initial meeting of what would become the American Indian Movement (AIM) occurred on July 28, 1968, in a church basement in Minneapolis. A primary concern leading to the meeting was police brutality, but a wide range of other issues would soon become part of the new organization's agenda, including better housing, employment opportunities, and education for Indians.

The turnout was large for that first meeting, about 200 people, and participants quickly got down to business. Clyde Bellecourt was made chairman and Banks field director. George Mitchell suggested naming the organization Concerned Indian Americans. That name prevailed for a time, but the initials CIA—evoking thoughts of a far different entity, the Central Intelligence Agency—would eventually lead to adoption of the group's current name.

The ongoing practice of rounding up Indians by the police, which Banks had experienced many times firsthand, led to AIM members, wearing red berets so that they could readily be identified, patrolling the streets where Indians tended to gather. Not only did they monitor the proceedings, but they also filmed police activity. Other early AIM activities included providing legal assistance, fostering better communications between Indians and the broader community, and establishing an alternative school for Indian children named the Red School House.

Federal Termination Policy

The federal termination and assimilation policy was designed to end special relationships between the federal government and Indian nations and encourage Indians to become assimilated into the larger American society. It involved dividing up communally held reservation land and pressuring Indians to move into cities and towns. However, many who attempted to relocate found themselves facing language barriers, having great difficulty finding jobs, and confronting considerable racism. The result was that often rural poverty was merely replaced by urban poverty.

Termination placed tribes under state jurisdiction, opened up previous reservation land to the highest bidder (including companies interested in mining and water rights), and ended tribal courts and police forces. The policy was a great blow to Indian sovereignty.

The movement toward termination grew rapidly after World War II as, influenced by Senator Joseph McCarthy's hunt for communists, Indian communal life on reservations was perceived by many as being too close to communism to be tolerated. In 1950, Dillon Myer, who had administered the relocation of Japanese Americans to internment camps during World War II, became Commissioner of Indian Affairs. His approach to relocation was to give Indians a one-way bus ticket to a city with little subsequent support.

Termination became official U.S. policy with passage of House Concurrent Resolution 108 in 1953. Shortly afterward, President Dwight Eisenhower signed Public Law 280, abolishing tribal courts and police on reservations in California, Minnesota, Nebraska, Oregon, and Wisconsin. By 1962, the government had succeeded in forcing termination on 61 tribes. The Menominees in Wisconsin finally were able to reverse termination in 1973.

Under President John Kennedy, the U.S. government largely abandoned the termination policy. Only when President Richard Nixon called for a definitive end to the termination program in 1970 would the policy be officially abolished, however.

Also established was an AIM radio station, KUXL. As a recruiter for the Honeywell Corporation, Banks helped other Indians to find jobs.

As Banks became increasingly involved in activist efforts to help other Indians, he nonetheless continued the heavy drinking that had marred his life since his Air Force days. That would change on New Year's morning, 1970. As Banks describes the moment in *Ojibwa Warrior*, drink, depression, and a sense of failure overwhelmed him during the final evening of 1969, and he thought that he might be dying.[3] He prayed fervently and resolved to quit drinking if he were spared. Finally, he fell asleep. The next morning he awoke, began fixing breakfast, and opened a can of beer. As he lifted the can to his mouth, he remembered his vow made the night before and emptied the beer down the sink. According to his account, he would not again have another drink. He also saw himself in a mirror—dressed in a white man's gray suit, white shirt, and tie—and resolved to begin dressing in a more traditional Indian way. He would let his hair grow long, and soon a headband became almost a constant part of his wardrobe.

The Spiritual Center

Although Banks quickly recognized the important work that AIM was doing, he also sensed that something was absent—"something," he wrote in his memoir, "that should be at the center of what we were doing."[4] That something was spirituality.

Learning of a spiritual reawakening that had been occurring on the Rosebud Reservation in South Dakota, especially through the efforts of the Crow Dog family, Banks drove there in 1969. He found his way to the Crow Dog home, where he was welcomed by a large sign reading "Crow Dog's Paradise." Banks met Henry Crow Dog, who invited him in but grilled him with a series of questions regarding religious experiences, among them the Sun Dance and sweat lodge purification. Banks understood how little he actually knew about Indian spirituality, but he was anxious to learn. With Crow Dog instructing him, he participated in two sweat lodge purifications.

On Banks's second trip to Rosebud the following year, this time accompanied by Clyde Bellecourt, he met Henry Crow Dog's son, Leonard. The younger man was playing a pivotal role in reestablishing the Sun Dance, which had been strongly discouraged since the late nineteenth century and was formally outlawed by the U.S. government in 1904. The Sun Dance had been legalized in 1934, but not until 1979, after the signing by President Jimmy Carter of the American Indian Religious Freedom Act, did the traditional dance with piercing become legal.

Banks and Bellecourt attended a Yuwipi ceremony conducted by Leonard Crow Dog, a ceremony intended to find out answers to certain important questions that one or more people had raised. Crow Dog, as the principal participant, had his hands tied and was wrapped in a star blanket; star blankets and quilts were a Lakota tradition hearkening back to early-morning awakenings to see the morning star, a symbol of not only a new day but also a new beginning. The ceremony involved prayers, songs, drumming, and ritualistic sharing of dog soup. It also included Crow Dog's answers to the questions raised by the Yuwipi sponsor. Leonard Crow Dog would soon become the spiritual leader of AIM and play major roles in various AIM events, including the occupation of Wounded Knee in 1973.

Banks also resolved to participate in a Sun Dance, which he did in 1971. Another prominent medicine man, John Fire Lame Deer, organized and led the Sun Dance for Banks; Bellecourt; Russell Means, also a major AIM leader; and Lee Brightman, a friend of Banks. The participants danced for three days, staring into the sun. On the fourth day, they were pierced as an act of sacrifice.

Lame Deer slit Banks's chest and inserted a wooden skewer that was attached to the skin, with the other end connected to a rawhide thong tied to the sacred cottonwood tree. Finally, the skewer tore free from his chest as he danced.

A New Political Force

The union of traditional Indian spirituality and culture with political action designed to advance civil rights has been a hallmark of Indian activism since the 1960s, and that combination was equally prominent in Dennis Banks's efforts within the American Indian Movement. One of the first actions by Banks to attract national attention, however, was not initially an AIM event. After a brief occupation of Alcatraz Island, site of the federal prison that had been closed in 1963, by a group headed by Mohawk Richard Oakes on November 9, 1969, a larger party of about 80 calling themselves Indians of All Tribes arrived on November 20. Their purpose was to reclaim the island under the Treaty of Fort Laramie of 1868, which provided for the return of abandoned federal land to the native peoples who previously owned it. The rationale was sweetly ironic— using a treaty, the weapon for dispossessing Indians of so much over the years, against those who had initially fashioned the weapon.

Banks, Bellecourt, Mitchell, and other AIM members heard of the occupation and headed to San Francisco to join those already on the island. They arrived near the end of November. Banks stayed only a couple of days, long enough to establish AIM support for the effort. The takeover convinced AIM leaders of the tactical usefulness of the 1868 treaty, which had created the Great Sioux Reservation in western South Dakota, while also setting aside hunting grounds in Montana and Wyoming so long as sufficient buffalo remained for hunting purposes, a condition that would not long prevail. The occupation of Alcatraz continued until June 11, 1971, when the remaining 15 occupiers were forcibly removed. Oakes, who was part of the original occupying force, had left in January 1970 after his 13-year-old stepdaughter, Yvonne, died in a fall on the island.

In 1970, again using the Treaty of Fort Laramie as justification, Banks and other AIM members occupied an abandoned naval station in Minnesota near the Minneapolis–St. Paul International Airport. When police and federal marshals arrived, they made their stand on the third floor of one of the buildings. In the ensuing battle, Banks was knocked unconscious.

The same year, a takeover of Mount Rushmore occurred. This effort was the brainchild of three Lakota women from Rapid City, South Dakota. The mountain, which is located within the sacred Black Hills, features the huge visages of Abraham Lincoln, George Washington, Thomas Jefferson, and Theodore Roosevelt. The point of the protestors was that four leaders of the nation that took the Black Hills from Indians and diverted portions of the area to such purposes as a World War II gunnery range and mining should not be represented there. Banks, Russell Means, and other members of AIM joined in the Lakota women's effort, taking their place atop the mountain as well.

AIM achieved national news coverage at Thanksgiving later that year with demonstrations at Plymouth Rock and aboard *Mayflower II*, a replica of the original Pilgrims' ship. The protest was led by Banks, Means, John Trudell, and Floyd Westerman in response to an invitation from the Wampanoag, Narragansett, and Passamaquoddy tribes; these tribes had proclaimed an Indian national day of mourning in conjunction with the 350th anniversary of the Pilgrims' landing.

AIM members took over *Mayflower II*, lowered the British flag, and hoisted the American flag upside down. The reversed flag became an AIM symbol, appropriate from AIM's point of view because an upside-down flag is an international symbol of distress. The protestors also dumped overboard dummies representing the Pilgrims. After two hours aboard the ship, they left peacefully when police arrived. Means and a few others then shoveled sand over Plymouth Rock, hiding the historic rock. Banks and other demonstrators also interrupted a costumed recreation of a Pilgrim feast at Plymouth Plantation.

Throughout 1970, AIM staged a variety of demonstrations against Bureau of Indian Affairs offices. BIA offices in Chicago, Cleveland, Minneapolis, and Littleton, Colorado, were occupied, as was a BIA warehouse in Gallup, New Mexico. Other demonstrations occurred at Fort Lawton in Washington State and on Ellis Island. The focus was on BIA abuses and the agency's alleged failure to adequately represent Indian rights and concerns.

The Littleton sit-in led to police arresting 12 demonstrators, who became known as the Littleton Twelve. Banks and AIM members actively supported the Littleton Twelve by occupying a BIA office in Minneapolis. There, another 12 protestors, including Banks, were arrested. Ultimately, the BIA decided to drop the trespassing charges against Banks and his associates.

Protesting policies, as important as such actions were, paled in comparison to the extreme violence that awaited American Indians at virtually every corner. One of those corners was Gordon, Nebraska, where on February 14, 1972, Raymond Yellow Thunder, a Lakota, was fatally beaten. The brothers Leslie and Melvin Hare, according to Banks, beat Yellow Thunder, dragged him into an American Legion dance, stripped him from the waist down, and forced him to dance. Then the Hare brothers and others beat him some more and stuffed him into the trunk of their car. According to differing reports, Yellow Thunder was found either in the trunk or in his own pickup after he was eventually released from the trunk and made his way back to the used-car lot where he lived. In either case, his dead body was not found until February 20.

The Hare brothers were arrested but charged with only second-degree manslaughter and released without bail. The case likely would have ended there if not for the decision of Yellow Thunder's family to ask AIM for help. Banks and other AIM members started for Gordon from South Dakota. Leonard Crow Dog prepared the AIM members by praying and sprinkling them with sacred gopher dust, Crazy Horse's standard preparation before battle. Hoping to avoid a violent confrontation, AIM informed governmental and law enforcement officials of the activists' pending arrival.

AIM took over the town hall and the mayor's office without resistance and conducted their own grand jury to hear testimony. Negotiations with Gordon officials followed, leading to an agreement that a Gordon Human Relations Council would be created to encourage cooperation and resolve problems between Indian and non-Indian members of the community.

The trial of the Hare brothers took place in Alliance, Nebraska, and resulted in convictions for both men. Leslie was sentenced to six years in prison for manslaughter, Melvin to two years. The punishments were inadequate but considerably more than the defendants likely would have received without AIM intervention. The outcome was especially significant for a people accustomed to seeing Indians beaten and even killed without any justice done. It gave them hope that they might stand up against oppression and seek justice with some hope of getting it. As Severt Young Bear said:

> People here still talk about Yellow Thunder and what happened in Gordon. When AIM came in and helped the family look into the death, that made the older people that are living out on the reservation out in the country—they kind of lifted up their heads, and were speaking out then. And they been talking against BIA, tribal government, law and order system on the reservation, plus some of the non-Indian ranchers that are living on the reservation and been abusing Indians.[5]

Banks mentions in *Ojibwa Warrior* that this early period of great political activity by the American Indian Movement was also very important personally to him, because he met a Lakota woman from Pine Ridge named Darlene Nichols, more commonly known as Kamook. Despite their age difference, 32 and 17, respectively, when they met, the two married and ultimately had four daughters and a son.

Trail of Broken Treaties

The primary AIM event of 1972 was the Trail of Broken Treaties. Its name was based on the Trail of Tears, the long forced journey of Cherokees from Georgia to Oklahoma between 1836 and 1840, as well as the long series of treaties that the U.S. government had violated over the years. Banks was one of the principal organizers of the event, which began with three caravans of Indians starting from Seattle, San Francisco, and Los Angeles and making their way toward Washington, D.C., while picking up additional participants along the way. Banks's caravan left San Francisco on October 6. The three groups met up in St. Paul, Minnesota, and arrived at Washington in the early morning of November 3; by that time, the caravan was some four miles long. Some of the participants continued on to the White House, circling it around 6:00 A.M. to alert President Richard Nixon to their presence.

Desperately in need of sleep, the participants were taken to a church and directed to its basement. Unfortunately, the basement was dark, dirty, and infested with rats. Angrily, they left the church and headed toward the Bureau of Indian Affairs building where they expected help. At the BIA building, Banks and the other leaders discovered from Bob Burnette, Anita Collins, and George Mitchell, who had gone ahead to set up meetings with government officials, that all of the meetings had been cancelled. Even a planned ceremony at the Arlington Cemetery graves of Pima Ira Hayes, who had helped to raise the flag on Mount Surabachi during the battle for Iwo Jima in World War II, and Winnebago John Rice, who was killed in action in 1950 during the Korean War after serving over three years in the Pacific during World War II, was first approved and then rejected by federal officials.

At first, no one—not even officials from the BIA—would talk with Banks and the other AIM members. Late in the morning, however, one official did come down to talk. Told that there was to be a meeting in the auditorium, he informed them that they were not to be inside the building. Not until the middle of the afternoon, when Commissioner of Indian Affairs Louis Bruce, of Lakota and Mohawk ancestry, arrived did anyone remotely supportive meet the new arrivals.

Bruce, whom Banks characterizes as "a fine and decent man,"[6] read a memo from Assistant Secretary of the Interior Harrison Loesch instructing Bruce to offer no assistance. Loesch and Bruce exchanged several telephone calls, with Loesch ordering Bruce to expel from the building all of the AIM members and everyone else from their group. Ultimately, Bruce refused and was fired.

Guards attempted to force the Indians out of the building later that day but were repulsed, although those occupying the building constantly expected other attempts to use force to evict them. The days dragged on with no resolution of the dispute in sight. Two White House aides, Leonard Garment and Brad Patterson, met with some AIM members but reached no agreement.

AIM had developed 20 demands that leaders wanted to discuss with the White House. These points included establishment of a treaty commission to negotiate with Indian nations, restoration of significant amounts of land, abolition of the Bureau of Indian Affairs, creation of a new unit within the Executive Office of the President to replace the BIA, protection of Indians' religious and cultural integrity, and advances in health, housing, education, and employment.

By November 6, the situation looked dire. There was no agreement, and U.S. District Court Judge John Pratt declared the Indians in contempt and ordered their arrest. He further gave the Indians a 6:00 P.M. deadline to leave the building. Also on November 6, Interior Secretary Rogers C. B. Morton, attempting to depict the occupiers of the BIA building as unrepresentative of most Indians, declared:

> For the honor and dignity of the 480,000 reservation Indians, all Americans should understand that the protesters are a small splinter group of militants. They do not represent the reservation Indians of America.[7]

Morton added that William Youpee, executive director of the National Tribal Chairmen's Association, had informed Morton that the protestors who had taken over the building had little support from other Indians.

In fact, a great many tribal leaders did denounce the takeover. Their reaction did not represent limited rank-and-file support for the effort, however, but rather reflected the fact that many tribal leaders had risen to their positions by forming strong alliances with U.S. government officials, often at the expense of the people whom they were expected to serve.

Almost at the last minute, the 6:00 P.M. deadline was extended for 48 hours, and the administration agreed to negotiations through Fred Carlucci, director of the Office of Management and Budget; Leonard Garment, the presidential advisor on minorities; and Secretary Morton. The motivation for both the extension and the negotiations may have been to avoid a potentially violent confrontation the evening before the presidential election.

An agreement was reached on November 10 providing for consideration of the 20 demands by a White House task force with a response within 30 days, a comprehensive review of Indian policy by the task force, and $66,000, a figure requested by AIM to defray the expenses of the Indians' return to their homes. The 20 demands ultimately were rejected, perhaps especially because they ultimately involved issues of Indian sovereignty. Nevertheless, Banks considered the Trail of Broken Treaties a great success, as it brought together members of about 200 tribes acting jointly for a just cause.

OCCUPATION OF WOUNDED KNEE

Murder of Wesley Bad Heart Bull

The prelude to the occupation of Wounded Knee was a legal case involving the murder of Wesley Bad Heart Bull, an Oglala who was killed in Buffalo Gap, South Dakota, on January 21, 1973. Bad Heart Bull had been in Bill's Bar the night before, where he had a confrontation with Darld Schmitz. The next day, he was found in front of the bar, fatally stabbed. He died shortly afterward, and Schmitz was arrested. Schmitz admitted stabbing Bad Heart Bull but was charged with second-degree manslaughter, with the killing being treated as more of a barroom brawl than a murder. Schmitz was released on bail.

Banks was notified that AIM might be able to help bring about justice for the family of the victim, including his mother, Sarah Bad Heart Bull. Banks flew to Rapid City, South Dakota, and then went to Custer, the county seat, for the arraignment. Banks and about 200 supporters arrived at Custer on February 6 in the early afternoon. Banks had notified officials of his planned arrival, which he anticipated to be about 9:00 A.M., but was delayed several hours because of a blizzard.

The planned meeting with County Attorney Hobart Gates quickly turned confrontational. Gates allowed only a small number of AIM representatives into the courthouse and refused to raise the charge to murder. When Russell Means attempted to bring Sarah Bad Heart Bull into the courthouse, they were stopped by state troopers. Many of those who arrived with Banks then attempted to enter but were also met by state police. As fighting broke out, a trooper threw the murder victim's mother down the steps.

The confrontation grew increasingly violent, with fighting continuing for the remainder of the afternoon. Unsuccessful attempts were made to burn down the courthouse, but a city sign reading "WELCOME TO CUSTER, THE TOWN WITH THE GUNSMOKE FLAVOR" and a small Chamber of Commerce building were burned. The riot resulted in 22 arrests, 20 of them involving Indians, including Banks, Means, and Sarah Bad Heart Bull. Sarah Bad Heart Bull eventually served five months in prison—five months more than the killer of her son served, as he was acquitted by an all-white jury.

Why Wounded Knee?

As bad as the situation was for Indians in much of South Dakota, conditions were little better for most on the Oglala Pine Ridge Reservation. There Richard Wilson, the tribal leader, ruled with an iron hand and, it was widely believed, enough fraud and intimidation to keep himself in power. Especially crucial to Wilson's success was his personal police force, the Guardians of the Oglala Nation, whose members were derisively known through an acronym for the hated group's name as Wilson's Goon Squad.

The Oglala Sioux Civil Rights Organization (OSCRO), which had been founded by Pedro Bissonette to support Oglala rights, maintain traditional values, and oppose Wilson's autocratic rule, appealed to AIM for help. Consequently, Banks attended a meeting on February 27, 1973, at the town of Calico, South Dakota, a few miles from Pine Ridge to discuss what action they might take. Among those arguing for action were Frank Fools Crow, an elderly and highly respected medicine man from Pine Ridge, and several women from the reservation.

Any confrontation at Pine Ridge would have likely resulted in considerable loss of life: Wilson, along with his goons, had mounted two machine guns atop the tribal council building. In addition, Wilson's federal allies, including the Federal Bureau of Investigation (FBI), were ready for any threat that AIM members might pose. One of the women at the meeting, Lou Bean, suggested going to Wounded Knee. The suggestion was quickly accepted, resonating with those in attendance as a fitting place to carry on the struggle.

Wounded Knee, South Dakota, was the site of a massacre of between 150 and 300 Lakota women, children, and men in 1890 by the Seventh Cavalry, Colonel George Armstrong Custer's former unit. Among the dead was Miniconjou chief Big Foot. The site of the massacre had become a tourist attraction, but for Lakotas especially it remained a deeply hallowed location.

Fifty-four cars long, with Banks and Fools Crow in the lead vehicle, the protestors' caravan made its way through Pine Ridge and to Wounded Knee.

The Occupation

Eighty-three years after the Wounded Knee massacre, Lakotas and members of other Indian nations were preparing for what they believed might well be another violent confrontation with the U.S. government. The AIM leaders, including Banks, Means, and Leonard Crow Dog, had to make many decisions quickly, as federal marshals surrounded the site within about an hour of their arrival. A defense perimeter consisting of a low wall of sandbags and cinder blocks was established, and various functions were allotted to the buildings: Sacred Heart Church became the command post, the museum the security office, the store a community center, and one of the houses the hospital. Leonard Crow Dog and Wallace Black Elk were the spiritual leaders, and Crow Dog also served as surgeon for bullet wounds, tending to several who were shot during the occupation. Means, an Oglala from Pine Ridge, served as primary spokesperson for the group.

The people who normally populated the site, including the parish priest and the individuals who ran the store and museum, were held for two days before being released. However, they chose to remain for much of the occupation.

The siege grew in intensity. FBI agents and the military—the latter under the command of Colonel Volney Warner, Chief of Staff of the 82nd Airborne Division—surrounded the compound. Banks credits Volney with resisting the FBI's directive to shoot to kill, instead opting to wait the occupiers out and try to avoid casualties. Nonetheless, considerable firing did occur throughout the siege.

AIM developed a set of demands, but the federal government exhibited little interest in negotiations. South Dakota Senators George McGovern and James Abourezk did visit the compound, but the discussions failed to produce any resolution of the standoff.

At one point, four men posing as postal inspectors were apprehended and disarmed. They subsequently identified themselves as federal agents. After being given breakfast and a lecture by Crow Dog about Pine Ridge and Wounded Knee, the men were escorted off the compound. The incident would later lead to legal charges of armed robbery and interfering with federal officers against several participants, including Crow Dog.

During the occupation of Wounded Knee, Leonard Crow Dog resurrected the Ghost Dance—the dance that had temporarily given Lakotas and other tribes hope in the late nineteenth century that they could reverse the Euro-American tide of history. It also was the government's fear of the dance that had brought the military to Wounded Knee in 1890. For four days, dancers performed the Ghost Dance, moving in a circle and holding hands in a hollow where the surrounding forces of the U.S. government could not see what they were doing.

Things looked up on April 5, when a preliminary agreement was apparently reached to end the siege. Kent Frizzell, a Justice Department official, helped consolidate AIM's 10 primary demands into 6 so that the set would more likely be accepted, and a four-man group was chosen to travel to Washington, D.C., supposedly to conclude final negotiations. The representatives were Crow Dog, Means, Tom Bad Cob, and Ramon Roubideaux. Ten days later, Crow Dog returned, as government officials refused to negotiate until those holding Wounded Knee laid down their weapons.

On April 11, Mary Ellen Moore (also known as Mary Crow Dog and Mary Brave Bird) gave birth to a son at Wounded Knee. Another happy event was the wedding of activist Anna Mae Pictou, a Micmac who later would be murdered in a case that continues to be shrouded in mystery, and Nogeeshik Aquash, an Ojibwa.

April 17 began with great excitement. Three Piper Cherokees arrived about 5:00 A.M., dropping supplies. The lead plane made a second pass, dropping another load. On the ground, there was a great rush to retrieve the bundles. About 9:30, as federal agents responded to the surprise drop with heavy firing, a bullet struck Frank Clearwater; Clearwater and his pregnant wife, Morning Star, had arrived at Wounded Knee only the night before. The bullet hit Clearwater in the back of his head. He was removed from the compound and airlifted to the Pine Ridge Reservation, and eventually flown to a Rapid City hospital, where he died about eight days later.

The second fatality occurred on April 26. The victim was Buddy Lamont, an uncle of Banks's wife, Kamook. He was shot in the back, with the bullet going through his heart and out the front of his body. Kamook accompanied her uncle's body; Mary Ellen Moore and her newborn son also went with her. All were arrested by tribal police, and Moore was separated from her baby while incarcerated for several days. Kamook later rejoined her husband.

By May, Banks knew that the occupation had to end. He hoped that the government would keep its commitment to redress the political corruption at Pine Ridge and hold hearings on the Fort Laramie Treaty of 1868. During the night of May 7, Banks, accompanied by six others, left the compound to avoid arrest and thus be able to continue his resistance efforts. The rest gave themselves over to the authorities the following day. There were 146 men and women, including the three remaining leaders of the occupation: Leonard Crow Dog, Carter Camp, and Wallace Black Elk. Crow Dog and Black Elk, handcuffed and chained, were put onboard a helicopter and flown to jail in Rapid City.

The occupation had lasted 71 days. Ultimately, no negotiated agreement had been realized, but the event had brought those at Wounded Knee considerable attention and support. It had also demonstrated Indian resolve in the face of injustice, whether perpetrated by the U.S. government or tribal governments more in league with federal authorities than committed to helping their own people. According to Banks, "Wounded Knee was the greatest event in the history of Native America in the twentieth century. It was our shining hour, and I am proud," he added, "to have been a part of it."[8] Gladys Bissonette, who stayed at Wounded Knee throughout the entire occupation, sounded a similar theme:

> Well, for myself, I think this was one of the greatest things that ever happened in my life . . . . I do think that people are beginning to realize—and I do know we have a lot of support on our own reservation. They have finally opened their eyes to what corrupt governing bodies we have on the reservation and they have finally realized that they should stand up to intimidation and stand up for their rights now. I do really think that we have brought a lot of people to sanity instead of letting everybody push them around.[9]

That opposition to intimidation bore fruit on Pine Ridge in the form of growing opposition to Richard Wilson. Although Wilson was reelected in a close win over Russell Means in 1974 in an election victory many considered fraudulent, he lost two years later to Al Trimble by a substantial margin. Wilson then left Pine Ridge, returning to run for the tribal council in 1990; however, he died before the election took place.

FIGHTING THE LEGAL SYSTEM

Wounded Knee Trial

After Wounded Knee, Banks stayed for a time on the Gosiute reservation near the Great Salt Lake and then moved north into Canada. When he learned that bail money had been accumulated, he returned to face trail. Initially, several AIM leaders were to be tried together: Banks, Leonard Crow Dog, Russell Means, Stan Holder, Carter Camp, and Pedro Bissonette. Bissonette, however, was murdered, allegedly by Richard Wilson's "goons." The prosecutions of the remaining five were separated, with Banks and Means facing trial together.

The Banks and Means trial opened on January 8, 1974. The venue was shifted from South Dakota to St. Paul, Minnesota, as U.S. District Judge Fred Nichol, a lifelong South Dakota resident who was intimately familiar with the strong sentiment against the American Indian Movement in the state, agreed with the argument of defense that the defendants could not get a fair trial in South Dakota. Nichol moved the trial but accompanied it as presiding judge.

Eleven charges were brought against the defendants, including assault, theft, interfering with federal agents, aiding and abetting crimes, arson, and conspiracy. As part of its rationale, the prosecution argued that even if Banks and Means did not personally commit criminal acts, they were leaders of the occupation of Wounded Knee and, therefore, directed and conspired with others to commit crimes.

Representing Banks were Larry Leventhal, Ken Tilsen, and Doug Hall; Mark Lane and William Kunstler were Means's attorneys. Ramon Roubideaux, an attorney for AIM, was in charge of the overall defense.

Nichol had a reputation among lawyers as "super fair," although he could be "tough as nails" upon sentencing.[10] Banks later expressed a similar judgment, writing that "Judge Fred Nichol was a decent, no-nonsense kind of person and open to reason," and that "he conducted the trial proceedings in a deliberate, sensitive, and fair manner."[11] Contributing to Banks's opinion of Judge Nichol was his ruling that the prosecution, which according to Banks had been withholding documents, had to hand over its files—more than 300,000 documents. After Brigadier General Volney Warner (a colonel during Wounded Knee) testified about the involvement of the U.S. military in the siege at Wounded Knee, Judge Nichol ruled that the military had been illegally involved in a civilian matter and dismissed five of the charges.

By September 17, the prosecution's case was teetering on the brink of failure. One of the jurors was ill, and the prosecution did not want the remaining 11 jurors to vote on the defendants' guilt, apparently for fear of losing. A mistrial appeared to be the prosecution's safest approach, but Judge Nichol dismissed the remaining charges. On April 16, 1975, the Eight Circuit Court of Appeals upheld Nichol's decision.

Attempts to prosecute participants in the occupation of Wounded Knee were largely unsuccessful. Attorney Tilsen summed up the results in 1976, pointing out that of 185 indictments, only 2 remained undisposed of. There had been only 15 convictions, and only 11 of them for felonies, while 10 of the convictions were currently being appealed. According to Tilsen, the U.S. District Court conviction rate was 78.2 percent, but the Wounded Knee trials had a conviction rate of just 7.7 percent, demonstrating the government's weak cases, presumably brought for political reasons.[12]

Custer Trial

Dennis Banks still had more trials to undergo, including one based on the events at Custer, South Dakota, in the aftermath of the killing of Wesley Bad Heart Bull. The Custer trial occurred in the same town and was prosecuted by William Janklow, an unrelenting opponent of the American Indian Movement. At the time, Janklow was state Attorney General; he would later serve as governor of South Dakota and as a member of the U.S. House of Representatives.

During the 1975 trial, Banks lived with his wife, Kamook, and their daughter, Tashina, on the Pine Ridge Reservation in a home owned by the Jumping Bull family near an AIM camp. During the trial, Leonard Peltier ran the camp for Banks. It was during the trial that a shooting occurred that would deeply affect Banks and many of his close associates.

On June 25, 1975, two FBI agents and two Bureau of Indian Affairs policemen arrived at the Jumping Bull ranch looking for Jimmy Eagle, who was wanted for allegedly stealing a pair of boots—an offense that hardly seemed to call for FBI intervention. The following day, June 26, according to Banks, two cars arrived at the Jumping Bull ranch. Two men got out: Ronald Williams and Jack Coler, the FBI agents who had appeared the day before.

Shooting broke out between the agents and a number of Indians, including Peltier. Other agents arrived quickly, perhaps indicating that they had been waiting nearby. By that time, both FBI agents were dead, as was Joe Stuntz Kills Right, Banks's bodyguard, whom Banks had given the day off. Firing continued well into the afternoon.

Meanwhile, the trial continued, and Banks was found guilty of assault and rioting charges on July 26. Sentencing was set for August 5, and Banks was allowed to remain free on bail until that time. Faced with the possibility of getting as much as 15 years in prison, he decided not to appear for the sentencing hearing. Instead, he, Kamook, and their daughter fled.

A Fugitive

The decision not to appear for sentencing would make Dennis Banks a fugitive from justice for almost a decade and pit prominent national politicians against one another regarding Banks's status. By the end of August, Banks was at Crow Dog's Paradise, rejoining his wife and a number of those persons who had been present for the shootout, including Leonard Peltier.

Banks and Peltier then drove to Los Angeles, where they sought help from a prominent supporter of AIM, the actor Marlon Brando. Brando gave them a motor home and $10,000. With some of the money, Banks and Peltier bought 10 rifles and then returned to South Dakota to give money to Kamook to help her with living expenses.

Banks, Peltier, Kenny Loud Hawk, Russ Redner, and Annie Mae Aquash (the only member of the group not wanted by law enforcement) headed toward the Northwest. They bought additional rifles as well as dynamite in preparation for any attempts to capture or kill them. They also bought a station wagon in which to carry the explosives. Kamook, now pregnant, and Tashina flew to Seattle to join Banks.

All went well for a time, but during November in eastern Oregon near the Idaho border on Interstate 84, a state trooper pulled the two vehicles over, unwittingly short-circuiting an FBI trap 15 miles along the highway. Another trooper arrived, and most of the occupants of the station wagon and motor home left their vehicles and followed orders to lie down on the ground. Banks, who was still in the motor home, pulled out, and Peltier, during the firing at the motor home, started running. Despite being wounded, Peltier escaped and made his way to Canada. Banks slowed down, opened the door, and jumped out. He escaped by running into the woods, although he cut himself badly on barbed-wire fences.

Banks took refuge in a farmer's barn. Four days later, when he finally approached the farmer, he discovered that the man was actually quite supportive and had met Banks previously in Lincoln, Nebraska, when Banks had given a speech at an event that also featured Marlon Brando. The farmer offered Banks a ride to Nevada; from there, two friends, John Trudell and Darrel Standing Elk, took him to the San Francisco area.

Banks stayed with Lee Brightman near Oakland until his presence was discovered and he was arrested by the FBI. Banks was released on bail. Kamook, who had been arrested and was being held in Wichita, Kansas, was bailed out with the financial help of Jim Jones, who later would lead a mass suicide of his followers in Guyana. Before being released, Kamook gave birth to another daughter, Tiopa Maza Win (Iron Door Woman), on December 30, 1975, the name reflecting the place of birth—the prison hospital.

Janklow tried to have Banks extradited to South Dakota, but Governor Edmund "Jerry" Brown, Jr., denied the request. Temporarily free in California, Banks was joined by his wife and their children and attempted to make a life there. He enrolled at D-Q University, an American Indian institution whose D-Q letters refer to an Iroquois prophet and an Aztec god of healing. He also received permission from school officials to hold a Sun Dance on campus. With the help of three medicine men—Leonard Crow Dog, Charlie Kills Enemy, and Archie Fire Lame Deer, all from South Dakota—the Sun Dance was not only successful but also enormously popular, as several hundred people participated.

As Banks's eight-year stay in California continued, he lectured at D-Q and other institutions, was hired as chancellor of D-Q, and with Kamook had another daughter (Tokala, meaning Kit Fox, but nicknamed Chubbs). His respite in his California sanctuary came to an end when Republican George Deukmejian was elected governor. Deukmejian had promised to extradite Banks to South Dakota if he received a request to do so, so Banks decided to move to New York City, where he hoped that the state's governor, Mario Cuomo, would also refuse extradition.

A longtime friend, Alice Papineau, persuaded Banks to stop at the Onondaga Reservation in Onondaga County, New York, rather than continue to New York City. Tribal leaders granted Banks sanctuary, and Governor Cuomo and other state officials respected the sovereignty of the Onondaga Nation regarding extradition.

During their stay at Onondaga, Dennis and Kamook had a fourth child, a son named Chanupa Washte (Good Sacred Pipe). Banks directed about 40 youngsters in running, developing an excited and talented cross-country team. He also organized a run from New York City to Los Angeles as part of the Jim Thorpe Games being held in California. Yet despite the relative safety and comfort of living on the Onondaga Reservation, Banks's freedom was limited by reservation boundaries. He decided that finally he had to resolve his legal issues and face prison.

Imprisonment

Banks returned to South Dakota for sentencing, which occurred on October 9, 1984. The sentence was three years, one year and two months of which he served in prison, first at the South Dakota State Penitentiary at Sioux Falls and later at the Springfield Correctional Facility in Springfield, South Dakota.

On the whole, Banks's incarceration went about as smoothly as being in prison can go. He was treated generally as any other prisoner, his AIM fame seemingly not eliciting special harshness. During April 1985, his paternal grandfather, Bijah, died. Despite the long-standing antagonism between William Janklow, the governor of South Dakota at the time, and Banks, the governor approved a leave for Banks to attend the funeral.

Banks's prison term came to an end when the parole board on August 6, 1985, approved parole, pending his ability to find employment. That did not prove difficult, as Banks found work on Pine Ridge Reservation and was soon free, albeit not entirely clear of legal troubles.

Banks had gone to Oregon in April 1976 to face firearms and explosives charges stemming from the ill-fated motor-home incident involving Peltier, Kamook, and others. The trial took place on May 12, but Judge Robert Belloni of the U.S. District Court for the District of Oregon dismissed the charges, but with prejudice, meaning that the charges could be reinstated. Like Governor Brown, Governor Robert Straub of Oregon had refused to extradite Banks to South Dakota.

New charges were filed several years later, but they were dismissed on May 2, 1983. The following year, an appeals court upheld the dismissal. Prosecution appeals continued into 1988, when, on March 8, Banks pleaded guilty to possessing dynamite. He was sentenced to five years' probation, and the case finally, for all practical purposes, ended.

NEW DIRECTIONS

Pine Ridge

Banks began his post-prison life working in education at the Lone Man School on Pine Ridge Reservation as a drug and alcohol counselor and a running coach. Drawing on his background as a recruiter for Honeywell (a Japanese business group), the school board added development of a business plan to boost employment on the reservation to his duties. Honeywell supported Banks's efforts by moving its computer circuit production to Pine Ridge and providing a training program. By agreement, ownership of the production business was transferred to the Loneman School after one year, the result being Loneman Enterprises.

Kamook started a business in which local women made quilts, shawls, and skirts. Kamook and Dennis Banks were not to be together much longer, however. By 1989, Banks had established a relationship with Alice Lambert, a photographer whom he met when she was covering a story involving him. He moved in with her at Newport, Kentucky, and they had a child on October 10, 1992—a son named Minoh (Good). In February 2004, Kamook testified that she had been a government informant since 1988 and asserted that she considered AIM leaders, including her former husband, to be implicated in or at least knowledgeable about the murder of Anna Mae Aquash.

Tim Giago

Resistance takes many forms, one of which is the printed word. No Indian journalist has contributed more to fostering understanding by and about Indians than Tim Giago (born 1934). A Lakota born on Pine Ridge Reservation, his Indian name, Nanwika Kciiji, which means "He Who Stands Up for You," is appropriate given the focus of his long career in journalism.

Giago has published several newspapers focusing on Indian news and issues, starting with the *Lakota Times* (later renamed *Indian Country Today*) in 1978 at Pine Ridge. A second paper, the *Pueblo Times*, was less successful, lasting only a year. After selling his first paper, Giago began the *Lakota Journal* in Rapid City, South Dakota; after selling it in 2005, he started *Indian Education Today*. He returned from a short-lived retirement in 2009 with *Native Sun News* in Rapid City.

Giago has attacked tribal mismanagement, use of derogatory Indian names such as *squaw*, false Indian medicine men, racist Indian mascots, fraudulent Indian charities, and other societal ills. He has been willing to take unpopular positions—for example, at times opposing the American Indian Movement or running an FBI ad against freeing Leonard Peltier.

Giago is a publishing traditionalist, an approach that seems more pragmatic than ideological. In a press release regarding the *Native Sun News,* he stated that his paper would have no web site because most Indian readers lacked access to the Internet or even a computer.

The Native American Journalists Association was Giago's creation in 1984. In addition, awards have come regularly, including the H. L. Mencken Award from the *Baltimore Sun*, a Gold Quill Award for Outstanding Editorial Writing, an award for promoting minority journalism and bringing more minorities into journalism from the National Education Association, and induction into the South Dakota Hall of Fame.

Sacred Runs and Other Activities

Banks became less confrontational regarding the U.S. government after his release from prison, but he remained committed to AIM and actively engaged in planning events that increasingly took a more cultural and spiritual direction rather than having a strong political bent. For example, Banks became involved in opposing desecration of Indian graves that had been occurring in Kentucky. He was asked to head up reburial ceremonies and was instrumental in both Kentucky and Indiana passing legislation to discourage further desecration of graves.

The longtime advocate for justice for Indians also continued to work to free Leonard Peltier, who was sentenced in April 1977 to two consecutive life terms for the deaths of FBI agents Williams and Coler. The conviction remains highly controversial, with many viewing Peltier as wrongfully convicted and a political prisoner.

The arts also attracted Banks. He appeared in the films *War Party*, *The Last of the Mohicans*, and *Thunderheart*, and he recorded both his own original songs and traditional American Indian music.

Banks had organized the first "Longest Walk" in 1978 and returned to the concept of sacred walks and sacred runs as a means to foster international peace and understanding and to recognize the sanctity of Mother Earth. Recent events of this type include the 2006 Sacred Run from San Francisco to Washington, D.C., and a "Longest Walk" from Alcatraz Island to Washington, D.C., in 2008. Banks was instrumental in creating a twenty-fifth anniversary celebration of the takeover of Wounded Knee that included four sacred runs from four directions, culminating at Wounded Knee. Participants included many who had been there in 1973, among them Russell Means and Leonard Crow Dog.

Back to Minnesota

The Wounded Knee celebration, Banks wrote, "completed one cycle of [his] life."[13] In 1999, he moved back to Minnesota with his son Minoh, his relationship with Alice having ended. Banks certainly did not retire, as he was involved in a number of activities, such as the sacred runs and walks mentioned earlier. He also served on the board of trustees of Leech Lake Tribal College, continued to counsel against drug and alcohol use, and traveled widely on speaking engagements.

Banks also returned to his roots in basic ways that he could share with Minoh. They hunted, trapped, and fished. They made canoes, drums, and other wooden items. They also harvested wild rice, tapped maple trees, and started a rice and maple syrup business.

On December 7, 2009, Banks was in an automobile accident, in which he suffered a compression fracture of the spine. He recovered, and has continued to be active in the American Indian Movement as National Field Director. He was scheduled to speak at the spring 2010 meeting of AIM but was forced to curtail his involvement in the meeting because of a commitment to attend a Hollywood showing of a recently completed documentary about his life, *A Good Day to Die*.

With additional plans under way, including a 2011 walk from California to Washington, D.C., Dennis Banks, one of the most significant figures in the Indian resistance movement of the twentieth century, was not yet ready to stop trying to make a difference in the twenty-first century.

NOTES

1. Dennis Banks with Richard Erdoes, *Ojibwa Warrior: Dennis Banks and the Rise of the American Indian Movement* (Norman: University of Oklahoma Press, 2004) 28.

2. Banks 57.

3. Banks 65–66.

4. Banks 95.

5. Peter Matthiessen, *In the Spirit of Crazy Horse: The Story of Leonard Peltier and the FBI's War on the American Indian Movement* (1983; New York: Penguin Books, 1992) 60.

6. Banks 134.

7. *Trail of Broken Treaties: B.I.A. I'm Not Your Indian Anymore*, rev. (Rooseveltown, NY: Akwesasne Notes, 1974) 24.

8. Banks 209.

9. *Voices from Wounded Knee, 1973* (Rooseveltown, NY: Akwesasne Notes, 1974) 244.

10. John William Sayer, *Ghost Dancing the Law: The Wounded Knee Trials* (Cambridge, MA: Harvard University Press, 1997) 71.

11. Banks 215.

12. Sayer 228.

13. Banks 360.

RECOMMENDED READING

Banks, Dennis, with Richard Erdoes. *Ojibwa Warrior: Dennis Banks and the Rise of the American Indian Movement.* Norman: University of Oklahoma Press, 2004.

Cheatham, Kae. *Dennis Banks: Native American Activist. Native American Biographies.* Berkeley Heights, NJ: Enslow Publishers, 1997.

Hendricks, Steve. *The Unquiet Grave: The FBI and the Struggle for the Soul of Indian Country.* 2006; New York: Thunder's Mouth Press, 2007.

Matthiessen, Peter. *In the Spirit of Crazy Horse: The Story of Leonard Peltier and the FBI's War on the American Indian Movement.* 1983; New York: Penguin Books, 1992.

Sayer, John William. *Ghost Dancing the Law: The Wounded Knee Trials.* Cambridge, MA: Harvard University Press, 1997.

Smith, Paul Chaat, and Robert Allen Warrior. *Like a Hurricane: The Indian Movement from Alcatraz to Wounded Knee.* New York: New Press, 1996.

Trail of Broken Treaties: B.I.A. I'm Not Your Indian Anymore, rev. Rooseveltown, NY: Akwesasne Notes, 1974.

Voices from Wounded Knee, 1973. Rooseveltown, NY: Akwesasne Notes, 1974.

Russell Means shakes hands with government negotiator Kent Frizzell on April 5, 1973, after coming to an agreement that, however, failed to end the stand-off at Wounded Knee. (AP Photo/Jim Mone)

Russell Charles Means (born 1939)

Russell Means has long been one of the most active and controversial leaders of the American Indian cultural and political movements. He joined the American Indian Movement (AIM) in 1969 and quickly became one of its top leaders, participating in such events as the takeover of the Bureau of Indian Affairs building in Washington, D.C., and the occupation of Wounded Knee in South Dakota.

A staunch traditionalist, Means has consistently attempted to persuade Indians to follow their traditions, including their ancestors' spiritual practices. At the same time, he has been harshly critical of the United States and Christianity as forces generally used to deprive Indians of their heritage, land, and self-respect.

Means's life has been a continuum of contrasts, alternating among idealism, strategic decisions, and personal shortcomings (including problems with alcohol and personal violence). In his autobiography, *Where White Men Fear to Tread*, Means forthrightly chronicles all aspects of his life, both positive and negative. In the twenty-first century he remains what he has been since the 1970s—one of the most important and unforgettable Indian leaders.

JOURNEY TO ALCATRAZ

Childhood

Little in Russell Means's early life would have indicated that he had a promising future as a leading Indian activist and advocate for Indian rights and self-determination. Although he was born on the Pine Ridge Reservation in South Dakota (on November 10, 1939), he moved with his parents, Walter "Hank" Means and Theodora Louise Feather, to California in 1942.

Hank Means was an Oglala born at Pine Ridge; Russell's mother was a Yankton from the Yankton Sioux Reservation, also in South Dakota. Hank, according to his son, was a traditional Indian, while Theodora Louise Feather became a Christian. Nonetheless, his mother also kept to some of the old ways. For example, she gave her son, in addition to the Euro-American name Russell, the name Wanbli Ohitika, which means "Brave Eagle." Both of Means's parents attended boarding schools, with the father later becoming a star basketball player at Pine Ridge High School. Means spent most summers of his early childhood with his maternal grandparents, John and Mabel Feather, at Greenwood on the Yankton Reservation, where his grandfather taught him much about the outdoors and his culture.

A brother, Dace, was born in 1941, followed by twin boys, Bill and Ted, in 1946. The Means family lived in Vallejo, California, where Hank worked as a welder in a U.S. Navy shipyard. That job lasted only until the end of World War II. At that point, the family returned to South Dakota, staying with Mabel and her new husband, Raymond Blacksmith, in Huron. Russell's grandmother, whom he and his siblings called Grandma Twinkle Star because of her fondness for the childhood song "Twinkle, Twinkle, Little Star," had divorced John Feather by that time.

Russell attended an almost all-white school in Huron for the remainder of the school year. After the twins' birth, the family returned to California, taking up residence in the same neighborhood in Vallejo. Hank was rehired as a welder at the shipyards, and Theodora went to work as a secretary at Travis Air Force Base, the type of work she had done earlier at Pine Ridge after attending Haskell Institute in Kansas.

Adolescence

Russell Means attended Franklin Junior High School, where he did well academically and participated in track and basketball. He also was baptized as an Episcopalian and attended a Baptist Sunday school, although he notes in his autobiography that he had lost his belief in Christianity as early as the second or third grade. At about the age of 13, he developed an interest in traditional Indian culture that would stay with him throughout his life.

By 1954, the Means family had moved into their own house in San Leandro, south of Oakland. In the fall, Russell entered San Leandro High, where, he writes, "almost every aspect of my life took a radical turn."[1] Many of those turns were far from positive.

He did well at San Leandro for a time, taking college-prep courses and earning good grades. Soon, however, he was drinking, stealing whiskey from a liquor store, skipping school, and hanging out with other rebellious kids. Arrests started coming—first for stealing beer, then for being in a car that a friend had stolen from his mother. Cutting classes led to suspensions.

Means's mother grew increasingly frustrated with her son's behavior. She sent him to live with an uncle on the Winnebago Reservation in Nebraska, but his behavior did not improve there. In fact, after being beaten up, Means found himself in a hospital. He then moved in with his Aunt Faith and her husband and informed his mother that he was planning to quit school. Thus began a long series of temporary jobs, starting with selling scrap iron to a junkyard.

Means returned to live with his parents in 1956 and enrolled in high school in San Leandro. There he joined with friends to sell "protection service" to other students and began selling drugs, moving steadily from marijuana to prescription pills and finally to heroin. He committed burglaries at pharmacies and even persuaded his brother Dace to sell drugs for him. When his family moved back to Vallejo, Means stayed behind in the house until it was sold and managed to graduate from high school in January 1958.

Moving into the Work Force

Over the next few months, Means periodically tried to move in positive directions. He attended Oakland City College and temporarily stopped dealing drugs, only to return to the practice after a few months. He decided not to continue with college and tried to enlist in the army, but was rejected by the recruiter when he showed up at the recruiting station still high from a series of parties.

In December, Means got a ride to his parents' home in Vallejo, just in time to accompany his mother and Dace to Los Angeles to visit relatives. When the pair returned home, Means stayed behind and found a job as a mail-room messenger with General Petroleum. While staying at the Kirby Hotel, he met Twila Smith, a Minniconjou who was attending Sawyer School of Business. The two established a relationship, and Twila became pregnant. She later returned home to the Cheyenne River Reservation to have the child.

By 1960, Means had decided to return to Pine Ridge and apply for the relocation program through the Bureau of Indian Affairs (BIA), hoping to return to Los Angeles with financial support and attend school. While awaiting a response to his application, Means visited Twila on the Cheyenne River Reservation to see her and their recently born daughter, Sherry.

In October 1960, Means returned to Los Angeles in the relocation program and applied to Sawyer School of Business. Twila and Sherry joined him there. He worked at a variety of jobs and then started at Sawyer. With Twila again pregnant, the couple decided to marry, which they did on November 10, 1961, Means's twenty-second birthday. The child, named Walter after Means's father, was born in February, but the marriage did not last much longer. Means acknowledges that he "was too young and ignorant, far too immature to be a husband, let alone a father."[2]

The following months included radically different pursuits: working hard at his accounting program but also teaming up with a prostitute to roll men. Means received straight A's in his courses but ran into trouble with the Bureau of Indian Affairs for not attending classes. As he explained, he was the only student still active in his program, and his instructors had him continue in what today would be called an independent-study course. That did not satisfy the BIA official, who argued that regular class attendance was required.

Dropped from the relocation program and without financial support, Means spent his time hustling money, sometimes sleeping outside, and getting arrested for public drunkenness. After receiving a letter demanding child support for his children, Means left Los Angeles for San Francisco.

In San Francisco, Means worked as a dance instructor, among other jobs. He also established a relationship with Betty Sinquah, a Hopi from Arizona who would become his second wife. In March 1964, with Betty now pregnant, Means's life would slowly start moving in the direction that would give it great meaning. His father arrived from South Dakota planning to participate in a demonstration at Alcatraz, the former federal prison, and invited his son to go with him.

The Takeover of Alcatraz

The federal government had closed the prison on Alcatraz Island in 1963. Under the 1868 Treaty of Fort Laramie, the government was obligated to permit land taken from Indians and later abandoned to revert to those who previously had lived on it. The point of occupying Alcatraz was thus more than symbolic. Although federal legislation had since removed the return provision of the treaty, Indians had not agreed to such a change in the treaty and, therefore, laid claim to the former prison grounds and the rest of the island.

On March 8, 1964, 40 Sioux led by Richard McKenzie and Mark Martinez, both welders, and Allen Cottier, descended from Crazy Horse, occupied the island for approximately 4 hours. Means and his father were among the group. Paul Chaat Smith and Robert Allen Warrior say in *Like a Hurricane: The Indian Movement from Alcatraz to Wounded Knee* that the leaders "saw the action as a publicity stunt, and never thought of a long-term occupation."[3] Smith and Warrior, though, recognized the serious impetus behind the event —the importance of honoring treaties. This theme would run throughout much of Indian political efforts throughout the next 20 years, including the Trail of Broken Treaties that Means would help lead 8 years later.

Also along for the takeover was a group of reporters, and soon U.S. marshals arrived. The occupiers' lawyers recommended avoiding a confrontation and pursuing claims in the courts. Not surprisingly, those claims were rejected. This would be Russell Means's first of many political actions on behalf of Indians. Despite the failure of the lawsuit, the initial event at Alcatraz would not be forgotten: Five years later, a much longer occupation of the island took place.

A second major influence that would have repercussions throughout Means's life occurred on the Hopi Reservation in Arizona. When Means had first visited Betty Sinquah's family there in 1962, he had been deeply impressed by the Hopis' traditional spiritual life. He had accompanied Betty's father to a kiva, for example, where they spent the night in prayer and meditation.

Means returned to the Hopi Reservation in 1964 as Betty was about to give birth to their child, Michele Bridget, who was born on September 10. Means then went to Albuquerque, where he danced professionally at various locations, including shopping centers, and Betty and Michele joined him there.

In the summer of 1965, Means moved to Rapid City, South Dakota, looking for work and stayed with his mother. With his brother Ted, Means continued dancing; among the places where he performed was a bar owned by James Abourezk, a law school student who would later become a United States senator. Another bartender for Abourezk was also a law student—William Janklow, later to figure prominently in Means's life. Means returned to Greenwood later that summer, where he received a new name from his mother's sister, his Aunt Evelyn: Cío, which refers to the prairie chicken, a connection perhaps being the animal's attractive mating dance.

THE AMERICAN INDIAN MOVEMENT

Finding His Way

From a retrospective view and in light of what Russell Means would later accomplish, he appears to have been largely treading water over the next few years. In reality, he was quite busy in a variety of ways and gradually moving toward a pattern of working to improve life, first for other Lakotas, and later for Indians from all nations.

Means had a second child with Betty, a boy they named Scott. He attended Iowa Technical College in Ottumwa, Iowa, studying a variety of subjects but especially accounting and computer programming. Means also played basketball for Iowa Tech and even filled in as coach when the regular coach resigned. He then attended Arizona State University in Tempe on scholarship, continuing to study computer programming.

When Means learned that his father was residing in the Felix Cohen Old Age Home at Pine Ridge, he wrote inviting his father to come to Arizona and stay with him and his family. Hank Means arrived on December 1, 1966. On January 6, 1967, Hank came back to Russell's home after having been drinking and went to bed. The next morning, when he did not get up early as he usually did, his son checked on him and found his father dead. When he called his mother, Russell learned that just the day before his Grandfather John also had died. Perhaps the most meaningful testimonial to Hank Means's life that his son could give appears in Russell Means's autobiography: "Of all the Means brothers, only my father had remained Indian all the way."[4]

Needing to find work after Arizona State, Means participated in rodeos and then, after suffering an infection that robbed him of his hearing in his left ear, got a job on the Rosebud Reservation as director of management information systems for the Community Action Program (CAP) operated by the Office of Economic Opportunity. At the time, William Janklow was the Legal Aid attorney on the reservation, and the two men became close friends and colleagues in trying to improve life for the Rosebud residents.

The Cleveland American Indian Center

In July 1968, after leaving his position with CAP, Means, Betty, and their children moved to Cleveland. After briefly working for an employment agency, Means became an accountant for the Council for Economic Opportunity, and Betty found employment as a secretary at the Cleveland Housing Authority.

In the spring of 1969, Means took a step that would lead before long to the American Indian Movement. Along with friends whom he had met in Cleveland, especially a Montana Crow named Sarge Old Horn, he decided to begin an Indian center where Indians in the Cleveland area could meet and interact, but that also could help with problems such as employment and securing funds to return home. By April 1969, a board of directors had been elected and the organization incorporated as the Cleveland American Indian Center. An Episcopalian priest offered the basement of his church as an office and the auditorium for events.

The Center obtained a $5,000 grant from the city and enlisted Jess Sixkiller, head of the National Urban Indian Council, to help the Cleveland American Indian Center get organized. It formally opened on January 2, 1970.

Introduction to AIM

Russell Means's introduction to the American Indian Movement, which was created in 1968 by Dennis Banks and other Indians from the Minneapolis area, was less than positive. In late 1969, Means attended a National Urban Indian Organization conference in San Francisco organized by Sixkiller and his associates. At the conference, Means noticed a group of attendees dressed in beaded belts, moccasins, headbands, and other Indian items of clothing. During that period of his life, Means was still wearing stylish Euro-American suits. Put off by their attire, he found himself on the opposite side when they attacked Sixkiller's organization, and Means spoke passionately in defense of the National Urban Indian Council.

Two of the AIM members who were present at the San Francisco conference were Dennis Banks and Clyde Bellecourt. Given Means's sharp response to the AIM members, he was surprised when a few weeks after the Cleveland American Indian Center opened for business he received a phone call from Dennis Banks. Banks asked Means to come to Detroit and support a confrontation with the National Council of Churches. It took no more than that one visit to Detroit to convince Means of the importance of AIM and the direction that his own life should take. On his way home from Detroit, he wrote his resignation letter from the Council for Economic Opportunity, where he had continued to work while starting the American Indian Center. Means recalls that moment as a great turning point in his life: "For the first time, I knew the purpose of my life and the path I must follow to fulfill it. At the age of thirty I became a full-time Indian."[5]

Means established in Cleveland the first AIM chapter outside Minneapolis: Cleveland AIM, or Claim. Through the dual organizations—Claim and the Center—Means helped develop a long list of programs to help Indians in the area. For example, Indians were provided with the means to get food stamps, travel home for family burials, receive job training, participate in cultural and educational programs, and seek employment and housing. Also established were a medical clinic and a Legal Aid service.

The Cleveland organizations actively opposed the Cleveland Indians baseball team mascot, a caricature named Chief Wahoo; persuaded the Cleveland schools to revise their curriculum; and demonstrated against the film *A Man Called Horse* for its distortion of Indian history and culture. Means also traveled to other areas for AIM events, including a confrontation with the National Congress of American Indians in Kansas City, Missouri, in May 1970. AIM viewed the much older organization, founded in 1944, as largely a sell-out to U.S. government interests. Also in 1970, Means participated in a demonstration atop Mount Rushmore designed to restate Lakota claims to the Black Hills.

All of these activities took their toll on Means's marriage. In the fall of 1970, Betty, with the children, returned to the Hopi Reservation in Arizona.

AIM ACTIVITIES

The Mayflower *and the First Thanksgiving*

The year 1970 was the 350th anniversary of the establishment of Plymouth Colony. To commemorate this anniversary, a reenactment of what has come to be known as the first Thanksgiving was planned. In addition, a replica of the *Mayflower* was moored in Plymouth Harbor, near Plymouth Rock, the purported landing site of the Pilgrims on the Massachusetts mainland (the Pilgrims actually landed near the tip of Cape Cod first).

AIM joined with Wampanoags to protest the continued retelling of American history from a strictly Euro-American perspective. First came a march replete with drumming and singing to where organizers of the anniversary celebration were staging a Thanksgiving dinner. Those in attendance were dressed as Pilgrims, and when Dennis Banks, Means, and other protesters entered, they were invited to join the dinner. Instead, Banks overturned one of the tables. Others followed suit and then set off for Plymouth Rock.

Banks suggested taking over the *Mayflower*. A group of demonstrators boarded the ship, tossed off the gangplank, and threw overboard mannequins dressed in period costumes. Leaving the ship after assurances from police that there would be no arrests, they gathered around a statue of Massasoit, who had befriended the Pilgrims, to listen to Means speak of Wampanoag generosity toward the Pilgrims.

The following spring, AIM held its first convention. The Saint Paul gathering was intended to establish AIM as a national organization, and Means was elected national coordinator. Later in 1971, Means returned to Mount Rushmore for another demonstration and participated in a Sun Dance at Pine Ridge. Guided by a highly respected Lakota holy man, Frank Fools Crow, Means participated in the dance and was pierced. During the ceremony, Fools Crow pierced Means's chest with a razor blade and inserted a stick. With a rope connecting the stick to the sacred Sun Dance tree, Means approached the tree several times before pulling away hard enough to cause the stick to rip out from his skin. The piercing served as a process of spiritual purification and sacrifice intended to benefit the community.

Justice for Raymond Yellow Thunder

Means was invited to attend a conference in Omaha, Nebraska, in February 1972 to address the special needs of urban Indians. Shortly before the conference, he learned of a killing that had occurred in Gordon, Nebraska. Raymond Yellow Thunder had been accosted by a group of whites, beaten, and forced to dance naked from the waist down before attendees at a dance at the local American Legion Hall. His body was discovered a few days later, and five people had been arrested, including Leslie and Melvin Hare, sons of a prominent area rancher.

Family members of Yellow Thunder were concerned that Raymond's death would be swept under the rug, a belief augmented by the authorities' refusal to let the family view Raymond's body. They approached AIM for help. Contributing to concern over a lack of justice was the reputation that Gordon police had for sexually assaulting Indian women with impunity. An important link to AIM was through Russell Means, whose mother had lived in the same community on Pine Ridge as the Yellow Thunder family.

In addition to AIM members, many others converged on Gordon. Ultimately, as many as 1,400 Indians from more than 80 tribes were present, leading many residents to hide indoors and merchants to shut their businesses.[6]

Means, Banks, and Leonard Crow Dog were among those leading a march into Gordon on March 8. Means, who had advised participants earlier to gather all the U.S. flags they could find and wear them upside down (the international distress signal that remains the AIM emblem), broke off from the group and took down the flag from the Post Office, draping it over himself. Means gave a captivating speech at the Neighborhood Center and then announced that the protestors would take over the city auditorium, a building that housed the city offices, including the mayor's office and the jail.

Ordered to appear to hear grievances, Mayor Bruce Moore, a local businessman, dutifully showed up. Stew Magnuson, writing in *The Death of Raymond Yellow Thunder*, describes the scene:

> The mayor, Britton [the city manager], and the three council members sat on their folding chairs as Means berated them, asking pointed questions but interrupting them before they could respond. The audience, packed all the way up the arena-style seats, looked down on them, some jeering like a Greek chorus. Soon, Means was shouting in Moore's face, calling him and his town "racist." The mayor tried to get a word in edgewise, but there was no talking to this angry man.[7]

In his tirade, Means several times referred explicitly to John Paul, the police officer accused but never convicted of sexually assaulting Indian women in his police car.

Clyde and Vernon Bellecourt then demanded that the mayor go with them to his office and call Governor J. J. Exon to demand a grand jury investigation. Moore made the call, and the governor responded by dispatching representatives to Gordon.

The following day, Means, Banks, and Clyde Bellecourt met with Mayor Moore, Police Chief Robert Case, County Attorney Michael Smith, and Governor Exon's representative, Clive Short. Several AIM demands were agreed to, including suspending Officer Paul, allowing access to the coroner's report, and allowing another autopsy arranged by AIM. In addition, a Gordon biracial committee was established to identify and oppose racism in the area.

The trial of the Hare brothers was moved to a different town, Alliance, where it was attended by Means and other AIM members. They expected the

Hares to get off, but instead the jury brought in a guilty verdict on charges of false imprisonment and manslaughter. Leslie received a sentence of 6 years, Melvin 2 years; the brothers would serve just 2 years and 10 months, respectively, before being released on parole. In a separate trial, Robert Bayliss received a sentence of 4 years for his participation in the crime, but, like the Hares, served only a portion of that time. The results were both gratifying and disappointing. It was not at all unusual for Euro-Americans to escape prison time entirely for crimes against Indians, even murder. Even so, the actual time that the men served was clearly inadequate given the serious nature of the crime.

AIM was taking up so much of Means's time by the middle of 1972 that he decided to leave the Cleveland American Indian Center and return to South Dakota to concentrate solely on working with AIM. Back at Porcupine on the Pine Ridge Reservation, he received a third name, Oyate Wacinyapi, which means "Works for the People"—by that time an appropriate name for Means.

The Trail of Broken Treaties

Also in the 1970s, Means was one of the leaders of the AIM-directed effort known as the Trail of Broken Treaties. The name derived from the forced journey of Cherokees from Georgia to Oklahoma between 1836 and 1840, known as the Trail of Tears, and the long series of treaties that the U.S. government had violated over the years. Means was charged with leading a caravan of cars from Seattle to Washington, D. C. Among those joining Means were members of the Survival of American Indians Association, including the organization's president, Hank Adams, who would play an important role in the event.

Although AIM had organized the Trail of Broken Treaties, large numbers of nonmembers joined on the way to Washington, D.C., as three caravans, originating in San Francisco, Los Angeles, and Seattle, made stops at various centers of Indian life along the way. During a stopover at the Minnesota state fairgrounds at Saint Paul, the group divided into workshops to address individual issues such as land rights, treaties, and tribal government. Hank Adams then took the results of the workshops and composed a set of 20 demands to be presented to government officials in Washington.

The merged caravans, now carrying approximately 1,000 people, arrived in Washington early in the morning on Friday, November 3, 1972. The effort to present a set of 20 points detailing failures of the federal government to uphold treaty provisions and generally treat Indians with some degree of justice quickly, by a chain of unintended events, led to the takeover of the Bureau of Indian Affairs building.

The chain reaction began with the failure of city or government authorities to provide promised housing. Instead, they sent the arrivals to a dilapidated church, where their proposed sleeping quarters in the basement were shared with rats. Angrily, everyone got back in their vehicles and headed to the BIA building. Directed by BIA officials, they next went to an armory, only to find

Henry Adams

Henry Adams (born 1944), usually referred to as Hank Adams, is an Assiniboine from Montana. He moved as a child to Washington State when his mother married a Quinault. Adams thus grew up on a reservation established where the Quinault people traditionally lived—a rarity for American Indians. The Quinaults had long fished for salmon and trout, but logging and government restrictions had impeded their ability to fish.

Adams was an outstanding student in high school and continued his education at the University of Washington. However, his growing awareness of the Indian struggle to maintain traditional ways of life, including the fish-ins that began in Washington in the early 1960s, especially by the Puyallup and Nisqually fishermen, drew him into political activism.

Adams helped organize a march by 1,000 Indians and the actor Marlon Brando to the Washington state capitol in 1964 to protest fishing policies. Eventually, his leadership on the fishing-rights issue bore fruit, as the Northwest tribes gained the right to half of the salmon catch in the region. Adams also worked with Ralph Nader, Vine Deloria at the National Congress of American Indians, and Robert Kennedy's presidential campaign of 1968.

In 1968, Adams became director of Survival of the American Indians Association, a position he continued to hold well into the twenty-first century. During the 1972 Trail of Broken Treaties, Adams composed the 20 points presented to the federal government as an attempt to further the quest for tribal sovereignty. As a presidential envoy, he helped to negotiate an end to the occupation and siege at Wounded Knee in 1973. Never a flamboyant figure, Adams has worked diligently, often behind the scenes, to improve life for American Indians throughout the country.

the housing there once again inadequate. That led to a second directive—to go to the BIA auditorium.

Packed into the auditorium, the large group awaited the arrival of federal officials to whom the 20 points could be presented. No one showed up, and eventually the protestors were told that the building was being closed for the day and they would have to leave. Means, obviously angered and frustrated over the repeated slights, stood up and yelled, "This is no longer the BIA building! This is now the American Indian embassy."[8] Suddenly, Indians went into action, barricading doors. Employees were allowed to leave, and AIM leaders directed that there be no stealing or damage, although those orders would be disobeyed as the occupation continued for the better part of a week.

The following day, Commissioner of Indian Affairs Louis Bruce added his support, resisting orders from his boss, Assistant Secretary of the Interior Harrison Loesch, to expel AIM and the others and offer no assistance. That support would cost Bruce his job.

Occupation leaders tried to negotiate, but the response from Interior Department officials was that they must first vacate the BIA building. Meanwhile, police ringed the building, with the occupants constantly expecting an attack to evict them by force. President Nixon at the time was away from Washington wrapping up his reelection bid in the final days before the 1972 presidential election.

According to Means, there was considerable disagreement over tactics. Hank Adams and others wanted to destroy the building rather than simply surrender. AIM leaders, including Dennis Banks and Clyde and Vernon Bellecourt, argued against that approach as counterproductive and certain to produce a public relations disaster. Means favored Adams's position but declined publically to disagree with other AIM leaders.[9]

With prospects for a peaceful settlement (short of surrender) looking increasingly dim, AIM leaders were contacted by White House officials about 5:00 P.M. on Friday, November 10, requesting a delegation to discuss the situation. According to Means, the group decided that the BIA building would be set on fire if no agreement were reached by 6:00 P.M. After the negotiation team left, others began looting items and destroying offices and bathrooms. Some started burning files, but Means directed them instead to take documents, hoping to find evidence of BIA wrongdoing. In fact, the stolen documents were later passed on to the muckraking columnist Jack Anderson, who used them as sources for writing exposés concerning the BIA.

As Means was about to order setting fire to the building, Vernon Bellecourt argued for waiting until the negotiators returned. A few minutes later, the negotiators phoned with the news that they had arrived at an agreement. The White House had agreed to consider the 20 points and respond within 30 days, and to provide travel money for members of the Trail of Broken Treaties to return home. Later that night, Caspar Weinberger and Leonard Garment arrived with approximately $66,000.

The next day, Means and the others who had remained in the BIA building left, feeling that they had accomplished a victory. That victory appeared less obvious later, when the government rejected all 20 demands.

THE OCCUPATION AND SIEGE OF WOUNDED KNEE

Pine Ridge Politics and the Death of Wesley Bad Heart Bull

Perhaps the most famous event in the history of both Russell Means and the American Indian Movement was the takeover of Wounded Knee, scene of the massacre of as many as 300 Lakota women, children, and men in 1890 by the Seventh Cavalry. Among those killed was Miniconjou chief Big Foot. Two other AIM concerns predated and to some extent led to the takeover.

One issue was tribal politics on the Pine Ridge Reservation, where tribal leader Richard Wilson had earned a reputation for corruption, authoritarian leadership, and a self-serving and overly cozy relationship with the federal government. His rule was reinforced by his own personal security and enforcement force, the Guardians of the Oglala Nation, commonly referred to, using an acronym for the group's name, as Wilson's Goon Squad.

Wilson's ire and allegedly violent repercussions were felt by those who opposed his rule, and AIM members came in for special animosity from him. In the fall of 1972, Wilson prohibited AIM activities at Pine Ridge, had Dennis Banks arrested and removed from the reservation, and forbade Means from holding any meetings on the reservation where he had been born. He threatened to cut off Means's braids if he returned and hung a poster up in his office offering $1,000 for his pickled body, an offer probably not entirely facetious.[10]

The Oglala Sioux Civil Rights Organization (OSCRO), led by Vernon Long and Pedro Bissonnette, had been formed in response to Wilson's actions. OSCRO sought help from the tribal council and succeeded in having Wilson face an impeachment trial. Wilson, who was supported by the Area BIA Superintendent Stanley Lyman, presided at his own trial and won acquittal. Wilson now felt confident of his position. According to Akim Reinhardt, federal marshals "were going to remain on the reservation, and the chairman was prepared to confront and attack his opponents."[11] That left AIM as the only remaining organization that might be able to go up against Wilson.

At about the same time, AIM learned of the stabbing death of Wesley Bad Heart Bull in Buffalo Gap, South Dakota. Members of the group decided to go to Custer, where the trial was to be held, to meet with the deputy state's attorney for the county, Hobart Gates, and try to convince him to raise the charge from second-degree manslaughter to murder.

A contingent including Means and Dennis Banks met with Gates on February 6, 1973, but Gates refused to raise the charge to murder. The meeting was highly confrontational. When Bad Heart Bull's mother, Sarah, was hit by a trooper when she tried to enter the courthouse where the meeting had occurred, the scene turned extremely violent. A trooper clubbed Means to the floor and dragged him by a braid. Recognizing him, the troopers, according to Means, repeatedly hit and taunted him. Along with 18 other Indians, among them Banks and Sarah Bad Heart Bull, Means was arrested and taken to jail in Rapid City. The next day, they were returned to Custer for arraignment. Means was released later that day on $35,000 bond.

The Custer charges were the second set of legal issues for Russell Means. In January, he had been arrested in Scottsbluff, Nebraska, while attending a conference hosted by a Chicano group. On what appeared to be trumped-up charges, Means was arraigned for supposedly illegally possessing a gun, engaging in disorderly conduct, resisting arrest, and assaulting police officers. Others attending the conference—Means's brothers Dace and Ted, and Leonard Crow Dog—also were charged with such offenses as assault, parking illegally, and driving without a license.

While Means and others faced probable jail time because of the confrontation at Custer, and even Sarah Bad Heart Bull was incarcerated for five months, the killer of her son was acquitted.

Facing two allied enemies—the federal government and Wilson—opponents of Wilson, including tribal elders, members of OSCRO, and AIM leaders, met to consider strategy. Means occupied an important role in these deliberations as both a prominent AIM figure and a native of Pine Ridge. Attempting direct action against Wilson was clearly suicidal, as the BIA agency building was heavily fortified, and Wilson was backed by federal agents as well his Goon Squad. Means reported to AIM, and several members, including Banks, attended another meeting at Calico. Elders, women, and various leaders agreed that something had to be done. Who first suggested going to Wounded Knee is unclear. Means reports that Frank Fools Crow made the suggestion,[12] while Dennis Banks suggests that the idea came from one of the women in attendance, Lou Bean.[13]

Once Wounded Knee was mentioned, the site of the earlier massacre seemed instantly to be the perfect destination, replete with historical and symbolic significance. Before the day was out, Wounded Knee would become the place where much of the United States finally got a good look at the Indian resistance effort. Vine Deloria, Jr., wrote that as the decision was being made to advance to Wounded Knee, "the coalition had finally been formed which was to shuffle Indian affairs beyond recognition. Urban Indian activists seeking an Indian identity and heritage and traditional Indians buttressed by the energies of the young combined forces and made ready to push the Indians who had accommodated the white man off the reservation."[14]

The Occupation and Siege

The occupation of the Wounded Knee compound—which consisted of a collection of houses, churches, a store, and a museum—began on February 27, 1973. In the early days of the occupation, the total number of Indians on site was about 350, with fewer than 100 of them being men. According to Means, fewer than two dozen of the protestors were AIM members. Although the group had some weapons and was able to get more from the store, the firepower of those at Wounded Knee was dwarfed by that of the federal agents and later military forces who surrounded the compound.

Security was an immediate concern, as fear of an attack was constantly present. Roadblocks were set up, and efforts were made to fortify the area as well as possible. The owners of the trading post and others living at Wounded Knee were moved and placed under guard, more to protect them than to prevent anyone from leaving. Leaders made it clear that the residents could, in fact, leave if they wished and deliberately avoided treating them as hostages.

Means and Pedro Bissonnette composed a set of demands to present to the FBI, drawing heavily on provisions of the 1868 Laramie Treaty. The demands, which included returning the Black Hills to Lakota control and establishing an

Vine Deloria, Jr.

Vine Deloria, Jr. (1933–2005), was a prominent and controversial figure throughout the second half of the twentieth century. His fame began with his book *Custer Died for Your Sins: An Indian Manifesto*, which he published in 1969. The book appeared as the Civil Rights movement was expanding into the world of the American Indian and the American Indian Movement was being born. In *Custer Died for Your Sins*, Deloria argues for a new analysis and more accurate understanding of American history, especially as it involves Indians. The book also focuses on Indian sovereignty, which would become a major concern as Indians attempted to regain the basic rights taken from them by Euro-American expansionism.

Deloria would go on to publish some 20 books, have a long academic career teaching at the Universities of Arizona and Colorado, and lead the National Conference of American Indians (NCAI) from 1964 to 1967. The NCAI was founded in 1944 and quickly aligned itself in opposition to termination and assimilation policies—the federal government's attempt to end formal relationships with Indian nations and assimilate Indians into the American mainstream. The NCAI, which is the country's oldest Indian organization, remains active today and, according to its web site, is the largest organization serving the American Indian.

Traditional Indian spirituality, according to Deloria, was as relevant in the twentieth century as ever, as he argued in *God Is Red* (1973). His most controversial stance, however, may have been his embrace of creationism. He came to deny that Indians crossed the Bering land bridge into America as well as generally held scientific views concerning the age of the planet and the time frame for humans as well as such animals as dinosaurs.

Oglala Nation, in reality had no chance of being accepted by the federal government, but at least could help sensitize the wider U.S. population to the American Indians' painful history with their oppressors.

The takeover of Wounded Knee immediately became a dual event, both an occupation and a siege. Federal officials and military personnel (wearing civilian clothes) ringed the area. Despite occasional heavy firing, they resorted to a prolonged siege rather than a direct attack to roust the occupying force. The siege would ultimately last for 71 days.

Members of the media periodically were allowed into the Wounded Knee compound, and a variety of visitors arrived. Early in the occupation, South Dakota Senators George McGovern and James Abourezk arrived, partly to ensure that the local inhabitants were not being held hostage. Other famous individuals, including the Reverend Ralph Abernathy, head of the Southern Christian Leadership Conference, and comedian Dick Gregory, visited. In fact, the perimeter, given the uneven terrain, was seldom completely blocked during the siege.

Negotiations began, ended, and began again, with various individuals representing the federal government. Ralph Erickson, and later Harlington Wood, both from the Justice Department, negotiated with a contingent that included Gladys Bissonnette, Pedro Bissonnette, Leonard Crow Dog, Wallace Black Elk, and Ellen Moves Camp. The basic federal position, however, was that those at Wounded Knee should surrender first before the government would make any concessions.

As the takeover reached two weeks, ominous signs were growing. Roadblocks established by the FBI, which had been taken down, went back up. Dick Wilson succeeded in getting a resolution passed forbidding anyone not Oglala from entering the Pine Ridge Reservation. Expecting an imminent attack, Leonard Crow Dog prepared a red paint that those willing to fight to the death could put on their faces. Means and others met at the mass grave where Big Foot and other victims of the 1890 massacre were buried and applied the paint. Nonetheless, the anticipated attack did not materialize.

Later in March, a third negotiator, Kent Frizzell, arrived. Others from the Wounded Knee group, including Means and Carter Camp, joined the negotiations. Still later that month, several prominent lawyers—William Kunstler, Mark Lane, and Ken Tilsen—arrived at Rapid City. Along with other attorneys, they formed the Wounded Knee Legal Defense/Offense Committee (WKLD/OC). AIM and other leaders of the Wounded Knee occupation would soon have great need of their services.

With supplies running out, Means and Dennis Banks managed to sneak out of Wounded Knee during the night of March 26 and make it 100 miles to Crow Dog's home on the Rosebud Reservation to let people know that they could get into the compound. Means was reunited with his children Michele and Scott, who had been brought to the area by Betty at Means's request. He continued to believe that he might not survive the siege.

After returning to Wounded Knee, Means found Frizzell seemingly more able or willing than his predecessors to negotiate seriously. Means and Bissonnette had drawn up 10 major demands, and Frizzell suggested the strategic approach of grouping them as 6 to give an impression of having dropped half of the demands. That, he argued, might be more appealing to his superiors in Washington, D.C.

The next step was to select a group of representatives to go to Washington to continue negotiations. Selected as emissaries were Means, Crow Dog, a lawyer named Ramon Roubideaux who was related to Means's mother, and a respected elder, Tom Bad Cob. The arrangement required Means to submit to arrest, after which he would immediately be released on bond. Means was then flown by helicopter to Rapid City. A wealthy man named Stan Adelstein agreed to put up $35,000 as bail, and Judge Andrew Bogue placed certain restrictions on Means, including prohibiting his return to Wounded Knee.

The four Wounded Knee negotiators then flew to Washington. The trip proved completely disappointing, as White House officials refused to negotiate until everyone at Wounded Knee turned in their weapons. Unable to return to

Wounded Knee, Means, at the suggestions of WKLD/OC, set out to raise money for the anticipated legal cases by speaking at universities. In Tulsa, Oklahoma, while responding to a reporter's question about future AIM actions, Means jokingly said that the group planned to take over western South Dakota militarily. Judge Bogue missed the humor and revoked his bond. Arrested on his way to the Los Angeles airport, Means was taken briefly to jail in Los Angeles, then flown to Sioux Falls, South Dakota, and later to Scotts-bluff, Nebraska, for a hearing in connection with his earlier arrest there.

By the time Means was finally freed, he had been in jail for 43 days. At that point, the occupation and siege of Wounded Knee had ended. Two Indians had been killed—Frank Clearwater (shot on April 17 but died on April 25) and Buddy Lamont (April 26)—and an agreement had been reached on May 4 providing for the federal government to hear grievances relating to the 1868 treaty once everyone had given up their weapons and left the compound. On May 8, the last holdouts departed Wounded Knee. Many immediately faced arrest, including Means, Banks, Crow Dog, Pedro Bissonnette, Clyde Bellecourt, Stan Holder, and Carter Camp. Means now faced charges from Wounded Knee as well as from Custer and Scottsbluff.

The Wounded Knee Trial

Means and Banks were tried together for their actions at Wounded Knee. The charges included, among other acts, burglary at the trading post, assault, wounding an FBI agent, arson, and conspiracy. Faced with a highly charged political climate in South Dakota, the trial was moved to Saint Paul, Minnesota, with the same judge, Alfred Nichol, presiding. Means's lead attorney was William Kunstler, and both Means and Banks acted as co-counsels. Other members of their legal team were Mark Lane, Ken Tilsen, Larry Leventhal, and Doug Hall. Leading the prosecution were Earl Kaplan, William Clayton, David Gienapp, and Richard Hurd.

Jury selection began on January 8, 1974, with the presentation of evidence commencing on February 12. In between those dates, Means ran for tribal chairman against Richard Wilson, who "told his people that electing Means was as good as giving their reservation to the Communists, the clergy, and the white hippie lawyers of WKLDOC."[15] Means came in first in the January 22 primary, outpolling Wilson 534 to 457. However, given the large number of candidates (12), no one received the majority required to avoid a run-off. The follow-up election took place on February 7, and Means again led Wilson in raw votes. However, the tribal electoral system relied on a winner-take-all approach that awarded the entire district to the top vote-getter. Wilson, helped by alleged voting violations, and undoubtedly assisted by a three-man election board that he personally had appointed, won more districts and hence the election.[16]

As the Wounded Knee trial proceeded, Means came increasingly to respect Judge Nichol, who was deeply offended by the prosecution's deceptive practices. The prosecution withheld files from the defense and allowed witnesses to engage in misstatements, if not outright lies. Denying that there had been wiretaps of phone calls made from Wounded Knee and that the military had played a significant role in the siege were among the government deceptions that came to light during the trial.

During an April recess in the Wounded Knee trial, Means attended a sacred pipe ceremony on the Cheyenne River Reservation and then went to the trial at Sioux Falls involving Sarah Bad Heart Bull and several other defendants. Prosecuting the case was Means's former friend, William Janklow, then running for Attorney General of South Dakota. The trial, presided over by Judge Joseph Bottum, had become contentious, with Bottum citing one of the defense lawyers, the only Indian on the defense team, Ramon Roubideaux, for contempt and jailing him. Indians at the trial responded by refusing to stand when the judge entered.

Judge Bottum summoned Means to his chambers and asked Means to try to persuade Indian spectators to show respect by standing. Although Means relayed the request, they remained seated. A large group of police then entered the courtroom in riot gear and attacked some of the seated Indians, including Means. Means responded physically, and the battle became extremely violent. When Lakotas outside started to break windows and doors, the police backed off, allowing those inside the courtroom to leave.

When Means arrived at the airport the following morning, he was arrested. Learning of the arrest, Judge Nichol angrily demanded that Means be released and returned so that the trial in Saint Paul could resume. It would not be the last that Means would hear from the Sioux Falls trial, however.

Back in Saint Paul, the Wounded Knee trial moved fitfully toward its conclusion. By August 16, the defense rested its case; on September 12, the jury began its deliberations. The verdict was clearly going the defense's way when one of the jurors, Therese Cerrier, suffered a stroke. The defense agreed to conclude the trial with 11 jurors, but the prosecution, hoping that a second try might be successful for its side, sought a mistrial. Judge Nichol sternly upbraided the prosecution for its behavior, saying, "I'm rather ashamed that our government was not represented better in the trial of this case."[17] He then dismissed all remaining charges against both Russell Means and Dennis Banks.

FIGHTING THE LEGAL SYSTEM

One Trial after Another

For the next few years after the Wounded Knee trial, Russell Means faced a series of legal charges and trials, resulting from a legal system that was soundly stacked against Indians in general and against activist AIM Indians in particular. Certainly Means's propensity for making threats rather than turning the other cheek was a contributing factor to his legal troubles. Sometimes the system eventually worked; other times it did not. In December 1974, about two months after the conclusion of the Wounded Knee trial, another legal entanglement came to an end for Means when charges relating to the Scotts-bluff incident were dropped.

The following March, Means and other AIM members drove to Scenic, a small town north of Pine Ridge Reservation. They stopped at the Longhorn Saloon, and Means went to the restroom. Dicky Marshall also entered, and a Lakota whom Means did not know followed them in. Means left but shortly afterward heard a gunshot: Marshall had shot and fatally wounded the other man.

The car Means was riding in, driven by Dave Clifford, was followed by police. When the vehicle got stuck in an effort to elude the police, the occupants were arrested. Means and Marshall were charged with attempted murder, a charge that would be elevated to murder later when the shooting victim, Martin Montileaux, died. Clifford was charged with felony possession of a gun and reckless driving.

Charges from the Custer confrontation also remained alive, but they were resolved when a new attorney general, Mark Meirhenry, was elected to replace Janklow, who had become governor of South Dakota. Meirhenry approved a plea bargain in which the felony charges were dropped in return for Means's agreement to plead guilty to misdemeanor assault. Means was sentenced to 30 days in jail, with the sentence to be suspended until his other trials were concluded.

That same spring, Means was attacked in a McLaughlin, South Dakota, bar by an off-duty police officer who came at him with a beer bottle. Means defended himself with a pool cue, and the officer subsequently pressed charges against Means. Judge Nichol, who had presided at the Wounded Knee trial, dismissed the charges.

Attempts to Kill Means

As Means attempted to deal with a series of legal trials, he also faced several attempts on his life. On June 7, 1975, while at Fort Rice, North Dakota, he and some of his friends were involved in a fight with locals. Their car was soon stopped by a Bureau of Indian Affairs policeman, Pat Kelly, who was accompanied by his son. Kelly grabbed the driver, Tom Poor Bear, by his hair, and knocked him onto the pavement. Means saw the younger man pointing a rifle at him and then felt a sharp pain in his back, having been shot by the father.

Means and Poor Bear were handcuffed, taken to jail, and put in a cell while Means continued losing blood. He was finally taken to a hospital on Standing Rock Reservation and then transferred to a hospital at Bismarck. Although badly wounded by Kelly, Means was charged with interfering with an officer.

On another occasion, while Means was returning to Rosebud, a car with three off-duty policemen inside pulled alongside him. One of them shot at Means, grazing his forehead, again sending Means to an emergency room.

The next trial for Means involved his alleged interference with Officer Kelly. Kelly testified that Means had assaulted him and his son, but Judge Bruce Van Sickle declared Means not guilty.

Next up was the Sioux Falls trial. Means waived his right to a jury trial, putting his fate in the hands of Judge Richard Braithwaite rather than a group of individuals who he thought would be even less likely than the judge to be impartial.

During a Thanksgiving recess in the Sioux Falls trial, Means went to Pierre, South Dakota, to face trial for another confrontation that had occurred during the Wounded Knee trial. In June, Means had stopped at Mission Golf Course in Mission, South Dakota, with other AIM members. They ordered food, testing whether the report that the private club routinely served whites but not Indians was true. The manager ordered them to leave; when they refused, he called the police. When Mission's police chief, Tom Rhoads, arrived, he put his gun to Means's head, but Means shoved the gun aside and hit Rhoads. After damaging the police car, the AIM members left. Ultimately, Means turned himself in and was arraigned and released on bond. The incident had led to several charges, but Judge Robert Merhige reduced them to simple assault and sentenced Means to 30 days in jail.

The Sioux Falls case would not end so easily. Braithwaite, employing a statute related to rioting to obstruct justice, found Means guilty in January 1976 and sentenced him to four years in prison. He remained free on bond, however, while he appealed the verdict.

Then came another shooting, this time on the Yankton Sioux Reservation in South Dakota. A confrontation developed between Means and his bodyguard, John Thomas, and two Indians named Weston and Weddell. In the scuffle, Weston shot Means in the chest, and Weddell shot Thomas under an eye. Luckily, both wounds were not as serious as they could have been.

Means's trial for the murder of Martin Montileaux opened in July 1976. Marshall already had been convicted in a separate trial and sentenced to life in prison, and Montileaux, just before dying, had told a deputy that Means was not involved in the shooting. Nonetheless, as Means writes in his autobiography, he had become convinced that he would be found guilty and had developed a plan with two other AIM members to shoot the jury and the judge when the guilty verdict was announced. The three succeeded in smuggling guns into the courtroom, but the "not guilty" verdict surprised and delighted Means. Whether the AIM members actually would have followed through with the shooting remains conjectural.

IMPRISONMENT

Remaining Days of Freedom

While imprisonment loomed ahead for Means, he continued to focus as much as possible on his work for AIM. In September 1976, after attending a centennial celebration of the victory over Custer at Little Bighorn and participating in a Sun Dance, during which Means was pierced in the chest on both the right and left sides, he turned himself in to serve the 30-day sentence from the Custer, South Dakota, case.

After his release, Means worked on the planning for an International Indian Treaty Council conference to be held in Geneva, Switzerland. He attended the conference in September 1977 with his new wife, Peggy Phelps, and his daughter Sherry. Among the issues to be decided was what to call themselves. AIM supported the term that finally was accepted: Indians. Representatives from approximately 35 countries attended the conference, which focused on matters relating to land ownership and treaty provisions.

In 1978, Means participated in the Longest Walk, organized by Dennis Banks, which started at Alcatraz and ended in Washington, D.C. Its purposes included protesting new federal legislation that undermined treaty provisions and Indian sovereignty. Means joined the walk in Pennsylvania. He also publicized the Indian Health Service program that focused on sterilizing Indian women,. According to Means, this program pressured women into agreeing to sterilization by threatening them with losing their children or welfare benefits. Means used the media effectively, even appearing on *Good Morning, America*, *Today*, and *CBS Morning News*. Senator Abourezk succeeded in having the sterilization program temporarily stopped, but according to Means it resumed under the term "family planning."

Behind Prison Walls

Means was ordered to report on July 27, 1978, to begin serving his sentence from the Sioux Falls trial at the South Dakota State Penitentiary. His fame preceded him, and many prisoners, especially other Indians, treated him royally, extending considerable respect and giving him gifts of magazines, cigarettes, and food. Among the prisoners there were Dicky Marshall and Vincent Bad Heart Bull, brother of Wesley Bad Heart Bull.

Means resolved to behave respectfully and politely, although he did not abandon his activism. He embarked on a spiritual fast that led to a weight loss of approximately 70 pounds. When prison officials became concerned for his life, he was sent to a Sioux Falls hospital. Circuit Judge Wayne Christensen ordered that he be force-fed if he refused to eat, and gradually Means regained his strength. He attempted to create a chapter of AIM in the prison; although the warden refused to recognize it as an official prison organization, Means led AIM meetings while incarcerated. He also participated in two meal boycotts to highlight abuses of prisoner rights.

Among those who came to visit Means were Governor Richard Kneip and Senator George McGovern. Means had been highly critical of McGovern previously, but he acknowledged that after the meeting he began to admire him. Means became a trusty after three months in the prison, which meant that he could work at jobs outside the prison and live in a trusty cottage also beyond the walls. Over the next nine months, he held jobs in Senator Abourezk's Sioux

Falls office, with the Rapid City Indian Service Council, and with the NAACP and Legal Aid.

Not everything went smoothly for Means, however, as he suffered yet another attempt on his life while in prison. One morning as he entered the prison yard for exercise, he was attacked by a man with a homemade knife. Another Indian grabbed a garbage can lid and hit the attacker over the head with it. Vincent Bad Heart Bull pursued the attacker and hit him until guards surrounded them. Marshall called out that it was a setup, and Means's supporters pulled back. A Sioux Falls grand jury ruled that the Indians were at fault, Bad Heart Bull was put in solitary confinement, and the man who attacked Means, a person named Schillinger, escaped punishment. Means argues in his autobiography that Schillinger was assigned to the prison at Sioux Falls to kill him.

Means received his release in August 1979, having served one year and three days of his four-year sentence.

RETURN TO THE LAND

The Black Hills Alliance

Means returned to Pine Ridge after his release from prison and set about attempting to strengthen AIM's activities on the reservation. The organization supported an effort by Means's brother Ted and Ted's wife to open a health center in Porcupine. Another brother, Dace, worked at a crisis center operated by AIM, and Means helped establish an AIM-run radio station, KILI.

Means also became deeply involved in the Black Hills Alliance, which sought to preserve the Black Hills from destruction through mining and development. Means's cousin Madonna had helped found Women of All Red Nations (WARN), which discovered that the water in Pine Ridge was contaminated with uranium and other toxic substances. The Black Hills Alliance sponsored a convention entitled the International Gathering for Survival in 1980 to consider how to best protect the land.

At that gathering, Means gave a speech, "For America to live, Europe must die." Means considers the speech to be his most famous. In the speech, which is reprinted in his autobiography, *Where White Men Fear to Tread*, he draws an important distinction between being (a spiritual process) and gaining (a material action). The Euro-American mentality, he argues, is about gaining— that is, acquiring wealth, land, and other possessions. The European mindset, he points out, is cultural rather than genetic. Indians can adopt it, and non-Indians can reject it. He concludes his speech by noting that he is not a leader (a statement with which a great many people would disagree) but rather "an Oglala Lakota patriot." In arguing against the European mindset, Means argues in favor of a Lakota (or more broadly, Indian) perspective, which respects the earth and is ultimately necessary for survival. Resisting the European attitude, he states, is a prerequisite for that survival. The attitude that

Means conveys in his speech perhaps resonates even more in the twenty-first century given the growing concern about climate change and other environmental issues.[18]

Also in 1980, Means's fifth child, and his first with Peggy, was born. She received the name Tatuye Topa Najinwin (Woman Who Stands Strong in the Four Winds), a name reflective of Means's mother, who had died also that year.

Yellow Thunder Camp

A major focus of the next several years for Means was a camp in the Black Hills named Yellow Thunder Camp. Its name came from Raymond Yellow Thunder, the man whose murder in Gordon had sparked such controversy. Means lived at the camp for the next two years and called that period "the finest and most important time of my life."[19]

The camp became a spiritual and educational experience, welcoming all, including non-Indians. The whole community and area became the classroom, and instruction included lessons in the Lakota language. Means and Ward Churchill developed a proposal to establish the camp as a youth camp, a proposal that local rangers supported but that Forest Supervisor James Mathers strongly opposed. Mathers further informed Means and the others at Raymond Yellow Thunder Camp that their fire permit would not be renewed and they would have to leave. They refused, and prepared for the threatened removal by the National Guard. The eviction did not materialize, but the camp leaders were subjected to a federal lawsuit, beginning a long period of legal action to retain the camp.

The first Sun Dance at the camp was held during the summer of 1982, led by Leonard Crow Dog. Meanwhile, legal action to preserve the camp continued, and Means turned to Congress for help. Representative Shirley Chisholm of New York sponsored a bill to set aside 800 acres for a spiritual youth camp, but opposition from the South Dakota congressional delegation helped prevent the bill from advancing.

A casualty of Means's focus on Raymond Yellow Thunder Camp was his marriage. Peggy taught on Pine Ridge Reservation, and commuting to her job from the camp would entail driving some 250 miles each day. In addition to the practical difficulty of living at the camp for her, Means felt that she considered the camp a rival for his affection.[20] Means would marry for a fourth time in 1984, to Gloria Grant Davis, and they would have a son, Tatanka Wanbli Sapa Xila Sábe (Black Buffalo Eagle) in February 1985.

EXPANDING THE FOCUS

Running for Vice President

Russell Means steadily expanded his focus in the 1980s to develop not only a national view of the U.S. government's treatment of their country's native peoples, but also an international perspective on how nations had repressed indigenous peoples. At the same time, he expanded his political activism from AIM and other Indian organizations within the United States to national efforts that transcended, while still encompassing, Indian issues. With that transition in mind, perhaps the most bizarre effort in Means's life possesses a logic that at first it seems to lack. That action was Means's seeking of the vice presidency of the United States on a ticket headed by pornographer Larry Flynt.

When Flynt proposed to Means that he join in Flynt's effort to win the Republican presidential nomination, Means already had sought political office. He had come close to winning the 1974 race for president of the Oglala Nation on Pine Ridge Reservation. He would again seek the position in 1984, only to be removed from the primary ballot on the grounds that he had been convicted of a felony.

Means received his invitation from Flynt in 1983.After seeking advice from his brother Bill and AIM associates, he accepted the offer. Means appeared to be attracted by Flynt's belief in First Amendment rights to self-expression, by his desire to defeat President Ronald Reagan, and by his belief that true obscenity lay in actions other than sexual ones. The political alliance did not last long, as Means became disillusioned not by Flynt's politics, but rather by his failure to put much effort into winning the nomination.

Nicaragua and the Miskito Indians

Also in the 1980s, AIM hoped to place the 1868 Fort Laramie Treaty before the International Court of Justice. The group sought the support of Nicaragua in this quest, as AIM needed a member nation to sponsor its case. Nicaragua declined to do so—a decision that offended Means and perhaps influenced his decision to investigate Nicaragua's treatment of its Miskito Indians. The Miskitos wanted autonomy within their region, and they and other Indian peoples in Nicaragua had formed a coalition called MISURASATA, led by Brooklyn Rivera, that was negotiating with the Sandinista government.

When Means announced his support for MISURASATA, some members of AIM strongly objected. AIM and the International Indian Treaty Council were supporting the Sandinistas at this point, consistent with their usual support for left-leaning organizations. Means, however, did not see himself as either liberal or conservative, Democrat or Republican. When he looked closely at the Nicaraguan Indians' relationship to the Nicaraguan government, he saw a parallel to American Indians' problems with the U.S. government.

In October 1985, Means flew to Costa Rica to meet with MISURASATA leaders and to visit Miskito refugee camps. After returning to the United States, he appeared on the *Larry King Show* to discuss what he had found and then returned to Costa Rica. On this trip, Means wanted to visit Miskito villages within Nicaragua. This dangerous enterprise, although successful, required Means to survive Sandinista bombing from planes (he received a shrapnel wound in his stomach) and a nighttime race by boat to reach a Colombian island, Puerto Cabezas, and safety.

Moonies

The short-lived Larry Flynt alliance demonstrated Means's willingness to accept allies wherever he could find them. In the spring of 1986, that willingness led him to the Unification Church (now called the Family Federation for World Peace and Unification), founded by Sun Myung Moon in 1954. Its members are commonly known, after the founder, as Moonies.

Means accepted an invitation to attend a convention of the political arm of the Unification Church in 1986. At the convention, Means rubbed shoulders with conservative Republicans who supported the pro-Contra position of the church. Again what might have seemed like an unusual coming together had its basis in shared views: The Contras were rebels who were opposing, with the support of the U.S. government, the Nicaraguan Sandinistas.

The Unification Church sponsored a speaking tour for Means and invited him to a conference in Korea. Means's friendship with the Moonies, like his opposition to the Sandinistas, elicited considerable opposition from longtime colleagues in AIM and supporters who usually championed liberal causes.

The Presidential Candidate

Means had sought important political offices, both tribal and national, but in 1986 he embarked on his most ambitious political quest yet: the presidency of the United States. Again his quest appeared unusually quixotic to many, as he ran as a Libertarian.

The impetus for his entry into the race came from Honey Lanham, who called Means after his return from Korea and raised the prospect of his running for president as a Libertarian candidate. After further conversations with Lanham and with a Libertarian from Montana, Larry Dodge, and visits to Libertarian groups in Texas, Means agreed to seek the nomination at the party's national convention in Seattle. The attraction for Means was such Libertarian characteristics as belief in limited governmental intrusion into people's lives, a commitment to the free market, and, as Means saw it, an unyielding loyalty to principle. According to Means, Libertarian ideology closely parallels Lakota culture.[21]

Means worked hard to earn delegates to the convention, visiting 46 states. He did well with state delegates but came up short at the convention, losing the nomination to Texas Congressman Ron Paul, still a favorite of Libertarians and Tea Party members well into the twenty-first century. Nonetheless, Means became the first Indian to run for president of the United States.

His failure to receive the Libertarian nomination was not Means's only loss in 1987. The struggle to keep Yellow Thunder Camp open finally came to an end when the U.S. Supreme Court refused to take up the case, and the camp was forced to close. At that point, Means and his wife, Gloria, decided to move to Arizona and live near her Navajo people. They took up residence in the town of Chinle.

A Movie Star

One of Russell Means's talents from his early days with AIM has been the ability to communicate eloquently and effectively. In 1991, he received an offer to communicate through, for him, a very new medium: film. Means was asked to play the role of Chingachgook, one of the "last of the Mohicans," in the film by that title based on the James Fenimore Cooper novel. Although completely unfamiliar with film acting and initially distressed by what he considered the unrealistic language of the script, Means quickly became absorbed with the project. He became convinced that the film depicted Indians faithfully as human beings rather than as the stereotypes presented in so many Westerns. In addition, his film character represented qualities that Means seemed to see in himself: a strong enemy when necessary, but also a loyal friend and honorable individual.

Means came to enjoy acting and followed *The Last of the Mohicans* with many other appearances in films and television shows. His film roles include appearances in Oliver Stone's *Natural Born Killers* (1994), *Wagons East* (1994), *Windrunner* (1995) as Jim Thorpe's ghost, *Buffalo Girls* (a 1995 television movie) playing Sitting Bull, *Wind River* (1998) as Washakie, *Pocahontas II: Journey to a New World* (1998) as the voice of Pocahontas's father, *Cowboy Up* (2000), *Black Cloud* (2004), *Pathfinder* (2005) as the title character, *Intervention* (2006), *Rez Bomb* (2008), *The Last Horseman* (2010), and *The Sasquatch and the Girl* (2010) as the narrator. In March 2010, Means was honored for his film accomplishments at the annual American Indian Stories N' Motion Film Festival at Haskell Indian Nations University.

Means has made appearances on many television series, including *Touched by an Angel* (1996), *Walker, Texas Ranger* (1996), *Profiler* (1997), *Nash Bridges* (1998), *Family Law* (2001), and *Curb Your Enthusiasm* (2004). In addition, Means has participated in a number of documentaries, including narrating *Paha Sapa: Struggle for the Black Hills* (1993), which appeared on HBO. He also has released two recordings of protest songs that he wrote: *Electric Warrior* (SOAR Records, 1993) and *The Radical* (American Indian Music Company, 1996), the latter for a company that he founded.

Even painting is a mode of communication that Means has taken up. His first show was in Santa Monica, California, in 1998. He followed it with another show in Southampton, New York, in 2000. In 2007, he participated in an international art show in Paris.

RESISTING AND SURVIVING

The Republic of Lakotah

With the dawn of a new century, Russell Means continued working on behalf of Lakotas and other Indians. As he pointed out in his speech "For America to Live, Europe Must Die," Indian survival requires resistance. This point is especially salient given that he considers survival not merely remaining alive, but also retaining one's culture, dignity, and self-worth as a people and as an individual.

That resistance led Means and some other Lakotas to withdraw from the treaties that Means had worked so hard to compel the U.S. government to enforce. In December 2007, a group of Lakotas traveled to Washington, D.C., to announce the withdrawal. They also declared their independence as a nation, establishing the Republic of Lakotah. The nation encompasses portions of Nebraska, Montana, and the Dakotas, although it is not recognized by tribal governments.

According to the Republic of Lakotah web site, the nation has a six-part strategy for its development: (1) political activism, including supporting tribal candidates who choose real freedom for their people; (1) education, especially through schools that employ total immersion in the Lakota culture; (3) improved health care; (4) use of sustainable energy; (5) continued awareness of international affairs and use of international bodies to combat U.S. genocidal policies; and (6) improved housing that is safe, sufficient, and energy efficient.

Means's political activism during the new century also involved candidacies for governor of New Mexico and president of the Oglala Nation. The former effort, which began in 2001, failed when procedural issues kept him off the ballot. His effort to win the Oglala presidency in 2004 came up short, although he finished first in the primary. He then lost the run-off election to Cecelia Fire Thunder, the first woman to head the Oglala Nation.

Means responded negatively to a listening session held by members of the U.S. State Department in Albuquerque on March 16, 2010, claiming that the government was using the session, and one the following day with members of the Navajo Nation, to argue that it has listened to Indians while it maintains its same policies. Means said that the Republic of Lakotah would submit its own report to the United Nations Human Rights Council detailing continued violation of treaties. Means promised, additionally, that he would communicate to the President of the United States and the Secretary of State the Republic's demand that the United States withdraw completely from the Republic of Lakotah.

The T.R.E.A.T.Y. Total Immersion School

A major Means goal, and an important element in furthering his plan for a successful Republic of Lakotah, has been establishing an approach to education that involves total immersion in Lakota culture. He has worked diligently with many others to establish such a school at Porcupine, South Dakota. The school, which was scheduled to admit its first students in the summer of 2010, is called the T.R.E.A.T.Y. Total Immersion School. The acronym refers to a "true revolution for the elders, ancestors, treaties, and youth." It also refers to the many treaties with native peoples signed, and then broken, by the U.S. government over the years.

Clyde Warrior

Clyde Warrior (1939–1968), a Ponca from Oklahoma, was called by Vine Deloria one of the three great Indians whom he knew. A brilliant student at Cameron Junior College in Lawton, Oklahoma, Warrior later attended the University of Oklahoma and Northeastern State College in Tahlequah, Oklahoma, earning a degree in education. He also was deeply influenced by Ponca culture, absorbing the history and stories of the Poncas from his grandparents.

While attending a conference heavily populated with members of the National Congress of American Indians (NCAI) in 1961, Warrior became convinced that members of NCAI were too cautious and too influenced by the Bureau of Indian Affairs. Consequently, he helped form the National Indian Youth Council, which encouraged self-determination and development of personal competence. From 1965 until his death, Warrior and his wife, Della, offered a series of summer training institutes for high school and college students, known as the Institute for American Indian Studies.

Clyde Warrior participated in the African American civil rights movement, represented NIYC at the March on Washington, D.C., in 1963, and studied the effects of schools on Indian children. His "We Are Not Free" speech, which he gave before the National Advisory Commission on Rural Poverty in 1967, was especially influential. In this address, he argued that Indian poverty is the result of the U.S. government administering Indian lands the way a colonial power manages a colony. Freedom for Indians to decide for themselves what is good, he argued, is a requirement for their advancement. Only then can Indians develop lasting competence and self-worth.

Clyde Warrior died of a heart attack on July 19, 1968, leaving behind an organization that would continue helping to empower Indians through such efforts as voter registration, job training, college preparation, and access to health care and social services.

The Total Immersion Educational Endowment Fund purchased an 85-acre ranch, including a house in which the Indian agent for Pine Ridge had lived. Means and his brothers donated an additional 160 acres. Solar panels were added to the building in 2009, consistent with Means's determination to be as respectful as possible toward the earth. Another addition to Pine Ridge was a youth center to help cure addictions among the reservation's young people.

The timeline for the T.R.E.A.T.Y. Total Immersion School calls for it to operate with a full attendance in years 2 to 5, and for students to begin graduating and applying what they learned in years 6 to 12. If the school is successful, it will be a lasting emblem of Russell Means's commitment, as his name indicates, to working for the people. Vine Deloria wrote, "I am thankful that in my time I have been allowed to know three great Indians—Clyde Warrior, Hank Adams, and Russell Means. If we had a hundred like them we would now rule the world. But every race is given only a few people of this stature in each century."[22] If Deloria got anything wrong about Means in his statement, it is his reference to ruling the world. Means's work has been devoted to preserving freedom, not rule; to being free to live as one wishes; to practicing one's religions, cherishing one's culture, holding close those one cares especially about. He surely has experienced too much of the negative effects of being controlled to want to rule anyone.

NOTES

1. Russell Means, with Marvin J. Wolf, *Where White Men Fear to Tread* (New York: St. Martin's Griffin, 1995) 44.
2. Means 86.
3. Paul Chaat Smith and Robert Allen Warrior, *Like a Hurricane: The Indian Movement from Alcatraz to Wounded Knee* (New York: The New Press, 1996) 10.
4. Means 128.
5. Means 153.
6. Smith and Warrior 115.
7. Stew Magnuson, *The Death of Yellow Thunder and Other True Stories from the Nebraska–Pine Ridge Border Towns* (Lubbock: Texas Tech University Press, 2008) 141.
8. Means 231.
9. Means 233.
10. Akim D. Reinhardt, *Ruling Pine Ridge: Oglala Lakota Politics from the IRA to Wounded Knee* (Lubbock: Texas Tech University Press, 2007) 153.
11. Reinhardt 185.
12. Means 253.
13. Dennis Banks, with Richard Erdoes, *Ojibwa Warrior: Dennis Banks and the Rise of the American Indian Movement* (Norman: University of Oklahoma Press, 2004) 161.
14. Vine Deloria, Jr., *Behind the Trail of Broken Treaties* (New York: Delacorte Press, 1974) 41.
15. Steve Hendricks, *The Unquiet Grave: The FBI and the Struggle for the Soul of Indian Country* (2006; New York: Thunder's Mouth Press, 2007) 117.
16. Means 304–05.
17. John William Sayer, *Ghost Dancing the Law: The Wounded Knee Trials* (Cambridge, MA: Harvard University Press, 1997) 196.
18. Means 545–54.
19. Means 408.
20. Means 418.
21. Means 482.
22. Smith and Warrior 274.

RECOMMENDED READING

Banks, Dennis, with Richard Erdoes. *Ojibwa Warrior: Dennis Banks and the Rise of the American Indian Movement*. Norman: University of Oklahoma Press, 2004.

Hendricks, Steve. *The Unquiet Grave: The FBI and the Struggle for the Soul of Indian Country*. 2006. New York: Thunder's Mouth Press, 2007.

Magnuson, Stew. *The Death of Yellow Thunder and Other True Stories from the Nebraska–Pine Ridge Border Towns*. Lubbock: Texas Tech University Press, 2008.

Means, Russell, with Marvin J. Wolf. *Where White Men Fear to Tread*. New York: St. Martin's Griffin, 1995.

Paha Sapa: Struggle for the Black Hills. HBO, 1993. Mystic Fire Video, 1998. VHS.

Reinhardt, Akim D. *Ruling Pine Ridge: Oglala Lakota Politics from the IRA to Wounded Knee*. Lubbock: Texas Tech University Press, 2007.

Russell Means. <http://wwww.russellmeansfreedom.com>.

Sayer, John William. *Ghost Dancing the Law: The Wounded Knee Trials*. Cambridge, MA: Harvard University Press, 1997.

Smith, Paul Chaat, and Robert Allen Warrior. *Like a Hurricane: The Indian Movement from Alcatraz to Wounded Knee*. New York: New Press, 1996.

Stern, Kenneth S. *Loud Hawk: The United States Versus the American Indian Movement*. Norman: University of Oklahoma Press, 1994.

The distress signal of an upside down flag, here hanging in front of a church at Wounded Knee, became the emblem of the American Indian Movement. Among those occupying Wounded Knee was Mary Brave Bird. (AP Photo/Jim Mone)

Mary Brave Bird
(born 1956)

Mary Brave Bird (formerly known as Mary Crow Dog) has been a prominent figure in the Indian struggle for justice and equal rights. A Brulé, one of the seven Lakota divisions, she participated in the Trail of Broken Treaties march on Washington, D.C., which culminated in the temporary takeover of the Bureau of Indian Affairs building. She later was a member of the group that under the leadership of the American Indian Movement occupied Wounded Knee, South Dakota.

Mary Brave Bird (the "Brave Bird" part of her name coming from her mother's father) was formerly married to Leonard Crow Dog, a prominent Lakota medicine man. After he was arrested on charges that seemed to have far more to do with his political activism than any lawbreaking, she loyally supported him and worked tirelessly to try to obtain his release. She also became a strong proponent of traditional Indian spirituality, including such important Indian religious practices as the Sun Dance and peyote rituals associated with the Native American Church.

Two books that Brave Bird wrote with the assistance of Richard Erdoes, *Lakota Woman* and *Ohitika Woman*, present her political and personal struggles and successes. In addition, the film *Lakota Woman, Siege at Wounded Knee*, was produced in 1994 by Jane Fonda for TNT.

"NATURAL-BORN REBEL"

Childhood

Mary Brave Bird was born Mary Ellen Moore in 1956 into a Lakota Brulé family on the Rosebud Reservation in South Dakota. The family resided in a small region named He-Dog after a former chief. Brave Bird traces her ancestry back to Chief Iron Shell, a respected leader and warrior in the mid-nineteenth century who distinguished himself in battle against the Pawnees. Iron Shell had seven sons, including Hollow Horn Bear and Stephen Brave Bird. Hollow Horn Bear achieved fame among both Indians and Euro-Americans, and was invited to ride in President Theodore Roosevelt's inaugural parade in 1905, along with five other Indian leaders including Geronimo and Quanah Parker. He also had his visage immortalized on a five-dollar bill and a postage stamp. Stephen, Mary Brave Bird's great-grandfather, was a cattle drover and rodeo rider.

Robert Brave Bird, son to Stephen and Zoe McKenzie, operated a farm and also hunted and trapped. He died in an accident during the 1930s, when a storm spooked the horses pulling his wagon. His widow, the former Louise Flood (descended from a family who had migrated from Ireland in the middle of the nineteenth century) and their children, among them Mary Brave Bird's mother, Emily, then lived with a relative. Louise Flood later married Noble Moore. According to Mary Brave Bird, the couple largely took care of her during her early childhood.

Mary had six siblings, one of whom died in infancy. Her other siblings were Kathie, Robert, Barbara, and Sandra—all older than Mary—and an adopted boy. The father, Bill Moore, left the family while Emily was pregnant with Mary. According to Brave Bird, he was vastly different from his kind and caring father, Noble Moore, who, she notes, was the only father she ever really had.

Both her Grandmother Louise and her mother Emily had attended mission school and embraced Catholicism rather than traditional Indian religious beliefs. Other relatives, however, kept more firmly to traditional spirituality. In particular, Dick Fool Bull, her grand-uncle, made Lakota courting flutes from which the music emanated through a bird's beak. Uncle Fool Bull took Brave Bird to her first peyote meeting and lived to be almost 100 years of age, dying in 1975.

Boarding School

Brave Bird followed her grandmother and mother to the St. Francis Mission School on the Rosebud Reservation. Typical of mission schools of the time (although they have changed considerably for the better in recent decades), St. Francis used strict discipline to try to impose a Euro-American set of values on the Indian students. The school was run by Jesuit priests and Sisters of St. Francis, who come in for harsh criticism in Brave Bird's first book, *Lakota Woman*. In that book, she describes herself as "a natural-born rebel,"[1] and that sense of rebellion manifested itself very directly at St. Francis.

With two friends, Brave Bird published a newspaper called *Red Panther* in which the authors sharply criticized the corporal punishment and food that they endured. The paper also characterized the principal as ignorant of Indian culture and charged the staff with improper sexual behavior. For punishment, Brave Bird was forced to scrub six flights of stairs daily, escaping harsher discipline when her mother intervened.

Brave Bird particularly chronicles an altercation with a young priest whom she hit in the face. After that incident, she demanded to return home and was permitted to do so. That priest, she notes without naming him, later became an advocate for Indian rights and defended the occupation of Wounded Knee before dying young of cancer.

In *Ohitika Woman*, Brave Bird acknowledges that substantial changes have occurred in the mission and school since her days there. The mission, as of 2010, included three Jesuit priests and one Jesuit brother working with a Lakota deacon and seven Lakota lay ministers. It offers a program in Lakota Studies directed by Deacon Ben Black Bear, Jr. The school, now known as St. Francis Indian School, has been run by the Lakotas of Rosebud since 1972.[2]

The next few years for Brave Bird were characterized by wandering, drinking, and uncertainty about her future. She ran away from home after repeated arguments with her mother and traveled with shifting groups of friends and acquaintances, combining drinking with driving—a mixture that she describes as deadly for many people on the reservation. She also engaged in small-time shoplifting and was raped while still in her early teens.

AMERICAN INDIAN MOVEMENT

Introduction to the Movement

The American Indian Movement (AIM) was created in 1968 in Minneapolis–St. Paul as a means to combat police brutality directed at Indian peoples. The founders were principally Chippewas (Ojibwas). According to the AIM web site, the organization is a spiritual movement that attempts to foster pride and dignity in people. Although also a civil rights movement, AIM has been more concerned with Indian sovereignty and reestablishing Indian culture than with desegregation and individual rights. The collective nature of AIM's focus reflects the deeply social nature of traditional Indian culture.

Brave Bird first encountered the American Indian Movement in 1971, when she attended a Sun Dance and powwow at Leonard Crow Dog's home. At the powwow, she heard a Chippewa give a speech advocating traditional culture and Indian self-rule rather than seeking to embrace Euro-American culture. As she learned more about AIM, she found it a good fit with her own personal yearning for meaning and identity.

AIM would have a significant impact on Brave Bird. As she became more involved with the movement, she quit drinking. She also entered into a relationship with a member of the movement and became pregnant with her first child, a child to whom she would courageously give birth during the later occupation of Wounded Knee.

Trail of Broken Treaties

Brave Bird attended another Sun Dance at the Rosebud Reservation in the summer of 1972 that became a turning point in her life. This sacred dance also occurred at Leonard Crow Dog's home, where a number of AIM members participated in the ritual. The power of the Sun Dance to unite participants coupled with growing anger against injustices against Indians gave additional impetus to organized activism, including the event known as the Trail of Broken Treaties. During this prolonged protest, groups of Indians from throughout the country gathered in Washington, D.C., the origin of most broken treaties. The name recalled the Cherokees' 800-mile Trail of Tears, a forced migration from Georgia to Indian Territory in the future state of Oklahoma between 1836 and 1840.

The demonstration originated with non-AIM leaders but quickly drew in the organization's leaders and other members. Brave Bird was among those traveling from Rosebud and Pine Ridge Reservations. By the time that the various groups reached Washington on November 3, 1972, the caravan stretched for four miles. Some 60 cars drove through the city honking and continued to

Wilma Mankiller

Wilma Mankiller (1945–2010) exercised more tribal power than almost any other woman in American Indian history. Despite her surname, which came from a traditional Cherokee military rank, she brought political activism and considerable visionary and administrative skill rather than violence to the Cherokee Nation.

Mankiller became involved in the battle for Indian rights by supporting those who occupied Alcatraz Island in 1969 to protest the federal government's treatment of Indians. She subsequently served in various roles to help expand Cherokee educational and economic opportunities. By 1983, she was deputy chief of the Cherokee Nation, headquartered in Tahlequah, Oklahoma. When Ross Swimmer left to join the Indian Affairs office in the Department of the Interior, she succeeded him as chief.

Mankiller was reelected in 1987 and 1991. During her years as chief (1985–1995), she combined guardianship of Cherokee traditions with progress in many areas of modern life. Under her leadership, the Cherokees diversified their revenue sources to include factories, a motel, a lumber company, gambling operations, and a variety of other businesses. Health care and job-training programs directed at Cherokees grew, and she helped improve education from Head Start through the Sequoyah High School in Tahlequah. In addition, the Cherokee population tripled in the face of improved health care and greater local economic opportunities.

Although Mankiller decided not to seek reelection in 1995, she continued to work on behalf of the Cherokee Nation, despite her own many health problems. President Bill Clinton awarded her the Presidential Medal of Freedom in 1998. Upon learning of her death in 2010, President Barack Obama noted that she had "served as an inspiration to women in Indian Country and across America." The story of her life is told in *Mankiller: A Chief and Her People*, which she co-wrote with Michael Wallis.

the White House, with some of the participants beating on drums as they drove by, hoping that President Richard Nixon might hear them.

The strong sense of unified purpose behind the Trail of Broken Treaties led Brave Bird to call it "the greatest action taken by Indians since the Battle of the Little Big Horn."[3] The trail led to the Bureau of Indian Affairs (BIA) building on Constitution Avenue. Brave Bird estimates that between 600 and 800 people crowded into the building. They forced the police and security guards outside and developed a set of 20 demands for the federal government. These points included recognition of Indian sovereignty, reconsideration of past treaties, elimination of all jurisdiction by states over Indian affairs, and substitution of a new Office of Federal Indian Relations and Community Reconstruction for the Bureau of Indian Affairs.

Police surrounded the building but did not attempt to enforce orders for the Indians to vacate it. As the occupation continued, Indians inside the BIA building readied for a possible effort to evict them. Dennis Banks recalled Brave Bird tying a letter opener to a broom handle to use as a weapon. When someone asked her intention, she reportedly replied that she would "get them in the balls before they get me."[4]

Finally, a compromise was reached, providing funds for those who had come to Washington to cover their return home and promising no legal prosecution of the protestors. The White House agreed to consider the 20 points, a consideration that did not lead to any subsequent action. Thus, after six days of occupying the BIA building, the siege was lifted and the occupation ended.

Native American Church

In addition to her growing political activism, Brave Bird by this time was strongly committed to traditional Indian culture—two directions in her life that she found complementary. In *Lakota Woman*, she refers to herself as a "half-breed," or "Iyeska," and notes that she had to turn to the "full-bloods" to truly become an Indian.[5] It is also clear in her autobiographical writing that she saw these matters of ethnicity not merely in terms of "blood," but even more so as cultural attitudes and practices grounded in traditional Indian spirituality.

Brave Bird's first spiritual mentor was her Uncle Fool Bull, who instructed her in Lakota history and religion and introduced her to peyote, recognized by many Indian peoples as a sacred medicine. At this time, she became involved with the Native American Church. These spiritual directions were sharply at odds with her mother's Catholicism and further separated mother and daughter, although later the two women were reconciled. Brave Bird's involvement in peyote rituals would increase after she married Leonard Crow Dog, who along with being a Lakota medicine man was a "peyote priest."[6] Brave Bird recalls proudly that she was one of the first women to be allowed to sing at peyote meetings.

Lakota religious belief holds that Wakantanka takes many forms, including peyote (*Lophophora williamsii*), a small cactus that grows in Mexico and southwestern Texas. The top of the cactus consists of small buttons that are harvested. They can be chewed or boiled in water and are used for their medicinal or spiritual effects. Peyote is used by some native peoples to treat a variety of ailments, including rheumatism, toothache, and post-childbirth pain.

Peyote has a psychoactive effect that within religious ceremonies can contribute to introspective and visionary experiences. The Native American Church makes extensive use of peyote in rituals that may begin at sundown and last through the night. The eating of peyote is combined with prayer, songs, a morning breakfast that includes ceremonial drinking of cold water, and a number of other ritual actions. Because of its psychoactive effects, peyote is generally outlawed in the United States except for use for religious purposes by Native Americans, although a few states also have legalized peyote use by non-Indian individuals.

WOUNDED KNEE

A Murder Trial

Wesley Bad Heart Bull, a Lakota, was killed by a Euro-American named Darld Schmitz (sometimes recorded as Darold Schmidt) in Buffalo Gap, near Rapid City, South Dakota, on January 21, 1973. Schmitz was charged with second-degree manslaughter and released on bail. A large number of Lakotas and other Indian leaders, including the prominent AIM leaders Russell Means and Dennis Banks, arrived in Rapid City in early February 1973 at the request of the victim's mother, Sarah Bad Heart Bull, to advocate for justice.

Approximately 200 advocates arrived in Custer on February 6, and several AIM leaders met with state's attorney Hobart Gates. Initially, only a handful of representatives was admitted into the courthouse. As others attempted to enter, however, state troopers moved in. They knocked down and arrested Sarah Bad Heart Bull and used tear gas and fire hoses to force the demonstrators away from the courthouse.

Some Lakotas threw gasoline on the courthouse door and attempted to set the building on fire. Firefighters and police kept the building from burning, but while they were occupied at the courthouse, a Chamber of Commerce building was ignited. Fighting continued for several hours. Mary Brave Bird escaped arrest, but her sister Barbara was arrested, although the latter was soon released. Sarah Bad Heart Bull was not only arrested but served several weeks in jail while the killer of her son was acquitted.

The Occupation of Wounded Knee

Angered by what they considered a great injustice regarding the acquittal of Wesley Bad Heart Bull's killer and determined to fight back against the government injustices, many of those who had been at Custer looked to a new means of resistance. Some suggested targeting Wounded Knee, where an estimated 150 to 300 Lakotas under Big Foot had been massacred by U.S. troops on December 29, 1890. The gathering at Wounded Knee also served as a protest against reservation dominance, especially at the Oglala Pine Ridge Reservation. There, tribal officials seemed primarily interested in maintaining their own power through intimidation and police brutality (by means of what were often referred to as "goon squads") and in eliminating influence by "traditionalists."

The occupation of Wounded Knee began on February 27, 1973, and ended 71 days later. Among those at Wounded Knee during the occupation was Brave Bird, whose Uncle Dick Fool Bull as a young boy had heard the army's shots at the site 83 years earlier from a camp two miles away. Although pregnant, Brave Bird did not hesitate to participate; in fact, she resolved that her child would be born at Wounded Knee.

The site included several buildings, among them Sacred Heart Church, the Gildersleeve Trading Post, and a museum. The men dug trenches around the perimeter and constructed bunkers for protection while an army of federal marshals and FBI agents surrounded the area. Periodic firing occurred, interrupted by occasional ceasefires to allow women and children to leave if they chose to do so. Brave Bird, however, remained committed to being part of the resistance effort.

Given the hills, gullies, and trees in the area, federal officials were not able completely to prevent movement into and out of the Wounded Knee complex. Reinforcements arrived, as did supplies. Among those who joined the group at Wounded Knee were two brothers, descendants of George Armstrong Custer and a young Cheyenne woman named Monahseetah whom he had taken as his mistress—ostensibly his interpreter despite her inability to speak English.

Brave Bird describes two airdrops that helped to supply those holding out at Wounded Knee. The first plane flew under a telephone wire and landed on a road, delivering some 400 pounds of supplies. The second, on April 17, was delivered by three planes that dropped supplies by parachute.

After the first airdrop, officials were ready. A helicopter flew over Wounded Knee shortly after the planes departed and a sniper fired from the helicopter at people carrying food from the drop site. One bullet went through a wall of the church and hit Frank Clearwater, who had arrived only the day before with his pregnant wife, Morning Star. The fatally wounded Clearwater was carried to a roadblock, and federal officials flew him to a Rapid City hospital, where he died on April 25. The second person to be killed was Buddy Lamont, an Oglala and former Vietnam War veteran who was shot through the heart during a firefight on April 26. Several others were wounded during the siege, while no law enforcement officers were killed and only one was seriously wounded.

The spiritual leader inside Wounded Knee, according to Brave Bird, was her future husband, Leonard Crow Dog. He revived the Ghost Dance, which had been outlawed for some 80 years; presided at religious ceremonies; and served as the group's primary healer, even operating on gunshot wounds.

By early May, negotiations to end the standoff were progressing. Those occupying Wounded Knee promised to lay down their weapons and come out, and the government agreed to investigate complaints regarding Pine Ridge. On May 8, those still at Wounded Knee, numbering approximately 120, left the compound. Government hearings were held later that year but proved unproductive.

A Birth at Wounded Knee

Brave Bird fulfilled her promise to herself to have her baby at Wounded Knee and to do so in the Lakota way with Indian women as midwives and accompanied by Lakota prayers. On April 11, her baby was born inside a trailer house. She named the baby Pedro after a friend, Pedro Bissonette. The birth occasioned the beating of drums and singing, along with tears from many, both women and men.

About a week before the siege ended, on the same day that Buddy Lamont was shot, Brave Bird left Wounded Knee with her son in response to a request from Lamont's family to help with the funeral. As she left, she was arrested, taken to the jail at Pine Ridge, and held there for about 24 hours before being released. She was then taken to the county jail at Rapid City, where she spent a few more hours.

Brave Bird was a very young woman at Wounded Knee, just 17 years old, and certainly not one of the primary leaders of the occupation. However, her determined and continued presence there for approximately two months under constant danger demonstrated remarkable courage. Her adamant commitment to giving birth among her fellow resisters had great symbolic value as a triumph for traditional Lakota culture even under the most difficult of circumstances. The response to Brave Bird's actions by those around her, including the most respected of AIM leaders, was an admiring recognition of her special role as a woman-warrior in her people's struggle for dignity and justice.

LEONARD CROW DOG

Marriage

Mary Brave Bird married Leonard Crow Dog in 1973 after the occupation of Wounded Knee. Not yet 18 years of age, she was about 12 years younger than her famous husband. In some ways, she was unprepared for what was to come. Leonard's parents, including his father, Henry Crow Dog, were initially uncertain that their son had made a wise choice. Leonard had been married before and had two daughters, Ina and Bernadette, and a son, Richard, who were old enough not to automatically accept a teenager as their new mother. Nor did the new wife have any special domestic skills: She admits in *Lakota Woman* that she did not even know how to make coffee.

In addition, Crow Dog's stature as a holy man attracted many people to their home, often seeking help of one sort or another, sometimes including money. That he was enormously generous fit well the old Lakota ideal but was not necessarily conducive to running a household efficiently. Brave Bird writes of the challenges in being married to a revered Wichasha Wakan, or holy man, noting that "confidentially, it can be hell on a woman to be married to such a holy one."[7]

The demands of her new life led Mary Brave Bird (now Mary Crow Dog) to become ill. She lost weight, had trouble sleeping, and regularly dreamed of the dead. Nonetheless, she tried hard and began to earn the respect of her husband's family and friends. Unfortunately, still greater trials lay ahead.

Arrest

Leonard Crow Dog's political activism, especially his role at Wounded Knee, had made him a marked man. In addition, a violent incident that occurred on June 26, 1975, which in no way involved him, would also help to deprive Crow Dog of his freedom. On that day, FBI agents Jack Coler and Ronald Williams were investigating an assault and robbery allegedly committed by Jimmy Eagle of Pine Ridge. The theft reportedly involved a pair of boots. The agents came under rifle fire from a pickup matching the description of the vehicle supposedly driven by Jimmy Eagle and called for backup. Both agents were killed, as was one of the shooters, Joe Stuntz.

A suspect in the crime, Leonard Peltier, an AIM activist, was arrested by the Royal Canadian Mounted Police in February 1976, extradited to the United States, tried and convicted, and in April 1977 sentenced to two consecutive life terms for the murders of Coler and Williams. Peltier is still in prison, but his conviction has been highly controversial. Many believe that he was falsely convicted based on fraudulent testimony and that he is essentially a political prisoner.

Leonard Crow Dog had been charged with interfering with federal officials because of an incident during the siege at Wounded Knee. Four agents pretending to be postal inspectors attempted to sneak into the compound during a truce but were caught and disarmed. Crow Dog lectured them on the reasons for the occupation before allowing the four to leave. However, he received a suspended sentence for these actions.

Then in March 1975, several Euro-Americans arrived at Crow Dog's home. After they used drugs openly and insulted Mary, Leonard ordered them to leave. One, a man named Pfersick, became violent but was subdued by several of Crow Dog's family and friends. Pfersick later charged Leonard with assault and battery, leading to a trial and his conviction the following January.

More was yet to come. On September 2, 1975, Robert Beck and William McCloskey arrived at the Crow Dog home, many believe at the instigation of the FBI. They drove through a fence into the Crow Dogs' yard. Leonard Crow Dog's nephew Frank Running, who had earlier been assaulted by Beck, and others beat up the intruders. Beck and McCloskey subsequently filed charges of assault and battery against Crow Dog.

Four days after the Beck and McCloskey incident, on September 5, a large number of FBI agents and U.S. marshals launched an assault on the Crow Dog home as well as on the home of Leonard's parents and the nearby Running home. According to Mary Brave Bird, one of the reasons for the military-type raid was that the FBI believed that Peltier might be hiding with Leonard Crow Dog.

Peter Matthiessen, writing in his book *In the Spirit of Crazy Horse*, describes the raid this way:

> The morning of September 5, an air-land-and-river operation had descended at daybreak on the Crow Dog and Running properties, in a massive racketing of helicopters that swept in over the dawn trees. More than fifty FBI agents in

combat dress, with four large helicopters, military vehicles, trucks, vans, cars, and even rubber boats—presumably to prevent aquatic escapes down the narrow creek called the Little White River—surrounded the houses and tents, shouting, "This is the FBI! Come out with your hands up!" No one was given time to dress—Crow Dog himself was marched out naked—and even the small frightened children were lined up against walls as the agents ransacked and all but wrecked every house, tent, cabin, and car on both properties.[8]

Mary Brave Bird puts the invading number even higher:

They came one hundred and eighty-five men strong, marshals, agents, SWAT teams, making an Omaha Beach-type assault on the home of a single medicine man.[9]

She offers very personal details of the raid, describing how agents threw her son, Pedro, across the room. Another threatened to shoot her, and two agents put their guns against her head.

A number of other people were also taken away, including a close friend of Brave Bird's, Annie Mae Aquash. On the way to Pierre, South Dakota, the state capital, agents stopped so that Leonard Crow Dog could relieve himself by the side of the road. They tossed a gun at his feet and dared him to pick it up, taunting him with the threat of spending the rest of his life behind bars. Despite the massive operation, the only actual charge was that Crow Dog had in some way been responsible for McCloskey's broken jaw. The arrest of her husband would soon propel Brave Bird into very public actions to try to obtain his release. She never again would be a strictly private person.

Fighting the System

Leonard Crow Dog was subsequently convicted at three trials and received sentences totaling 23 years. He was moved repeatedly as a prisoner. Brave Bird lists the places of incarceration as "Pennington County Jail in Rapid City; Pierre, South Dakota; legendary Deadwood in the Black Hills; Minnehaha County Jail in Sioux Falls; Oxford and Cedar Rapids in Iowa; Terre Haute in Indiana; Leavenworth in Kansas; Chicago; Sioux City in Iowa; Lewisburg in Pennsylvania; Richmond in Virginia; and for a short time a holding tank in New York City."[10]

Mary followed her husband as well as she could, although both she and their attorneys had difficulty even keeping track of where he was being held at any given moment. Fortunately, various organizations and prominent individuals helped. The National Council of Churches, Amnesty International, and other organizations contributed money to Crow Dog's defense. A team of lawyers that included William Kunstler and Sandy Rosen worked hard on appeals. Such celebrities as Harry Belafonte, Marlon Brando, Ossie Davis, Ruby Dee, and Rip Torn got involved. Richard Erdoes, a book and magazine illustrator, and his wife served as defense coordinators and also took Brave

Bird into their apartment in New York City. She, along with baby Pedro, stayed with the Erdoes for about a year to be relatively close to her husband when he was being held in the prison at Lewisburg.

Crow Dog suffered a level of discrimination in prison that in certain ways exceeded what most prisoners faced. While Christian and Jewish inmates were allowed access to clergy and their sacred books, American Indians who practiced traditional spirituality often found themselves denied the means with which to practice their religion. Crow Dog, for example, was denied his sacred pipe. When the warden at Terre Haute finally was forced to comply with his request for his pipe, the warden still withheld the red willow tobacco that he used in it, claiming that the tobacco might be an illegal drug.

Brave Bird did far more than simply follow her husband from prison to prison. She gave talks on his behalf, granted interviews to the press, consulted with lawyers, and raised money to help defray legal expenses. Leonard Crow Dog was finally released pending appeal in the spring of 1976, but his appeal was ultimately rejected. After three months of uncertain freedom, Crow Dog returned to prison. The extensive legal activity and outpouring of support, much of it due to Mary's consistent efforts, ultimately prevailed, however. Judge Robert Merhige, who had presided over Crow Dog's assault-and-battery cases, reduced his sentence to time served.

Three more months passed before Leonard Crow Dog was released on parole in 1977, having served 27 months behind bars. Brave Bird and her husband returned to Rosebud amid great jubilation, and the former prisoner was honored with music, dance, and feasting. Brave Bird also was honored for her great struggle against a system that had imprisoned her husband. Led forward by two medicine men, Wallace Black Elk and Bill Eagle Feathers, she was given an eagle plume for her hair and a new name: Ohitika Win, which means Brave Woman. *Ohitika Woman* would become the title of her second book of memoirs.

TROUBLE IN PARADISE

Marital Difficulties

Back at Crow Dog's Paradise, the name of the Crow Dog home complex, which included Henry Crow Dog's main house as well as the small building in which Leonard and Mary Crow Dog lived, life continued to be a struggle for Mary. Leonard Crow Dog eked out a living by conducting religious rituals throughout the country. Because he did not charge for his services, he had to rely on support from foundation grants and friends.

There was much traveling for the growing family, with the children not able to receive much time in school. On one trip, they met the director Oliver Stone, who was working on the film *The Doors* about Jim Morrison. The Crow Dogs were invited to appear in the film and traveled to San Francisco, participating in a dance scene.

In addition to the traveling, there was little privacy back home. People were constantly appearing at the door to ask for money or some other sort of help. Mary describes her deteriorating relationship with Crow Dog in *Ohitika Woman*. The couple gradually grew apart, living together but no longer sharing the same bed. The small building in which they lived was actually stolen, and the family made do, at times camping outside, later sleeping in a U-Haul trailer.

The growing family came to include, in addition to Mary's first child Pedro, three more children with Crow Dog. There were two boys—Anwah, born in 1979; and Leonard Eldon, called Junior, then June, and ultimately June Bug, who was born in 1981—and a girl, Jennifer. Life became no easier with the growing family, and Brave Bird reached the difficult decision to leave her husband. She moved several times, with Leonard in pursuit trying to persuade her to return. Her odyssey took her to Marshall, Minnesota; Sioux Falls, South Dakota; Omaha, where she had an unsuccessful and very brief reunion with her father; Denver; Tucson; and Phoenix. At Phoenix, Crow Dog caught up with her, and they lived together there for about three years.

Descent into Alcohol

Brave Bird began drinking heavily. She vividly and frankly describes in her second book this period of her life. The drinking accelerated as she returned to Rosebud. During the stretch from summer of 1990 to spring 1991, she was consistently, in her own words, "in a haze."[11]

The appearance of her first book did not deter Brave Bird from immersing herself in alcohol. Richard Erdoes, before meeting Brave Bird, had collaborated with a medicine man named John Fire Lame Deer on the book *Lame Deer, Seeker of Visions*. The book proved commercially successful, and Erdoes' publisher approached him about doing another book. At the time, Brave Bird was staying with Erdoes and his wife to be near her incarcerated husband, and a book about her life seemed like a natural project.

Erdoes and Brave Bird worked together taping and transcribing the story of her life. After Leonard's release and the couple's return to Rosebud, Erdoes continued to work on the manuscript, pulling it together from the many tapes that had been recorded. The editor, however, had a change of heart regarding the finished manuscript, which he considered too politically controversial. For more than 10 years, the manuscript awaited a publisher. Finally, in 1989, an editor at Grove Press became interested and published the book in 1990. This account of Brave Bird's life until 1977 became a best-seller, won the American Book Award, and was made into a film, *Lakota Woman, Siege at Wounded Knee* (1994) produced by Jane Fonda for Turner Network Television (TNT).

Publication of *Lakota Woman* led to a book tour for Brave Bird. In New York, she went out drinking before an interview; she was sober for interviews in Washington, D.C., and for an interview with talk-show host Larry King. Back in her hotel, however, she drank heavily from the liquor in her room's mini-bar and was still feeling the effects of her drinking during interviews back in New York at the Grove offices.

Then came an automobile accident that almost resulted in Brave Bird's death. On March 28, 1991, back on the Rosebud Reservation, she was driving drunk after an evening of partying. On a gravel road, she lost control of her car and hit a utility pole. She details her injuries as six broken ribs (including one that punctured a lung and another that cut into her aorta), a nearly severed ear, and multiple cuts on her face. Brave Bird was flown from the local hospital to one in Sioux Falls, where her mother had a priest administer the last rites. Surgery was performed to repair the aorta, and a series of operations included removal of one of her ovaries. Finally, after a month in the hospital, she was released.

Even after the accident, Brave Bird acknowledges, she continued drinking. That began to change, however, when a friend of hers, Pewee Leader Charge— a Vietnam veteran, poet, and artist—committed suicide, the victim of alcoholism and depression. His death brought home to Mary the realization that drinking simply made her more depressed.

A New Beginning

On August 24, 1991, Brave Bird married Rudi Olguin, a Chicano who had been engaged in working for Chicano rights. He also had become associated with the American Indian Movement. Because her marriage to Leonard Crow Dog had been in an Indian ceremony, one not recognized by civil authorities, she did not need to obtain a legal divorce from her first husband.

Olguin had become a close friend of Mary's sister Barbara and Barbara's husband, Jim. During his visits to them, he and his future wife had become acquainted. Mary and Rudi moved to Phoenix, but after a few months returned to Rosebud with her children. Although Brave Bird had been told after her accident that she could not become pregnant again, in fact she did just that after her marriage to Olguin. When the time came for the birth, there was no pediatrician at the Rosebud hospital, so she had to be flown to a hospital at Yankton to deliver her child. Brave Bird (who dropped the Crow Dog name after separating from Leonard) chose for their daughter a name recommended by Barbara—Summer Rose. A second child was eventually born to the couple and named after Rudi.

Brave Bird and Olguin later separated. *Ohitika Woman* makes it clear, however, that Brave Bird's second marriage played an important role in her healing from her extended battle with alcohol.

CONTINUING THE STRUGGLE

Big Mountain

Brave Bird remained a strong advocate for Indian religious traditions. She conducted sweat baths, conducting her first one at Big Mountain, also known as

Black Mesa, in Navajo country in Arizona. That commitment to Indian religion, she wrote in *Ohitika Woman*, is central to her life. It is part of her heritage, an integral dimension of who she is, and therefore inseparable from her other efforts to reclaim basic Indian rights and Indian culture.

An especially significant battle that Brave Bird took on both spiritually and politically was at Big Mountain. Big Mountain lies in both traditional Navajo (more accurately known as Diné) and Hopi land. As a "joint land use area," as Brave Bird explains in her *Ohitika Woman*, the area was long shared by the two peoples for pasturing their sheep. In addition, the area included substantial deposits of both coal and uranium. The Peabody Energy Company, formerly known as the Peabody Western Coal Company, contracted with the Navajo nation in 1964 for mineral rights and for the right to use water from an underground aquifer to transport the coal to a Nevada generating station that produces electricity. Peabody added a contractual arrangement with the Hopis two years later.

The aquifer, however, also serves as the primary water supply (for drinking, farming, and watering animals) for both tribes. Considerable opposition existed among the rank-and-file Navajos and Hopis against the decisions by their tribal leaders to enter into the agreements with Peabody. Further anger arose when a federal relocation plan was developed to move Navajos and Hopis, mainly into nonreservation towns.

Brave Bird was among those who responded to the Navajos' call for help. She participated in political action, such as removing fences around mining areas, lying in front of bulldozers, and publicizing what was happening at Big Mountain. She also helped bring Sun Dances to the region in the 1980s; along with organizing sweat baths during these rituals, she led and taught Sun Dance songs. She was one of the dancers in 1987 and 1988 and participated both times in piercings. She describes the initial piercing, the first that she had undergone in about six years, in *Ohitika Woman*:

> They took me to the sacred pole and I stretched out beneath it, face down. A Big Mountain Navajo woman, Sarah Katenay, pierced me with a skewer on one side, high up on my back. A young mixed-blood guy, my own age, pierced me on the other side. They pierced me real deep. They attached ropes to the skewers in my flesh and threw them over the crotch of the tree, and men on the other side pulled me up, ever so slowly. I was hanging there for a while, suspended in the air, about seven or eight feet above the ground. I had an eagle wing in each hand and fanned the air with it, hoping that the movement would make me break free. Suddenly, the skewer on my right side broke and I was spinning around wildly, like a tumbleweed in a whirlwind. Finally the other side broke. I was pretty high up in the air and all I could think about was to try landing on my feet.[12]

Brave Bird repeated the piercing the following year after having a vision of a dancing red horse. This time, the rope was thrown over the crotch of the tree and tied to a horse. The horse was slowly walked away from the tree, pulling Brave Bird into the air, and then ridden back to the tree, jerking her and

Women of All Red Nations

Women of All Red Nations (WARN) was founded in 1974 by Madonna Gilbert, a former state coordinator for the American Indian Movement, and a number of other Indian women activists. The group hoped to fill an important need by focusing on issues confronting Indian women, such as inadequate health care, denial of reproductive rights, domestic violence, and a lack of educational opportunities.

WARN increasingly became involved in other issues as well, such as trying to protect the sacred Black Hills of South Dakota from extensive coal, gas, and uranium mining as well as from development projects that threatened the water supply for Indians and non-Indians alike. Its members also became deeply concerned about the large number of spontaneous abortions and birth defects occurring at Pine Ridge Reservation in South Dakota.

WARN, finding that many of its goals relate directly to other groups as well, has formed alliances with such organizations as the National Organization for Women and has established particular solidarity with other minority women.

applying pressure to the skewers. After this action was repeated several times, the horse, according to Brave Bird, started dancing, and the movements finally caused the skewers to break through her skin.

Despite Brave Bird's efforts and those of many others, the mining continued. The Peabody web site currently notes with pride its Kayenta Mine on Black Mesa and the 8 million tons of coal the mine supplies annually to the Navajo Generating Station. The adjacent Black Mesa Mine is not running at this time.

Finally, the Land

The land, especially the Black Hills of South Dakota, has long been sacred to Lakotas. Because of efforts to strip the land of coal, uranium, and other minerals, the land, from the perspective of the Lakotas, is under serious attack. Various organizations—among them the Black Hills Alliance, Women of All the Red Nations (WARN), and the American Indian Movement (AIM)—have tried to preserve the Black Hills as well as reservation and nonreservation land throughout the areas that lie within the American Indians' traditional cultural homes. Brave Bird has been part of that effort.

Looking at her life as a grandmother who has fought many battles, Brave Bird writes that she wants her children to "understand what it means to be Indian." To do so, she believes, she must fight for the land, by being an environmentalist. If the term "environmentalist" sounds non-Indian, she quickly corrects that possible misconception. "[I]t is over the environment," she says, "that the last Indian Wars will be fought."[13]

NOTES

1. Mary Crow Dog, with Richard Erdoes, *Lakota Woman* (1990; New York: HarperCollins, 1991) 15.
2. St. Francis Mission. <http://www.sfmission.org>.
3. *Lakota Woman* 84.
4. Dennis Banks, with Richard Erdoes, *Ojibwa Warrior: Dennis Banks and the Rise of the American Indian Movement* (Norman: University of Oklahoma Press, 2004) 139.
5. *Lakota Woman* 93.
6. *Lakota Woman* 98.
7. *Lakota Woman* 176.
8. Peter Matthiessen, *In the Spirit of Crazy Horse: The Story of Leonard Peltier and the FBI's War on the American Indian Movement* (1983; New York: Penguin Books, 1992) 224–25.
9. *Lakota Woman* 218.
10. *Lakota Woman* 224.
11. Mary Brave Bird, with Richard Erdoes, *Ohitika Woman* (New York: Grove Press, 1993) 163.
12. *Ohitika Woman* 130.
13. *Ohitika Woman* 274.

RECOMMENDED READING

Banks, Dennis, with Richard Erdoes. *Ojibwa Warrior: Dennis Banks and the Rise of the American Indian Movement.* Norman: University of Oklahoma Press, 2004.

Brave Bird, Mary, with Richard Erdoes. *Lakota Woman.* 1990. New York: Harper-Collins, 1991.

Brave Bird, Mary, with Richard Erdoes. *Ohitika Woman.* New York: Grove Press, 1993.

Lakota Woman, Siege at Wounded Knee. Dir. Frank Pierson. Turner Home Entertainment, 1994.

Mankiller, Wilma, and Michael Wallis. *Mankiller: A Chief and Her People.* 1993. New York: St. Martin's Griffin, 1994.

Matthiessen, Peter. *In the Spirit of Crazy Horse: The Story of Leonard Peltier and the FBI's War on the American Indian Movement.* 1983. New York: Penguin Books, 1992.

Bibliography

PRINT

Adams, Alexander B. *Geronimo: A Biography*. New York: G. P. Putnam's Sons, 1971.

Ambrose, Stephen E. *Crazy Horse and Custer: The Parallel Lives of Two American Warriors*. 1975. New York: Anchor Books, 1996.

Banks, Dennis, with Richard Erdoes. *Ojibwa Warrior: Dennis Banks and the Rise of the American Indian Movement*. Norman: University of Oklahoma Press, 2004.

Bemrose, John. *Reminiscences of the Second Seminole War*. Ed. John K. Mahon. Gainesville: University of Florida Press, 1966.

Betzinez, Jason, with Wilbur Sturtevant Nye. *I Fought with Geronimo*. Harrisburg, PA: Stackpole, 1959.

Black Hawk. *An Autobiography*. Ed. Donald Jackson. 1955. Urbana: University of Illinois Press, 1990.

Bourne, Russell. *The Red King's Rebellion: Racial Politics in New England 1675–1678*. New York: Atheneum, 1990.

Brand, Johanna. *The Life and Death of Anna Mae Aquash*. 2nd ed. Toronto: James Lorimer, 1993.

Brave Bird, Mary, with Richard Erdoes. *Lakota Woman*. 1990. New York: Harper-Collins, 1991.

Brave Bird, Mary, with Richard Erdoes. *Ohitika Woman*. New York: Grove Press, 1993.

Bray, Kingsley M. *Crazy Horse: A Lakota Life*. Norman: University of Oklahoma Press, 2006.

Britt, Albert. "King Philip: The Wampanoag Mystery." *Great Indian Chiefs: A Study of Indian Leaders in the Two Hundred Year Struggle to Stop the White Advance*. 1938. Freeport, NY: Books for Libraries Press, 1969. 29–66.

Brown, Dee Alexander. *Bury My Heart at Wounded Knee: An Indian History of the American West*. 4th ed. New York: H. Holt, 2007.

Calloway, Colin G. *Crown and Calumet: British–Indian Relations, 1783–1815*. Norman: University of Oklahoma Press, 1987.

Calloway, Colin G. *The Shawnees and the War for America*. The Penguin Library of American Indian History. New York: Viking, 2007.

Cave, Alfred A. "The Delaware Prophets." *Prophets of the Great Spirit: Native American Revitalization Movements in Eastern North America.* Lincoln: University of Nebraska Press, 2006. 11–44.

Chavers, Dean. *Modern American Indian Leaders: Their Lives and Their Works.* 2 vols. Lewiston, NY: Edwin Mellen Press, 2007.

Cheatham, Kae. *Dennis Banks: Native American Activist. Native American Biographies.* Berkeley Heights, NJ: Enslow Publishers, 1997.

Chief Joseph. *Chief Joseph's Own Story.* St. Paul: Great Northern Railway, 1925.

Clum, Woodworth. *Apache Agent: The Story of John P. Clum.* 1936. Lincoln: University of Nebraska Press, 1978.

Debo, Angie. *Geronimo: The Man, His Time, His Place.* Norman: University of Oklahoma Press, 1976.

Dowd, Gregory Evans. *War Under Thunder: Pontiac, the Indian Nations and the British Empire.* 2002. Baltimore: Johns Hopkins University Press, 2004.

Drake, Benjamin. *Life of Tecumseh, and of His Brother the Prophet; with a Historical Sketch of the Shawanoe Indians.* 1841. New York: Arno Press and *The New York Times*, 1969.

Eckert, Allan W. *A Sorrow in Our Heart: The Life of Tecumseh.* 1992. New York: Bantam Books, 1993.

Edmunds, R. David. *The Shawnee Prophet.* 1983. Lincoln: University of Nebraska Press, 1985.

Edmunds, R. David. *Tecumseh and the Quest for Indian Leadership.* Boston: Little, Brown, 1984.

Faulk, Odie B. *The Geronimo Campaign.* New York: Oxford University Press, 1969.

Gatewood, Charles B. *Lt. Charles Gatewood and His Apache Wars Memoir.* Ed. Louis Kraft. Lincoln: University of Nebraska Press, 2005.

Geronimo. *Geronimo: His Own Story.* Ed. S. M. Barrett. Newly edited with Introduction and Notes by Frederick Turner. 1970. New York: Meridian, 1996.

Gilpin, Alec R. *The War of 1812 in the Old Northwest.* East Lansing: Michigan State University Press, 1958.

Gray, John S. *Centennial Campaign: The Sioux War of 1876.* Ft. Collins, CO: Old Army Press, 1976.

Greene, Jerome A. *Nez Perce Summer, 1877: The U.S. Army and the Nee-Me-Poo Crisis.* Helena: Montana Historical Society Press, 2000.

Hardorff, Richard G., ed. *The Surrender and Death of Crazy Horse: A Source Book About a Tragic Episode in Lakota History.* Spokane: Arthur H. Clark, 1998.

Hartley, William, and Ellen Hartley. *Osceola: The Unconquered Indian.* New York: Hawthorn Books, 1973.

Hendricks, Steve. *The Unquiet Grave: The FBI and the Struggle for the Soul of Indian Country.* 2006. New York: Thunder's Mouth Press, 2007.

Howard, Helen Addison. *Saga of Chief Joseph.* 1941. Lincoln: University of Nebraska Press, 1978.

Howard, Oliver O. *My Life and Experiences Among Our Hostile Indians.* 1907. New York: Da Capo Press, 1972.

Howard, Oliver O. *Nez Perce Joseph: An Account of His Ancestors, His Lands, His Confederates, His Enemies, His Murders, His War, His Pursuit and Capture.* 1881. New York: Da Capo Press, 1972.

Hubbard, William. *A Narrative of the Troubles with the Indians in New-England* (1677). Ed. Samuel G. Drake as *The History of the Indian Wars in New England from the First Settlement to the Termination of the War with King Philip, in 1677.* 2 vols. 1865. New York: B. Franklin, 1971.

Jennings, Francis. *Empire of Fortune: Crowns, Colonies, and Tribes in the Seven Years War in America.* New York: Norton, 1988.

Josephy, Alvin M., Jr. *The Nez Perce Indians and the Opening of the Northwest.* New Haven: Yale University Press, 1965.

Jung, Patrick J. *The Black Hawk War of 1832.* Norman: University of Oklahoma Press, 2007.

Kadlecek, Edward, and Mabell Kadlecek. *To Kill an Eagle: Indian Views on the Last Days of Crazy Horse.* 1981. Boulder, CO: Johnson Books, 2008.

Laumer, Frank. *Dade's Last Command.* Gainesville: University Press of Florida, 1995.

Leach, Douglas Edward. *Flintlock and Tomahawk: New England in King Philip's War.* 1958. New York: Norton, 1966.

Library of American Indian History. New York: Penguin, 2007.

MacEwan, Grant. *Sitting Bull: The Years in Canada.* Edmonton: Hurtig Publishers, 1973.

Magnuson, Stew. *The Death of Yellow Thunder and Other True Stories from the Nebraska–Pine Ridge Border Towns.* Lubbock: Texas Tech University Press, 2008.

Mahan, Bruce E. *Old Fort Crawford and the Frontier.* 1926. Prairie du Chien, WI: Prairie du Chien Historical Society, 2000.

Mahon, John K. *History of the Second Seminole War: 1835–1842.* Gainesville: University of Florida Press, 1967.

Mankiller, Wilma, and Michael Wallis. *Mankiller: A Chief and Her People.* 1993. New York: St. Martin's Griffin, 1994.

Matthiessen, Peter. *In the Spirit of Crazy Horse: The Story of Leonard Peltier and the FBI's War on the American Indian Movement.* 1983. New York: Penguin Books, 1992.

McLaughlin, Benjamin. *In Black Hawk's Footsteps: A Trail Guide to Monuments, Museums, and Battlefields of the Black Hawk War of 1832.* 3rd ed. Santa Fe: B. McLaughlin Publishing, 2005.

McMurtry, Larry. *Crazy Horse.* New York: Lipper/Viking, 1999.

McWhorter, Lucullus Virgil. *Yellow Wolf: His Own Story.* 1940. Caldwell, ID: Caxton Printers, 1948.

Means, Russell, with Marvin J. Wolf. *Where White Men Fear to Tread.* New York: St. Martin's Griffin, 1995.

Miles, Nelson A. *Personal Recollections and Observations of General Nelson A. Miles.* 1896. New York: Da Capo Press, 1969.

Miles, Nelson A. *Serving the Republic: Memoirs of the Civil and Military Life of Nelson A. Miles.* 1911. Freeport, NY: Books for Libraries Press, 1971.

Nerburn, Kent. *Chief Joseph and the Flight of the Nez Perce: The Untold Story of an American Tragedy.* New York: HarperSanFrancisco, 2005.

Nichols, Roger L. *Black Hawk and the Warrior's Path.* American Biographical History Series. Wheeling, IL: Harlan Davidson, 1992.

Olson, James S., and Raymond Wilson. *Native Americans in the Twentieth Century.* 1984. Urbana: University of Illinois Press, 1986.

Parkman, Francis. *The Conspiracy of Pontiac.* 10th ed. New York: Collier Books, 1962.

Peckham, Howard H. *Pontiac and the Indian Uprising.* 1947. Chicago: University of Chicago Press, 1961.

Philbrick, Nathaniel. *Mayflower: A Story of Courage, Community, and War.* New York: Viking, 2006.

Quaife, Milo Milton, ed. *The Siege of Detroit in 1763: The Journal of Pontiac's Conspiracy and John Rutherfurd's Narrative of a Captivity.* Chicago: R. R. Donnelley, 1958.

Reinhardt, Akim D. *Ruling Pine Ridge: Oglala Lakota Politics from the IRA to Wounded Knee.* Lubbock: Texas Tech University Press, 2007.

Rielly, Edward J. *Sitting Bull: A Biography.* Westport, CT: Greenwood Press, 2007.

Rowlandson, Mary. *A True History of the Captivity and Restoration of Mrs. Mary Rowlandson. Women's Indian Captivity Narratives.* Ed. Kathryn Zabelle Derounian-Stodola. New York: Penguin Books, 1998. 1–51.

Sajna, Mike. *Crazy Horse: The Life Behind the Legend.* 2000. Edison, NJ: Castle Books, 2005.

Sandoz, Mari. *Crazy Horse: The Strange Man of the Oglalas.* 1942. Lincoln: University of Nebraska Press, 1961.

Sayer, John William. *Ghost Dancing the Law: The Wounded Knee Trials.* Cambridge, MA: Harvard University Press, 1997.

Schultz, Eric B., and Michael J. Tougias. *King Philip's War: The History and Legacy of America's Forgotten Conflict.* 1999. Woodstock, VT: Countryman Press, 2000.

Simpson, Alan, and Mary Simpson, eds. *Diary of King Philip's War 1675–1676*, by Colonel Benjamin Church. Chester, CT: Pequot Press, 1975.

Sitting Bull. *Three Pictographic Autobiographies of Sitting Bull*, ed. M. W. Stirling. Washington, DC: Smithsonian Institution, 1938.

Smith, Paul Chaat, and Robert Allen Warrior. *Like a Hurricane: The Indian Movement from Alcatraz to Wounded Knee.* New York: New Press, 1996.

Sprague, John T. *The Origin, Progress, and Conclusion of the Florida War.* 1848. Gainesville: University of Florida Press, 1964.

Stern, Kenneth S. *Loud Hawk: The United States Versus the American Indian Movement.* Norman: University of Oklahoma Press, 1994.

Sugden, John. *Tecumseh: A Life.* New York: Henry Holt, 1997.

Sweeney, Edwin R. *Mangas Coloradas: Chief of the Chiricahua Apaches.* Norman: University of Oklahoma Press, 1998.

Tebbel, John, and Keith Jennison. *The American Indian Wars.* 1960. Edison, NJ: Castle Books, 2003.

Thayer, Crawford B., ed. *Hunting a Shadow: The Search for Black Hawk. Black Hawk War Eye-Witness Series.* Menasha, WI: Banta Press, 1981.

Todish, Timothy J., and Todd E. Harburn. *A "Most Troublesome Situation": The British Military and the Pontiac Indian Uprising of 1763–1764.* Fleischmanns, NY: Purple Mountain Press, 2006.

Trail of Broken Treaties: B.I.A. I'm Not Your Indian Anymore. Rev. Rooseveltown, NY: Akwesasne Notes, 1974.

Trask, Kerry A. *Black Hawk: The Battle for the Heart of America.* New York: Henry Holt, 2007.

Utley, Robert M. *The Lance and the Shield: The Life and Times of Sitting Bull.* 1993. New York: Ballantine Books, 1994.

Vestal, Stanley. *Sitting Bull: Champion of the Sioux.* 2nd ed. 1957. Norman: University of Oklahoma Press, 1989.

Voices from Wounded Knee, 1973. Rooseveltown, NY: Akwesasne Notes, 1974.

West, Elliott. *The Last Indian War: The Nez Perce Story*. New York: Oxford University Press, 2009.

Whitney, Ellen M., ed. *The Black Hawk War 1831–1832*. 4 vols. Springfield: Illinois State Historical Library, 1970–78.

Wickman, Patricia Riles. *Osceola's Legacy*. Rev. ed. Tuscaloosa: University of Alabama Press, 2006.

Yenne, Bill. *Sitting Bull*. Yardley, PA: Westholme Publishing, 2008.

NONPRINT

American Indian Movement. <http://www.aimovement.org>.

Buffalo Bill Historical Center. <http://www.bbhc.org/home/index/cfm> (information about the Plains Indians, William F. Cody, and other aspects of Western life).

Crazy Horse: The Last Warrior. Biography Series. A&E Television Networks, 1993. DVD.

Geronimo: The Last Renegade. Executive producers, Craig Haffner and Donna E. Lusitana. A&E Television Networks, 1996.

Lakota Woman, Siege at Wounded Knee. Dir. Frank Pierson. Turner Home Entertainment, 1994.

Last Stand at Little Big Horn. Dir. Paul Stekler. *American Experience*. WGBH Educational Foundation and Thirteen/WNET, 1992.

Little Bighorn National Monument. <http://www.nps./libi/index.htm>.

Ohio Historical Society. "Tecumseh" (and related links). *Ohio History Central: An Online Encyclopedia of Ohio History*. <http://www.ohiohistorycentral.org/entry.php?rec=373>.

Paha Sapa: Struggle for the Black Hills. HBO, 1993. Mystic Fire Video, 1998. VHS.

Russell Means. <http://wwww.russellmeansfreedom.com>.

Standing Rock Sioux Tribe. <http://www.standingrock.org/> (information about the history of the Sioux and the reservation).

Index

In the following entries, "b" indicates boxed material and "f"indicates a figure.

Abenaki, Maine, 3, 15–16

Abiákî (Abèca, "Sam Jones"), Creek medicine man, 93, 95–96, 103

Abourezk, Senator James, 262, 277, 287, 293

Adams Henry (Hank), Assiniboine activist, 283b, 284

Additional Treaty (1833), Indian Removal treaty, 95

Adobe Walls, 244b

Akicitas, warrior societies, 111

Alcatraz, 237; 1970s occupation, 250, 256, 276–77

Alderman, Wampanoag informant, 14–15

Aleshire, Peter, 222

Algonquian language family tribes, 3

Allen, Charles Wesley, 152b

Alligator, Creek war leader, 99, 101, 103

Allison, Senator William Boyd, 159

Allison Commission, 159

Alope, Geronimo's wife, 217–18

American Fur Company, 74; whiskey trade, 75

American Indian Movement (AIM), 250, 253–60, 270, 274, 277–79,
306; distress signal emblem, 257, 281, 303f; *Mayflower II* demonstration, 257, 280; Mount Rushmore takeover, 256; Raymond Yellow Thunder murder, 257, 280–81; Trail of Broken Treaties, 258–60, 282–84, 306–8; Wounded Knee Occupation (1973), 260–64, 286–89

American Indian Religious Freedom Act, 255

Amherst, Sir Jeffery, 22

Amherstburg, Canada, 48, 53, 57, 59

Andros, Edmund, New York governor, 7, 11, 16

Anishinabeg, 25

Annawon, Wampanoag warrior, 15

Apache, 216–17

Aquash (Pictou), Anna Mae, 263, 266, 268, 313

Aquash, Nogeeshik, 263

Arapaho, 150, 152

Astor, John Jacob, 74

Atkinson, General Henry, 76, 80

Autobiography of Red Cloud (Paul), 152b

Awashons, Sakonnet chief, 8, 16

Bad Cob, Tom, 263, 288

Bad Heart Buffalo, Amos, 143f

Bad Heart Bull, Sarah, 260, 261, 285, 309

Bad Heart Bull, Vincent, 293

Bad Heart Bull, Wesley, 250, 260, 265, 285, 309

Bailey, Major David, 81

Baker, Major Eugene M., 118, 156

Baldwin, Lt. Frank D., 132

Banks, Dennis James (Nowa-Cumig), 249f, 279, 281, 284, 293; AIM, 253–61, 270; Custer trial, 265–66; early life, 250–51; imprisonment, 267–68; Pine Ridge Reservation, 268; sacred runs, 270; U.S. Air Force, 252–53; Wounded Knee Occupation, 262–64; Wounded Knee trial, 264–65

Barclay, Captain Robert, 59

Barrett, Stephen M., 245

Barron, Joseph, 49

Bascom, Lt. George, 222

Battle of Apache Pass, 222–24

Battle of Arrow Creek, 118, 156

Battle of Bear's Paw, 202

Battle of Black Point, 98

Battle of Bloody Bridge, 28

Battle of Brownstown, 54

Battle of Bushy Run, 29

Battle of Canyon Creek, 199

Battle of Cedar Creek, 131

Battle at Clearwater River, 192

Battle of Fallen Timbers, 44–45

Battle of Killdeer Mountain, 113

Battle of Little Bighorn, 125–30, 143f, 158–66

Battle of New Orleans, 73

Battle of Pecatonica, 82

Battle of Point Pleasant, 41

Battle of the Rosebud, 124–25, 160–63

Battle of Sink Hole, 73

Battle of the Thames, 59–60, 72

Battle of Tippecanoe, 52, 69–70

Battle of Wahoo Swamp, 101

Battle of Welika Pond, 101

Battle of White Bird Canyon, 191–92

Battle of Wolf Mountain, 167–68

Baylor, Confederate Colonel John B., 222

Bean, Lou, 261, 286

Bear's Paw, 202

Bear's Rib, 112

Bedonkohe Apache band, 217

Bellecourt, Clyde, 253, 255, 279, 281, 284

Bellecourt, Vernon, 279, 284

Bemrose, John, 96

Benteen, Captain Frederick, 126, 128–29, 163–64

Betzinez, Jason, 229, 233

Big Foot, 138b

Big Hole, Montana, 195–96

Big Indian Creek, attack, 82

Big Mountain, Black Mesa, 316–18

Bissonette, Gladys, 264, 288

Bissonette, Pedro, 261, 264, 285–86, 288

Bitterroot Mountains, Montana Territory, 194

Black Dog, Peoria chief, 34, 36

The Black Drink, Catlin painting, 105

Black Elk, Wallace, 262, 288

Black Elk Speaks, 253

Black Fish, Shawnee war chief, 41

Black Hawk (Makataimeshekiakiak), Sauk warrior, 58–59; autobiography, 85–86; British alliance, 69, 79; death of, 86; early life, 64–68; Fort Madison raid, 70; imprisonment, 84–85; retreat, 82–84; Saukenuk loss, 75–78; war, 79–82; War of 1812 involvement, 71–73; whiskey trade objections, 75

Black Hawk War of 1832, 63f, 79–84

Black Hills (*Paha Sapa*), Dakota
  Territory, 120, 147, 158–59;
  Crazy Horse Memorial, 178–79;
  Mount Rushmore takeover, 256
Black Hills Alliance, 294–95, 318
Black Hoof (Catahecassa), 47
Black Moon, Sitting Bull's cousin,
  115, 124
Black Shawl, Crazy Horse's wife,
  156, 169, 172
Bliss, Major John, 80
Blue Jacket, war chief, 45
Blue Snake, Seminole leader, 103
Boone, Daniel, 41
Bordeaux, Louis, translator, 173,
  175–76
Bouquet, Colonel Henry, 29, 31
Bourke, Captain John G., 161, 164,
  170, 235
Bowman, Colonel John, 41
Bozeman, John M., 150
Bozeman Trail, 116–17, 150–51
Braddock, Edward, 20
Bradford, William, Plymouth
  Colony governor, 4
Bradley, Lt. Colonel Luther P., 171,
  173–76
Bradstreet, Colonel John, 31
Brando, Marlon, 266, 283b
Brave Bird, Mary (Mary Ellen
  Moore, Mary Crow Dog), 263,
  304; AIM, 306–8; Black Hills
  Alliance, 318; early years, 304–6;
  FBI raid, 312–13; Native
  American Church, 308–9; Women
  of All Red Nations (WARN), 319;
  Wounded Knee, 309–11
Brave Bird, Robert, Mary Brave
  Bird's grandfather, 304
Bray, Kingsley M., 146–47
Brightman, Lee, 267
Brininstool, E. A., 173
British attitudes and policies, 21–22;
  Sauk alliance, 69, 79; Shawnee
  alliance, 53, 55b

Brock, Major General Isaac, 54, 56
Brotherton, Major David, 134–35
Brown, Edmund ("Jerry")
  Brown, Jr., 267
Brown, James, 6
Bruce, Louis, 259
Bruguier, Johnny, 132
Brulè Sioux, 145, 304
Brush, Captain Henry, 54
Buffalo Calf Road Woman,
  Cheyenne, 163b
Bureau of Indian Affairs (BIA):
  demonstrations, 257; occupation,
  259, 307–8. *See also* Trail of
  Broken Treaties
Burke, Captain Daniel, 175–76

Caballo, Juan (John Horse), 104
Camas Meadows, Idaho
  Territory, 197
Camp Robinson, 169, 171, 173, 175
Campbell, Captain Donald, 25–27
Canonchet, 12
Carleton, General James H., 223
Carlisle Indian Industrial School,
  243, 246
Carr, Colonel Eugene Asa, 230–31
Carrasco, General José María,
  217–18
Carter, Jimmy, 255
Casey, Captain James, 168
Cass, Lewis, Michigan Territory
  governor, 56, 75
Catch the Bear, 137–38
Catlin, George, 105
Cayuse, 183, 184
*Centennial Campaign: The Sioux
  War of 1876* (Gray), 165
Chaine, Isadore, Wyandot, 53, 55b
Chanku wakan (sacred road), into
  Canada, 133
Chapman, Ad, 210
Chappo, Geronimo's son, 237
Chato, Apache leader, 234–35, 237
Chattahoochee River, 91

Cheyenne, 117, 121, 150, 152, 167–68
Chickasaw, 50
Chief Elias, Chihenne leader, 222
Chief Joseph (Hin-mah-too-yah-lat-kekht, Thunder Rising in the Mountain), Nez Perce, 173, 181f, 182; Colville, 211–12; early life, 182–87; flight to Canada, 197–205; and General Howard, 188–89; Indian Territory, 209–11; Lolo Trail, 194–95; return, 206–8; war, 190–94; Yellowstone National Park, 197–99
Chief Moses, Columbia Nez Perce, 211
Chihuahua, Apache leader, 231, 234–35, 240
Chiksika, Tecumseh's brother, 42
Chippewa, 84, 250
Chiricahua Apache, 217; population by 1890, 243
Chiricahua Reservation, 228
Choctaw, 50
Church, Benjamin, 8, 12–13, 15; on death of Philip, 14
Clark, George Rogers, 42
Clark, William, 70, 73, 75–77
Clark's Fork Canyon, 198
Claus, William, 48
Clay, General Green, 58
Clearwater, Frank, 263, 289, 310
Cleveland, Grover, 241–43
Cleveland American Indian Center, 278
Clifford, Captain Walter, 134
Clinch, General Duncan, 100
Clum, John, agent, 227–28
Coacoochee, Philip's son, 103–4
Cochise, Chokonen Apache chief, 218, 221; death of, 227
Cochise Wars, 222–28. *See also* Geronimo
Cody, Buffalo Bill, 135
Cole, Hugh, 6

Cole, Colonel Nelson, 151
Coler, Jack, 265, 269, 312
Columbia (Sqinkquaius), Nez Perce, 211
Colville Reservation, 211–12
Comanche, 244b
A Concise Account of North America (Rogers), 34
Conner, General Patrick, 151
Conspiracy of Pontiac, The (Parkman), 20, 37
Conquering Bear, Brulè leader, 145–46
Consensus, 24, 206
Coppinger, José, Osceola's grandfather, 90
Cornstalk, Shawnee leader, 41
Covenant Chain, Iroquois/England, 31
Cow Island, Nez Perce crossing, 200–1
Crawford, Captain Emmett, 236–38
Crawford, Hugh, 34
Crazy Horse (Tasunke Witko, "Curly Hair"), 121–22, 125; burial, 177–78; captivity, 170–74; death of, 174–77; early years, 144–46; Indian wars, 148–50; Little Big Horn, 158–66; memorial, 178–79; reputation, 166–67; Shirt Wearer, 155–56; and Sitting Bull, 147, 154, 156, 166–67; surrender, 169–70; U.S. military wars, 150–54; warrior, 146–50
Creek, 50–51, 90; Florida population 1850s, 107
Creek War (1813–1814), 90–91
Croghan, George, 20, 32–33
Crook, General George: and Apache, 226, 234–36, 239–40, 243; and Sioux, 122, 124–25, 131, 159–63, 167, 172–74
Crow, 111, 112, 118, 120, 147, 155, 162, 198

Crow Dog, Henry, 255, 311
Crow Dog, Leonard, 255, 257, 262, 267, 285, 295, 304, 310; arrest, 311–13; imprisonment, 313–14
Crow Dog, Mary. *See* Brave Bird, Mary
Crow Foot, Sitting Bull's son, 137–38
Crozier, Leif N. F., Northwest Mounted Police, 134
Cuillerier, Alexis, 35–36
Cuillerier, Antoine, 26, 35
Curtis, Robert John, 105
Custer, Colonel George Armstrong, 120, 123, 126–28, 157–58, 160, 165; last stand, 129, 166
Custer (South Dakota), trial, 250, 265, 285, 293
Custer Died for Your Sins: An Indian Manifesto (Deloria), 287b

Dade's column, battle, 99
Daklugie, Asa, 246
Dakota Sioux, 112
Dalyell, Captain James, 28
Dancing Horseman, Crazy Horse's vision, 149–50
Davenport, George, 76–77
Davis, Lt. Britton, 236–37
Davis, Jefferson, 84, 222
Dawes Act (1887), 212b
de Belestre, François-Marie Picoté, 26, 35
De Smet, Fr. Peter John, 115–16
The Death of Raymond Yellow Thunder (Magnuson), 281
Debo, Angie, 218, 237
Delassus, Charles Dehault, Spanish governor of Louisiana, 68
Delaware, 30–31
Deloria, Vine, Jr., 283b, 286, 287b, 300–1
Dement, Major John, 82
Detroit, British–Shawnee attack on, 54–57

Dewolfe, M. A., 5
Dickson, Robert, 71
Diyim, Apache medicine man, 218
Dodge, Henry, 82–84
Dohnsay, Geronimo's daughter, 230, 240
Dowd, Gregory Evans, 21
D-Q University, 267
Drake, Benjamin, 44, 58, 72
Drumbeater, Jenny and Josh, Dennis Banks' grandparents, 250–251
Dudley, Colonel William, 57–58

Easton, John, 4, 7
Eckert, Allan W., 41, 60, 72
Edmunds, R. David, 48
Edwards, Ninian, 76
Elliott, Matthew, agent, 44, 50
Emathla, Charley, 98
Environmentalism, and Indian struggle, 319
Erdoes, Richard, 251, 315
Euro-Americans: expansionism, 30, 34, 46, 57, 61, 75–76, 184; fear of revitalization messages, 230; gaining mindset, 294; 1670s population, 3; treatment of native population, 4
Eustis, William, 49, 51
Eyre, Lt. Colonel E. E., 223

"Factory system" trading, 74
Feather, Theodora Louise, Russell Means' mother, 274
Federal termination and assimilation policy, 254b
Fetterman, Captain William J., 152–153
Fisher, Elizabeth (Betty), 26, 35
Fisher, James, 26
Fisk, Captain James L., 114
Five Nations, 30
Flatheads, 192, 195, 198
Flood, Louise, Mary Brave Bird's grandmother, 304

Florida, invasion of, 92
Flynt, Larry, 296
Fonda, Jane, 304, 315
Fools Crow, Frank, 261–62, 280, 286
Ford, R. Clyde, 24b
Forsyth, Lt. Colonel George, 232–33
Forsyth, Colonel James, 138b
Forsyth, Thomas, 75–77
Fort Abraham Lincoln, 207
Fort Apache, 230
Fort Armstrong, 73, 78, 80
Fort Berthold, 207
Fort Bowie, 224, 226, 239–40, 242
Fort Brooke, 103
Fort Buford, 117, 134, 207
Fort de Chartres, 26, 32, 36
Fort Dearborn, 56
Fort Defiance, Maumee River, 44
Fort Detroit, 25, 28, 43; siege, 27–28
Fort Dilts, 114
Fort Ellis, 120–21
Fort Fetterman, 161
Fort Harrison, 52
Fort King, 96
Fort Laramie, 146, 150–51. *See also* Treaty of Fort Laramie
Fort Leavenworth, 208
Fort Madison, 70
Fort Malden, 48, 54, 70
Fort Marion, 103–4, 242
Fort Meigs, 57–58, 71–72
Fort Mellon, 102
Fort Miami, 27–28, 44, 57–58
Fort Michilimackinac, 28, 43
Fort Monroe, Virginia, 85
Fort Moultrie, 104–5, 106b
Fort Niagara, 28–29, 31
Fort Pease, 121
Fort Peck, 132
Fort Phil Kearny, 151–52, 154
Fort Pickins, Florida, 243
Fort Pitt (Fort Duquesne), 28–29
Fort Presque Isle, 28, 31
Fort Recovery, 44–45

Fort Reno (Camp Connor), 151–54
Fort Stephenson, 58
Fort Washington, 43
Fort Yates, 139
Four Horns, Sitting Bull's uncle, 113, 115, 118, 127
Fox, Illinois, 49; population in 1845, 86; revenge, 79; Sioux attacks, 77
The Fox and the Whirlwind: General George Crook and Geronimo (Aleshire), 222
Fraser, Lieutenant Alexander, 32
Free, Mickey, 237
French, Indian alliance, 21–22
French and Indian War (1756–1763), 16, 20–21, 40
Frizzell, Kent, 263, 273f, 288
Fur trade, "factory system," 74

Gadsden, James, 94, 221
Gadsden Purchase, 221
Gage, Thomas, 31, 33
Gaines, Major General Edmund, 78, 101
Gaining mindset, 294
Gall, Hunkpapa chief, 115–16, 136
García, Colonel Lorenzo, 233
Garland, Brevet Major John, 85
Garment, Leonard, 259–60, 284
Garnett, Billy, 172
Gates, Hobart, 260, 285
Gatewood, Lt. Charles, 241
Geronimo (Goyahkla), 215f, 216; autobiography, 245–46; death of, 245; final breakout, 237–39; in Mexico, 231–35; return to reservation, 236–37; San Carlos Reservation, 228–31; surrender, 239–43; warrior, 216–27
Ghost Dance, 45, 136–37; resurrection, 262
Ghost Owing Ceremony, 177
Giago, Tim (Nanwika Kciiji), 269b
Gibbon, Colonel John, 126, 195–96
Gift giving, 22

Gilbert, Madonna, 318b
Gladwin, Major Henry, 19f, 25–29
Glegg, Captain John, 55
God Is Red (Deloria), 287b
Gold mining: Black Hills, 120, 167;
  New Mexico, 221
A Good Day to Die, Banks
  documentary, 270
Goslin, François, 26
Goulding, Captain Roger, 14
Graham, John, 96
Grant, Ulysses, 122, 159, 187
Gratiot, Henry, 80
Grattan Massacre, 146
Gray, John, 165
Gray Eagle, Clarence, 139
Great Sauk Trail, 50
Great Sioux Reservation,
  South Dakota, 256
Great Swamp Fight, 10
Green Corn Ceremony, 92–93
Greene, Jerome, 193
Gros Ventre (Atsina, Hidatsa), 148
Grouard, Frank, 121–22, 131, 160,
  167, 170, 173
Grummond, Lt. George, 152–53

Habitants, Detroit-area French
  population, 26–27
Hahtalekin, Palouse leader, 191, 196
Hajo, Coe, 104
Hamilton's Diggings, mining
  settlement, 74
Hamtramck, Major John, 43
Haozous, Sam, 218
Hare brothers, trial, 257–58, 281–82
Harmar, General Josiah, 43
Harney, General William, 102–3,
  146, 155
Harrington, M. R., 67b
Harrison, William Henry, 40, 47,
  49, 57, 68; Battle of Tippecanoe,
  52–53, 69–70; meeting with
  Tecumseh, 49–50
Hawkins, Benjamin, agent, 51

Hay, Lieutenant Jehu, 36
Hayes, Ira, Pima World War II
  veteran, 259
Hayes, Rutherford B., 210, meeting
  with Chief Joseph, 210
Hayt, A. E., 209
He Dog, 147, 159
Henry, Benjamin Tyler, 164b
Hernandez, Brigadier General
  Joseph, 104
Hicks, John (Euchee Billy), 95
High Backbone, 145, 148, 151–52
High Forehead, Miniconjou, 145–46
Hill, Tom, 204
Hinman, Elinor, 145
Homestead Act of 1862, 184
Hopi, 317
Hotchkiss guns, 203
Howard, Helen Addison, 186–87
Howard, General Oliver Otis, 188–
  90, 193–94, 204–5; Chief Joseph
  pursuit, 197–202; and Geronimo,
  226–27, 243
Hubbard, William, 6–7, 13
Hull, William, Michigan Territory
  governor, 53–54, 56
Hunkpapa, 110, 115; at Standing
  Rock Reservation, 136
Huron, gunboat, 26–28
Husis Kute, Nez Perce leader,
  191, 202

In the Spirit of Crazy Horse
  (Mathiessen), 312
Indian confederacy, 48–49
Indian Country Today, 269b
Indian graves reburial
  ceremonies, 269
Indian Removal Act (1830),
  94, 208b
Indian scouts, Fort Apache, 230–31
Indian Territory, 208b, 209
*Indian Wars: The Campaign for the
  American West* (Yenne), 163
Indians of All Tribes, 256

Inkpaduta, Dakota Sioux
leader, 113b
International Gathering for Survival
(1984), 294
International Indian Treaty Council,
Geneva (1977), 293
Iroquois League, 30–31
Iyeska, "half-breed,"308

Jackson, Andrew, 73, 79, 85, 208b;
Creek/Seminole Wars, 91–92;
presidency, 94
Jackson, J. W., 106b
Janklow, William, 265, 267–68,
277–78, 290–91
Jefferson, Thomas, 68
Jeffords, Thomas, 226–27, 230
Jessup, Brevet Major General
Thomas S., 102–3
Johnson, John, agent, 49
Johnson, Colonel Richard, 60
Johnson, Sir William, 20, 30–31,
33–35, 41
Jones, Hiram, agent, 209–10
Jones, Jim, 267
Jones, Sam. *See* Abiákî
Juana, Geronimo's mother, 217–18
Jumper, Creek war leader, 99,
101–3
Jumping Bull, Sitting Bull's brother,
111, 114, 124, 131, 137
Jumping Bull Ranch, shooting,
265–66
Jun, Nednai Apache chief, 218–19,
227, 230–31, 233–34, 236

Kamiah, Christian Nez Perce
settlement, 193–204
Katenay, Sarah, 317
Kaytennae, Apache leader, 235,
237, 239
Kelly, Fanny, 114
Kennington, Captain James, 175–76
Kenton, Simon, 43–44, 60
Keogh, Captain Myles W., 128

Keokuk, Sioux war chief, 76, 78,
80, 85
Kickapoos, 32, 49, 57
King, Thomas, Oneida chief, 31
King Philip (Metacom, Metacomet),
5. *See also* Philip
King Philip's War, 8–14, 15–16
Kirker, Thomas, Ohio governor,
47–48
Kneebingkemewoin, Black Hawk's
mother, 64
Kunstler, William, 264, 288

La Gouthrie, Edward, trader, 70
Lakotah, Republic of, 298–99
Lakota Sioux, 110, 137, 147, 152,
178; in Canada, 132–33; at
Standing Rock Reservation,
135–37
Lakota Woman (Brave Bird/Erdoes),
304–5, 311, 315
*Lakota Woman, Siege at Wounded
Knee* (1994), film, 315
Lakota women, Mount Rushmore
takeover, 256
Lalawethika, Tecumseh's brother,
42, 44–46
Lame Deer, John Fire, 255, 315
Lamont, Buddy, 263, 289
Land grants, War of 1812
veterans, 74
L'Anse aux Feuilles, 31
Lapwai reservation, 186, 189, 211
Larrabee, Nellie, 172
Last Stand Hill, 129
Lavalie, Louis, 133
Lawyer, Nez Perce treaty
signer, 186
Leach, Douglas Edward, 4
Leader Charge, Peewee, 316
LeClaire, Antoine, 76, 85
Lee, Lt. Jesse, 175
Leech Lake Chippewa
Reservation, 250
Lewis, Colonel Andrew, 41

Like a Hurricane: The Indian Movement from Alcatraz to Wounded Knee (Smith and Warrior), 277

Lincoln, Abraham, 81–82

Little Bighorn (Greasy Grass): attack, 127, 165; village, 125, 163

Littleton Twelve, 257

Loco, Chihenne leader, 226, 231–32, 235

Loesch, Harrison, 259, 283

Logan, Benjamin, 42

Lolo Trail, 194–95

Lone Man School, Pine Ridge Reservation, 268

Long, Vernon, 285

Long Holy, 157

Longest Walk, sacred run, 270, 293

Looking Glass, Nez Perce leader, 191–92, 195–96, 199, 201–3

Louisiana Purchase, 68

Lozen, Apache woman warrior, 238, 239b

Madison, James, 49–50, 53, 70

Magnuson, Stew, 281

Mahon, John, 107

Maiet, Jean, 35

Main Poc, Potawatomis chief, 48, 50, 53

Makes the Song, Crazy Horse's grandfather, 144

Male Crow, Crazy Horse's uncle, 144

Man Afraid of His Horse, Oglala leader, 151, 154–55

Mangas Coloadas, Chiricahua leader, 217–19, 221, 223; death of, 224–25

Mangas Coloradas: Chief of the Chiricahua Apaches (Sweeney), 217

Mangus, Apache leader, 229, 235, 238, 240, 243

Mankiller, Wilma, Cherokee chief, 307b

Marsh, John, 76, 77

Marshall, Dicky, 291, 293

Marshall, Chief Justice John, 22

Mascoutens, 32

Maskókî (Muskoke) clan, Creek, 90

Mason, John, 9b

Massachusetts Bay Colony, 3, 5

Massasoit (Ousamequin), Philip's father, 2, 4

Master of Life: Lalawethika's vision, 46; Neolin's story, 24–25

Mather, Increase, 2, 13

Mattachunnamo, execution, 7

Matthiessen, Peter, 312–13

Matoonas, Nipmuc sachem, 9, 13

Maus, Lt. Marion, 239–40

Mayflower II demonstration, 257, 280

McArthur, Duncan, 56

McClelland, Robert, 43

McComas, Charlie, 234

McConville, Colonel Edward, 192–93

McDougall, Lieutenant John, 26–27

McDougall, Captain Thomas, 126, 163–64

McIntosh, Archie, 236, scout, 236

McKee, Alexander, 44

McLaughlin, Major James, agent, 135–37, 211–12

McLenmore, Captain John, 98

McLeod, Norman, 35

McQueen, Peter, Creek leader, 91–92

Means, Hank, Russell Means' father, 274–75, 278

Means, Russell Charles (Wanbli Ohitika), 249f, 255, 261–62, 264, 273f, 274; acting, 298; AIM, 278–90; alliances, 295–97; attempts on life, 291–92; early years, 274–76; imprisonment, 292–94; legal troubles, 290–91;

Libertarian presidential candidate, 297; Oyate Wacinyapi, 282; resistance and survival, 298–99

Medicine bundle, 64, 67b

Menominee, 79

Mescalero Apache, 229, 245

Methotasa, Tecumseh's mother, 42

Mexican–American War, 220–21

Mexico, Apache raids, 219–20, 226–28

Micanopy, Seminole leader, 94, 99, 102–3

Michigan, gunboat, 26–28

Mide, holy man, 23

Miles, Colonel Nelson A. ("Bear Coat"), 131, 167–68, 198, 200, 202–3, 210; and Geronimo, 241

Miller, Lt. Colonel James, 54, 57

Mills, Captain Anson, 131, 162, 167

Minavavana, Chippewa chief, 37

Miniconjou, 117, 121, 131, 145; at Wounded Knee, 138b

Miskito, Nicaragua, 296

Mitchell, George, 253, 256

Modoc, 290

Mohawk, 11

Monoco, Nipmuc sachem, 11, 15

Monteith, John, agent, 187

Montileaux, Martin, 291–92

Moraviantown, 59

Moore, Mary Ellen. *See* Brave Bird, Mary

Morris, Lieutenant Thomas, 31, 34

Morrison, Captain Pitcairn, 105

Morton, Rogers C. B., 259–60

Mott, Dr. Valentine, 106

Mount Rushmore takeover, AIM, 256

Moves Camp, Ellen, 288

Muir, Brevet Major Adam, 54, 56–57

Muttawmp, Nipmuc sachem, 11–12, 15

My Life and Personal Experience Among Our Hostile Indians (Howard), 200

Mystic Massacre (1638), 9b

Naiche, Cochise's son, 226, 228, 235, 240, 242

Nana, Chihenne leader, 224, 229, 234–35

Nanabush, Trickster figure, 23

Nanámakee, Black Hawk's grandfather, 64

Narragansett, 2, 5, 8–9, 11, 247

National Conference of American Indians (NCAI), 287b, 300b

Native American Church, 244b, 308

Native American Journalists Association, 269b

Native Sun News, 269b

Navajo, 317

Neapope, Sauk war chief, 79, 83, 85

Neolin, Delaware Prophet, 23–24

Nerburn, Kent, 193, 198, 209

New Madrid earthquakes, 51

Neyon de Villiers, Pierre Joseph, 26–27, 29–30

Nez Perce, 182; population at siege end, 207–8; splitting of, 186

Nez Perce Summer 1877 (Greene), 193

Nichol, Judge Alfred, 264–65, 289–90

Nichols, Darlene (Kamook), 258, 263, 266, 268

Niehardt, John, 253

Nipmuc, 9, 13

Nochaydelklinne, Prophet, 230

Nocona, Peta, Quahada Comanche leader, 245b

Noise of Running Feet (Sarah Moses), Chief Joseph's daughter, 202, 212

Northern Pacific Railroad, 156

Northwest Territory, area of, 43

Nunnuit, Peter, 8

Oakes, Richard, 256

Oakley, Annie, 135

Oglala Sioux, 114, 116, 121, 130, 144, 167–68

Oglala Sioux Civil Rights Organization (OSCRO), 261, 285

Ohitika Woman (Brave Bird/ Erdoes), 304–5, 314–17

Ojibwa (Chippewa), 27–28, 250

Ojibwa Warrior (Banks/Erdoes), 251, 254, 258

Olguin, Rudi, 316

Ollokot, Chief Joseph's brother, 183, 189, 197, 202

On the Border with Crook (Bourke), 161, 164, 170, 235

Once They Moved Like the Wind: Cochise, Geronimo, and the Apache Wars (Roberts), 246

Onondaga Reservation, New York, 267

Oregon Compromise of 1846, 184

Origin, Progress and Conclusion of the Florida War (Sprague), 95

Osage, 68

Osceola (Billy Powell), 89; arrest, 97; burial place, 89f, 90; capture, 103–4; death and burial, 105; early life, 92–93; health, 101–3; imprisonment, 104–5; missing rifle, 106b; removal opposition, 94–97; war, 99–103

Osceola, the Black Drink, a Warrior of Great Distinction, Catlin painting, 105

Osceola's Legacy (Wickman), 90, 106b

Ottawa, 30; French alliance, 20–21; gift giving, 22; "trade," 24

Overhunting, 74

Owen, Colonel Abraham, 52

Owens, Robert M., 52

Palouse, 191, 196

Panasoffke Swamp, 102

Panther clan, Shawnees, 40

Papineau, Alice, 267

Parker, Cynthia Ann, Quanah's mother, 244b, 245b

Parker, Quanah, Comanche leader, 243b

Parkman, Francis, 20, 37

Pasamaquoddy, 247

Patterson, John B., 85

Patuckson, 7

Paukeesaa, Tecumseh's son, 59

Paul, R. Eli, 152b

Pawnee, 146

Pease, Fellows D., 121

Peckham, Howard, 20–21, 25, 29, 35–37

Peltier, Leonard, 265–66, 269–70, 312

Peoria, 34, 36–37

Pequot War, 9b

Perry, Captain David, 191

Perry, Captain Oliver, 59

Peskeompskut Massacre, 13

Peyote, 308

Phagan, John, agent, 95

Phelps, Peggy, 293, 295

Philip (Metacom, Metacomet), Pokanoket sachem, 1f, 1–5; death of, 14–15; King Philip, 6; relationship with English, 7–8; war, 8–14, 15–16

Pierce, Lt. Colonel Benjamin, 101

Pilgrims, Plymouth Colony, 2, 16

Pine Ridge Oglala Sioux Reservation, corruption, 261, 263, 284

Pinos Altos, 221, 224

Pipestone board schools, 251

Place of the Manure Fires, 202

Plains Wars, 146

Plymouth Colony, 3, 5–6

Plymouth Rock demonstrations, 257, 280

Pocasset, 8

Poinsenay, Chokonen Apache, 227, 229
Pokanoket, 2, 3
Poker Joe, Nez Perce warrior, 196, 198, 200–202
Pontiac, Ottawa war chief, 19f, 20–22; 1763 speech, 24b; and Alexis Cuillerier, 35–36; beliefs, 23; and Black Dog, 34, 36; French alliance, 21; murder of, 36–37; peace agreement, 32–33; and Robert Rogers, 34; and Thomas Morris, 34; war, 26–30; war preparations, 23–25; and William Johnson, 35
Pontiac and the Indian Uprising (Peckham), 20
Poor Bear, Tom, 291
Potawatomi, 48, 82
Powder River Battle, 160
Powell, Billy. *See* Osceola
Powell, William, Osceola's father, 90
Prairie du Chien, peace conferences, 75–77
Proctor, Colonel Henry, 54, 58–59, 71
Prophetstown, 48–49, 52
Pucksinwah, Tecumseh's father, 41
Puritans (Separatists), 2, 5
Pyesa, Black Hawk's father, 64–67

Quapaw Agency, 209–10
Quashquame, Sauk, 69
Quinapin, 11–12

Rawn, Captain Charles, 195–96
Red Cloud, Oglala Sioux chief, 116, 151, 152b, 153–55, 169–71, 177
"Red Napoleon," Chief Joseph, 182, 197, 209
"Red sticks," 51
Red Tomahawk, 137–38
A Relacion of the Indyan Warre (Easton), 8

Reno, Major Marcus, 127–30, 143f, 163–64
Reno Hill, 127–28
Repeating rifles, 164b
Republic of Lakotah, 298–99
Reuben, James, 210
Reynolds, John, Illinois governor, 77–78, 81
Reynolds, Colonel Joseph J., 160
Riche, John, Winnebago World War II veteran, 259
Rivera, Brooklyn, 296
Roberts, David, 246
Roberts, Captain Thomas L., 223
Rogers, Erastus, 98–99
Rogers, Robert, 34
Roosevelt, Theodore, 243, 246
Rope, John, scout, 234
Rosebud Reservation, 255, 278, 288, 305–6, 316
Roubideaux, Ramon, 263–64, 288–89
Rowlandson, Mary, 11–13
Royal Proclamation of 1763, 30, 40
Running, Frank, 312

Sacred Bundles of the Sac and Fox Indians (Harrington), 67b
Sacred runs, 270
San Carlos Reservation, 227–29; breakout, 237–38; Geronimo's return to, 236–37
Sandoz, Mari, 145–47, 150
Sassacus, Pequot sachem, 9b
Sassamon, 6–7
Sauk, 49, 64–65; population in 1845, 86
Saukenuk: attack on, 78; Euro-American intrusion, 75–78; summer home, 65, 69, 73
Sauwauseekau, Tecumseh's brother, 44
Schmitz, Darld, 260
Schultz, Eric, 4
Scott, General Winfield, 84

Seminole, 92; Florida population in the 1850s, 107

Seminole War: First, 91–92; Second, 98–103, 106–7

Seneca, 31, 49

Serving the Republic (Miles), 168

Seventh Cavalry: Custer's command, 126–27, 157; fatalities, 129

Shawnee, 30–31, 36, 40; British alliance, 53, 55b

Sheridan, General Philip, 120, 122, 158, 207, 241

Sherman, General William Tecumseh, 122, 194

Shirt Wearers, 155

Shoshone, 144, 148, 162

"Showing the rifle," 190

Sibley, General Henry, 112

Sieber, Al, scout, 232, 235

The Siege of Detroit in 1763 (Milton), 24

Sioux Wars, 146

Sitting Bull (Tatanka-Iyotanka), 45, 109f, 157; arrest and death, 137–39; counting coup, 110–11, 114; in Canada, 132–34; and Crazy Horse, 147, 154, 156, 166–67; family, 110–11; Little Bighorn, 122–32; peace initiative, 115–16; Standing Rock Reservation, 135–36; surrender, 134–35; unification attempts, 118, 121; visions, 123–24, 161; war, 112–15, 117–22

Six Nations of the Iroquois Treaty, 31, 41

Sixkiller, Jess, 278–79

Skinya, Chokonen Apache, 227

Slim Buttes, Dakota Territory, 130–31, 167

Smith, Charles, "white Shawnee," 45

Smith, Paul Chaat, 277

Smoholla, Wanapam Dreamer, 184, 185b, 189

Sonora, raids, 217–19

Spafford, Omri, 82

Spaulding, Henry, 183

Spotted Eagle, Sans Arc leader, 121

Spotted Tail, Brulè leader, 145–46, 151, 154, 177

Sprague, John, 95

St. Ange de Bellerive, Louis, 32, 37

St. Clair, Arthur, Northwest Territory governor, 43–44

St. Francis Mission School, 305

St. Vrain, Felix, 77, 80–81

Standing Bear, Henry, Brulé chief, 178–79

Standing Rock Reservation, Sitting Bull at, 135–37

Stevens, Issac, Washington Territory governor, 184, 186

Stillman's Run, 81

Stone, John, 9b

Straub, Robert, 268

Street, Joseph, agent, 77, 84–85

Strobel, Dr. Benjamin Beard, 105–6

Sturgis, Colonel Samuel, 198–99

Sugden, John, 58, 60

Sully, General Alfred, 112

Sun Dance, Lakota ceremony, 119b; of 1875, 121–22, 161; of 1877, 123–24, 171; legalization, 255

Survival of the American Indians Association, 283b

Sutherland, Thomas, 193

Swansea, shooting, 8

Sweeney, Edwin R., 217, 221

T.R.E.A.T.Y., total immersion school, 299–301

Tachnedorus (John Logan), Mingo chief, 41

Taklishim, Geronimo's father, 217

Taunton Agreement, 6

Taylor, Major Charles, 246

Taylor, Captain Zachary, 57, 80, 84, 106

Taza, Cochise's son, 226–28

Teck, Charles, 117
Tecumseh, Shawnee chief, 31, 37, 39f; Battle of Tippecanoe, 52–53, 69–70; British alliance, 53–54, 55b, 69; death of, 59–60; Indian confederacy, 48–50, 69; prisoner protection, 57–58; resistance, 45–47; southern recruiting, 50–51; warrior, 43–44; William Henry Harrison meeting, 49–50; youth, 41–43
Tenskwatawa (Lalawethika), Prophet, 46–47, 49–50, 52, 56–57
Terrazas, Colonel Joaquin, 229
Terry, General Alfred, 123, 126, 160
Thompson, Wiley, agent, 96–99, 104
Thorpe, Jim, 86
Throckmorton, Joseph, 83
Thunder Head Mountain, 178
Tiffany, Joseph, agent, 230
Tiffin, Edward, Ohio governor, 47
Tilsen, Ken, 264–65, 288–89
Tispaquin, Philip's brother-in-law, 15
Tisquantum (Squanto), 2
Tobias, execution, 7
Toohoolhoolzote, Nez Perce Dreamer, 190–91, 202
Touch the Clouds, 173, 175–77
Tougias, Michael, 4
Trail of Broken Treaties, 250, 258–60, 282–84
Trail of Tears, Cherokee, 258
Treaty of 1804, Sauk land sale, 67–68
Treaty of 1816, 73
Treaty of 1855, 184–86
Treaty of 1863, 185
Treaty of Casco, 16
Treaty of Fort Jackson, 91
Treaty of Fort Laramie (1851), 111, 116–17, 145

Treaty of Fort Laramie (1868), 154–55; return provision and Alcatraz, 256, 263, 276–77
Treaty of Fort Stanwix, 41
Treaty of Fort Wayne, 49
Treaty of Greenville, 45, 46
Treaty of Payne's Landing, 94
Trimble, Al, 264
Trudell, John, 257
Tuekakas, Chief Joseph's father, 182–84, 186–87
Tupper, Captain Tullius, 232
Turner, Captain William, 13
Tustennuggee, 94
Tyler, John, 52, 70

Unceded land ultimatum, Black Hills, 122–23
Unification Church, 297
Usen, Apache creative spirit, 239
Utley, Robert, 110, 114, 117

Van Horne, Major Thomas, 54
Vestal, Stanley, 110, 138
Victorio, Chiricahua leader, 226; death of, 228–29

Wabokieshiek, Winnebago Prophet, 76, 79–80, 84–85
Wagon Box Fight, 154
Wagon Road and Prospecting Expedition, 120–21
Wahlitis, 191
Wakantanka, forms of, 308
Walker, Colonel Samuel, 151
Wallowa Valley: Nez Perce, 182, 186; settlers, 187
Walsh, Major James M., Northwest Mounted Police, 133–35
Wampanoag, 2, 4, 8, 257
Wampapaquan, execution, 7
Wampum, 55b
Wamsutta (Alexander), Philip's brother, 2, 4; death of, 5
War of 1812, 53–61, 69–71, 73

War Under Heaven: Pontiac, the Indian Nations and the British Empire (Dowd), 21

Ward, John, "white Shawnee," 44

Warner, General Volney, 262, 265

Warner, Wyncoop, agent, 77

Warrior, Clyde, Ponca activist, 300b

Warrior, Robert Allen, 277

Warrior, steamboat, 63f, 83–84

Wasson, Chippewa chief, 27

Wayne, Major General Anthony, 44–45

"We Are Not Free," Clyde Warrior, 300b

Weedon, Dr. Frederick, 104–5, 106b

Weetamoe, female sachem, 8, 12, 14

Weir, Captain Thomas, 129

Wergild ("man price"), 68

West, Elliott, 199

Wheeler's Surprise, 10

Where White Men Fear to Tread (Means), 274, 294

White, Dr. Elijah, 183

White Bird, 191–92, 195–96, 202–4

White Buffalo Woman, 115

White Bull, Sitting Bull's nephew, 113, 119, 127, 131

Whitman, Marcus, 183

Wichasha Wakan (holy man): Leonard Crow Dog, 311; Sitting Bull, 111, 116

Wickman, Patricia Riles, 90, 106b

Willcox, Major General Orlando, 231

Williams, Roger, Rhode Island, 5–6

Williams, Ronald, 265, 269, 312

Wilson, Richard, 261, 264, 284–85, 289

Winchester, General James, 56–57, 71

Winchester, Oliver, 164b

Winchester rifles, 164b

Winnebago, 49, 57

Winslow, Edward, Plymouth Colony governor, 4

Winslow, Josiah, Plymouth Colony governor, 7, 10–11

Withlacoochee, First Battle of, 99–100

Woman Dress, Red Cloud's cousin, 174

Women of All Red Nations (WARN), 294, 318b, 319

Wood, Lt. Charles Erskine Scott, 205

Wootonekanuska, 13

Worm, Crazy Horse's father, 148, 169, 174, 177

Wounded Knee, 250, 284–86; celebration in 2008, 270

Wounded Knee Massacre (1890), 45, 138b, 230, 261

Wounded Knee Occupation (1973), 260–64, 286–89, 309–11; trial, 264, 289–90

Wovoka (Jack Wilson), Paiute holy man, 45, 136, 230

Wratten, George, 241

Wyandot, 25–26, 49

Yale, Skull and Bones suite, 216

Yankton Sioux Reservation, 292

Yanktonai, 113

Yates, Captain George, 128

Yellow Bull, 204–5, 208, 210

Yellow Grizzly Bear, 191

Yellow Thunder, Raymond, 257, 280–81

Yellow Thunder Camp, 295

Yellowstone National Park, Nez Perce, 197–99

Yenne, Bill, 163

Young Bear, Severt, 258

Ziolkowski, Korczak, 139, 178–79

About the Author

Edward J. Rielly is professor of English at Saint Joseph's College of Maine, Standish, Maine. His published works include approximately 20 books, including *F. Scott Fitzgerald: A Biography; Sitting Bull: A Biography*; and *The 1960s.*